D0928142

NONLINEAR METHODS IN ECONOMETRICS

CONTRIBUTIONS
TO
ECONOMIC ANALYSIS

77

Honorary Editor

J. TINBERGEN

Editors

D. W. JORGENSON
J. WAELBROECK

NORTH-HOLLAND PUBLISHING COMPANY
AMSTERDAM · LONDON

NONLINEAR METHODS
IN
ECONOMETRICS

STEPHEN M. GOLDFELD

and

RICHARD E. QUANDT

Princeton University

with a contribution by

Dennis E. Smallwood

1972

NORTH-HOLLAND PUBLISHING COMPANY
AMSTERDAM · LONDON

© NORTH-HOLLAND PUBLISHING COMPANY, 1972

Library of Congress Catalog Card Number: 77 - 157013

ISBN: 0 7204 3177 8

Publishers:

NORTH-HOLLAND PUBLISHING COMPANY – AMSTERDAM
NORTH-HOLLAND PUBLISHING COMPANY, LTD. – LONDON

Printed in Germany

INTRODUCTION TO THE SERIES

This series consists of a number of hitherto unpublished studies, which are introduced by the editors in the belief that they represent fresh contributions to economic science.

The term *economic analysis* as used in the title of the series has been adopted because it covers both the activities of the theoretical economist and the research worker.

Although the analytical methods used by the various contributors are not the same, they are nevertheless conditioned by the common origin of their studies, namely theoretical problems encountered in practical research. Since for this reason, business cycle research and national accounting, research work on behalf of economic policy, and problems of planning are the main sources of the subjects dealt with, they necessarily determine the manner of approach adopted by the authors. Their methods tend to be "practical" in the sense of not being too far remote from application to actual economic conditions. In addition they are quantitative rather than qualitative.

It is the hope of the editors that the publication of these studies will help to stimulate the exchange of scientific information and to reinforce international cooperation in the field of economics.

The Editors

TO LAURA AND MIDGE

PREFACE

The last several years have been characterized by increasing acceptance on the part of statisticians and econometricians of the fact that nonlinear models and nonlinear estimation problems can be handled, if not quite as routinely as linear problems, at least in a reasonably effective manner.

The present volume is intended as a contribution to the growing list of works on nonlinear problems and covers areas in which we have had particularly strong interest in the past few years. The coverage of this volume is not intended to be exhaustive. It is rather selective and emphasizes those areas in which we have accumulated relatively abundant experience. The first two chapters are devoted to a systematic discussion of (a) maximization techniques and (b) least squares and maximum likelihood methods from the statistical point of view. The remaining chapters, an overview of which is provided at the end of chapter 2, deal with particular nonlinear estimation problems. Two of these chapters, namely chapters 5 and 8, are extended and revised versions of two articles written by us in recent years.[1] Chapter 6 was contributed by Dennis E. Smallwood.

The list of friends and colleagues from whose advice we have benefited at various stages of our work is long. We are indebted most heavily to Ray C. Fair, who has read the entire manuscript. We have received helpful advice on various portions of or particular problems contained in this volume from Gregory C. Chow, J. Durbin, John Hartigan, Harry H. Kelejian, L. R. Klein, Dwight M. Jaffee, M. J. D. Powell, Dennis E. Smallwood, Hale F. Trotter, and A. Zellner. We are also grateful to the National Science Foundation for support through various grants. Finally, we have benefited greatly from the

---

[1] S. M. Goldfeld and R. E. Quandt, The estimation of Cobb-Douglas type functions with multiplicative and additive errors. *International Economic Review* **11** (1970), 251–7; and Nonlinear simultaneous equations: estimation and prediction. *International Economic Review* **9** (1968), 113–36.

stimulating environment and the congenial intellectual atmosphere at Princeton University and at the Center for Operations Research and Econometrics,
Catholic University of Louvain, where the various parts of the book were
written.

Princeton, N.J.   STEPHEN M. GOLDFELD
1971   RICHARD E. QUANDT

TABLE OF CONTENTS

CHAPTER 1

NUMERICAL OPTIMIZATION

1.1. Introduction

A problem that frequently presents itself in a wide variety of applications is the maximization or minimization of a function $y = f(x_1, \ldots, x_n)$.[1] In the econometric problems that shall be our concern in this volume, we are interested in obtaining estimates for the parameters of nonlinear functions. In these cases one usually attempts either to maximize an appropriate likelihood function or to minimize an error sum of squares. In the first case a global maximum is sought, and this may be achieved, in principle, by finding all local maxima and choosing the *maximum maximorum*.

A local maximum is attained at the point $x^0 = (x_1^0, \ldots, x_n^0)$ if there exists an ε-neighborhood about x^0, such that

$$f(x_1^0, \ldots, x_n^0) \geq f(x_1, \ldots, x_n) \tag{1.1}$$

for all x satisfying the conditions $|x_1^0 - x_1| < \varepsilon, \ldots, |x_n^0 - x_n| < \varepsilon$. If the function $f(x)$ is continuous and has continuous first and second partial derivatives, sufficient conditions for a maximum are given by the usual conditions that the first partial derivatives be equal to zero

$$\frac{\partial f}{\partial x_i} = 0, \quad i = 1, \ldots, n \tag{1.2}$$

and that the Hessian

$$\left\| \frac{\partial^2 f}{\partial x_i \, \partial x_j} \right\|$$

be a negative definite matrix. The standard maximum problem is solved by finding all solutions to eqs. (1.2) such that the Hessian, evaluated at the solu-

---

[1] Henceforth it will be sufficient to speak of maximizing a function, since minimizing $f(x)$ is equivalent to maximizing $g(x) = -f(x)$.

1

tion point, is indeed negative definite and then choosing the point corresponding to the largest maximum.

In practice it may often be extremely difficult analytically to solve eqs. (1.2)
and thus recourse must be made to numerical methods. Numerous algorithms
exist for maximizing, and they differ from each other in many ways, both
theoretically and practically. The largest class of numerical methods consists of choosing a starting-point and then iterating according to the scheme

$$x^{p+1} = x^p + h^p D^p, \tag{1.3}$$

where x^p is the approximation to the maximum at the pth iteration, D^p is a
direction vector and h^p is a positive scalar. The iterative scheme is permitted
to continue until some convergence criterion is satisfied. Individual methods
differ in the choice of h^p, D^p, and the convergence criterion. Some of these
possible choices are discussed below. Other types of methods, such as the
random search are also briefly treated.

At a practical level, differences among the various algorithms arise on
several possible levels:

(a) some algorithms tend to locate inappropriate stationary points, i.e.,
cannot guarantee that the stationary point found is a maximum rather than a
saddle point;

(b) some algorithms converge more slowly than others in terms of the
number of iterations performed[2], particularly when employed with functions exhibiting narrow ridges;

(c) some algorithms have a relatively higher failure rate than others in the
sense that convergence criteria may become satisfied at points which are not
stationary points at all[3];

(d) some algorithms place a heavy demand on computer time by requiring
the evaluation at each iteration of first and second derivatives whereas others
have no such requirements; if analytic derivatives are desired further human
effort in programming may be involved.

The main purpose of this chapter is not to present an exhaustive list of
algorithms or even of all major types but to describe briefly some particularly
effective algorithms for *unconstrained* optimization and some of the practical

---

[2] An iteration is not necessarily a well-defined concept and it may be more useful to use as
a measure of 'work performed' in locating the stationary point the number of times the
function has to be evaluated.
[3] As a rough generalization, this tends to occur relatively more frequently in situations
when the Hessian is (nearly) singular.

difficulties encountered in using them.[4] It should be noted at the outset that we will discuss the theoretical questions associated with convergence of various methods only in a limited way.[5]

1.2. Ordinary gradient methods

As before, let the function to be maximized be $y = f(x)$, where x is the vector $(x_1, x_2, \ldots, x_n)$; denote the gradient $(\partial f/\partial x_1, \partial f/\partial x_2, \ldots, \partial f/\partial x_n)$ evaluated at the point $a = (a_1, a_2, \ldots, a_n)$ by F_a and denote the matrix of second partial derivatives evaluated at that point by S_a. We assume that we are given a starting-point $x^0 = (x_1^0, x_2^0, \ldots, x_n^0)$ and iterate according to (1.3). In gradient methods the direction vector D^p is usually chosen to be

$$D^p = B^{p-1} F_{x_p}, \tag{1.4}$$

where B is some positive definite weighting matrix.

The method of steepest ascent

The simplest choice of B is given by $B = I$. The rationale for this choice is the fact that the gradient points in the direction of the maximum increase of the best local linear approximation to $f(x)$.

For h^p one may use some predetermined constant. This is not likely to work well since a small value for this constant is likely to make convergence slow and a large value may cause the method not to converge at all. Alternately a suitable value for h^p may be determined by requiring h^p to be such as to maximize the improvement in the function at each iteration. Assuming that $f(x)$ admits of a second-order Taylor series expansion around x^p,

$$f(x^{p+1}) = f(x^p) + (x^{p+1} - x^p)' F_{x^p} + \tfrac{1}{2} (x^{p+1} - x^p)' S_{x^p} (x^{p+1} - x^p). \tag{1.5}$$

---

[4] For a good survey article see H. A. Spang, III, A review of minimization techniques for nonlinear functions. *SIAM Review* **4** (1962), 343–65. For an excellent survey of the most recent developments see M. J. D. Powell, A survey of numerical methods for unconstrained optimization, paper presented at the 1968 SIAM Annual Meeting, Toronto, Canada, and Recent advances in unconstrained optimization, paper presented at the 7th Mathematical Programming Symposium, 1970, The Hague, Netherlands.

[5] Relatively little is known about convergence of various methods under assumptions that are realistically verifiable. In addition, convergence results typically insure only that a stationary point is reached. Indeed, the steepest ascent algorithm which is one of the few methods supported by convergence theorems is typically rejected in practical situations because of its unsatisfactory convergence properties. See M. J. D. Powell, *op. cit.*

Substituting from (1.3) and (1.4) we obtain

$$f(x^{p+1}) - f(x^p) = h^p F'_{x^p} F_{x^p} + \tfrac{1}{2}(h^p)^2 F'_{x^p} S_{x^p} F_{x^p}. \qquad (1.6)$$

In order to maximize the left-hand side we differentiate with respect to h^p and set the result equal to zero.

$$F'_{x^p} F_{x^p} + h^p F'_{x^p} S_{x^p} F_{x^p} = 0,$$

and hence

$$h^p = -(F'_{x^p} S_{x^p} F_{x^p})^{-1} F'_{x^p} F_{x^p}.$$

This value of h^p will yield a maximum if and only if the second derivative of (1.6) is negative, i.e., if $F'_{x^p} S_{x^p} F_{x^p} < 0$. It follows that S_{x^p} must be a negative definite matrix. Since the negative definiteness of S_{x^p} is necessary and sufficient for $f(x)$ to be concave in some neighborhood of x^p, it follows that this method, known as the 'optimum gradient method'[6], will break down if x^p is not sufficiently close to the maximum to insure the concavity of the function. A further theoretical difficulty of steepest ascent methods is that they may converge to a saddle point rather than the maximum. A final and practical disadvantage of these methods is that they may, if the maximum lies on a narrow ridge, oscillate back and forth across it, thus making convergence slow. The reason for this is easily seen from fig. 1.1.

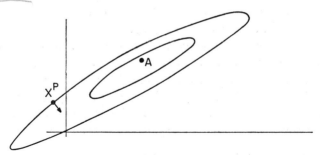

Fig. 1.1. Contours of a narrow ridge.

In two dimensions the contours corresponding to the case in which the maximum lies on a narrow ridge appear (approximately) as elongated ellipses with the maximum at A. Starting with x^p, the gradient (arrow) points in a direction which is roughly perpendicular to the desired direction.

Newton's method

We may maximize the quadratic approximation (1.5) with respect to the

---

[6] T.L.Saaty and J.Bram, *Nonlinear mathematics*. New York, McGraw–Hill, 1964.

unknown point x^{p+1} by differentiating with respect to x^{p+1}. Setting the result equal to zero we obtain

$$F_{x^{p+1}} = F_{x^p} + S_{x^p}(x^{p+1} - x^p) = 0, \qquad (1.7)$$

and thus

$$x^{p+1} = x^p - S_{x^p}^{-1}F_{x^p}. \qquad (1.8)$$

If the function to be maximized is quadratic, the approximations (1.5) and (1.7) become exact and (1.8) yields the maximum in a single step. If the function is not quadratic but the point x^p is close to the maximum, the approximation is likely to be very good and convergence may be expected to be fast. A serious difficulty, however, is that if the point x^p is sufficiently far from the maximum so that the function at that point is not concave, Newton's method will not converge and keep moving in the wrong direction. The reason for this is essentially the same as the reason for the breakdown of the optimum gradient method: the second order conditions for a maximum require that S_{x^p} be negative definite.

The quadratic hill-climbing method[7]

The essence of this method, which is a modification of the Newton method and has been called 'quadratic hill-climbing', is to take that step at each iteration that maximizes a quadratic approximation to the function $f(x)$ on a sphere of suitable radius. The method is designed to cope with the problem that arises if the initial approximation to the maximum is sufficiently far from its true location, so that the application of Newton's method does not guarantee convergence. Since the method is based on a quadratic approximation, the theorems that give it theoretical justification deal with a quadratic function $g(x)$. For a quadratic function, the matrix S is a constant and the expansion in (1.5) is exact. Furthermore, if S is negative definite (1.8) gives the unique global maximum to $g(x)$. Denote the length of a vector x by $\|x\|$ and define

$$x^{p+1} = x^p - (S_{x^p} - \alpha I)^{-1} F_{x^p} \qquad (1.9)$$

$$r_\alpha = \|x^{p+1} - x^p\|, \qquad (1.10)$$

where α is some scalar. The basic results for the method are as follows:

LEMMA 1: *If α is any number such that $S_{x^p} - \alpha I$ is negative definite, then $g(x^{p+1}) \geq g(x)$ for all x such that $\|x - x^p\| = r_\alpha$.*

---

[7] S. M. Goldfeld, R. E. Quandt, and H. F. Trotter, Maximization by quadratic hill-climbing. *Econometrica* 34 (1966), 541–51. A new method, belonging to the same family of algorithms, has been proposed by R. Fletcher in "An efficient, globally convergent, algorithm for unconstrained and linearly constrained optimization problems", paper presented at the 7th Mathematical Programming Symposium, 1970. The Hague, Netherlands. Fletcher's method maximizes a quadratic approximation to the function on a hypercube.

PROOF: We consider the quadratic

$$h(x) = g(x^p) + (x - x^p)' F_{x^p} + \tfrac{1}{2}(x - x^p)'(S_{x^p} - \alpha I)(x - x^p)$$

$$= g(x) - \tfrac{1}{2}\alpha \|x - x^p\|^2.$$

Since $(S_{x^p} - \alpha I)$ is negative definite, (1.8) with S_{x^p} replaced by $(S_{x^p} - \alpha I)$ applies to show that $h(x)$ has a global maximum at x^{p+1} and thus

$$g(x^{p+1}) - \tfrac{1}{2}\alpha \|x^{p+1} - x^p\|^2 = h(x^{p+1}) \geq h(x) = g(x) - \tfrac{1}{2}\alpha \|x - x^p\|^2.$$

It follows that if $\|x - x^p\| = \|x^{p+1} - x^p\| = r_\alpha$ then $g(x^{p+1}) \geq g(x)$.

LEMMA 2: *If $F_{x^p} \neq 0$ then r_α is a strictly decreasing function of α for all $\alpha > \lambda_1$, where λ_1 is the largest eigenvalue of S_{x^p}.*

PROOF: For a symmetric matrix S the squared norm $\|Sx\|$ can be written as $\sum_{i=1}^{n} \lambda_i^2 c_i^2$, where $\lambda_1 \geq \lambda_2 \geq \cdots \geq \lambda_n$ are the eigenvalues of S, and c_i certain constants. Combining (1.9) and (1.10) thus implies

$$r_\alpha^2 = \sum_{i=1}^{n} c_i^2 (\lambda_i - \alpha)^{-2},$$

since $(S_{x^p} - \alpha I)^{-1}$ has the same eigenvectors as S_{x^p} and has eigenvalues $(\lambda_i - \alpha)^{-1}$. The stated conclusion is immediate for $\alpha > \lambda_1$.

THEOREM 1.1: *Let $F_{x^p} \neq 0$ and let R_α be the region of all x values satisfying $\|x - x^p\| \leq r_\alpha$. The maximum of $g(x)$ on R_α is then attained at x^{p+1} if $\alpha \geq 0$ and in the interior of R_α at $x^p - S_{x^p}^{-1} F_{x^p}$ if $\alpha < 0$.*

PROOF: Two cases are distinguished:
(i) S_{x^p} is not negative definite. Then lemma 1 applies and the conclusion follows.
(ii) S_{x^p} is negative definite. Then $g(x)$ has a global maximum at $x^p - S_{x^p}^{-1} F_{x^p}$, which is in the interior of R_α by Lemma 2 if $\alpha < 0$. If $\alpha \geq 0$, $x^p - S_{x^p}^{-1} F_{x^p}$ is not in the interior of R_α and the maximum on R_α occurs at x^{p+1}, as before.

THEOREM 1.2: *If $F_{x^p} = 0$, the maximum of $g(x)$ on a region R defined by $\|x - x^p\| \leq r$ occurs at $x^p \pm r u_1$ if $\lambda_1 > 0$ and at x^p otherwise, where λ_1 is the maximum eigenvalue of S_{x^p} and u_1 the corresponding unit eigenvector.*

PROOF: The result follows from the observations that

$$g(x) = g(x^p) + \tfrac{1}{2}(x - x^p)' S_{x^p} (x - x^p)$$

in this case and that the maximum of a quadratic form $x'Sx$ on the unit sphere is attained for $x = u_1$.

These results provide the basis for an iterative algorithm for finding the maximum of a general function. Given a point x^p at which first and second partial derivatives are evaluated, one defines x^{p+1} as the maximum of the quadratic approximation on a spherical region centered at x^p. Ideally the region should be taken as large as possible, provided that it is small enough so that in the region the quadratic approximation is a satisfactory guide to the actual behavior of the function.

In practice then two cases may arise at the pth iteration:

(a) F_{x^p} is different from the null vector. In that case we obtain a number

$$\alpha = \lambda_1 + R \, \|F_{x^p}\|, \tag{1.11}$$

where λ_1 is the largest eigenvalue of S_{x^p}, and R is a parameter discussed below. We then compute

$$x^{p+1} = x^p - (S_{x^p} - \alpha I)^{-1} F_{x^p}$$

or

$$x^{p+1} = x^p - S_{x^p}^{-1} F_{x^p},$$

according to whether α is positive or not. By theorem 1.1, x^{p+1} is the maximum of the quadratic approximation to the function on a region of radius $\|(S_{x^p} - \alpha I)^{-1} F_{x^p}\|$. For $\alpha = 0$, we simply have a Newton method. For very large α the method tends to move in the direction of the gradient (although, as lemma 2 assures us, within a relatively small sphere). Consequently, the present method can be regarded as an interpolation between the method of steepest ascent and the Newton method.[8]

It is clear that the radius of the sphere on which we are maximizing is less than or equal to R^{-1}, and although the strict inequality may well hold, it is reasonable to expect in practice that the two quantities will be of comparable order of magnitude. Thus, alterations of R will affect the radius of the sphere. We can therefore allow R to be automatically adjusted, increasing it when the quadratic approximation is poor and reducing it in the converse case. We can thus avoid one of the difficulties of Newton's method which may call for a step so large that the quadratic approximation at x^p has no validity at x^{p+1}.

---

[8] This in a sense is also the spirit of Marquardt's method. See Donald W. Marquardt, An algorithm for least squares estimation of nonlinear parameters. *Journal of the Society of Industrial and Applied Mathematics* **11** (1963), 431–41.

(b) $F_{x^p} = 0$. In that case a step is taken in the direction of the eigenvector u_1 if $\lambda_1 > 0$, as described by theorem 1.2. This part of the algorithm guarantees that it will not converge to a saddle point.

The modified quadratic hill-climbing method[9]

The theorems which justify the use of (1.9) remain valid if the identity matrix I in that equation is replaced by an arbitrary positive definite matrix A. Employing (1.9) with I replaced by A is equivalent to maximizing the quadratic approximation $g(x)$ on an ellipsoid. The size of the ellipsoid is a function of α, but it is now possible to alter the shape and orientation of the ellipsoid. These latter two are chosen on the heuristically plausible assumption that the most useful direction of search at any point is close to the direction of the immediately preceding step.

A suitable ellipsoid can be chosen in the following manner. Assume that p iterations have been completed. Any vector can be decomposed into its orthogonal projection on the vector representing the last step $x^p - x^{p-1}$ and its orthogonal complement. The coordinate system can then be mapped into a new coordinate system by requiring that the component of every vector in the direction of $x^p - x^{p-1}$ be stretched by some factor. Defining δ as $x^p - x^{p-1}$ in the coordinate system at the pth iteration, this defines a transformation of the coordinate system prevailing at the pth iteration given by

$$x^p_{\text{new}} = \left[I - \frac{(\beta - 1)\,\delta\delta'}{\delta'\delta} \right] x^p_{\text{old}} = B^p x^p_{\text{old}}, \qquad (1.12)$$

where $0 < \beta < 1$.

At each iteration a new B-transformation takes place. Let them be denoted by $B_0, B_1, \ldots$, and for any vector let x_k stand for its coordinates in the system used to make the kth step. Then

$$x_k = B_{k-1}B_{k-2} \cdots B_1 B_0 x_0.$$

(We take $B_0 = I$, since there is no previous step and δ is undefined.) For the $(k+1)$th iteration we maximize over a 'sphere'

$$x'_{k+1}x_{k+1} = (B_k x_k)'\,(B_k x_k) = \text{constant},$$

which is in general an ellipsoid in the original coordinate system. The new step computed at this point may be expressed easily in terms of the original

[9] S.M.Goldfeld, R.E.Quandt, and H.F.Trotter, Maximization by improved quadratic hill-climbing and other methods. Econometric Research Program Research Memo. No. 95, Princeton University, 1968.

coordinate system prevailing at the beginning of the process. Setting $B_{k-1} \cdots B_1 B_0 = B$, it is easy to verify that the gradient evaluated at x^k and expressed in the original coordinates is $(B^{-1})' F_{x^k}$ and the matrix of second partial derivatives is $(B^{-1})' S_{x^k} B^{-1}$. The step in the new coordinate system is clearly

$$-((B^{-1})' S_{x^k} B^{-1} - \alpha I)^{-1} (B^{-1})' F_{x^k},$$

and premultiplication by B^{-1} yields the step in the old coordinates and it equals $-(S_{x^k} - \alpha B'B)^{-1} F_{x^k}$. Thus $B'B$ is the positive definite matrix A mentioned at the beginning of this section.

As for β, its magnitude determines the amount of stretching. It has seemed reasonable on pragmatic grounds to modify the magnitude of β at each iteration according to the same principle that was applied to the modification of R in the basic quadratic hill-climbing method, namely the success of the quadratic approximation. We now turn to some illustrative examples.[10]

Some examples

This section has considered four types of gradient methods—steepest ascent, Newton, quadratic hill-climbing, and modified quadratic hill-climbing. A comparison of the effect of these methods can perhaps best be provided by some simple examples.

Consider the function $f(x, y) = e^{-x^2 - 2y^2}$, which has a maximum at $x = 0$, $y = 0$. For this function the vector F_x and the matrix S_x are given by

$$F_x = \begin{bmatrix} -2x \\ -4y \end{bmatrix} f(x, y)$$

and

$$S_x = \begin{bmatrix} -2 + 4x^2 & 8xy \\ 8xy & -4 + 16y^2 \end{bmatrix} f(x, y).$$

---

[10] Another variant of the Newton method that deserves mention is that of Greenstadt. As with quadratic hill-climbing, the essence of the method involves replacing the matrix of second partials by a negative definite matrix. In particular Greenstadt computes $S = \Omega D \Omega'$, where Ω is orthogonal and D is a diagonal matrix. In place of S Greenstadt then uses $\Omega D^* \Omega'$, where D^* is the diagonal matrix obtained by replacing the positive elements of D by their negative and leaving the negative elements as is. See John Greenstadt, On the relative efficiencies of gradient methods. *Mathematics of Computation* **21** (1967), 360–67.

Let us assume that we start at the point (3, 2). At this point we have

$$S_x = f(3, 2) \begin{bmatrix} 34 & 48 \\ 48 & 60 \end{bmatrix},$$

which is not negative definite. As a result Newton's method, which takes a step given by $-S_x^{-1}F_x$, can be expected to go in the wrong direction. Indeed the first step is (24/264, 16/264) and takes us to the point (3.091, 2.061), which is clearly away from (0, 0). A similar difficulty will arise in the case of the 'optimum gradient' version of method of steepest ascent. Table 1.1 lists the successive iterations of the various methods. Both the steepest ascent and the Newton method steadily diverge from the optimum, while both versions of the quadratic hill-climbing algorithm attain the optimum in six

TABLE 1.1

Function $= e^{-x^2 - 2y^2}$

Itera-tion	Steepest ascent		Newton		Quadratic hill-climbing			Modified quadratic hill-climbing		
	x	y	x	y	x	y	α	x	y	α
Start	3.000	2.000	3.000	2.000	3.000	2.000	—	3.000	2.000	—
1	3.062	2.083	3.091	2.061	0.570	−1.177	0.4×10^{-5}	0.570	−1.177	0.4×10^{-5}
2	3.121	2.163	3.179	2.119	0.318	−0.210	1.1	0.404	−0.143	1.2
3	3.178	2.241	3.264	2.176	−0.193	0.127	0.0	−0.278	0.098	0.0
4	3.232	2.318	3.348	2.232	0.031	−0.021	0.0	0.066	−0.023	0.0
5	3.284	2.392	3.429	2.286	0.000	0.000	0.0	−0.001	0.000	0.0
6	3.334	2.465	3.508	2.338	0.000	0.000	0.0	0.000	0.000	0.0

iterations. The table lists the values of α (see (1.11)) used by the hill-climbing methods. A positive value appears for the first two iterations indicating that at each of these steps the matrix of second partials is not negative definite. The use of $\alpha > 0$ in (1.9) causes an iteration to be taken in the general direction of the maximum, but the precise path taken by successive iterations depends on the sequence of values assigned to α, not only because the radius of the sphere (ellipsoid) of maximization is affected but the actual direction is as well. After the second iteration the x-vector is sufficiently close to the optimum so that S_x is negative definite. Indeed from this point on $\alpha = 0$ and the hill-climbing algorithms proceed essentially as would a Newton method.

For this particular example, both hill-climbing methods tend to behave in the same way.

Table 1.2 contains the iterations produced in maximizing the function

$$f(x, y) = \frac{1}{Q (1 + x^k)} \exp \left\{ - \frac{(y - x^2)^2}{Q^2 (1 + x^k)^2} \right\}$$

for $Q = 0.1$ and $k = 2$. The function is a parabolic Gaussian ridge achieving a maximum at $(0, 0)$. As the results indicate, after the third iteration the modified hill-climbing method is uniformly closer to the maximum at each iteration[11], although ultimately of course, both methods achieve the maximum.[12]

TABLE 1.2

$$\text{Function} = \frac{10}{1 + x^2} \exp \left\{ - 100 \left(\frac{y - x^2}{1 + x^2} \right)^2 \right\}$$

Quadratic hill-climbing		Modified quadratic hill-climbing	
x	y	x	y
3.000	2.000	3.000	2.000
2.119	2.472	2.119	2.472
1.685	2.629	1.636	2.662
1.634	2.642	1.623	2.655
1.612	2.625	1.352	1.752
1.431	1.991	1.187	1.445
1.379	1.926	0.853	0.634
1.091	1.106	0.834	0.660
0.979	1.031	0.638	0.397
0.990	0.976	0.475	0.206
0.773	0.561	0.283	0.070
0.457	0.186	0.123	0.001
0.171	0.012	0.087	0.007
0.107	0.018	0.008	−0.006
0.038	−0.003	0.004	0.000
0.018	0.000	0.000	0.000
0.001	0.000		
0.000	0.000		

[11] The value of β (see (1.12)) produced at each iteration for modified hill-climbing reflects an increased degree of 'stretching' after the third iteration. This, in turn, stems from the relatively good quality of the quadratic approximation.

[12] Although not readily apparent in table 1.2 (since the results are terminated after three decimals) the modified method took 15% fewer iterations to achieve the same degree of accuracy.

A final example which illustrates the operation of theorem 1.2 above is contained in table 1.3. The function considered is

$$f(x, y) = (2x^2 + 3y^2) \exp(-x^2 - y^2),$$

which has maxima at $(0, 1)$ and $(0, -1)$, saddle points at $(1, 0)$ and $(-1, 0)$, and a minimum at $(0, 0)$.

TABLE 1.3

Function $= (2x^2 + 3y^2) \exp(-x^2 - y^2)$

Simple quadratic hill-climbing	
x	y
4.000	0.000
2.000	0.000
1.000	0.000
1.000	−0.500
0.584	−1.015
0.051	−1.020
0.004	−1.000
0.000	−1.000

The table reports the results for the basic method (the modified method performs essentially the same) from the starting-point $(4, 0)$. The algorithm takes us straight to a saddlepoint from which we move counterclockwise, substantially along the rim of the crater. This example points up the virtues of having an algorithm that is robust with respect to saddlepoints.

These examples are merely meant to be illustrative of the operational characteristics of the several gradient methods we have discussed. Both the appendix to this chapter and the remainder of this book contain numerous additional applications of the hill-climbing methods. In practice both versions of the algorithm are relatively expensive to compute because of the need to compute first and second partial derivatives and also eigenvalues. Nevertheless it is a desirable algorithm in many instances because it is a robust procedure that rarely accepts a nonstationary point as optimal. We now turn to a class of methods that are generally much less costly to compute.

1.3. Conjugate gradient methods

The methods included in this broad class are based on searching the function along mutually conjugate directions. Two direction vectors p_i and p_j are termed conjugate if, for a quadratic function $g(x) = x'Ax + b'x + c$, we have $p_i'Ap_j = 0$. In practice, of course, the function to be maximized is not quadratic and thus the various methods are based on pseudo-conjugate directions. Among others, the several approaches which use conjugate directions differ from each other in the way in which the conjugate directions are selected.[13] Conjugate gradient methods have been quite successful although it is not entirely clear theoretically why this should be so.[14]

One of the most powerful methods of this type, which involves no evaluation of derivatives, is the conjugate gradient method of Powell.[15] As other members of this class, it is based on solving a sequence of one-dimensional maximization problems. Each iteration consists basically of maximizing the function sequentially in n conjugate directions. At the end of such an iteration either the original n conjugate directions are retained or one of them is eliminated and a new conjugate direction is computed.

The essential features of the algorithm may be summarized by considering a single iteration. Let the function under consideration be $f(x_1, x_2, \ldots, x_n) = f(x)$. Assume we have completed k iterations and let $d_1^k, d_2^k, \ldots, d_n^k$ be n linearly independent search directions starting from the most recent estimate of the optimum $x^k = (x_1^k, x_2^k, \ldots, x_n^k)$. The steps of an iteration are as follows[16]:

(a) For $r = 1, 2, \ldots, n$ sequentially calculate λ_r, so as to maximize the objective function

$$f(x^k + \sum_{j=1}^{r} \lambda_j d_j^k). \quad \text{Let} \quad \bar{x}^k = \sum_{j=1}^{n} \lambda_j d_j^k + x^k.$$

(b) The displacement $\delta = \sum_{j=1}^{n} \lambda_j d_j^k$ is used as a search direction: i.e., a value of λ is chosen to maximize $f(\bar{x}^k + \lambda\delta)$.

---

[13] Some worthwhile methods not dealt with in detail are R. Fletcher and M. J. D. Powell, Function minimization by conjugate gradients. *Computer Journal* 6 (1963), 163–68, and W. C. Davidon, Variable metric method for minimization. AEC Research and Development Report, ANL-5990, 1959.

[14] See M. J. D. Powell, A survey..., *op. cit.*

[15] M. J. D. Powell, An efficient method for finding the minimum of a function of several variables without calculating derivatives. *Computer Journal* 7 (1964), 155–62.

[16] See *ibid.*, p. 156.

(c) The starting-point for the next iteration is taken as $x^{k+1} = \bar{x}^k + \lambda \delta$.

(d) The search directions are replaced by the set

$$d_i^{k+1} = d_{i+1}^k$$
$$\qquad\qquad\qquad\qquad i = 1, 2, \ldots, n-1.$$
$$d_n^{k+1} = \delta.$$

Initially, the search directions are chosen as the coordinate directions. Given the manner of altering directions [in (d)], if a quadratic function is being maximized, after k iterations the last k of the n directions chosen for the next step are mutually conjugate. Hence, after n iterations all the directions are mutually conjugate.

In consequence it can be shown that if the function is quadratic, at most n iterations are required for finding the maximum. The proof of this assertion is contained in three theorems due to Powell.

THEOREM 1.3: *Let $d_1, \ldots, d_n$ be mutually conjugate, and linearly independent directions. The maximum of $x'Ax + b'x + c$ can be found by searching in each of the n directions only once.*

PROOF: Starting from the initial approximation x^0, the location of the maximum may be expressed as $x^0 + \sum_{i=1}^{n} \alpha_i d_i$. The value of the quadratic at that point is

$$\left(x^0 + \sum_{i=1}^{n} \alpha_i d_i\right)' A \left(x^0 + \sum_{i=1}^{n} \alpha_i d_i\right) + b' \left(x^0 + \sum_{i=1}^{n} \alpha_i d_i\right) + c$$

$$= (x^{0\prime} A x^0 + b' x^0 + c) + \sum_{i=1}^{n} \alpha_i^2 d_i' A d_i + 2x^0 A \sum_{i=1}^{n} \alpha_i d_i,$$

where terms involving d_i and d_j vanish by the assumption that the d_i are conjugate. Clearly, the values of α_i ($i = 1, \ldots, n$) that maximize the function are independent of the values assigned to the remaining α_j, which proves the assertion.

THEOREM 1.4: *If the general quadratic function achieves a maximum at x^0 when searched in the direction d and also at x^1 when searched in the same direction, then the directions d and $x^1 - x^0$ are conjugate.*

PROOF: The point x is the maximum in the direction d if

$$\frac{\partial}{\partial \lambda} [(x + \lambda d)' A (x + \lambda d) + b' (x + \lambda d) + c] = 0 \quad \text{at} \quad \lambda = 0.$$

Performing the differentiation, substituting x^0 and x^1, in turn, for x and setting $\lambda = 0$ implies

$$d'A(x^1 - x^0) = 0,$$

which proves the theorem.

THEOREM 1.5: *The maximum of the general quadratic is reached in at most n iterations.*

PROOF: Assume that after k iterations the last k directions employed were mutually conjugate. By theorem 1.3 both the x^k with which the $(k+1)$st iteration starts and the $\bar{x}^k$ which is defined in it represent maxima in the space involving these last k directions. By theorem 1.4 the new direction $\bar{x}^k - x^k$ is conjugate to the last k (already mutually conjugate) directions. The same reasoning establishes that after the first two iterations a pair of conjugate directions will exist. Hence, after n iterations all directions will be conjugate and will have been searched once; thus by theorem 1.3 the maximum is reached.

This method has the very great advantages of not needing the computation of derivatives and of ensuring quadratic convergence.[17] It is simple to implement (the original directions may be taken to be parallel to the coordinate axes), but it does not guarantee that we shall not converge to a saddlepoint. Special refinements are occasionally necessary when a new direction to be introduced turns out to be (nearly) linearly dependent on the other directions retained for the subsequent iteration. A particular aspect of this and other methods[18] is the reliance placed upon maximizing over a line (once or several times) during each iteration. This aspect of the algorithm is flexible since there are various ways to accomplish maximization over a line; one of the simplest being the iterative scheme by which (a) the function is evaluated at three points on the line, (b) a quadratic is fitted to the three points and the exact maximum of the fitted quadratic determined, (c) one of the three points is replaced by the maximum of the quadratic and the preceding is repeated until satisfactory convergence is achieved.[19]

---

[17] Powell has recently shown convergence when the function has a strictly negative definite second derivative matrix. See M. J. D. Powell, On the convergence of the variable metric algorithm. T-P. 382, Harwell, October 1969.

[18] See, for example, H. A. Spang, III, *op. cit.*

[19] See also P. D. Flanagan, P. A. Vitale, and J. Mendelsohn, A numerical investigation of several one dimensional search procedures in nonlinear regression problems. *Technometrics* **11** (1969), 265–84.

Computational experience with the method is good and is a particularly useful alternative to the algorithms discussed in the previous section when derivatives cannot be evaluated with sufficient precision. Such cases arise, for example, when the function to be maximized cannot be evaluated exactly but only as a numerical approximation.[20]

1.4. Direct search methods

The methods comprising this class search the function directly in the sense that they make no reference to the gradient or to conjugate gradients, nor do they maximize the function at any one iteration along the direction selected for that iteration. Essentially they explore the function step by step, where a step is accepted if it results in an improvement and where the proposed direction for a step is selected either independently at each iteration or perhaps by reference to the computational experience of recent iterations.

The simplest, but very inefficient, approach is to explore at each iteration in the (at most) $2n$ directions that are parallel to the coordinate axes. Any exploratory step that results in an improvement is accepted and the process repeated. A vast improvement over this is achieved by the pattern search method of Hooke and Jeeves.[21] Their algorithm consists of a combination of exploratory moves (parallel to the axes) and pattern moves (incorporating the aggregate of directions found successful in recent iterations). A pattern move is made and is followed by an exploratory move. If the two together result in an improvement, they are accepted and the process is repeated. Otherwise they are both rejected and only an exploratory move is made. It is an essential feature of the pattern move-exploratory move combination that the function value may diminish as a result of the pattern move alone. It is this characteristic that allows the Hooke and Jeeves method to follow ridges successfully. Unlike gradient or conjugate gradient methods, however, convergence does not tend to speed up when the current estimate of the location of the maximum is good enough so that the quadratic approximations on which the gradient methods are based become reasonable.

---

[20] See, for example, chapter 5.

[21] R. Hooke and T. A. Jeeves, Direct search solution of numerical and statistical problems. *Journal of the Association of Computing Machinery* **8** (1961), 212–21.

An alternative to pattern search is random search, which consists of generating random points on a sphere centered on the current estimate of the location of the maximum. The function is evaluated at these points until one is found to yield an improvement. If such a point is found, the center of the sphere is relocated to it and the process is repeated.

In some ways random search methods can be quite economical because the number of function evaluations required to effect an improvement does not increase with the dimensionality of the problem. They (as well as pattern search methods) have an advantage over Newton-type methods when the function is quite flat and the Hessian matrix is (nearly or apparently) singular. Random search methods will tend, however, to converge slowly along ridges because there is only a small probability in such cases that a random point on a sphere will lie on a contour of the function that is higher than the one passing through the center of the sphere.

1.5. Iteration methods for systems of equations

The methods considered to date have been motivated by the inherent difficulty in directly solving the first-order conditions (1.2). Indirectly of course, all these methods do produce solutions of these equations. However, one class of methods for optimization proceeds by directly trying to solve the first-order conditions. This, indeed, is the approach taken by Chow in computing full-information maximum likelihood estimates.[22]

There is, of course, a substantial literature on iterative methods for solving systems of equations.[23] Consider the case of two equations (generally non-linear) and two unknowns given by

$$f(x, y) = 0 \qquad\qquad (1.13)$$
$$g(x, y) = 0.$$

Most methods involve rewriting the equations in the form

$$x = F(x, y) \qquad\qquad (1.14)$$
$$y = G(x, y)$$

[22] Gregory C. Chow, Two methods of computing full-information maximum likelihood estimates in simultaneous stochastic equations. *International Economic Review* **9** (1968), 100–12.

[23] See, for example, Peter Henrici, *Elements of numerical analysis*. New York, John Wiley, 1964.

and iterating according to

$$x^{k+1} = F(x^k, y^k) \tag{1.15}$$

$$y^{k+1} = G(x^k, y^k).$$

In the economics literature an iterative scheme such as (1.15) is often called a Seidel or a Gauss-Seidel method.[24]

Several things should be noted about these methods. First, there is typically more than one way to obtain eqs. (1.14) from (1.13). For example, one may either solve the first or the second equation in (1.13) for x. This can be critical since the convergence properties of (1.15) depend on the nature of (1.14). Second, while there exists a significant number of convergence theorems for these iteration methods, as a practical matter, as with the steepest ascent algorithms, convergence is often difficult to achieve.[25] Nevertheless, such methods have been extremely useful in solving dynamic macroeconometric systems where one can use last period's value as a reasonable starting-point for the iterations.

1.6. The use of derivatives

Maximization algorithms differ with respect to whether they require the computation of derivatives. Newton-type methods need first and second partial derivatives, steepest ascent and Davidon's method require first partial derivatives, and finally Powell's conjugate gradient procedure and the Hooke and Jeeves pattern search method use no derivatives.

Apart from such qualitative characteristics as the ability of an algorithm to distinguish a saddlepoint from a genuine extremum—and this ability may cause one to employ a particular method, all other considerations notwithstanding—the various methods differ greatly in the amount of work that has to be performed by both the user of a method and the computer. If derivatives are to be evaluated exactly, one first has to develop expressions for them by differentiating and these expressions must then be translated into computer

---

[24] See, for example, Morris Norman, Solving a nonlinear econometric model by the Gauss-Seidel iterative method, paper presented to Econometric Society Meetings, December 1967. The Seidel method was originally developed for the linear case. See D. K. Faddeev and V. N. Faddeeva, *Computational methods of linear algebra*. New York, Freeman and Co., 1963.

[25] See chapter 6.

programs. The number of first partials is n and the number of distinct second partials is $n(n + 1)/2$ in general. Except in the most special cases the labor involved will be deemed excessive by most individuals for $n > 10$.

If such large amounts of work are to be avoided, first derivatives may be evaluated numerically as the slope of the secant over some interval and second derivatives as a change in first derivatives over some interval. As a compromise between the two extremes, first derivatives may be evaluated exactly and second derivatives numerically by employing the expressions for the first derivatives. The first derivative at a point a may be obtained from the approximation

$$f(x) = f(a) + (x - a)f'(a). \tag{1.16}$$

Since, for a function continuously differentiable in a suitable interval, the mean value theorem states that there exists θ, $0 < \theta < 1$, such that

$$f(x) = f(a) + (x - a)f'(a + \theta(x - a)),$$

a better approximation can be obtained for the derivative at a than is given by (1.16) if one evaluates the function symmetrically about a. Thus $f'(a)$ would be estimated by

$$f'(a) = \frac{f(a + \Delta x) - f(a - \Delta x)}{2\Delta x}. \tag{1.17}$$

Although (1.17) is theoretically more accurate, it requires in general twice as many function evaluations as does (1.16) since the value of the function at a is usually already available when the gradient is required.

A similar problem arises with respect to second derivatives. Employing for illustration a function of two variables, the second direct partials may be evaluated by

$$\left.\frac{\partial^2 f(x, y)}{\partial x^2}\right|_{\substack{x=a \\ y=b}} = \frac{f(a - \Delta x, b) - 2f(a, b) + f(a + \Delta x, b)}{(\Delta x)^2}.$$

In the case of the cross partial we may compute

$$\left.\frac{\partial^2 f(x, y)}{\partial x \, \partial y}\right|_{\substack{x=a \\ y=b}} = \frac{1}{\Delta y}\left(\frac{f(a + \Delta x, b + \Delta y) - f(a, b + \Delta y)}{\Delta x}\right.$$

$$\left. - \frac{f(a + \Delta x, b) - f(a, b)}{\Delta x}\right)$$

requiring three additional function evaluations, or, evaluating it analogously to (1.17) we may use

$$\frac{\partial^2 f(x, y)}{\partial x \partial y}\bigg|_{\substack{x=a \\ y=b}} = \frac{1}{2\Delta y}\left(\frac{f(a + \Delta x, b + \Delta y) - f(a - \Delta x, b + \Delta y)}{2\Delta x}\right.$$
$$\left. - \frac{f(a + \Delta x, b - \Delta y) - f(a - \Delta x, b - \Delta y)}{2\Delta x}\right)$$

requiring four additional function evaluations. The total number of function evaluations is $3n(n + 1)/2$ by the asymmetrical procedure and $2n^2 + 4n$ by the symmetrical procedure. The latter can be substantially more expensive if the function is complicated, as is often the case with likelihood functions in statistics and econometrics, and the process of evaluating the function may take up a substantial fraction of computing time. However, neither the choice between analytically computed or numerically estimated derivatives, nor, if the latter are chosen, the choice between the symmetrically or asymmetrically constructed numerical derivatives can be settled *a priori*. *Ceteris paribus*, of course, analytic derivatives are preferred over numerical ones and symmetrically constructed numerical derivatives over asymmetrically constructed ones.

A further difficulty with numerically evaluated derivatives is that the 'proper' value of the intervals Δx and Δy is not defined. In the implementation of some algorithms the displacement in the ith direction is taken as a fixed fraction of the current value of the ith variable.[26] This is somewhat arbitrary and needs special adjustments in order to avoid the undesirable consequence that the denominator $\Delta x \to 0$ if the value of the variable approaches 0. More sophisticated is the approach based on the observation that the error in a derivative comes from two sources: the truncation error, which is caused by the fact that derivatives are estimated from truncated Taylor series, and the cancellation error due to cancellation of significant digits when fixed word length computation is undertaken. Increasing Δx increases the truncation error but reduces the cancellation error, and conversely. An elegant solution of this problem is to find that value of Δx for which the two types of error are equal in size.[27] Less sophisticated

---

[26] D.W.Marquardt, *op. cit.*, and *Least-squares estimation of nonlinear parameters*. Wilmington, E.I. DuPont de Nemours and Company, Inc.

[27] G.W.Stewart, III, A modification of Davidon's minimization method to accept difference approximations of derivatives. *Journal of the Association of Computing Machinery* **14** (1967), 72–83.

but adequate in many cases is to set the interval at the pth iteration over which the difference in function values is computed in the ith principal direction equal to max $(|f(x^p)| \varepsilon_1, |\delta_i| \varepsilon_2, (|x_i| + \varepsilon_3) \varepsilon_4)$, where $\varepsilon_1, \varepsilon_2, \varepsilon_3$ and ε_4 are preassigned small positive constants and $\delta_i = x_i^p - x_i^{p-1}$ Thus, unless either the absolute value of a variable or the value of the function becomes very large, the size of the interval is governed by the amount of change in the ith variable since the last iteration. A final possibility is to approximate the first partial derivatives with the calculated coefficients of a hyperplane obtained as the least squares fit of $m \ (\geq n)$ function values to m points in the space of variables.

1.7. Global maxima

It is only in the rarest cases that it can be ascertained with certainty that a local maximum is a global maximum as well, i.e., a case in which $f(x^0) \geq f(x)$ for all x. Of course, such a situation exists if $f(x)$ is a quadratic function. It is reasonably easy to exhibit simple and relatively realistic cases in which multiple maxima occur.

Consider a set of n observations $x_1, \ldots, x_n$ on an independent variable and corresponding observations $y_1, \ldots, y_n$ on a dependent variable. Assume that the y's were generated by the linear regression equation

$$y_i = a_0 + a_1 x_i + u_i, \tag{1.18}$$

where the u_i are unobservable error terms distributed normally with mean zero and variance σ^2, and where a_0, a_1 and σ^2 are unknown parameters to be estimated by the data. Thus the u_i have the density

$$f(u_i) = \frac{1}{\sqrt{2\pi\sigma}} \exp\left(-\frac{u_i^2}{2\sigma^2}\right). \tag{1.19}$$

Assume further that *a priori* information is available to the effect that $a_0^2 = a_1$. Eq. (1.18) can then be written

$$y_i = a + a^2 x_i + u_i. \tag{1.20}$$

From (1.19) the likelihood function is obtained as

$$= (2\pi)^{-n/2} \sigma^{-n} \exp\left(-\frac{1}{2\sigma^2} \Sigma u_i^2\right)$$

and substituting from (1.20)

$$= (2\pi)^{-n/2}\sigma^{-n} \exp\left(-\frac{1}{2\sigma^2}\Sigma(y_i - a - a^2 x_i)^2\right)$$

and taking logarithms

$$L = -\frac{n}{2}\log 2\pi - n\log\sigma - \frac{1}{2\sigma^2}\sum_{i=1}^{n}(y_i - a - a^2 x_i)^2. \quad (1.21)$$

Differentiating with respect to a and σ,

$$\frac{\partial L}{\partial a} = \frac{1}{\sigma^2}\sum_{i=1}^{n}(y_i - a - a^2 x_i)(1 + 2ax_i) = 0 \quad (1.22)$$

$$\frac{\partial L}{\partial \sigma} = -\frac{n}{\sigma} + \frac{1}{\sigma^3}\sum_{i=1}^{n}(y_i - a - a^2 x_i)^2 = 0. \quad (1.23)$$

From (1.23) we have as an estimate for $\hat{\sigma}^2$

$$\hat{\sigma}^2 = \frac{\sum\limits_{i=1}^{n}(y_i - a - a^2 x_i)^2}{n} \quad (1.24)$$

and $\hat{a}$ is obtained as a solution of the cubic (1.22). Consider the simple case in which $n = 3$ and the observations are $x_1 = 1, x_2 = 2, x_3 = 3, y_1 = 2 + \varepsilon$, $y_2 = 3 + \varepsilon$, $y_3 = 4 - \varepsilon$, where ε represents some small positive number. Eq. (1.22) then has three real roots for a at approximately -1.4, -0.4 and 1.0. The second-order conditions which must be satisfied for a maximum are that $\partial^2 L/\partial\sigma^2 < 0$, $\partial^2 L/\partial a^2 < 0$ and $(\partial^2 L/\partial\sigma^2)(\partial^2 L/\partial a^2) - (\partial^2 L/\partial\sigma\,\partial a)^2 > 0$. Some manipulation shows that these conditions are satisfied for the largest and smallest values of a, whereas the likelihood function possesses a saddlepoint at the intermediate value.[28]

Another somewhat more standard case which may produce multiple maxima is the estimation of the correlation parameter ϱ from n observations from the standardized bivariate normal distribution. The standardized joint normal density can be written as

$$f(x, y) = \frac{1}{2\pi(1 - \varrho^2)^{1/2}}\exp\left\{-\frac{1}{2(1 - \varrho^2)}(x^2 - 2\varrho xy + y^2)\right\}, \quad (1.25)$$

---

[28] The second-order condition for the sample in the text is $\dfrac{\partial^2 L}{\partial a^2} = -\dfrac{1}{\hat{\sigma}^2}(84a^2 + 36a$

$- 37) < 0$. This incidentally, underscores the importance of having a maximization algorithm which is robust with respect to saddlepoints.

and hence the logarithm of the likelihood function is

$$\log L = -n \log 2\pi - \frac{n}{2} \log (1 - \varrho^2) - \frac{1}{2 (1 - \varrho^2)} (\Sigma x^2 - 2\varrho \Sigma xy + \Sigma y^2).$$

(1.26)

The first-order condition $(\partial \log L)/\partial \varrho = 0$ reduces to the cubic equation

$$\varrho (1 - \varrho^2) + (1 + \varrho^2) \frac{\Sigma xy}{n} - \varrho \left(\frac{\Sigma x^2}{n} + \frac{\Sigma y^2}{n} \right) = 0, \qquad (1.27)$$

which may have three real roots.

The possibility of multiple maxima is particularly serious if we are dealing with likelihood functions since solutions that do not correspond to the largest maximum do not have the property of consistency.[29] It is therefore desirable to ascertain whether a local maximum is in fact a *maximum maximorum*.

Of course, there cannot ever exist an algorithm that guarantees to discover all maxima of an arbitrary function since the number of maxima need not be finite. But even in the case in which it is known *a priori* that the number of maxima is finite there exist only heuristic methods for locating more than one.

Some heuristic methods

The simplest procedure rests on the observation that in most realistic cases *a priori* information will be available to bound the region R in which the maximum is thought to occur. Thus suppose that a starting-point is chosen in R and one of the algorithms for finding local maxima locates a relative maximum at x^0. One might then restart the procedure from a number of different starting-points in R and compare the newly computed answer to x^0. The larger the number of such attempts that all lead to x^0 as the location of the maximum, the greater the subjective certainty that it is the only one.

An alternative procedure is also based on first finding any local maximum at, say, x^0 with value $f(x^0) = M$. We then select a small positive quantity ε

---

[29] We shall return to the question of multiple maxima in the context of maximum likelihood estimation in the next chapter.

and ask whether there exists an x such that

$$f(x) = M + \varepsilon. \tag{1.28}$$

This is tantamount to passing a plane over the function at its last known peak and seeing if it intersects the function. Fig. 1.2 represents this in two dimensions.

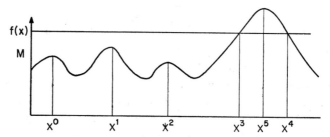

Fig. 1.2. Illustration for finding a global maximum.

Starting from x^0, we are attempting to get to either x^3 or x^4 and consequently, via hill-climbing, to x^5. Of course, solving (1.28) is a problem in itself. In practice, what one can do is to minimize the function[30]

$$g(x) = (f(x) - M - \varepsilon)^2. \tag{1.29}$$

In fig. 1.2, it is clear that x^0, x^1 and x^2 are all local minima for (1.29), so that one may not find x^3 or x^4. Indeed, in two dimensions the starting-points for minimizing (1.29) which produce x^3 or x^4, most probably would yield x^5 as a solution to maximizing the original function $f(x)$. In more than two dimensions, however, this is no longer the case, so that the method may be of significant assistance in locating points like x^3 and x^4, which can then be used as starting-points in maximizing $f(x)$.

We have done some experimentation with combining the two suggestions made above. More explicitly the 'global routine' involved the following steps:

(i) From a starting-point, find a local maximum.

(ii) Randomly generate n_1 new starting-points.[31] If any of these produce a higher function value than in (i) go back to (i) and use this point as a starting value.

---

[30] This suggests that one can use the various methods described above also to solve equations, although there are some additional difficulties noted in the text.

[31] The range of the randomly generated points was made a function of the maximum distance between starting-points and termination points. As new maxima are found, the range automatically was varied.

(iii) Minimize (1.29), n_2 times. If a function value higher than the previous peak is obtained go to (i) with the new starting-point.

(iv) Finally, choose n_3 starting-points and remaximize $f(x)$. If any of these improve over the current maximum go back to (i).

We applied this routine to several function with considerable success. For example, we examined the function

$$f(x, y) = -\left(\frac{x^6}{6} - \frac{37x^5}{5} + 106x^4 - \frac{1828x^3}{3} + 1520x^2 - 1600x\right)$$
$$- 4\left(\frac{y^6}{6} - \frac{37y^5}{5} + 106y^4 - \frac{1828y^3}{3} + 1520y^2 - 1600y\right).$$

The first-order conditions for this are

$$f_x = (x - 1)(x - 2)(x - 4)(x - 10)(x - 20) = 0$$
$$f_y = (y - 1)(y - 2)(y - 4)(y - 10)(y - 20) = 0.$$

Of the 25 points which satisfy the first-order conditions there are 9 maxima [(1, 1), (1, 4), (4, 1), (1, 20), (20, 1), (4, 4), (4, 20), (20, 4), (20, 20)], 4 minima, and 12 saddlepoints, with a global maximum at (20, 20). The above-described routine found all maxima with 18 uses of the quadratic hill-climbing algorithm, where each of the steps (i)–(iv) yielded one or more of the local maxima.

The method was subsequently applied to a number of other simple test functions and it worked nearly as well on these. In short, heuristic methods such as those described may work reasonably well in assisting one in attaining a global maximum.

1.8. Concluding remarks

The probable success of any one method of maximization is difficult to predict in a realistic case. Some rough expectations concerning performance in a variety of conditions can be and have been generated by experimenting with varieties of functions and algorithms. However, unlike a standard sampling procedure in which the population to be sampled is well defined, this is not the case when functions are chosen for experimental purposes from the population of all functions. By the very nature of the situation, the characteristics of a function to be maximized in a realistic situation are not sufficiently well known to allow immediate application of the algorithm most 'likely' to maximize it successfully. As a result of the large element of ignorance that remains inherent in a realistic situation, in spite of all elegant theorems, the maximization of functions of many variables remains an art as much as it is a science. In these concluding remarks we list and discuss briefly some of the most frequent stumbling blocks and some possible remedies. Some actual computational experience is reported in appendix A.

(1) The function may possess narrow ridges with steep sides. Although the steepest ascent method may converge very slowly in these cases, conjugate gradient, quadratic hill-climbing and pattern search methods tend to perform quite well. All methods tend to encounter severe difficulties, however, if the ridge line is severely curved and describes a twisting path.

(2) The problem may be more severe if the function is very flat. Flatness may cause difficulties arising from various sources.

(a) If the algorithms require derivatives, their numerical evaluation may involve large cancellation errors (as two nearly identical function values are subtracted from each other) leading to erroneous estimates of the derivatives.

(b) Whether evaluated numerically or exactly, first derivatives may be very close to zero, resulting in a step-size that is below the preset tolerance used as a criterion for termination. The step-size may also be small for conjugate gradient methods not requiring derivatives. As a result of this the estimated location of the maximum is likely to be sensitive to the initial approximation employed.

(c) In Newton-type methods the inversion of the matrix S may fail because of its apparent singularity. Quadratic hill-climbing may fail if the rank of S is very small since then S will have a repeated root of zero which may cause the computation of eigenvalues to fail. Clearly both of these difficulties may be minimized by employing robust procedures for matrix inversion and eigenvalue computation.

(3) The speed of convergence and the accuracy of the maximum may depend in any event on (a) the initial approximation, (b) the method employed for calculating derivatives, (c) the values selected for the several tolerances and parameters required by the algorithms.

(4) The path and speed of convergence are affected by the manner in which certain constraints are handled. It happens frequently that some range of values for a variable, say x_i, violate the pre-suppositions of the model. Thus, the model may require that x_i be a positive (or non-negative) variable. At least three procedures are possible without inviting the further complica-

tions that would result from reformulating the problem as one in nonlinear programming.

(a) The variable x_i may be replaced by e^y and the function $f(x_1, \ldots, e^y, \ldots, x_n)$ is maximized with respect to $x_1, \ldots, y, \ldots, x_n$.

(b) The function may be left in its original form but whenever an iteration is proposed that would take x_i into the prohibited range the value of the function is set equal to a very small negative number (say -10^{30}), thus causing any algorithm from shying away from accepting such an iteration.

(c) The proposed step size may be shortened (maintaining the same direction) until an acceptable step is produced.

(5) A local maximum may be attained reliably, but there may be no information about the presence of other maxima and even if there is, it may be difficult or impossible to locate all alternatives.

As a result of these and other difficulties a subjective sense of reliability may be achieved by the arduous and inelegant procedure of maximizing each function several times, employing different algorithms and initial approximations. To the extent that the final answers from the several attempts agree, one's confidence is usually greatly increased.

Appendix A: Comparison of maximization algorithms: some numerical results

The efficiency of an algorithm is a composite of at least three types of factors: (1) its reliability which might be measured by the probability that convergence to a true maximum ultimately does take place; (2) its cost in terms of human effort required to make the algorithm 'work' on a given problem; and (3) its cost in terms of the computer time required to achieve a solution. The choice among competing algorithms must be based on an evaluation of at least these three factors. The present appendix deals only with the first and last of these.

The numerical results have been obtained by maximizing a number of functions with several algorithms employing a variety of initial approximations.[32] The algorithms employed were the two versions of the quadratic hill-climbing algorithm discussed in chapter 1, the Powell conjugate gradient

---

[32] Some preliminary results of this type were reported in S. M. Goldfeld, R. E. Quandt, and H. F. Trotter, Maximization by improved quadratic hill-climbing and other methods. Princeton University, Econometric Research Program, Research Memorandum No. 95, April 1968.

method, the Davidon variable metric algorithm, and the Hooke and Jeeves pattern search method.

The reliability of an algorithm may be measured by the relative frequency of cases in which it terminates within an ε-distance of the true location of the extremum. Clearly, different answers may be obtained depending on the specification of ε. Moreover, there are generally two ways in which an algorithm may fail to come within the desired ε-distance. The first is a fatal and abnormal termination such as occurs when a matrix to be inverted is singular and the algorithm cannot proceed further. The second way is a case in which the algorithm mistakenly satisfies its own conditions for a successful termination. We employed two sets of ε-values: (a) $\varepsilon = 0.01 \sqrt{n}$ and (b) $\varepsilon = 10.0 \sqrt{n}$, where n is the number of variables. The first value of ε will tend to catch all instances in which the algorithm fails; the second value passes all cases except those that have failed in an abnormal way. For most of the test functions a large number (25) of starting-points was generated and the failure rate for each algorithm was obtained. We report results based on the smaller of the two ε-values.

The comparison of the algorithms from the point of view of the computing time required for satisfactory convergence is a difficult matter. Computing requirements will generally depend not only upon the intrinsic characteristics of the algorithm but also upon the efficiency with which the necessary computer programs have been prepared. Although it would be desirable to program the various algorithms with 'equal efficiency', this term is not well defined. Thus, even though the time required for computation may be the most relevant measure of efficiency, the reliability of this measure is questionable.

As an additional measure of efficiency one may employ the number of times the function is evaluated in the course of computations. Since much of the computational work is in evaluating the function, this will shed new light on the efficiency question. In particular, it may be that certain methods perform faster only because we are dealing with simple functions and the rank ordering of methods with respect to efficiency will, in general, vary with the nature of the functions. Of course, by itself the number of function evaluations is not a completely suitable measure. If first and second derivatives are evaluated analytically, it is not clear how the work performed in these evaluations should be counted relative to the work involved in function evaluations. Only some measure of time can provide a common denominator. In the work reported here the derivatives are evaluated numerically so that this problem did not arise.[33] Both of these measures of efficiency have been used.

The functions employed are partly well-known test functions that had already been employed by other investigators and partly new functions we devised for test purposes. Sampling experiments were performed with the following functions:

(1) Rosenbrock's function

$$z = 100\,(y - x^2)^2 + (1 - x)^2,$$

which has a single minimum at $(1, 1)$ and resembles a U-shaped valley with steep walls.[34]

(2) The function

$$z = (x_1 + 10x_2)^2 + 5\,(x_3 - x_4)^2 + (x_2 - 2x_3)^4 + 10\,(x_1 - x_4)^4$$

with a single minimum at $(0, 0, 0, 0)$.[35]

(3) The function

$$z = \exp\,(\exp\,(\exp\,(\exp\,(\exp\,(\exp\,(\exp\,(-x^2 - 3y^2)/10)/10)/10)/10)))$$

with a single maximum at $(0, 0)$.

(4) Beale's function, given by

$$z = (1.5 - x\,(1 - y))^2 + (2.25 - x\,(1 - y^2))^2 + (2.625 - x\,(1 - y^3))^2,$$

which is a narrow curving valley with a minimum at $(3, 0.5)$.[36]

(5) A three-dimensional Rosenbrock function

$$z = 100\,(x_3 - x_1^2)^2 + 100\,(x_2 - x_1^2)^2 + (1 - x_1)^2$$

with a minimum at $(1, 1, 1)$.

---

[33] The intervals over which function values were evaluated for the purpose of obtaining approximate derivatives were computed as fractions of the last step in each of the n principal directions. It subsequently emerged that the quadratic hill-climbing algorithms have superior performance if the ith derivative is calculated over an interval that is a fraction of the absolute value of the current value of the ith variable. The present results therefore understate the speed with which the quadratic hill-climbing algorithms converge.

[34] Investigated previously by R. Fletcher and M. J. D. Powell, A rapidly convergent descent method for minimization. *Computer Journal* 6 (1963), 163–68; A. Leon, A comparison among eight known optimizing procedures. Space Sciences Laboratory, Working Paper No. 20, University of California, Berkeley, August 1964; M. J. D. Powell, An efficient method for finding the minimum of a function of several variables without calculating derivatives. *Computer Journal* 7 (1964), 155–62.

[35] Investigated by M. J. D. Powell, *op. cit.*

[36] Investigated by A. Leon, *op. cit.*

(6) The function

$$z = \frac{1}{Q(1 + x^k)} \exp\left\{-\frac{(y - x^2)^2}{(Q(1 + x^k))^2}\right\} \quad \begin{array}{l} Q > 0 \\ k > 0 \text{ and even,} \end{array}$$

which is a parabolic Gaussian ridge, achieving its maximum at $(0, 0)$. It has the particular advantage that the computational characteristics of this function can be radically altered by varying the quantities Q and k.

Each of these functions was maximized or minimized by each of the five algorithms, and 25 randomly chosen starting-points were employed. The algorithms employed were as follows: (1) the simple (spherical) quadratic hill-climbing algorithm; (2) the modified (ellipsoidal) quadratic hill-climbing algorithm; (3) the Powell conjugate gradient algorithm; (4) the Davidon variable metric algorithm; and (5) the Hooke and Jeeves pattern search algorithm. Wherever relevant, derivatives were computed by numerical evaluation. The results are reported in detail in tables 1.4 to 1.15. These tables present for each method (a) the mean time and the standard deviation of

TABLE 1.4

The function $z = 100 (y - x^2)^2 + (1 - x)^2$.
Numerical derivatives. 25 random starting-points in the cube $-2 \leq x, y \leq 2$

		Simple quadratic hill-climbing	Modified quadratic hill-climbing	Davidon	Powell	Hooke and Jeeves
Time (seconds)	Mean	0.021	0.023	0.038	0.031	0.018
	Stand. dev.	0.008	0.010	0.012	0.010	0.011
Number of	Mean	204	187	451	382	462
function	Stand. dev.	78	70	143	117	279
evaluations						
Function value	Mean	0.26×10^{-10}	0.23×10^{-10}	0.39×10^{-9}	0.13×10^{-10}	0.60×10^{-8}
Distance from	Mean	0.92×10^{-6}	0.12×10^{-5}	0.17×10^{-4}	0.35×10^{-5}	0.61×10^{-4}
true extremum						
Failure rate		0.0	0.0	0.040	0.0	0.0

time, in seconds; (b) the mean and the standard deviation of the number of function evaluations; (c) the mean value of the function at the point of convergence; (d) the mean distance of the alleged location of the extremum from the true location; and (e) the failure rate of the algorithm. Computer

TABLE 1.5

The function $z = (x_1 + 10x_2)^2 + 5(x_3 - x_4)^2 + (x_2 - 2x_3)^4 + 10(x_1 - x_4)^4$.
Numerical derivatives. 25 random starting-points in the hypercube $-3 \leq x_i \leq 3$

		Simple quadratic hill-climbing	Modified quadratic hill-climbing	Davidon	Powell	Hooke and Jeeves
Time (seconds)	Mean	0.071	0.075	0.050	0.080	0.058
	Stand. dev.	0.012	0.012	0.013	0.017	0.037
Number of function evaluations	Mean	665	668	551	956	1607
	Stand. dev.	115	117	153	198	1061
Function value	Mean	0.73×10^{-17}	0.44×10^{-16}	0.11×10^{-7}	0.14×10^{-7}	0.37×10^{-7}
Distance from true extremum	Mean	0.24×10^{-4}	0.25×10^{-4}	0.51×10^{-2}	0.40×10^{-2}	0.72×10^{-2}
Failure rate		0.0	0.0	0.0	0.080	0.160

TABLE 1.6

The function $z = \exp(\exp(\exp(\exp(\exp(\exp(\exp(-x^2 - 3y^2)/10)/10)/10)/10)))$.
Numerical derivatives. 25 random starting-points in the cube $-2 \leq x, y \leq 2$

		Simple quadratic hill-climbing	Modified quadratic hill-climbing	Davidon	Powell	Hooke and Jeeves
Time (seconds)	Mean	0.018	0.020	0.002	0.010	0.022
	Stand. dev.	0.002	0.003	0.002	0.003	0.002
Number of function evaluations	Mean	80	81	10	44	120
	Stand. dev.	10	14	6	12	11
Function value	Mean	21.3204	21.3204	21.3191	21.3131	21.3204
Distance from true extremum	Mean	0.20×10^{-5}	0.13×10^{-5}	0.13×10^{-2}	0.20	0.29×10^{-1}
Failure rate		0.0	0.0	0.0	0.280	0.0

programs were written in Fortran and the computations were performed on an IBM 360/91.

Some general conclusions from these experiments are as follows:

(1) The two versions of the quadratic hill-climbing method are of substantially comparable performance.

TABLE 1.7

The function $z = (1.5 - x(1 - y))^2 + (2.25 - x(1 - y^2))^2 + (2.625 - x(1 - y^3))^2$.
Numerical derivatives. 25 random starting-points in the cube $-2 \leq x, y \leq 2$

		Simple quadratic hill-climbing	Modified quadratic hill-climbing	Davidon	Powell	Hooke and Jeeves
Time (seconds)	Mean	0.012	0.014	0.018	0.019	0.013
	Stand. dev.	0.003	0.003	0.002	0.004	0.002
Number of function evaluations	Mean	118	118	204	225	323
	Stand. dev.	27	26	24	47	47
Function value	Mean	0.83×10^{-12}	0.74×10^{-10}	0.76×10^{-11}	0.28×10^{-11}	$0.32 \times 10^{-}$
Distance from true extremum	Mean	0.17×10^{-5}	0.22×10^{-5}	0.41×10^{-5}	0.18×10^{-5}	$0.92 \times 10^{-}$
Failure rate		0.160	0.160	0.240	0.120	0.200

TABLE 1.8

The function $z = 100(x_3 - x_1^2)^2 + 100(x_2 - x_1^2)^2 + (1 - x_1)^2$.
Numerical derivatives. 25 random starting-points in the hypercube $-2 \leq x_1, x_2, x_3 \leq 2$

		Simple quadratic hill-climbing	Modified quadratic hill-climbing	Davidon	Powell	Hooke and Jeeves
Time (seconds)	Mean	0.038	0.049	0.067	0.052	0.051
	Stand. dev.	0.016	0.020	0.015	0.021	0.057
Number of function evaluations	Mean	425	402	802	659	1430
	Stand. dev.	173	147	185	225	1593
Function value	Mean	0.12×10^{-9}	0.24×10^{-10}	0.20×10^{-8}	0.53×10^{-7}	$0.27 \times 10^{-}$
Distance from true extremum	Mean	0.33×10^{-5}	0.13×10^{-5}	0.53×10^{-4}	0.50×10^{-4}	$0.29 \times 10^{-}$
Failure rate		0.0	0.0	0.040	0.040	0.0

(2) These two methods have a smaller overall failure rate than the other three methods and are quite substantially better than Davidon and Powell in this respect.[37]

---

[37] Some limited experimentation with analytically evaluated derivatives indicates modest improvement in the time required by the quadratic hill-climbing and the Davidon algorithms. Davidon's method also seems to perform very much better in the case of numerically evaluated derivatives if Stewart's modification is employed. See G. W. Stewart, III, *op. cit.*

TABLE 1.9

The function $z = (1/(Q(1 + x^2)))\exp\{-(y - x^2)^2/(Q(1 + x^2))^2\}$ for $Q = 1$.
Numerical derivatives. 25 random starting-points in the cube $-5 \leqq x, y \leqq 5$

		Simple quadratic hill-climbing	Modified quadratic hill-climbing	Davidon	Powell	Hooke and Jeeves
Time (seconds)	Mean	0.012	0.015	0.042	0.015	0.36
	Stand. dev.	0.030	0.004	0.034	0.010	1.72
Number of function evaluations	Mean	104	111	393	142	6070
	Stand. dev.	24	30	328	91	29 369
Function value	Mean	1.00000	1.00000	0.99999	1.00000	1.00000
Distance from true extremum	Mean	0.11×10^{-5}	0.18×10^{-5}	0.12×10^{-2}	0.50×10^{-3}	0.48×10^{-3}
Failure rate		0.0	0.0	0.040	0.360	0.0

TABLE 1.10

The function $z = (1/(Q(1 + x^2)))\exp\{-(y - x^2)^2/(Q(1 + x^2))^2\}$. $Q = 0.5$.
Numerical derivatives. 10 random starting-points in the cube $-5 \leqq x, y \leqq 5$

		Simple quadratic hill-climbing	Modified quadratic hill-climbing	Davidon	Powell	Hooke and Jeeves
Time (seconds)	Mean	0.018	0.022	0.047	0.020	0.013
	Stand. dev.	0.004	0.007	0.029	0.022	0.003
Number of function evaluations	Mean	146	154	414	208	224
	Stand. dev.	31	42	207	224	51
Function value	Mean	1.99999	1.99999	1.99999	2.00000	2.00000
Distance from true extremum	Mean	0.10×10^{-5}	0.15×10^{-5}	0.13×10^{-2}	0.44×10^{-3}	0.45×10^{-3}
Failure rate		0.0	0.0	0.400	0.920	0.0

(3) They usually require fewer function evaluations than the other three methods, sometimes by substantial margins. However, for 10-variable or larger problems (not reported here), Powell is often the best method.

(4) Their superiority in terms of time is less uniform, this being due to the greater expense of time per iteration.

(5) Davidon, Powell, and Hooke and Jeeves each become worst performers with respect to time for some case with the latter achieving the overall worst record.

TABLE 1.11

The function $z = (1/(Q(1 + x^2))) \exp\{-(y - x^2)^2/(Q(1 + x^2))^2\}$. $Q = 0.1$.
Numerical derivatives. 25 random starting-points in the cube $-5 \leq x, y \leq 5$

		Simple quadratic hill-climbing	Modified quadratic hill-climbing	Davidon	Powell	Hooke and Jeeves
Time (seconds)	Mean	0.064	0.091			0.653
	Stand. dev.	0.048	0.094			3.015
Number of	Mean	334	389			10973
function	Stand. dev.	112	206			50811
evaluations						
Function value	Mean	10.00000	9.99903			10.00000
Distance from	Mean	0.22×10^{-5}	0.21×10^{-3}			0.49×10^{-3}
true extremum						
Failure rate		0.080	0.120	1.000	1.000	0.0

(6) The parabolic Gaussian ridge seems to be a severe test, causing Davidon and Powell to have 100% failure rates for $Q = 0.1$ and causing excessive computation time for Hooke and Jeeves and some failures for the quadratic hill-climbing algorithms.

We also employed some of the methods on some more realistic examples. The modified quadratic hill-climbing method and Powell's method were used for maximizing the likelihood function associated with a small econometric model of the U.S. economy (Klein's Model I). After eliminating identities, the equations of this model are[38]:

$$u_{1i} = -y_{1i} + \beta_{12}y_{2i} + \beta_{13}y_{3i} + \beta_{12}x_{1i} + \gamma_{12}x_{2i} - \beta_{13}x_{3i} - \beta_{13}x_{5i} + \beta_{13}x_{6i}$$

$$u_{2i} = \beta_{21}y_{1i} \quad - y_{2i} \quad\quad\quad + \gamma_{24}x_{4i} + \beta_{?1}x_{5i} + \gamma_{27}x_{7i} \quad (1.30)$$

$$u_{3i} = \beta_{31}y_{1i} \quad\quad\quad - y_{3i} \quad\quad + \gamma_{32}x_{2i} + \gamma_{33}x_{3i},$$

where (i) $x_{1i}, x_{2i}, \ldots, x_{7i}$ are assumed to be nonstochastic (ii) u_{1i}, u_{2i} and u_{3i} are (unobservable) stochastic terms assumed to be jointly normally

[38] G.C.Chow, Two methods of computing full information maximum likelihood estimates in simultaneous stochastic equations. *International Economic Review* **9** (1968), 100–12; and L.R.Klein, *Economic fluctuations in the United States*. Cowles Commission Monograph No. 11. New York, Wiley, 1950.

TABLE 1.12*

The function $L = -\frac{1}{2}\log(\frac{1}{21}\det(U'U)) + \log(\det(B))$

		Modified quadratic hill-climbing	Powell
Time (seconds)	Start 1	41.55	64.48
	Start 2	23.52	63.78
Number of function	Start 1	3289	6324
evaluations	Start 2	1830	6233
Function value	Start 1	-2.75562	-2.75797
	Start 2	-2.75581	-2.75625

* These computations were performed on an IBM 7094.

TABLE 1.13*

Location of maximum for the function $L = -\frac{1}{2}\log(\frac{1}{21}\det(U'U)) + \log(\det(B))$

Para- meter	Modified quadratic hill-climbing		Powell		Chow's estimate**
	Start 1	Start 2	Start 1	Start 2	
β_{12}	-0.16426	-0.16957	-0.15926	-0.15295	-0.16079
β_{13}	0.82053	0.85037	0.81734	0.77604	0.81144
γ_{12}	0.31561	0.30402	0.29741	0.31927	0.31295
β_{21}	0.31122	0.31977	0.28905	0.29574	0.30569
γ_{24}	0.30674	0.30357	0.31245	0.31191	0.30662
γ_{27}	0.37202	0.36948	0.36366	0.36714	0.37170
β_{31}	-0.77638	-0.72073	-0.79786	-0.89165	-0.80099
γ_{32}	1.05149	1.02007	0.99084	1.07300	1.0519
γ_{33}	0.85120	0.84839	0.85150	0.85300	0.85190

* These computations were performed on an IBM 7094.
** From G.C. Chow, *op. cit.*

distributed with mean vector $\mu = 0$ and covariance matrix Σ; (iii) observations are available[39] on all $y_{1i}, y_{2i}, y_{3i}, x_{1i}, \ldots, x_{7i}, i = 1, \ldots, 21$; and (iv) the β's, γ's and the elements of Σ are to be estimated. The system given by (1.30) can be written more compactly as

$$U = YB + XA, \qquad (1.31)$$

[39] See L.R.Klein, *op. cit.*

TABLE 1.14

The function $\sum_{i=1}^{6} (y_i - \theta_1 - \theta_2 e^{\theta_3 x_i})^2$

	Number of function evaluations	Function value at minimum	Location of minimum		
			θ_1	θ_2	θ_3
Simple quadratic hill-climbing	1698	13 639	560.30	− 197.05	−0.1690
Modified quadratic hill-climbing	1047	13 710	565.78	− 203.86	−0.1633
Davidon	221	13 393	526.74	− 160.89	−0.1962
Powell	578	13 390	523.38	− 157.05	−0.1995
Hooke and Jeeves	1999	13 552	551.83	− 189.51	−0.1735
Vitale and Taylor estimates using analytic derivatives	−	13 390	523.31	− 156.95	−0.1997
Vitale and Taylor estimates using numerical derivatives	−	13 421	514.11	− 145.49	−0.2105

where Y is the (21×3) matrix of observations on the jointly dependent variables, X is the (21×7) matrix of observations on the predetermined variables, B and A are the corresponding coefficient matrices, and U is the (21×3) matrix of error terms.

It is easy to show that the logarithm of likelihood function for y_1, y_2 and y_3 can be condensed to the following form

$$L = -\tfrac{1}{2} \log \left(\tfrac{1}{21} \det (U'U)\right) + \log (\det (B)). \qquad (1.32)$$

The function (1.32) was maximized employing two starting-points: Start 1 is the point $(0, 0, 0, 0, 0, 0, 0, 0, 0)$ and Start 2 is the point $(0.20410, 0.10250, 0.22967, 0.72465, 0.23273, 0.28341, 0.23116, 0.54600, 0.85400)$.[40] The results are displayed in tables 1.12 and 1.13. Inspection of these tables reveals that the modified quadratic hill-climbing algorithm performs substantially better

---

[40] This point represents the parameter estimates by the method of limited information maximum likelihood and is in effect a maximum likelihood estimate taking the equations of the model one at a time and disregarding the *a priori* restrictions on the remaining equations.—Since the logarithm of a negative number is not defined, both algorithms were slightly modified in order to avoid generating steps that would take one into a forbidden region in the parameter space.

TABLE 1.15

The function $S = \sum_{i=1}^{n} [(x_i - x)^2 + (y_i - y)^2]^{k/2}$

	x	y	S	Number of function evaluations	Iterations
Problem 1-1					
$n = 10, \quad k = 1$					
Simple quadratic hill-climbing	28.814	49.051	303.261	86	6
Modified quadratic hill-climbing	28.814	49.051	303.261	86	6
Davidon	28.819	49.082	303.261	107	5
Powell	28.837	49.053	303.261	108	3
Hooke and Jeeves	28.808	49.045	303.261	147	29
Cooper	28.814	49.053	303.261	—	27
Problem 1-2					
$n = 10, \quad k = 2.5$					
Simple quadratic hill-climbing	32.604	56.201	82459.0	41	3
Modified quadratic hill-climbing	32.604	56.201	82459.0	41	3
Davidon	32.601	56.201	82459.0	86	5
Powell	32.610	56.185	82459.0	110	3
Hooke and Jeeves	32.597	56.193	82458.9	144	28
Cooper	32.604	56.201	82459.0	—	9
Problem 2–1					
$n = 20, k = 1.0$					
Simple quadratic hill-climbing	52.180	52.312	793.067	71	5
Modified quadratic hill-climbing	52.180	52.312	793.067	71	5
Davidon	52.158	52.338	793.065	66	3
Powell	52.162	52.316	793.065	133	3
Hooke and Jeeves	52.174	52.329	793.065	164	31
Cooper	52.178	52.318	793.065	—	20
Problem 2–2					
$n = 20, k = 2.5$					
Simple quadratic hill-climbing	45.271	49.476	255069.4	41	3
Modified quadratic hill-climbing	45.271	49.476	255069.4	41	3
Davidon	45.275	49.480	255068.8	100	5
Powell	45.270	49.469	255068.8	137	4
Hooke and Jeeves	45.280	49.463	255068.9	135	28
Cooper	45.271	49.476	255069.0	—	8

than Powell in terms of time which is not surprising since it is often true that Powell requires more function evaluations. In terms of accuracy, both seem to give results that compare well with the independently computed results of Chow.

A second test case was Hartley's function given by

$$S = \sum_{i=1}^{6} (y_i - \theta_1 - \theta_2 e^{\theta_3 x_i})^2,$$

where the six x and y values are $(-5, -3, -1, 1, 3, 5)$ and $(127, 151, 379, 421, 460, 426)$ respectively.[41] This function was minimized by all five methods discussed in this appendix, and the results are contrasted with the independently obtained results of Vitale and Taylor.[42] Table 1.14 reveals the following conclusions: (a) the two versions of the quadratic hill-climbing method do not do as well as the others in terms of accuracy; (b) Powell and Davidon perform as well as Vitale and Taylor's modified Davidon method using analytic derivatives; (c) using numerical derivatives the latter method is worse than Davidon or Powell.

A third class of problem investigated is the generalized Weber problem which consists of minimizing

$$S = \sum_{i=1}^{n} [(x_i - x)^2 + (y_i - y)^2]^{k/2}$$

with respect to x and y, where x_i and y_i are given numbers. These problems have most often been solved by *ad hoc* methods that are basically Newton-Raphson type approaches to solving the equations representing the first-order conditions for a minimum.[43] Four of the many problems solved by Cooper were solved by the methods discussed here. All methods do very well with the two quadratic hill-climbing methods holding the edge in terms of the number of function evaluations. Unfortunately none of them can be compared easily with Cooper's procedure for the latter measures work performed in terms of the number of iterations which is an ambiguous measure.

---

[41] P. Vitale and G. Taylor, A note on the application of Davidon's method to nonlinear regression problems. *Technometrics* **10** (1968), 843–49.

[42] The results of Vitale and Taylor do not include the number of times the function was evaluated, but only the number of iterations performed.

[43] See H. W. Kuhn and R. E. Kuenne, An efficient algorithm for the numerical solution of the generalized Weber problem in spatial economics. *Journal of Regional Science* **4** (1962), 21–34; and L. Cooper, An extension of the generalized Weber problem. *Journal of Regional Science* **8** (1968), 181–98.

CHAPTER 2

LEAST SQUARES THEORY, CONFIDENCE INTERVALS, AND MAXIMUM LIKELIHOOD ESTIMATION

2.1. Introduction

The previous chapter dealt with the problem of optimizing a given objective function and presented several alternative algorithms for use in numerical analysis. The present chapter is concerned with estimation and hypothesis testing in econometric models and its focus is on the steps preceding and following the actual optimization process. The step prior to estimation consists of adopting a criterion for estimation. That is, one must develop an objective function, one whose optimization will produce estimates of unknown parameters with desirable statistical properties. The present chapter considers two of these criteria, least squares and maximum likelihood. The step following estimation consists of testing statistical hypotheses about the true parameter values or providing confidence intervals for them. As we shall see, in situations involving nonlinearities this may be quite complex and we shall be forced to examine several alternative approximative methods.

The discussion in the first parts of the chapter focuses on the general regression model of the form

$$y = f(x, \theta) + u, \tag{2.1}$$

where $x = (x_1, \ldots, x_k)$ is a k-component vector of non-stochastic independent variables, $\theta = (\theta_1, \ldots, \theta_p)$ is a p-component vector of population parameters to be estimated, y is the dependent variable, and u is an unobservable error term. Given n observations on y and on the k x's denoted by y_i and $x^i = (x_{1i}, \ldots, x_{ki}), (i = 1, \ldots, n)$, least squares estimates for θ are those that minimize the expression

$$S(\theta) = \sum_{i=1}^{n} (y_i - f(x^i, \theta))^2. \tag{2.2}$$

The least squares estimates are denoted by $\hat{\theta}$ and the minimum value of (2.2) by $S(\hat{\theta})$.

Principal differences among models of type (2.1) depend on whether the function $f(x, \theta)$ is linear in θ or not.

The computation of both the $\hat{\theta}$'s (by least squares) and of a joint confidence region for the $\hat{\theta}$'s on the assumption of normally distributed errors is a straightforward matter in the linear case. Neither of these is likely to be easy in the presence of nonlinearities. In addition, once one leaves the realm of linearity, the least squares principle has no general optimum properties. As a consequence, in section 2.4 of this chapter we consider the maximum likelihood principle. It should be noted that if the disturbances in model (2.1) are normally and independently distributed, then least squares and maximum likelihood estimates are identical. Maximum likelihood estimation can, of course, be applied to models of the type (2.1) even if the u's do not follow the normal distribution. Moreover, maximum likelihood estimation can readily be applied to models that are considerably more general than (2.1)—indeed to models for which the least squares principle is not even well-defined. We shall meet examples of this later.

The outline of this chapter is as follows. We first briefly review the essential details of estimation and hypothesis testing in the linear model.[1] We then examine the corresponding procedures in the more general model given by (2.1) and (2.2). We subsequently turn our attention to maximum likelihood estimation. The chapter concludes with a brief survey of our aims and objectives in the following chapters.

2.2. Linear models

As indicated above, linearity in the context of model (2.1) will always be taken to refer to linearity in θ; thus a model will be called linear if it can be written as

$$y = \sum_{i=1}^{p} \theta_i z_i + u \tag{2.3}$$

after suitable redefinition of the original variables $x_1, \ldots, x_k$, where $z_i = g_i(x_1, \ldots, x_k)$ $(i = 1, \ldots, p)$. If the model is linear in θ as well as in

---

[1] For relatively complete treatments of the linear model see F. A. Graybill, *An introduction to linear statistical models*. New York, McGraw–Hill, 1961, ch. 6; A. S. Goldberger, *Econometric theory*. New York, Wiley, 1964, ch. 7; J. Johnston, *Econometric methods*. New York McGraw–Hill, 1963, ch. 4.

the original variables x, it can be written in shorthand form as

$$Y = X\theta + U, \tag{2.4}$$

where X is the $n \times k$ matrix of observations on the independent variables, Y is the $n \times 1$ vector of observations on the dependent variable, U is the $n \times 1$ vector of unobservable error terms, and $k = p$.

Preliminaries

In this part we state without proof a number of well-known theorems that are used in the development of the theory of least squares. In what follows Z will denote a $k \times 1$ vector of random variables. It will be assumed that Z is distributed as $N(\mu, \Omega)$; i.e., Z has the normal distribution with mean vector μ and covariance matrix Ω. The symbol $t(r)$ will denote the t-distribution with r degrees of freedom, $\chi^2(r)$ will denote the (central) chi-square distribution with r degrees of freedom, and $F(n_1, n_2)$ will denote the (central) F-distribution with (n_1, n_2) degrees of freedom.

THEOREM 2.1: *If Z is distributed as $N(0, \sigma^2 I)$ and if A is a symmetric idempotent matrix of rank $r \leq k$, then the quadratic form $(Z'AZ)/\sigma^2$ has the $\chi^2(r)$ distribution.*

THEOREM 2.2: *If the random variables u_1 and u_2 have independent χ^2 distributions with n_1 and n_2 degrees of freedom respectively, the quantity $(u_1/n_1)/(u_2/n_2)$ has the $F(n_1, n_2)$ distribution.*

THEOREM 2.3: *If Z is distributed as $N(0, I)$ and if A and B are positive semidefinite matrices of order k, the quadratic forms $Z'AZ$ and $Z'BZ$ are independent if (and only if) $AB = 0$.*

THEOREM 2.4: *If Z is distributed as $N(\mu, \Omega)$ and A is a matrix, the vector AZ is distributed as $N(A\mu, A\Omega A')$.*

THEOREM 2.5: *If the random variable u_1 is normally distributed with mean μ and standard deviation σ and if u_2 has independent $\chi^2(k)$ distribution, the quantity*

$$\frac{(u_1 - \mu)/\sigma}{\sqrt{u_2/k}}$$

is distributed as $t(k)$.

THEOREM 2.6: *If Z is distributed as $N(\mu, \sigma^2 I)$, and if A and B are two matrices, the linear form AZ and the quadratic form $Z'BZ$ are independent if $AB = 0$.*

Basic least squares theory

The statistical model to be discussed is given by (2.4)

$$Y = X\theta + U$$

and where we assume that $E(U) = 0$ and $E(UU') = \sigma^2 I$.

The expression for the sum of squares, (2.2), is given in matrix form by

$$S(\theta) = (Y - X\theta)'(Y - X\theta). \tag{2.5}$$

In order to minimize (2.5) we set the partial derivatives of $S(\theta)$ with respect to the elements of θ equal to zero, yielding

$$-X'Y + X'X\hat{\theta} = 0,$$

and, provided that no linear dependencies exist among the columns of X,

$$\hat{\theta} = (X'X)^{-1} X'Y. \tag{2.6}$$

A number of important results are summarized in

THEOREM 2.7 (Gauss-Markov): *The least squares estimates* (2.6) *are the only best, linear, unbiased estimates.*

PROOF: Construct an estimator $\tilde{\theta}$, linear in the dependent variable Y, by

$$\tilde{\theta} = [(X'X)^{-1} X' + A] Y$$

where A is a $k \times n$ matrix. Requiring $\tilde{\theta}$ to be unbiased implies

$$E(\tilde{\theta}) = E\{[(X'X)^{-1}X' + A][X\theta + U]\} = \theta + AX\theta = \theta,$$

which restricts A to the class of matrices for which $AX = 0$.

The covariance matrix of $\tilde{\theta}$ is given by

$$E[(\tilde{\theta} - \theta)(\tilde{\theta} - \theta)']$$

$$= E\{([(X'X)^{-1}X' + A]Y - \theta)([(X'X)^{-1}X' + A]Y - \theta)'\},$$

which, substituting $X\theta + U$ for Y and using $AX = 0$, simplifies to

$$\sigma^2 [(X'X)^{-1} + AA']. \tag{2.7}$$

The diagonal elements of (2.7), being the variances of the elements of $\tilde{\theta}$, are minimized with respect to the elements of A by setting A equal to the null matrix, since the contribution of A to the ith diagonal term is $\sum_{j=1}^{n} a_{ij}^2$. This proves the theorem. It also follows that the covariance matrix of least squares estimates is $\sigma^2 (X'X)^{-1}$.

Confidence regions

The question of establishing confidence regions for regression coefficients can be handled by the same procedures as the question of testing hypotheses about them. We first deal with a single coefficient. We denote by θ_i and $\hat{\theta}_i$ the ith component of θ and $\hat{\theta}$ respectively, by σ_i^2 we denote the true variance of $\hat{\theta}_i$, and by $\hat{\sigma}_i^2$ the estimated variance of $\hat{\theta}_i$.

The minimum value of $S(\theta)$, denoted by $S(\hat{\theta})$, is obtained by substituting (2.6) into (2.5):

$$S(\hat{\theta}) = (Y - X(X'X)^{-1}X'Y)'(Y - X(X'X)^{-1}X'Y)$$

$$= Y'(I - X(X'X)^{-1}X')'(I - X(X'X)^{-1}X')Y$$

$$= Y'(I - X(X'X)^{-1}X')Y \tag{2.8}$$

since $I - X(X'X)^{-1}X'$ is idempotent. Further, substituting $X\theta + U$ for Y in (2.8) yields

$$S(\hat{\theta}) = U'(I - X(X'X)^{-1}X')U, \tag{2.9}$$

which is quadratic a form in the random variable U.

THEOREM 2.8: *The expected value of* $S(\hat{\theta})$ *is* $\sigma^2(n - k)$.

PROOF: Since the elements of U are independent of each other, $E(U'AU) = \sigma^2 \operatorname{tr}(A)$, where tr is the trace, for any quadratic form with matrix A. But

$$\operatorname{tr}[I - X(X'X)^{-1}X'] = \operatorname{tr}(I) - \operatorname{tr}[X(X'X)^{-1}X']$$

$$= \operatorname{tr}(I) - \operatorname{tr}[(X'X)^{-1}(X'X)] = n - k,$$

which proves the theorem. It follows that an unbiased estimate of the error variance σ^2 is obtained by $S(\hat{\theta})/(n - k)$.

Up to now we have not assumed a specific distribution for the disturbances in (2.4). In what follows we shall assume that the vector U is normally distributed. We, of course, retain the assumptions that $E(U) = 0$ and $E(UU') = \sigma^2 I$.

THEOREM 2.9: *The quantity* $S(\hat{\theta})/\sigma^2$ *has the* $\chi^2(n - k)$ *distribution.*

PROOF: U is distributed as $N(0, \sigma^2 I)$. The matrix of the quadratic form (2.9) is idempotent and of rank $n - k$. The theorem then follows from theorem 2.1. It further follows that if we estimate the error variance $\hat{\sigma}^2$ by $S(\hat{\theta})/(n - k)$ then the quantity $\hat{\sigma}^2/\sigma^2$ is distributed as $\chi^2(n - k)/(n - k)$.

THEOREM 2.10: *The vector* $\hat{\theta} - \theta$ *is distributed as* $N(0, \sigma^2(X'X)^{-1})$.

PROOF: Since $\hat{\theta}$ is the least squares estimate, $\hat{\theta} - \theta = (X'X)^{-1}X'U$, where U is distributed as $N(0, \sigma^2 I)$. The assertion then follows from theorem 2.4. As a corollary, it immediately follows that $(\hat{\theta}_i - \theta_i)/\sigma_i$ is distributed as $N(0, 1)$, where σ_i represents the square root of the ith diagonal element of $\sigma^2(X'X)^{-1}$.

Since the estimate $\hat{\sigma}^2$ of σ^2 is obtained by calculating $S(\hat{\theta})/(n - k)$, the estimate $\hat{\sigma}^2$ of σ_i^2 is obtained by replacing in the ith diagonal element of $\sigma^2(X'X)^{-1}$ the quantity σ^2 by $\hat{\sigma}^2$. From this we can deduce

THEOREM 2.11: *The quantity $(\hat{\theta}_i - \theta_i)/\hat{\sigma}_i$ has the $t(n - k)$ distribution.*

PROOF: Divide numerator and denominator by σ_i, yielding the quantity

$$\frac{(\hat{\theta}_i - \theta_i)/\sigma_i}{\hat{\sigma}_i/\sigma_i}.$$

By theorem 2.10 the numerator has the $N(0, 1)$ distribution. The denominator is equal to $\hat{\sigma}/\sigma$, which is the square-root of a random variable with $\chi^2(n - k)$ distribution divided by the degrees of freedom. Moreover, the product of the matrices of the linear form in U and the quadratic form in U is zero, i.e.,

$$(X'X)^{-1}X'[I - X(X'X)^{-1}X'] = 0.$$

The theorem then follows as a direct application of theorems 2.5 and 2.6. It follows that if we denote by $t_\alpha(n - k)$ the critical value from the $t(n - k)$ distribution at a significance level α, then $100(1 - \alpha)$ percent confidence limits for θ_i are given by $\hat{\theta}_i \pm t_\alpha(n - k)\hat{\sigma}_i$. It further follows that the k intervals for θ_i, $(i = 1, \ldots, k)$ cannot be asserted simultaneously with a confidence of $100(1 - \alpha)^k$ %, since the intervals established disregard the covariance between $\hat{\theta}_i$ and $\hat{\theta}_j$. If (and only if) the $\hat{\theta}_i$ $(i = 1, \ldots, k)$ are all independent (which will be the case if the independent variables are all mutually orthogonal), the intervals hold simultaneously with a confidence of $100(1 - \alpha)^k$ %.

The construction of a simultaneous confidence region for a subset of the elements of θ is most easily approached from the point of view of testing hypotheses about them. Let the vector θ be partitioned $(\theta_1 \theta_2)$ and let X be partitioned conformably $(X_1 X_2)$, so that (2.4) becomes

$$Y = X_1\theta_1 + X_2\theta_2 + U, \tag{2.10}$$

where θ_1 contains $k - q$ and θ_2 contains q elements. Assume that a hypothesis is to be tested about the elements of θ_2 simultaneously. The test is based upon the reduction in the residual sum of squares resulting from replacing the hypothesized values of θ_2 by their least squares values. If the reduction turns out to be large, the hypothesis is considered untenable.

Utilizing the partitioned form (2.10), least squares estimates are given by[2]

$$\hat{\theta} = \begin{bmatrix} \hat{\theta}_1 \\ \hat{\theta}_2 \end{bmatrix} = \begin{bmatrix} X_1'X_1 & X_1'X_2 \\ X_2'X_1 & X_2'X_2 \end{bmatrix}^{-1} \begin{bmatrix} X_1'Y \\ X_2'Y \end{bmatrix}$$

$$= \begin{bmatrix} (X_1'X_1)^{-1} X_1' (I - X_2 V^{-1} X_2' W) Y \\ V^{-1} X_2' W Y \end{bmatrix}, \quad (2.11)$$

where

$$W = I - X_1 (X_1'X_1)^{-1} X_1'$$

$$V = X_2' W X_2.$$

These estimates are clearly the same as those given by (2.6). If, on the other hand, the elements of θ_2 were set at fixed values, least squares estimates for θ_1 denoted by $\hat{\theta}_1(\theta_2)$, could be derived as functions of θ_2:

$$\hat{\theta}_1(\theta_2) = (X_1'X_1)^{-1} X_1' (Y - X_2\theta_2). \quad (2.12)$$

To each of these cases there corresponds a sum of squares of residuals. The sum of squares corresponding to (2.11) is

$$S(\hat{\theta}) = S(\hat{\theta}_1, \hat{\theta}_2) = U' (I - X(X'X)^{-1}X') U,$$

which is the same as (2.9). The one corresponding to (2.12) is

$$S(\hat{\theta}_1(\theta_2), \theta_2) = U' (I - X_1 (X_1'X_1)^{-1} X_1') U. \quad (2.13)$$

THEOREM 2.12: *The quantity*

$$\frac{[S(\hat{\theta}_1(\theta_2), \theta_2) - S(\hat{\theta}_1, \hat{\theta}_2)]/q}{S(\hat{\theta}_1, \hat{\theta}_2)/(n - k)}$$

has the F $(q, n - k)$ distribution.

---

[2] It is well known that the inverse of the partitioned matrix $\begin{bmatrix} A & B \\ C & D \end{bmatrix}$ can be expressed as

$$\begin{bmatrix} A^{-1} [I + B (D - CA^{-1}B)^{-1} CA^{-1}] & - A^{-1}B (D - CA^{-1}B)^{-1} \\ - (D - CA^{-1}B)^{-1} CA^{-1} & (D - CA^{-1}B)^{-1} \end{bmatrix}$$

PROOF: Except for the scalar q, the numerator is a quadratic form in U with matrix $[X(X'X)^{-1}X' - X_1(X_1'X_1)^{-1}X_1']$. It is easy to verify that this matrix is idempotent of rank q. The denominator is also a quadratic form in U with an idempotent matrix of rank $n - k$. Hence the numerator and denominator are distributed as $\sigma^2\chi^2(q)$ and $\sigma^2\chi^2(n - k)$ respectively by theorem 2.1. Moreover, the two quadratic forms are independent since

$$[X(X'X)^{-1}X' - X_1(X_1'X_1)^{-1}X_1'][I - X(X'X)^{-1}X'] = 0.$$

The theorem then follows as a direct application of theorem 2.2.

A particular hypothesis $\theta_2 = \theta_2^*$ is tested at the α level of significance by comparing the quantity in theorem 2.12

$$\frac{[S(\hat{\theta}_1(\theta_2^*), \theta_2^*) - S(\hat{\theta}_1, \hat{\theta}_2)]/q}{S(\hat{\theta}_1, \hat{\theta}_2)/(n - k)}$$

with the critical value $F_\alpha(q, n - k)$. If this critical value is exceeded, the hypothesis is rejected.

The locus of points which separates the acceptance and rejection regions is then defined by

$$\frac{[S(\hat{\theta}_1(\theta_2), \theta_2) - S(\hat{\theta}_1, \hat{\theta}_2)]/q}{S(\hat{\theta}_1, \hat{\theta}_2)/(n - k)} = F_\alpha(q, n - k) \qquad (2.14)$$

and gives a confidence contour with a $1 - \alpha$ degree of confidence.

THEOREM 2.13: *The confidence region given by* (2.14) *is ellipsoidal in the space of θ_2 with center at $\hat{\theta}_2$.*

PROOF: The two sums of squares in the numerator of (2.14) may be expressed alternatively in the following way. First,

$$S(\hat{\theta}_1(\theta_2), \theta_2) = (Y - X_1\theta_1 - X_2\theta_2)'(I - X_1(X_1'X_1)^{-1}X_1')(Y - X_1\theta_1 - X_2\theta_2)$$

$$= (Y - X_2\theta_2)'(I - X_1(X_1'X_1)^{-1}X_1')(Y - X_2\theta_2)$$

$$= Y'WY - 2Y'WX_2\theta_2 + \theta_2'X_2'WX_2\theta_2$$

using the definition of W employed in (2.11). To express $S(\hat{\theta}_1, \hat{\theta}_2)$, we first observe that the residuals $Y - X\hat{\theta}$ may be written as

$$Y - X_1(X_1'X_1)^{-1}X_1'Y + X_1(X_1'X_1)^{-1}X_1'X_2V^{-1}X_2'WY - X_2\hat{\theta}_2,$$

where V is as defined in (2.11), from which it follows that

$$S(\hat{\theta}_1, \hat{\theta}_2) = Y'WY - 2Y'WX_2\hat{\theta}_2$$
$$+ Y'WX_2V^{-1}X_2'X_1(X_1'X_1)^{-1} \times$$
$$X_1'X_2V^{-1}X_2'WY$$
$$- 2Y'WX_2V^{-1}X_2'X_1(X_1'X_1)^{-1} \times$$
$$X_1'X_2\hat{\theta}_2 + \hat{\theta}_2'X_2'X_2\hat{\theta}_2$$
$$= Y'WY - 2Y'WX_2\hat{\theta}_2$$
$$- \hat{\theta}_2'X_2'X_1(X_1'X_1)^{-1}X_1'X_2\hat{\theta}_2$$
$$+ \hat{\theta}_2'X_2'X_2\hat{\theta}_2.$$

The difference between the two sums of squares becomes

$$S(\hat{\theta}_1(\theta_2), \theta_2) - S(\hat{\theta}_1, \hat{\theta}_2) = 2Y'WX_2(\hat{\theta}_2 - \theta_2) + \theta_2'X_2'WX_2\theta_2$$
$$- \hat{\theta}_2'X_2'X_2\hat{\theta}_2 + \hat{\theta}_2'X_2'(I - W)X_2\hat{\theta}_2$$
$$= 2Y'WX_2(\hat{\theta}_2 - \theta_2) + \theta_2'V\theta_2 - \hat{\theta}_2'V\hat{\theta}_2$$
$$= 2\hat{\theta}_2'V(\hat{\theta}_2 - \theta_2) + \theta_2'V\theta_2 - \hat{\theta}_2'V\hat{\theta}_2$$
$$= (\hat{\theta}_2 - \theta_2)'V(\hat{\theta}_2 - \theta_2). \tag{2.15}$$

Eq. (2.14) may then be written as

$$(\hat{\theta}_2 - \theta_2)'V(\hat{\theta}_2 - \theta_2) = \frac{q}{n-k}S(\hat{\theta})F_\alpha(q, n-k). \tag{2.16}$$

Since $V = X_2'X_2 - (X_2'X_1)(X_1'X_1)^{-1}(X_1'X_2)$, V is the inverse of the lower right-hand $q \times q$ principal submatrix of $(X'X)^{-1}$, as may be verified from (2.11) and the inversion formula for partitioned matrices. Since $X'X$ is a positive definite matrix, so is $(X'X)^{-1}$ and any principal submatrix of it. This establishes that (2.16) defines an ellipsoid, which is clearly centered on $\hat{\theta}_2$.

A special form of (2.14) is obtained as a corollary for the case in which θ_1 is the (scalar) constant term in the equation. In that case X_1 is a column of ones and $V = (X_2 - \bar{X}_2)'(X_2 - \bar{X}_2)$, where $\bar{X}_2$ represents a matrix in which every element of a particular column is equal to the mean value of the elements of the corresponding column of X_2.

Denote the matrices of the variables expressed as deviations from sample means by $Y_d = Y - \bar{Y}$ and $X_{2d} = X_2 - \bar{X}_2$. An equivalent formulation of the problem is to find simultaneous confidence limits for, or test a hypothesis about, all the coefficients of the modified system

$$Y_d = X_{2d}\theta_2 + U_d. \tag{2.17}$$

One may define the coefficient of determination R^2 by

$$R^2 = 1 - \frac{S(\hat{\theta}_2)}{Y_d'Y_d},$$

where $S(\hat{\theta}_2)$ is the sum of the squares of the residuals based on (2.17). In the case in which we wish to make a simultaneous test for all the coefficients of the modified model (2.17), the numerator of (2.14) becomes

$$[S(\theta_2) - S(\hat{\theta}_2)]/(k-1).$$

But by definition, $S(\theta_2) = Y_d'Y_d + \theta_2'X_{2d}'X_{2d}\theta_2 - 2\theta_2'X_{2d}'Y_d$ and $S(\hat{\theta}_2) = Y_d'Y_d - \hat{\theta}_2'X_{2d}'Y_d$. Thus, the difference $S(\theta_2) - S(\hat{\theta}_2)$ of (2.14) becomes

$$\theta_2'X_{2d}'X_{2d}\theta_2 - 2\theta_2'X_{2d}'Y_d + \hat{\theta}_2'X_{2d}'Y_d$$

$$= \theta_2'X_{2d}'X_{2d}\theta_2 - 2\theta_2'X_{2d}'Y_d + \hat{\theta}_2'X_{2d}'Y_d + \hat{\theta}_2'X_{2d}'X_{2d}\hat{\theta}_2 - \hat{\theta}_2'X_{2d}'X_{2d}\hat{\theta}_2$$

$$= \theta_2'X_{2d}'X_{2d}\theta_2 - 2\theta_2'X_{2d}'Y_d + \hat{\theta}_2'X_{2d}'X_{2d}\hat{\theta}_2 \tag{2.18}$$

since $X_{2d}'Y_d - X_{2d}'X_{2d}\hat{\theta}_2 = 0$. But (2.18) is clearly the same as

$$S(\theta_2) - S(\hat{\theta}_2) = (\hat{\theta}_2 - \theta_2)' X_{2d}'X_{2d} (\hat{\theta}_2 - \theta_2)$$

$$= (\hat{\theta}_2 - \theta_2)' V (\hat{\theta} - \theta_2). \tag{2.19}$$

Consider now the hypothesis that $\theta_2 = 0$. Under this hypothesis. since $S(\hat{\theta}_2) = Y_d'Y_d - \hat{\theta}_2'X_{2d}'Y_d$, the definition of R^2 implies that $S(\theta_2) - S(\hat{\theta}_2) = \hat{\theta}_2'X_{2d}'Y_d = R^2 Y_d'Y_d$. Thus, (2.14) becomes

$$\frac{(\hat{\theta}_2 - \theta_2)' X_{2d}'X_{2d} (\hat{\theta}_2 - \theta_2)/(k-1)}{S(\hat{\theta}_2)/(n-k)} = \frac{R^2 Y_d'Y_d/(k-1)}{(1-R^2) Y_d'Y_d/(n-k)}$$

$$= \frac{R^2/(k-1)}{(1-R^2)/(n-k)}$$

$$= F_\alpha (k-1, n-k),$$

which will be recognized as a standard formula in elementary regression theory.

2.3. Nonlinear models

The general nonlinear model (2.1) is estimated by minimizing the sum of squares

$$S(\theta) = \sum_{i=1}^{n} (y_i - f(x^i, \theta))^2, \tag{2.2}$$

with respect to the p elements of the vector θ. Differentiating (2.2) with respect to the components of θ provides p normal equations which take the form

$$\partial S / \partial \theta_j = 2 \sum_{i=1}^{n} \left[(y_i - f(x^i, \theta)) \frac{\partial f(x^i, \theta)}{\partial \theta_j} \right] = 0 \quad (j = 1, \dots, p). \tag{2.20}$$

When the model (2.1) is nonlinear in the θ's, the partial derivatives appearing in the middle of (2.20) will also involve the θ's, and as a result the normal equations will be nonlinear. Consider, e.g., the relatively simple model, involving two variables x and y, given by

$$y = \theta_1 e^{\theta_2 x} + u. \tag{2.21}$$

The normal equations corresponding to this model are

$$\sum_{i=1}^{n} (y_i - \theta_1 e^{\theta_2 x_i}) (e^{\theta_2 x_i}) = 0$$

$$\sum_{i=1}^{n} (y_i - \theta_1 e^{\theta_2 x_i}) (\theta_1 x_i e^{\theta_2 x_i}) = 0,$$

which clearly do not admit of a simple analytic solution. As indicated earlier, however, our concern in this chapter is not with the explicit solutions of such equations. Rather, it will be assumed throughout this section that the methods of chapter 1 or other methods have yielded an estimate $\hat{\theta}$ that minimizes (2.2). Since, as was discussed in section 1.6, optimization algorithms yield only a local optimum, there is no guarantee that $\hat{\theta}$ corresponds to a global minimum.[3] It will be further assumed that $\hat{\theta}$ corresponds to the smallest minimum.

---

[3] Since the sum of squares $S(\theta)$ is quadratic in θ for the case of linear $f(x, \theta)$, any minimum will be a global minimum.

Exact confidence contours

Assume that it is desired to establish a simultaneous confidence contour for all p parameters of (2.1). The analogue of (2.14) is

$$\frac{[S(\theta) - S(\hat{\theta})]/p}{S(\hat{\theta})/(n - p)} = F(p, n - p), \qquad (2.22)$$

and has a similar interpretation to that of (2.14). Eq. (2.22) describes a locus in the parameter space that has the characteristic that the reduction of the residual sum of squares obtained by replacing a point θ on the locus by the least squares estimate $\hat{\theta}$ is a constant figure. This is as far as the formula emerging from the linear theory may be applied directly. In particular one must note the following:

(1) Employing the critical values of the $F(p, n - p)$ distribution on the right-hand side of (2.22) is valid only to an approximation (the quality of which will vary from case to case) since the numerator and denominator no longer have independent χ^2 distributions.

(2) The shape of the confidence contours will no longer be ellipsoidal. The contours are not even necessarily closed curves.

(3) The computation of confidence contours for various subsets of elements of θ is no longer a routine one since $\hat{\theta}_1(\theta_2)$ cannot be expressed as a linear function of θ_2, as was done in (2.12). Thus the computation of $S(\hat{\theta}_1(\theta_2), \theta_2)$ will in general involve a separate numerical minimization problem for every possible choice of θ_2. The problem of finding a confidence contour for a subset θ_2 of the whole set of parameters reduces to the possibly very difficult problem of finding the set of θ_2 on which the minimum of the function $S(\hat{\theta}_1(\theta_2), \theta_2)$ is a constant.

Approximate confidence contours

There are several ways in which an approximation can be obtained to the confidence contours. These procedures differ from the earlier ones in that not only the confidence level but the contours themselves are approximate. It is perhaps easiest to motivate the first approximate procedure if we consider an iterative scheme for the minimization of (2.2).

The scheme rests on linearizing $y = f(x, \theta)$ by expanding the function in a Taylor series about a given estimate of θ, say θ^*. We thus have

$$y - f(x, \theta^*) = \sum_{i=1}^{p} \frac{\partial f(x, \theta^*)}{\partial \theta_i} (\theta_i - \theta_i^*), \qquad (2.23)$$

where $\partial f(x, \theta^*)/\partial \theta_i$ denotes the partial derivative of $f(x, \theta)$ with respect to θ_i, evaluated at the point $\theta = \theta^*$. Considering these partials to be constant, (2.23) may be employed as an iterative scheme for computing the value $\hat{\theta}$ that minimizes the sum of squares in the following manner. Denoting by θ^t the estimate for θ available at the start of the tth iteration, (2.23) can be written as

$$Y - F^t = Z^t \Phi^t + v, \tag{2.24}$$

where Y is the vector of observations on the dependent variable, F^t is the vector of predicted values for Y, Z^t is the matrix (assumed constant) the ijth element of which is $[\partial f(x^i, \theta^t)]/\partial \theta_j$, Φ^t is $\theta - \theta^t$, and v is the usual error term. Using the linear theory, (2.24) can be used to determine Φ^t by

$$\Phi^t = (Z^{t'} Z^t)^{-1} Z^{t'} (Y - F^t).$$

A new estimate θ^{t+1} can then be obtained from

$$\theta^{t+1} = \Phi^t + \theta^t,$$

which can then be used to compute new F^{t+1}, Z^{t+1}, yielding a new version of (2.24). Convergence will have occurred in this process if, eventually, Φ^t is sufficiently close to zero, i.e., if successive values θ^t, θ^{t+1} differ only negligibly from each other.

There is, of course, no guarantee that this process converges at all or, if it does, that it converges in an efficient manner.[4] It is easy to show, however, that if the process converges at all to some estimate $\hat{\theta}$, that estimate satisfies the first order conditions for S to be a minimum. Convergence implies

$$0 = \Phi^t = (Z^{t'} Z^t)^{-1} Z^{t'} (Y - F^t)$$

and hence

$$Z^{t'} (Y - F^t) = 0. \tag{2.25}$$

Taking the jth partial derivative of (2.2) and setting it equal to zero yields (2.20) or

$$\partial S/\partial \theta_j = 2 \sum_{i=1}^{n} (y_i - f(x^i, \theta)) \frac{\partial f(x^i, \theta)}{\partial \theta_j} = 0,$$

which is clearly the same, as the jth row of $Z^{t'}$ multiplied into $Y - F^t$. Thus, one may conclude that if the process converges at all, it converges to a point satisfying the first order conditions for a minimum.[5]

---

[4] For a further discussion of this method see N.R. Draper and H. Smith, *Applied regression analysis*. New York, Wiley, 1966, ch. 10, and references contained therein.

[5] We are, of course, ignoring the possibility of multiple roots of the normal eq. (2.20). That is, the iterative technique need not converge to the global minimum.

It immediately follows (see (2.19)) that the joint confidence contours from the linear theory for the set of all Φ^t are given by

$$\frac{(\hat{\Phi} - \Phi)' \, Z'Z \, (\hat{\Phi} - \Phi)/p}{S(\hat{\Phi})/(n - p)} = F \, (p, n - p),$$

where

$$S(\hat{\Phi}) = (Y - F \, (x, \hat{\theta}) - Z\hat{\Phi})' \, (Y - F \, (x, \hat{\theta}) - Z\hat{\Phi}),$$

i.e., the sum of squared residuals of (2.24). Since $\hat{\Phi} = 0$ at the minimum we have $S(\hat{\Phi}) = S(\hat{\theta})$, where $S(\hat{\theta})$ is given by (2.2). The confidence contours are then given by

$$\frac{(\hat{\theta} - \theta)' \, Z'Z \, (\hat{\theta} - \theta)/p}{S(\hat{\theta})/(n - p)} = F \, (p, n - p). \tag{2.26}$$

Eq. (2.26) describes ellipsoids in the original parameter space and represents the approximate confidence contours. Of course, while (2.26) was motivated by the iterative scheme described above, the use of (2.26) is hardly dependent on obtaining $\hat{\theta}$ in that way. One may also use the techniques of chapter 1 to obtain $\hat{\theta}$ and then compute (2.26) directly.

The second procedure for obtaining approximate contours starts from (2.22) and involves finding a quadratic Taylor Series approximation to $S(\theta)$ about the estimate $\hat{\theta}$ (which we again assume is available from direct minimization of (2.2)):

$$S(\theta) = S(\hat{\theta}) + \sum_{i=1}^{p} \frac{\partial S \, (\hat{\theta})}{\partial \theta_i} \, (\theta_i - \hat{\theta}_i) + \frac{1}{2} \sum_{i=1}^{p} \sum_{j=1}^{p} \frac{\partial^2 S \, (\hat{\theta})}{\partial \theta_i \, \partial \theta_j} \times$$

$$\times \, (\theta_i - \hat{\theta}_i) \, (\theta_j - \hat{\theta}_j). \tag{2.27}$$

The first summation on the right vanishes by the first order conditions for a minimum. From (2.27) we have

$$S(\theta) - S(\hat{\theta}) = \tfrac{1}{2} (\hat{\theta} - \theta)' \, S_{\theta\theta} \, (\hat{\theta} - \theta), \tag{2.28}$$

where $S_{\theta\theta}$ denotes the matrix of second partial derivatives of S.

Eq. (2.22) then becomes

$$\frac{\tfrac{1}{2} (\hat{\theta} - \theta)' \, S_{\theta\theta} \, (\hat{\theta} - \theta)/p}{S(\hat{\theta})/(n - p)} = F \, (p, n - p). \tag{2.29}$$

It is clear that (2.26) and (2.29) do not represent the same ellipsoids in general. The term in the ith row and jth column of $Z'Z$ is

$$\sum_{k=1}^{n} \frac{\partial f(x^k, \hat{\theta})}{\partial \theta_i} \frac{\partial f(x^k, \hat{\theta})}{\partial \theta_j}.$$

The corresponding term in $\frac{1}{2}S_{\theta\theta}$ is obtained by differentiating $\frac{1}{2}S(\theta)$ twice, and is

$$\frac{1}{2} \frac{\partial^2 S(\hat{\theta})}{\partial \theta_i \partial \theta_j} = \sum_{k=1}^{n} \left[\frac{\partial f(x^k, \hat{\theta})}{\partial \theta_i} \frac{\partial f(x^k, \hat{\theta})}{\partial \theta_j} - (y_k - f(x^k, \hat{\theta})) \frac{\partial^2 f(x^k, \hat{\theta})}{\partial \theta_i \partial \theta_j} \right].$$

This will equal the corresponding term of $Z'Z$ if the model is linear to begin with, i.e., if $\partial^2 f(x^k, \hat{\theta})/\partial \theta_i \partial \theta_j = 0$.

In nonlinear models the choice between (2.26) and (2.29) will rest on which can provide the better approximation. Since the quadratic approximation to $S(\theta)$ includes the terms $\partial^2 f/\partial \theta_i \partial \theta_j$ which are excluded from the linear approximation to $f(x, \theta)$, (2.29) may be expected to be more accurate in general.

An example

The differences among the contours corresponding to the various methods are most easily illustrated by a concrete example. We assume for this purpose that the function to be estimated is as given by (2.21):

$$y = \theta_1 e^{\theta_2 x} + u,$$

and that the three available observations on the variables x and y are as given in the following table:

x	y
0	1
0	2
1	3

The sum of squares $S(\theta)$ is given by

$$S(\theta) = (1 - \theta_1)^2 + (2 - \theta_1)^2 + (3 - \theta_1 e^{\theta_2})^2. \tag{2.30}$$

It may be verified easily that (2.30) attains a global minimum at the point $\hat{\theta}_1 = 1.5$, $\hat{\theta}_2 = 0.693$ approx. (i.e., $e^{\hat{\theta}_2} = 2.0$). The sum of squares of residuals, $S(\hat{\theta})$, becomes 0.5. The matrix $Z'Z$ is easily seen to be

$$\begin{bmatrix} 6 & 6 \\ 6 & 9 \end{bmatrix}$$

and, in the present example[6], $\frac{1}{2}S_{\theta\theta}$ is also given by

$$\begin{bmatrix} 6 & 6 \\ 6 & 9 \end{bmatrix}$$

Employing a 95% (pseudo-)confidence level, $F(2, 1) = 18.51$ and the possible confidence regions discussed in this section are given by

(A) $$\frac{(S(\theta) - 0.5)/2}{0.5} = 18.51$$

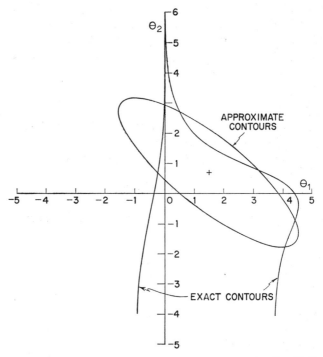

Fig. 2.1. Exact and approximate confidence contours for $F = 18.51$.

---

[6] The reader may verify that the reason for this is as follows: the term $\partial^2 f/\partial\theta_i\,\partial\theta_j$ is zero for the first two observations; $y_k - f(x, \hat{\theta})$ happens to equal zero for the last observation. As a consequence (2.26) and (2.29) imply the same contours.

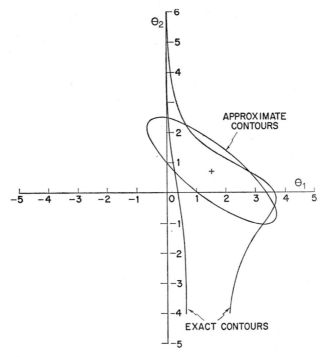

Fig. 2.2. Exact and approximate confidence contours for $F = 9.5$.

for exact contours and by

(B)
$$\frac{[\theta_1 - 1.5 \quad \theta_2 - 0.693] \begin{bmatrix} 6 & 6 \\ 6 & 9 \end{bmatrix} \begin{bmatrix} \theta_1 - 1.5 \\ \theta_2 - 0.693 \end{bmatrix} \Big/ 2}{0.5} = 18.51$$

for the elliptical approximate contours.
The contours are depicted in figs. 2.1 and 2.2 for two different values of F.

Beale contours[7]

It was shown earlier that the contours given by

$$\frac{[S(\theta) - S(\hat{\theta})]/p}{S(\hat{\theta})/(n - p)} = F_{\hat{\alpha}}(p, n - p) \qquad (2.22)$$

---

[7] See E.M.L.Beale, Confidence regions in non-linear estimation. *Journal of the Royal Statistical Society*, **B22** (1960), 41–76; and I.Guttman and D.A.Meeter, On Beale's measures of non-linearity. *Technometrics* **7** (1965), 623–37.

are themselves exact but that the confidence level $1 - \alpha$ is approximate. It is clear that the approximation is likely to be relatively good if $f(x, \theta)$ is nearly linear and will tend to deteriorate with the degree of nonlinearity. Beale has developed a procedure that accomplishes at least two important tasks: (a) he has devised a measure of nonlinearity by which one may judge the appropriateness of using (2.22), and (b) he has constructed an adjustment procedure that yields as a second approximation a conservative confidence region in the sense that the probability is at least $1 - \alpha$ that the true θ vector is contained in the region. We shall consider only the first of these in any detail.

The measure of nonlinearity is based upon the curvature of the solution locus $f(x, \theta)$ near the estimate $\hat{\theta}$. This is computed by preselecting some points in θ-space and finding the sum of the normalized distances for these points between the solution locus and the plane tangent to it at $\hat{\theta}$. Let the points at which these distances are evaluated be θ_l $(l = 1, \ldots, m)$. The tangent plane has the equation

$$\eta_i = a_{i0} + \sum_{j=1}^{p} a_{ij}(\theta_j - \hat{\theta}_j) \quad (i = 1, \ldots, n),$$

where the a's are obtained from the Taylor expansion of $f(x, \theta)$ and the n observations. The (unnormalized) distance then is

$$Q = \sum_{l=1}^{m} \sum_{i=1}^{n} (f(x^l, \theta_l) - a_{i0} - \sum_{j=1}^{p} a_{ij}(\theta_{lj} - \hat{\theta}_j))^2,$$

where θ_{lj} represents the jth component of θ_l. This distance will increase both with the distance between $\hat{\theta}$ and θ_l and with the number m of points used. To hold these factors constant, Beale recommends dividing Q by the quantity

$$D = \sum_{l=1}^{m} \left[\sum_{i=1}^{n} (f(x^l, \theta_l) - a_{i0})^2 \right]^2.$$

The estimated measure of nonlinearity is

$$\hat{N}_\theta = \frac{p}{n - p} S(\hat{\theta}) \frac{Q}{D}.$$

Beale suggests that the approximation of (2.22) is acceptable if $\hat{N}_\theta < 0.01/F_\alpha(p, n - p)$ and that the model is too nonlinear for (2.22) to be acceptable if $\hat{N}_\theta > 1.0/F_\alpha(p, n - p)$, with intermediate values of $\hat{N}_\theta$ suggesting the desirability of further analysis. In the example of the function

$y = \theta_1 e^{\theta_2 x}$ discussed earlier, $\hat{N}_\theta = 0.011$, which represents an intermediate case, being neither disastrously nonlinear, nor acceptably linear.[8]

It may be noted that the empirical measures of nonlinearity will be somewhat sensitive to the actual points θ_i for which the relevant distances are evaluated. In order to standardize the procedure it has been suggested that the θ_i should be chosen as the $2p$ endpoints of the principal axes of the ellipsoid that may be computed from (2.29).

So far we have considered the application of least squares to the general nonlinear regression model given by (2.1). While we have made little explicit use of distributional assumptions concerning the error term in (2.1), we have certainly made implicit use of the assumption of normality in considering the analogy between confidence intervals in the linear and nonlinear cases. Furthermore, as suggested earlier, while least squares estimates possess no general optimum properties for nonlinear models, it will be seen that least squares estimates are maximum likelihood estimates for model (2.1) if the disturbances are normally distributed. Since this fact is the main virtue of least squares applied to (2.1), it suggests that we ought directly to consider the use of maximum likelihood estimates. In the first instance, this will substantially broaden the class of models we may estimate—indeed it will allow us to consider models for which least squares is not even well-defined.[9] In the second instance, it will provide us with further (albeit asymptotic) ammunition to attack the problem of confidence intervals and/or hypothesis testing.

2.4. The maximum likelihood approach

Given a sample of n independent observations $x = (x_1, \ldots, x_n)$ from the density function $f(x, \theta)$, the likelihood function is defined as the joint density function of the observations conditional on the parameter vector θ:

$$L(x \mid \theta) = \prod_{i=1}^{n} f(x^i, \theta). \qquad (2.31)$$

---

[8] For the case in which the model is too nonlinear to allow direct application of (2.22), Beale has developed a technique for appropriately adjusting the right-hand side of (2.22).

[9] E.g., in chapter 5 we consider a model of the form $y = ax^\beta e^u + v$, which has two disturbance terms u and v. It is not obvious how one would apply least squares to such a model.

It will be assumed throughout this section that the first two derivatives of L exist everywhere. A relationship between least squares estimation and maximum likelihood estimation is established in the case in which the errors u in (2.1) are assumed to be normally distributed with zero mean and constant variance σ^2. In that case the relevant likelihood function is

$$L = \frac{1}{(\sqrt{2\pi}\sigma)^n} \exp\left\{ -\frac{1}{2\sigma^2} \sum_i (y_i - f(x^i, \theta))^2 \right\}. \qquad (2.32)$$

Differentiating (2.32) with respect to σ^2 produces a maximum likelihood estimate of σ^2 given by $\hat{\sigma}^2 = S(\hat{\theta})/n$, where $\hat{\theta}$ is the maximum likelihood estimate of θ and $S(\theta)$ is as in (2.2). Substituting this back into (2.32) yields the condensed logarithmic likelihood function given by

$$\log L = -\frac{n}{2}\left(1 + \log \frac{2\pi}{n}\right) - \frac{n}{2} \log S(\hat{\theta}),$$

from which it is clear that the same values of θ that minimize $S(\theta)$ also maximize the likelihood function. It is also clear that the confidence contours discussed in section 2.3 are isolikelihood contours under the present assumptions. Further results, useful for establishing confidence intervals and testing hypotheses, will be obtained below by exploiting the properties of the likelihood function.

We begin by consideration of a very general variance bound estimate.

The Cramer-Rao bound[10]

We first consider the estimation of a single parameter θ. On the assumption that the first two derivatives of the likelihood function exist and that the range of variation of the random variable x is independent of θ, we may establish a lower bound for the variance of an unbiased estimator $\hat{g}$ of a function $g(\theta)$.

THEOREM 2.14: *The variance of $\hat{g}$ is bounded from below by*

$$-[g'(\theta)]^2 / E\left(\frac{\partial^2 \log L}{\partial \theta^2}\right).$$

PROOF: The expected value of $\hat{g}$ is, by definition,

$$E(\hat{g}) = \int \cdots \int \hat{g} L(x|\theta)\, dx_1 \ldots dx_n = g(\theta),$$

---

[10] For details far beyond the present development see M.G. Kendall and A. Stuart, *The advanced theory of statistics*, vol. 2. New York, Hafner Publishing, 1961, ch. 17.

where the last equality follows from the assumption of unbiasedness. Differentiating both sides of the right-hand equality,

$$g'(\theta) = \int \cdots \int \hat{g} \frac{\partial L\,(x \,|\, \theta)}{\partial \theta}\, dx_1 \ldots dx_n$$

$$= \int \cdots \int \hat{g} \frac{\partial \log L\,(x \,|\, \theta)}{\partial \theta}\, L\,(x \,|\, \theta)\, dx_1 \ldots dx_n \qquad (2.33)$$

Since $L\,(x \,|\, \theta)$ is a joint density

$$\int \cdots \int L\,(x \,|\, \theta)\, dx_1 \ldots dx_n = 1$$

and differentiating,

$$\int \cdots \int \frac{\partial L\,(x \,|\, \theta)}{\partial \theta}\, dx_1 \ldots dx_n = \int \cdots \int \frac{\partial \log L\,(x \,|\, \theta)}{\partial \theta}\, L\,(x \,|\, \theta)\, dx_1 \ldots dx_n$$

$$= E\left(\frac{\partial \log L\,(x \,|\, \theta)}{\partial \theta}\right) = 0. \qquad (2.34)$$

The middle term in (2.34) can be rewritten

$$0 = \int \cdots \int \frac{\partial \log L\,(x \,|\, \theta)}{\partial \theta}\, L\,(x \,|\, \theta)\, dx_1 \ldots dx_n$$

$$= \int \cdots \int \frac{1}{L\,(x \,|\, \theta)} \frac{\partial L\,(x \,|\, \theta)}{\partial \theta}\, L\,(x \,|\, \theta)\, dx_1 \ldots dx_n$$

and differentiating the right-hand side of the last expression

$$\int \cdots \int \frac{1}{L\,(x \,|\, \theta)} \left[\frac{\partial L\,(x \,|\, \theta)}{\partial \theta}\right]^2 dx_1 \ldots dx_n + \int \cdots \int \frac{\partial^2 \log L\,(x \,|\, \theta)}{\partial \theta^2} \times$$

$$\times L\,(x \,|\, \theta)\, dx_1 \ldots dx_n = \int \cdots \int \left[\frac{1}{L\,(x \,|\, \theta)} \frac{\partial L\,(x \,|\, \theta)}{\partial \theta}\right]^2 \times$$

$$\times L\,(x \,|\, \theta)\, dx_1 \ldots dx_n + \int \cdots \int \frac{\partial^2 \log L\,(x \,|\, \theta)}{\partial \theta^2}\, L\,(x \,|\, \theta)\, dx_1 \ldots dx_n$$

$$= E\left[\left(\frac{\log L\,(x \,|\, \theta)}{\partial \theta}\right)^2\right] + E\left[\frac{\partial^2 \log L\,(x \,|\, \theta)}{\partial \theta^2}\right] = 0. \qquad (2.35)$$

Multiplying (2.34) by $g(\theta)$, which is a constant with respect to integration and subtracting from (2.33),

$$g'(\theta) = \int \cdots \int (\hat{g} - g(\theta)) \frac{\partial \log L(x|\theta)}{\partial \theta} L(x|\theta) \, dx_1 \ldots dx_n.$$

Squaring both sides and applying Schwarz's inequality for integrals,

$$[g'(\theta)]^2 \leq \int \cdots \int (\hat{g} - g(\theta))^2 L(x|\theta) \, dx_1 \ldots dx_n \times$$

$$\times \int \cdots \int \left(\frac{\partial \log L(x|\theta)}{\partial \theta}\right)^2 L(x|\theta) \, dx_1 \ldots dx_n$$

$$= \text{var}(\hat{g}) \, E\left[\left(\frac{\partial \log L(x|\theta)}{\partial \theta}\right)^2\right]. \tag{2.36}$$

Applying (2.35) we have

$$\text{var}(\hat{g}) \geq -[g'(\theta)]^2 \Big/ E\left[\frac{\partial^2 \log L(x|\theta)}{\partial \theta^2}\right], \tag{2.37}$$

which proves the theorem.

The right-hand side of (2.37) is typically termed the minimum variance bound (MVB) and an estimator that attains the bound (for all θ) is called an MVB estimator. Several further observations on the MVB are relevant.

(1) Theorem 2.14 considers an unbiased estimator $\hat{g}$ of some function $g(\theta)$. This permits one to treat both biased and unbiased estimators of θ itself. If an unbiased estimator of θ itself is being considered then $g(\theta) = \theta$ and $g'(\theta) = 1$, so that (2.37) assumes the form

$$\text{var}(\hat{\theta}) \geq -\frac{1}{E\left[\dfrac{\partial^2 \log L(x|\theta)}{\partial \theta^2}\right]}. \tag{2.38}$$

(2) The MVB is actually attained if (2.37) holds as an equality, i.e., if Schwarz's inequality is satisfied as an equality. This will be the case if the integrands in (2.36) are proportional and thus if

$$\frac{\partial \log L(x|\theta)}{\partial \theta} = k(\hat{g} - g(\theta)), \tag{2.39}$$

where k is independent of the sample but will in general depend on θ. Expression (2.39) thus implies

$$E\left[\left(\frac{\partial \log L}{\partial \theta}\right)^2\right] = k^2(\theta)\, \text{var}\, (\hat{g})$$

and, since (2.37) and (2.36) hold as an equality, we find

$$\text{var}\, (\hat{g}) = \frac{g'(\theta)}{k(\theta)}. \tag{2.40}$$

(3) It follows from (2.39) that, when an MVB estimator exists, it will exist for one and only one specific function $g(\theta)$.[11]

These several points can be simply illustrated with the aid of an example. We consider the estimation of the variance of a normal density with mean equal to zero. The log-likelihood function can then be written

$$\log L = -\frac{n}{2} \log (2\pi\theta^2) - \frac{\Sigma x^2}{2\theta^2}.$$

Then

$$\frac{\partial \log L}{\partial \theta} = -\frac{n}{\theta} + \frac{\Sigma x^2}{\theta^3} = \frac{n}{\theta^3}\left(\frac{1}{n}\Sigma x^2 - \theta^2\right). \tag{2.41}$$

The right-hand side of (2.41) is clearly of the form (2.39), where $k(\theta) = n/\theta^3$. Consequently $\Sigma x^2/n$ is an MVB estimator of θ^2 with sampling variance $2\theta^4/n$ (from (2.40)). It should be noted, however, that there is no MVB estimator for θ itself, or indeed, any other function of θ other than θ^2.

Up to this point the discussion has concentrated on a scalar parameter θ, but the results are easily generalized to the many-parameter case. For simplicity we focus on the case in which we are interested in estimating a p-component vector $(\theta_1, \ldots, \theta_p)$ rather than some function of θ. If we denote the estimator by $\hat{\theta} = (\hat{\theta}_1, \ldots, \hat{\theta}_p)$ and the covariance matrix of $\hat{\theta}$ by V, we have for an arbitrary vector a that

$$a'\, [V - R^{-1}(\theta)]\, a \geq 0, \tag{2.42}$$

---

[11] M. G. Kendall and A. Stuart, *op. cit.*, p. 11. What is meant is that for no other linearly independent function will there be an MVB estimator.

where

$$R(\theta) = -E\left[\frac{\partial^2 \log L\,(x\,|\,\theta)}{\partial\theta\,\partial\theta'}\right]. \tag{2.43}$$

Expression (2.43) is the matrix generalization of the right-hand side of (2.38), while (2.42) simply states that $V - R^{-1}(\theta)$ is a positive semi-definite matrix. A more concise way of stating this is $V \geq R^{-1}(\theta)$ which is the matrix version of (2.38).

As an illustration of this consider the estimation of the mean and variance (μ and σ^2) for the normal density. The log-likelihood can be written

$$\log L = -\frac{n}{2} \log 2\pi - \frac{n}{2} \log \sigma^2 - \frac{1}{2\sigma^2} \sum_{i=1}^{n} (x_i - \mu)^2. \tag{2.44}$$

The matrix of second partial derivatives with respect to μ and σ^2 is

$$\begin{bmatrix} \dfrac{\partial^2 \log L}{\partial\mu^2} & \dfrac{\partial^2 \log L}{\partial\mu\,\partial\sigma^2} \\[2ex] \dfrac{\partial^2 \log L}{\partial\sigma^2\,\partial\mu} & \dfrac{\partial^2 \log L}{\partial(\sigma^2)^2} \end{bmatrix} = \begin{bmatrix} -n/\sigma^2 & -\dfrac{1}{\sigma^4} \sum (x_i - \mu) \\[2ex] -\dfrac{1}{\sigma^4} \sum (x_i - \mu) & \dfrac{n}{2\sigma^4} - \dfrac{1}{\sigma^6} \sum (x_i - \mu)^2 \end{bmatrix}$$

From (2.43) we have

$$R(\theta) = \begin{bmatrix} n/\sigma^2 & 0 \\ 0 & n/2\sigma^4 \end{bmatrix}$$

so that

$$V \geq \begin{bmatrix} \sigma^2/n & 0 \\ 0 & 2\sigma^4/n \end{bmatrix}. \tag{2.45}$$

However, it is worth noting that the use of the Cramer-Rao bound for assessing the sampling variability of the estimated variance is only valid in large samples. This follows from the fact that the maximum likelihood estimates are given by $\hat{\mu} = \bar{x}$ and $\hat{\sigma}^2 = s^2 = \sum (x - \bar{x})^2/n$. The variance of $\bar{x}$ is indeed given by the first diagonal element in (2.45), but we know from other considerations that the exact sampling variance of s^2 is $2\sigma^4(n-1)/n^2$, not $2\sigma^4/n$.

Properties of maximum likelihood estimators

The maximum likelihood principle of estimation involves choosing as an estimator of a parameter θ (which may be a vector) that admissible value of θ, which makes the likelihood function as large as possible. In other words we choose $\hat{\theta}$ such that

$$L(x|\hat{\theta}) \geq L(x|\theta). \tag{2.46}$$

Under suitable regularity conditions (e.g., the existence of relevant derivatives) this problem is characteristically approached by finding all solutions to

$$\frac{\partial L(x|\theta)}{\partial \theta} = 0 \tag{2.47}$$

that satisfy the second-order conditions for a maximum and taking the estimate which yields the highest value of the likelihood function. Under suitable regularity conditions, the maximum likelihood estimator possesses a number of extremely desirable properties. In particular, we have the following well-known results[12]:

(i) The estimator $\hat{\theta}$ in (2.46) is a consistent estimate of the true value of the parameter θ_0.

(ii) There is at most one root of (2.47) that is a consistent estimator of θ_0 and that root corresponds to a maximum of the likelihood function with probability one.[13]

(iii) The maximum likelihood estimator is asymptotically normally distributed with mean θ_0 and covariance matrix given by $R^{-1}(\theta)$ (2.43).

(iv) The maximum likelihood estimator is asymptotically efficient in the sense that it (asymptotically) attains the Cramer-Rao bound.

(v) If the density $f(x|\theta)$ admits a sufficient statistic, then the maximum likelihood estimator is a function of the sufficient statistic[14] and is indeed a sufficient statistic itself.

(vi) If the maximum likelihood estimator is sufficient then

$$E\left(\frac{\partial^2 \log L}{\partial \theta \, \partial \theta'}\right) = \frac{\partial^2 \log L}{\partial \theta \, \partial \theta'}\bigg|_{\hat{\theta}=\theta},$$

---

[12] For detailed statements and proofs of these results see *ibid*.

[13] If $\hat{\theta}_n$ and $\hat{\theta}_n^*$ are roots of (2.47), which are both consistent estimators for θ_0, then (ii) states that for $\varepsilon > 0$ and all sufficiently large n $\Pr\{|\hat{\theta}_n - \hat{\theta}_n^*| < \varepsilon\} = 1$ and

$$\Pr\left\{\frac{\partial^2 \log L(\hat{\theta}_n)}{\partial \theta^2} < 0\right\} = 1.$$

The latter condition is written in a form valid for a scalar θ. If θ is a vector, the matrix generalization must be used.

[14] A statistic $T = T(x)$ is sufficient if and only if the likelihood function can be written $L(x|\theta) = h_1(T|\theta) h_2(x)$. Then maximizing the likelihood function is equivalent to maximizing $h_1(T|\theta)$, so that $\hat{\theta} = \hat{\theta}(T)$.

so that $R^{-1}(\theta)$ may be consistently estimated by

$$-\left\|\frac{\partial^2 \log L}{\partial\theta \, \partial\theta'}\right\|^{-1}_{\theta = \hat{\theta}}. \tag{2.48}$$

These several properties clearly make the maximum likelihood method a highly desirable estimation technique—at least for large samples. There are, however, several further things to be said about these properties.

First, we shall sketch the argument concerning the asymptotic normality of maximum likelihood estimators since this will be useful in the subsequent construction of confidence intervals. For simplicity we consider the case of a single parameter θ with true value θ_0 and maximum likelihood estimator $\hat{\theta}$. Using Taylor's theorem we can write

$$\left(\frac{\partial \log L}{\partial\theta}\right)_{\hat{\theta}} = \left(\frac{\partial \log L}{\partial\theta}\right)_{\theta_0} + (\hat{\theta} - \theta_0)\left(\frac{\partial^2 \log L}{\partial\theta^2}\right)_{\theta*},$$

where $\theta*$ lies between θ_0 and $\hat{\theta}$. Since the left side of this expression is zero ($\hat{\theta}$ satisfies the first-order condition) we can rewrite this as

$$(\hat{\theta} - \theta_0)\,B(\theta_0) = \frac{\left(\dfrac{\partial \log L}{\partial\theta}\right)_{\theta_0}\Big/ B(\theta_0)}{\left(\dfrac{\partial^2 \log L}{\partial\theta^2}\right)_{\theta*}\Big/ (-R(\theta_0))}, \tag{2.49}$$

where $R(\theta)$ is given by

$$R(\theta) = -E\left(\frac{\partial^2 \log L}{\partial\theta^2}\right) = E\left\{\left(\frac{\partial \log L}{\partial\theta}\right)^2\right\} \tag{2.50}$$

and $B(\theta) = \sqrt{R(\theta)}$. The numerator of the right side of (2.49) is the ratio of the sum of n independent identical variates $\log f(x^i | \theta_0)$ to $B(\theta_0)$. By (2.34) this sum has zero mean and by (2.50) it has variance $R(\theta_0)$. Consequently, one may apply the central limit theorem to show that the numerator of (2.49) is asymptotically $N(0, 1)$. Since $\hat{\theta}$ is a consistent estimate of θ_0 and $\theta*$ lies between the two, the probability limit of the denominator of (2.49) is unity. Consequently, the left-hand side of (2.49) is asymptotically $N(0, 1)$, i.e. $\hat{\theta}$ is asymptotically $N(\theta_0, 1/R(\theta_0))$.

The asymptotic nature of the normality should be clear from the example given above in (2.44). That example implies that s^2 is asymptotically normally distributed with variance $2\sigma^4/n$. However, we know that ns^2/σ^2 is distributed exactly as $\chi^2(n-1)$. We also know that as n tends to infinity the χ^2 distribution approaches the normal, so that the nature of the approximation is readily apparent in the present case. In more general cases, however, little may be known about the nature of convergence to normality.

The second consideration concerns the use of (2.48) to evaluate or estimate $R(\theta)$. To illustrate the point let us reconsider the estimation of the variance from a normal distribution with mean zero. Letting $\theta = \sigma^2$, we can write the log-likelihood function as

$$\log L = -\frac{n}{2} \log (2\pi\theta) - \frac{\Sigma x_i^2}{2\theta}.$$

Whence

$$\frac{\partial \log L}{\partial \theta} = -\frac{n}{2\theta} + \frac{\Sigma x_i^2}{2\theta^2}$$

and

$$\frac{\partial^2 \log L}{\partial \theta^2} = \frac{n}{2\theta^2} - \frac{\Sigma x_i^2}{\theta^3} = \frac{n}{\theta^2} \left(\frac{1}{2} - \frac{\Sigma x_i^2/n}{\theta} \right). \qquad (2.51)$$

If we let $\hat{\theta} = \Sigma x_i^2/n$, i.e. the maximum likelihood estimate of θ, then we can rewrite (2.51) as

$$\frac{\partial^2 \log L}{\partial \theta^2} = \frac{n}{\theta^2} \left(\frac{1}{2} - \frac{\hat{\theta}}{\theta} \right). \qquad (2.52)$$

Quite evidently, whether we evaluate the expectation of (2.51) or simply set $\hat{\theta} = \theta$ in (2.52), we arrive at the same asymptotic result, namely $n/2\theta^2$, so that the variance of our estimate is given by $2\theta^2/n = 2\sigma^4/n$, which accords with our earlier result. Thus in the present instance we can dispense with the expectation. The resulting quantity of course still depends on the unknown σ^2. However, from (2.48) and from (2.52), a consistent estimate of the variance is provided by $2\hat{\theta}^2/n$, where $\hat{\theta} = \Sigma x_i^2/n$. Now characteristically, (2.48) is often employed without explicit verification of the joint sufficiency of the elements of $\hat{\theta}$, which may be a difficult task. This task may be approached in several ways: (a) if it can be shown that the estimator's variance attains the Cramer-Rao bound, sufficiency follows[15] and (2.48) may be applied; (b) sufficiency may be established directly by exhibiting that $L(x|\theta)$ can be appropriately factored; (c) the inappropriateness of applying (2.48) may be shown

---

[15] M.G. Kendall and A. Stuart, *op. cit.*, p. 24.

by determining that the likelihood function has more than one maximum, for in that case sufficiency does not hold.[16]

This brings us to a further point—the possibility of multiple maxima of the likelihood function. Proposition (ii) above, which stems from the work of Huzurbazar[17], loosely states that a consistent root of the likelihood equation (2.47) is unique. Although there has been considerable confusion on this point, this proposition does not rule out the possibility of multiple maxima. Indeed, as Perlman has pointed out, the confusion in part stems from the ambiguity of the phrase 'consistent root of the likelihood equation'.[18] The nature of the ambiguity can be seen as follows.

Given a sample of size n, let $S(n)$ denote the set of solutions to the likelihood equation (2.47). To interpret the phrase 'root of the likelihood equation' we let n increase and consider a sequence of solutions $\{\theta_n\}$ such that, for each n, θ_n is the set $S(n)$. Such a sequence is a 'root'. As a result, if $S(n)$ generally contains more than one point, there are infinitely many 'roots' (i.e., sequences). Furthermore, since consistency is a limiting property of a sequence of estimators we may alter the initial terms in such a sequence without destroying consistency. Hence, there may be many consistent roots. As Perlman shows, these ambiguities are easily avoided. He obtains a more precise statement of proposition (ii) by considering the limiting behavior of $S(n)$, as n goes to infinity and shows (under suitable regularity conditions) that all but one element of $S(n)$ is bounded away from the true parameter value and the remaining element approaches the true parameter value.

While this serves to clarify proposition (ii), as indicated before, it does not rule out the possibility of multiple maxima. In one instance, Perlman has provided conditions which produce a unique maximum.[19] However, the results to date only apply to the scalar case and only yield sufficient conditions so that they are of limited practical use. One must in practical problems attempt to assure that the *maximum maximorum* is attained, for it is only this root which is consistent.

To illustrate these points we reconsider the two examples given in section 1.7 above. Eq. (1.27), reproduced below, is the first-order condition for

[16] *Ibid.*, p. 53.

[17] V.S.Huzurbazar, The likelihood equation, consistency and the maxima of the likelihood function. *Annals of Eugenics 14* (1948), 185–200.

[18] M.D.Perlman, The limiting behavior of multiple roots of the likelihood equation. Technical Report 125, University of Minnesota, July 1969.

[19] *Ibid.*

estimation of the correlation parameter ϱ from the standardized bivariate normal distribution.

$$\varrho (1 - \varrho^2) + (1 + \varrho^2) \frac{1}{n} \Sigma xy - \varrho \left(\frac{1}{n} \Sigma x^2 + \frac{1}{n} \Sigma y^2 \right) = 0. \quad (1.27)$$

As indicated earlier, this cubic equation may well have three real roots. However, for large samples there will tend to be only one real root of (1.27). Although one can deduce this from Perlman's results, it can also be verified directly. If we define $\lambda = \varrho - \Sigma xy/3n$ and substitute for ϱ, (1.27) reduces to

$$\lambda^3 + q\lambda + r = 0,$$

where

$$q = \frac{1}{n} \Sigma x^2 + \frac{1}{n} \Sigma y^2 - \frac{1}{3} \left(\frac{1}{n} \Sigma xy \right)^2 - 1. \quad (2.53)$$

The requirement that there be only one real root is

$$4q^3 + 27r^2 > 0, \quad (2.54)$$

which will be met if $q > 0$. Now the sample moments in (2.53) are consistent estimators of the corresponding population moments. Since x and y follow the bivariate standardized normal we have that q converges in probability to

$$(1 + 1 - \tfrac{1}{3}\varrho^2 - 1) = 1 - \tfrac{1}{3}\varrho^2 > 0,$$

so that in large samples (1.27) will only have one real root.

The other example considered above was that of estimating the parameter a in the regression model given by

$$y_i = a + a^2 x_i + u_i. \quad (1.20)$$

The first-order condition for this example (given in (1.22)) also reduces to a cubic equation, which may have three real roots. Unlike the previous case, however, as n tends to infinity there is no guarantee that conditions (2.54) will be met. Indeed, whether the condition is met depends on the constellation of values (a, μ_x, σ_x^2), and it is possible to find values of these parameters that yield either one or three real roots.[20] Nevertheless, it is easy to verify

---

[20] The actual expressions are quite cumbersome. They can be simplified somewhat if $\mu_x = 0$. In that case

$$27r^2 + 4q^3 = \frac{15a^2}{4\sigma_x^4} + \frac{1}{2\sigma_x^6} + \frac{6a^4}{\sigma_x^2} - 4a^6,$$

which can be either positive or negative.

that the root corresponding to the maximum of the likelihood function tends to the true value of the parameter a.[21]

Confidence intervals and hypothesis testing

It was shown in section 2.3 that the precise confidence intervals (both in sense of shape and significance level) that are used in linear models will not, in general, be usable in nonlinear models. In particular situations, of course, one may obtain exact results. However, when this is not possible, it is desirable to work with confidence intervals that are at least asymptotically valid. As suggested earlier, if a maximum likelihood estimator is available, its asymptotic normality may be invoked for this purpose. Furthermore, while exact tests of hypotheses are desirable, in their absence one would at least hope for asymptotically valid tests. As is well known, likelihood ratio tests provide us with such a procedure. We shall discuss each of these problems in turn.

We first consider the case of a single parameter θ. From (2.49) it follows that $(\theta - \theta_0) B(\theta_0)$ and $((\partial \log L)/\partial \theta)/B(\theta_0)$ are both asymptotically distributed as $N(0, 1)$. We may thus determine confidence intervals for either of these quantities by using the normal distribution. Furthermore, if the relevant quantity is monotonic in θ, we may transform these confidence inequalities into corresponding confidence intervals for θ. This can best be illustrated by two examples.

Consider first establishing a confidence interval for the mean of a normal distribution, μ, with known variance σ^2. The log-likelihood function is

$$\log L = -\frac{n}{2} \log (2\pi\sigma^2) - \frac{1}{2\sigma^2} \Sigma (x_i - \mu)^2,$$

from which we have

$$\frac{\partial \log L}{\partial \mu} = \frac{n}{\sigma^2} (\bar{x} - \mu)$$

and $\partial^2 \log L/\partial \mu^2 = -n/\sigma^2$. Then by (2.50) $R(\mu) = n/\sigma^2$ and

$$\psi = \frac{\partial \log L/\partial \mu}{B(\mu)} = \frac{n}{\sigma^2} \frac{(\bar{x} - \mu)}{\sqrt{n/\sigma^2}} = (\bar{x} - \mu) \sqrt{n/\sigma^2}$$

---

[21] It can be shown, again if $\mu_x = 0$, that the roots of (1.22) tend to a and $\dfrac{-a \pm \sqrt{a^2 - 2/\sigma^2}}{2}$.

is asymptotically $N(0, 1)$. Consequently a 95% confidence interval for μ is $\bar{x} \pm 1.96\sigma/\sqrt{n}$. In the present case, of course, the normality holds for all sample sizes so this confidence interval is exact for small samples as well.

While this seems relatively straightforward, a second example will illustrate that this is not always the case. Consider the Poisson distribution

$$f(x, \lambda) = \frac{e^{-\lambda}\lambda^x}{x!} \qquad (x = 0, 1, ...),$$

where we wish to establish a confidence interval for λ. It is easily checked that

$$\frac{\partial \log L}{\partial \lambda} = \frac{n}{\lambda}(\bar{x} - \lambda)$$

and

$$\frac{\partial^2 \log L}{\partial \lambda^2} = -\frac{n\bar{x}}{\lambda^2}.$$

Consequently $R(\lambda) = n/\lambda$ and for 95% confidence limits we have[22]

$$(\bar{x} - \lambda)\sqrt{n/\lambda} = \pm 1.96. \tag{2.55}$$

Now to obtain confidence limits comparable to those obtained in the previous example, we must solve (2.55) for λ. This obviously reduces to solving a quadratic in λ, which can be seen to imply confidence limits of[23]

$$\bar{x} + \frac{1.92}{n} \pm \sqrt{\frac{3.84}{n}\bar{x} + \frac{3.69}{n^2}}.$$

To order $n^{-1/2}$ this expression is equivalent to the confidence limits

$$\bar{x} \pm 1.96\sqrt{\bar{x}/n}. \tag{2.56}$$

In the present instance, (2.56) could also have been arrived at more directly. In particular, since $\bar{x}$ is sufficient for λ, we may consistently estimate the variance of $\hat{\lambda}$ by $1/R(\bar{x}) = \bar{x}/n$. We could then use the asymptotic $N(0, 1)$

---

[22] Eq. (2.55) follows either from the right-hand side of (2.49) or the left-hand side. In fact (2.55) is precisely the left-hand side. In some instances (e.g., establishing a confidence interval for the standard deviation of a normal distribution) the resulting expression will depend on whether one uses the right or left side of (2.49).

[23] For details see M. G. Kendall and A. Stuart, *op cit.*, pp. 106–7. It should also be noted that in general the 'inversion' of expressions like (2.55) may present some conceptual difficulties. See *ibid.*, and S. S. Wilks, *Mathematical statistics*. New York, Wiley, 1962.

feature of $(\hat{\lambda} - \lambda) B(\bar{x}) = (\bar{x} - \lambda)/\sqrt{\bar{x}/n}$ to obtain (2.56) directly. In actual econometric applications, this is typically the procedure that is followed so that the same *caveats* noted above concerning the use of (2.48) must be cited here.

Up to this point we have treated the case of a single parameter. It is actually fairly simple to use the asymptotic normality of maximum likelihood estimators to derive confidence ellipsoids that are asymptotically equivalent to those considered above (e.g. (2.26) or (2.29)). The procedure can be sketched as follows.[24]

Let $\hat{\theta}$ be a p-component vector that is a maximum likelihood estimator of a vector θ. Then, asymptotically, $\hat{\theta}$ is distributed as $N(\theta, R^{-1}(\theta))$, where $R^{-1}(\theta)$ is given by (2.43). Letting $\Sigma = R^{-1}(\theta)$, we can write the asymptotic joint normal density of $\hat{\theta}$ as

$$f(\hat{\theta}) = (2\pi)^{-p/2} |\Sigma|^{-1/2} \exp\left\{-\tfrac{1}{2}(\hat{\theta} - \theta)' \Sigma^{-1}(\hat{\theta} - \theta)\right\}. \quad (2.57)$$

The exponent in (2.57) $Q = (\hat{\theta} - \theta)' \Sigma^{-1}(\hat{\theta} - \theta)$ can easily be seen to have a χ^2 distribution.[25] Consequently, one may compute confidence intervals by using the χ^2 distribution to find Q_1 and Q_2 such that $\Pr\{Q_1 < Q < Q_2\}$ is some chosen confidence level. Again, in practical situations we must replace Σ by a consistent estimate of Σ.

As an illustration consider the sum-of-squares minimization problem (2.2) with likelihood function given in (2.32). The log-likelihood function can be written as

$$\log L = -\frac{n}{2} \log 2\pi - n \log \sigma - S(\theta)/2\sigma^2$$

$$= -\frac{n}{2} \log 2\pi - n \log \sigma - \frac{1}{2\sigma^2} \sum_{k=1}^{n} [y_k - f(x^k, \theta)]^2.$$

The relevant first-order conditions are given in (2.20), and one may compute the Cramer-Rao bound as follows. The required second derivatives are

---

[24] For a detailed formal justification see S.S. Wilks, *op. cit.*, pp. 384–8.

[25] Since Σ is symmetric and positive definite, there exists a nonsingular matrix A such that $A\Sigma A' = I$ or $\Sigma = (A'A)^{-1}$. If we define $Z = A(\hat{\theta} - \theta)$, then Z is normally distributed with $E(Z) = 0$ and $E(ZZ') = E[A(\hat{\theta} - \theta)(\hat{\theta} - \theta)' A'] = A\Sigma A' = I$. Furthermore $Z'Z = Q$. Consequently, Q is a sum of squares of p independent $N(0, 1)$ variables and is distributed as $\chi^2(p)$.

given by

$$\frac{\partial^2 \log L}{\partial \theta_i \, \partial \theta_j} = \frac{1}{\sigma^2} \sum_{k=1}^{n} \left[(y_k - f(x^k, \theta)) \frac{\partial^2 f(x^k, \theta)}{\partial \theta_i \, \partial \theta_j} - \frac{\partial f(x^k, \theta)}{\partial \theta_i} \frac{\partial f(x^k, \theta)}{\partial \theta_j} \right]$$

$$(i, j = 1, \ldots, p). \tag{2.58}$$

$$\frac{\partial^2 \log L}{\partial (\sigma^2)^2} = \frac{n}{2\sigma^4} - \frac{1}{\sigma^6} \sum_{k=1}^{n} (y_k - f(x^k, \theta))^2 \tag{2.59}$$

$$\frac{\partial^2 \log L}{\partial \theta_i \, \partial (\sigma^2)} = -\frac{1}{\sigma^4} \sum_{k=1}^{n} \left[(y_k - f(x^k, \theta)) \frac{\partial f(x^k, \theta)}{\partial \theta_i} \right]. \tag{2.60}$$

Taking expected values of the negatives of (2.58)–(2.60) (i.e. computing (2.43)) yields

$$R = \begin{bmatrix} \dfrac{1}{\sigma^2} \sum_k \dfrac{\partial f(x^k, \theta)}{\partial \theta_i} \dfrac{\partial f(x^k, \theta)}{\partial \theta_j} & 0 \\ \hline 0 & \dfrac{n}{2\sigma^4} \end{bmatrix} \tag{2.61}$$

the inverse of which is the Cramer-Rao bound.

Of course, (2.61) is not observable in practice and must be estimated. If we let $\hat{\theta} = (\hat{\theta}_1, \ldots, \hat{\theta}_p)$ be the maximum likelihood estimate, then $\hat{\sigma}^2 = S(\hat{\theta})/n$, and we can estimate R by evaluating the derivatives in (2.61) at $\hat{\theta}$ and replacing σ^2 by $\hat{\sigma}^2$. It is clear that R then has the form

$$\hat{R} = \begin{bmatrix} \dfrac{1}{\hat{\sigma}^2} Z'Z & 0 \\ \hline 0 & \dfrac{n}{2\hat{\sigma}^4} \end{bmatrix}, \tag{2.62}$$

where Z is as in (2.26). From (2.57) we have a confidence ellipsoid for θ given by

$$\frac{(\hat{\theta} - \theta)'(Z'Z)(\hat{\theta} - \theta)}{\hat{\sigma}^2} = \chi^2(p). \tag{2.63}$$

The relation between the contours given by (2.26) and (2.63) becomes apparent from the following theorem: given the distribution $F(d_1, d_2)$ if the degrees of freedom $d_2 \to \infty$, then $d_1 F(d_1, d_2) \to \chi^2(d_1)$. Hence, as the number of observations n goes to infinity, (2.26) and (2.63) are seen to be asymptotically equivalent.

Alternatively one may estimate the covariance matrix by use of (2.48). If one substitutes $(\hat{\theta}, \hat{\sigma}^2)$ into (2.58)–(2.60), one obtains

$$\hat{R} = \begin{bmatrix} S_{\theta\theta}(\hat{\theta})/2\hat{\sigma}^2 & 0 \\ \hline 0 & \dfrac{n}{2\hat{\sigma}^4} \end{bmatrix}$$

An alternate set of confidence ellipsoids is then obtained by

$$\frac{(\hat{\theta} - \theta)'S_{\theta\theta}(\hat{\theta} - \theta)}{2\hat{\sigma}^2} = \chi^2(p). \tag{2.64}$$

By the same theorem as was used in the case of (2.63), the contours implied by (2.64) are asymptotically equivalent to those of (2.29).[26]

We turn now from the problem of confidence intervals to that of hypothesis testing. Our primary concern will be with the likelihood ratio test—a technique that is closely related to the maximum likelihood method of estimation. We again consider a likelihood function given by

$$L(x \mid \theta) = \prod_{i=1}^{n} f(x^i \mid \theta), \tag{2.65}$$

where θ is a p-component vector. Let us partition $\theta = (\theta_r, \theta_s)$, where θ_r and θ_s each contain r and s components respectively. Let us further suppose that we wish to test the hypothesis that $\theta_r = \bar{\theta}_r$. The likelihood ratio for this problem is given by

$$\lambda = \frac{L(x \mid \bar{\theta}_r, \hat{\hat{\theta}}_s)}{L(x \mid \hat{\theta}_r, \hat{\theta}_s)}, \tag{2.66}$$

where $(\hat{\theta}_r, \hat{\theta}_s)$ corresponds to the unconditional maximum of (2.65) and $\hat{\hat{\theta}}_s$ is the conditional maximum of (2.65) given that $\theta_r = \bar{\theta}_r$. It follows that $0 \leq \lambda \leq 1$. Clearly, if $s = 0$, there is no maximization process needed for the numerator of (2.66).

While λ is an intuitively appealing statistic, we need to know something about the distribution of λ. In practice we have two alternatives. For particular problems we may be able to derive the exact distribution of λ. Even

---

[26] See chapter 6 for an application of alternative methods of estimating variance bounds.

when this cannot be done, however, we have the rather remarkable fact that under suitable regularity conditions[27] $-2\log\lambda$ is distributed as $\chi^2(r)$, i.e.,

$$-2\log\lambda \sim \chi^2(r). \tag{2.67}$$

The regularity conditions are essentially those that assure the asymptotic normality and efficiency of the maximum likelihood estimator. We shall illustrate both the exact and asymptotic use of the likelihood ratio test.

Consider a normal distribution with unknown mean μ and unknown variance σ^2. Given a sample $\{x_i\}$ we wish to test the hypothesis that $\mu = \bar{\mu}$. The log-likelihood function for this problem is given above in (2.44), and we have also indicated that the unconditional maximum likelihood estimators are given by $\hat{\mu} = \bar{x}$ and $\sigma^2 = \Sigma(x - \bar{x})^2/n = s^2$. Consequently, we have

$$L(x|\hat{\mu}, \hat{\sigma}^2) = (2\pi s^2)^{-n/2} \exp\left(-\frac{n}{2}\right).$$

It is easy to verify that when the condition $\mu = \bar{\mu}$ is imposed
$$\hat{\sigma}^2 = \Sigma(x - \bar{\mu})^2/n = s^2 + (\bar{x} - \bar{\mu})^2.$$
Consequently

$$L(x|\bar{\mu}, \hat{\sigma}^2) = [2\pi(s^2 + (\bar{x} - \bar{\mu})^2)]^{-n/2} \exp\left(-\frac{n}{2}\right)$$

and

$$\lambda = \left\{\frac{s^2}{s^2 + (\bar{x} - \bar{\mu})^2}\right\}^{n/2}$$

or

$$\lambda^{2/n} = \frac{1}{1 + t^2/(n-1)},$$

where t is a t-statistic with $n - 1$ degrees of freedom. Since λ is a monotonic function of t^2, we may use the known distribution of t^2 to find significance points for λ.

There are numerous other problems for which the exact distribution of λ (or of some monotonic function of λ) can be derived. Of perhaps most interest in the present content is the fact that all of the hypothesis tests mentioned in our discussion of the linear model can be shown to be likelihood ratio

---

[27] M.G. Kendall and A. Stuart, *op. cit.*; and S.S. Wilks, *op. cit.*

tests. E.g., the likelihood ratio for testing $\beta = \beta^*$ in $Y = X\beta + U$ can easily be shown to be a monotonic function of the F statistic that is conventionally employed in the linear model.[28]

We turn now to the asymptotic use of the likelihood ratio and we consider, once again, our sum-of-squares minimization problem. The likelihood function is given in (2.32) and as above let $\hat{\theta}$ and $\hat{\sigma}^2 = \sum_{i=1}^{n} (y_i - f(x^i, \hat{\theta}))^2/n = S(\hat{\theta})/n$ be the unconditional maximum likelihood estimates. If we wish to test the hypothesis $\theta = \bar{\theta}$, then we need to maximize (2.32) with respect to σ^2, with θ set equal to $\bar{\theta}$. This produces

$$\hat{\bar{\sigma}}^2 = \frac{1}{n} \sum_{i=1}^{n} (y_i - f(x^i, \bar{\theta}))^2 = S(\bar{\theta})/n.$$

The likelihood ratio is then

$$\lambda = \frac{\hat{\sigma}^n}{\hat{\bar{\sigma}}^n}$$

or

$$-2 \log \lambda = n \log [S(\bar{\theta})/n] - n \log [S(\hat{\theta})/n]. \tag{2.68}$$

There is an obvious similarity between (2.68) and (2.22) and they may be shown to be asymptotically equivalent.

We may conclude that maximum likelihood estimation offers a highly attractive mode of estimation from a variety of viewpoints—especially in large samples. In subsequent chapters we shall assess its behavior in small samples in a variety of applications. In the remaining section of this chapter we give a brief overview of these applications

2.5. Overview of remaining chapters

The material presented so far has been primarily technique-oriented. We have discussed in a general way the principles and practice of estimation and hypothesis testing. The remaining chapters of this book consist of applications of these general principles to a number of specific econometric problems.

All subsequent chapters deal with problems in which there are nonlinearities. The term 'nonlinearity' is used here in a rather broad sense. More

---

[28] For details see F. A. Graybill, *op. cit.*

particularly, it is meant to cover situations in which there are either non-linearities in the parameters (including those of the error structure) or in the variables or in the estimating equations.[29] In the chapters to follow, there will appear examples of all three types of nonlinearities—often in conjunction with each other.

The practical difficulties of dealing with nonlinearities have constrained econometricians in the past in two different ways. In the first place econometricians have tended to ignore maximum likelihood or generalized least squares estimating methods. In some cases this has led to the development of other attractive estimating methods, but in other cases an obviously inferior estimator (at least for large samples) is accepted because of its computability. The second impact of the practical difficulties of handling nonlinearities is more subtle in that it has influenced the character of models that econometricians are willing to put forth as maintained hypotheses. E.g., macroeconometric model builders have often linearized relationships that theory (i.e., microtheory) tells us should be nonlinear. In addition, there is a general tendency among model builders to specify an error structure that will minimize computational difficulties.[30]

As indicated earlier, maximum likelihood methods can be applied to a wide variety of econometric problems; and in what follows we shall present seven such applications. While not all of these chapters will have the same degree or type of detail, the general problems that will be our concern can be briefly described.

Computability: Several questions arise under this heading. First, do the methods of chapter 1 provide a reasonable set of tools for attacking non-linear econometric problems? Second, do the methods work equally well and, if not, can one characterize the specific situations in which one method is better than another? Finally, how do problems of multiple solutions impinge on computability?

Estimator properties: Most of the known, desirable properties of maximum likelihood estimators are asymptotic, and so the question arises as to how these estimators behave in small samples. The small-sample behavior of

---

[29] Nonlinearities in the estimating equations can appear in essentially linear problems, e.g., in applying full information maximum likelihood to a system of simultaneous linear equations.

[30] This typically means that linear models have additive disturbances while exponential models have multiplicative disturbances. See chapter 5 for more detailed consideration of this problem.

maximum likelihood estimators should be contrasted with the behavior of other estimating methods for the same sample size and with the behavior of the maximum likelihood estimators themselves as the sample size is increased. In other words one would like to know how large is 'large'. A related question is how different estimating methods are affected by misspecification.

Confidence intervals and hypothesis testing: As indicated above, in general we can consistently estimate only the asymptotic covariance matrix of the maximum likelihood estimator. (The same is often true for other methods we shall consider as well.) In addition, we can construct likelihood ratios whose distribution is only known asymptotically. If maximum likelihood is to be useful in practice, we need to know how the Cramer-Rao bound compares with the variance of the actual sampling distribution of the estimator. Furthermore, we need to know the extent to which we can rely on the asymptotic χ^2 character of the logarithmic likelihood ratio in small samples.

These then are the general problems that will be our concern in subsequent chapters. No chapter will treat all of these problems by itself, but the remaining chapters taken as a whole provide a considerable amount of evidence on these questions.

One further point should be noted. In principle, the properties of the estimators and the procedures for testing hypotheses could be handled analytically. E.g., for a particular problem, one might hope to derive exact small sample distributions for various estimating methods. In practice, as is well known, this is extremely difficult. As a consequence, virtually all small sample properties presented below are derived from sampling experiments. The shortcomings of sampling experiments for adequately characterizing the small sample distributions (or the moments of such distributions) are too well known to elaborate here in detail. Suffice it to say that, despite our awareness of these difficulties, we felt that there was much to be gained from sampling experiments. The alternative would have been to discuss computability and estimator properties only in general terms—a position we found unattractive in view of the rapidly growing appearance of nonlinearities in econometric work.

The outline of the remaining chapters is as follows. Chapter 3 concerns itself with a single equation linear regression model with a heteroscedastic error term in which the variance of the error term is postulated to be a function of a given variable. Alternative ways of estimating the parameters of this function (as well as the basic parameters of the model) are considered and a number of tests for heteroscedasticity are examined. The next chapter deals with two different models for handling binary dependent variables—the linear probability model and the probit model. Again, alternative ways of estimating the models are considered. Chapter 5 treats the estimation of Cobb-Douglas type functions with both multiplicative and additive error terms, while chapter 6 examines the estimation of a vintage model of production. This latter chapter goes far beyond estimating the vintage model, however, in that it provides a good example of the use of alternative ways to estimate variance bounds in nonlinear situations. Chapters 7 and 8 both consider simultaneous equation systems. The former examines alternative estimators in a linear model with autocorrelated disturbances while the latter does the same for nonlinear simultaneous equation models without autocorrelation of error terms. Finally, chapter 9 examines ways to estimate models in the face of structural shifts in the parameters. A brief overall conclusion is provided at the end of chapter 9.

CHAPTER 3

ANALYSES OF HETEROSCEDASTICITY

3.1. Introduction

A very interesting and important econometric question that can be formulated as a problem in nonlinear estimation is the treatment of heteroscedasticity in regression analysis. The disturbances in a regression model are said to be heteroscedastic if they do not have a constant variance for each observation. This problem arises characteristically in cross-sectional models where a significant variation exists in the size distribution of the units considered. For example, heteroscedasticity has been encountered in consumer budget studies utilizing observations on individuals with diverse incomes and in analyses of the investment behavior of firms of different sizes.[1]

As is well-known, one generally obtains inferior parameter estimates if ordinary least squares is applied to a model with heteroscedastic disturbances. Furthermore, the presence of heteroscedasticity may invalidate standard tests of statistical significance. It is the purpose of this chapter to spell out these shortcomings and to gauge their quantitative significance. In addition, we shall be concerned with tests for heteroscedasticity and with its cure.

3.2. Statement of the problem

We consider a generalized linear regression model, which can be written in the usual matrix notation as

$$Y = X\beta + U, \qquad (3.1)$$

where X is a nonstochastic $n \times k$ matrix of rank k, β is a $k \times 1$ vector of parameters, and U is the $n \times 1$ vector of disturbances with $E(U) = 0$ and

---

[1] S.J.Prais and H.S.Houthakker, *The analysis of family budgets*. Cambridge, University Press, 1955; J.R.Meyer and E.Kuh, *The investment decision: an empirical study*. Cambridge, Mass., Harvard University Press, 1957.

$E(UU') = \sigma^2 \Omega$ (Ω positive definite). In the simple case in which Ω is the identity matrix the best linear unbiased estimate (BLUE) of β is given by the ordinary least squares (OLS) estimator[2]

$$\hat{\beta} = (X'X)^{-1} X'Y \tag{3.2}$$

and its covariance matrix is

$$\Sigma = \sigma^2 (X'X)^{-1}. \tag{3.3}$$

An unbiased estimate of σ^2 is provided by

$$\hat{\sigma}^2 = \frac{e'e}{n-k}, \tag{3.4}$$

where e is the vector of residuals, and hence an unbiased estimate of (3.3) is given by $\hat{\sigma}^2 (X'X)^{-1}$.

In the more general case, the BLUE of β is provided by Aitken's generalized least squares (GLS) given by

$$\tilde{\beta} = (X'\Omega^{-1}X)^{-1} (X'\Omega^{-1}Y) \tag{3.5}$$

with covariance matrix

$$\tilde{\Sigma} = \sigma^2 (X'\Omega^{-1}X)^{-1}. \tag{3.6}$$

Corresponding to (3.4) we have an unbiased estimate of σ^2 given by

$$\tilde{\sigma}^2 = \frac{e'\Omega^{-1}e}{n-k}. \tag{3.7}$$

We next consider the consequences of estimating β by (3.2), where $\Omega \neq I$, i.e., where the appropriate estimator is given by (3.5). As is well known, $\hat{\beta}$ is still an unbiased estimator of β but it no longer has minimum variance.[3] Its covariance matrix is now

$$\Sigma_{\hat{\beta}} = E(\hat{\beta} - \beta)(\hat{\beta} - \beta)' = E[(X'X)^{-1} X'UU'X(X'X)^{-1}]$$
$$= \sigma^2 (X'X)^{-1} (X'\Omega X)(X'X)^{-1}, \tag{3.8}$$

---

[2] See chapter 2.

[3] That is, any other unbiased linear estimator of β has a covariance matrix equal to (3.6) plus a positive semi-definite matrix. In particular, an arbitrary linear estimator of β can be written

$$[(X'\Omega^{-1}X)^{-1} X'\Omega^{-1} + A] Y$$

and its covariance matrix can be derived, analogously to theorem 2.7 above, to be

$$\sigma^2 (X'\Omega^{-1}X)^{-1} + \sigma^2 A\Omega A'$$

or (3.6) plus a positive semi-definite matrix.

from which it follows that the usual formula for the covariance matrix is no longer appropriate. Furthermore, it can be shown that the usual estimate of σ^2 given by (3.4) is no longer unbiased.

To see this we first substitute (3.1) into (3.2) to obtain

$$\hat{\beta} = \beta + (X'X)^{-1} X'U. \tag{3.9}$$

Substituting (3.9) into the definition of the residual e produces

$$e = X\beta + U - X\hat{\beta} = X\beta + U - X[\beta + (X'X)^{-1} X'U]$$

$$= [I - X(X'X)^{-1}X'] U = MU. \tag{3.10}$$

The matrix M is symmetric and idempotent so that

$$e'e = U'M'MU = U'M^2U = U'MU.$$

Taking expected values we have

$$E(e'e) = E(U'MU) = E[\text{tr}(U'MU)] \tag{3.11}$$

where tr is the trace operator. Since the trace of a product is invariant with respect to cyclic permutations of the multiplicands,

$$E(e'e) = \text{tr}[ME(UU')].$$

Now $E(UU') = \sigma^2\Omega$ and $M = I - X(X'X)^{-1}X'$, so

$$E(e'e) = \sigma^2 \text{tr}(M\Omega) = \sigma^2 \text{tr}[\Omega - X(X'X)^{-1}X'\Omega]$$

$$= \sigma^2 [\text{tr}\,\Omega - \text{tr}(X'X)^{-1}(X'\Omega X)]. \tag{3.12}$$

Expression (3.12) can be simplified by observing that

$$X'\Omega X = X'X - X'(I - \Omega) X,$$

and hence

$$(X'X)^{-1}(X'\Omega X) = I - (X'X)^{-1}X'(I - \Omega) X. \tag{3.13}$$

Taking the trace of (3.13) we have

$$\text{tr}(X'X)^{-1}(X'\Omega X) = k - \text{tr}[(X'X)^{-1}X'(I - \Omega) X]. \tag{3.14}$$

Assuming Ω is normalized so that $\text{tr}\,\Omega = n$, and substituting (3.14) into (3.12) yields

$$E(e'e) = \sigma^2 [n - k + \text{tr}(X'X)^{-1}X'(I - \Omega) X]$$

and from (3.14) we have

$$E(\hat{\sigma}^2) = \sigma^2 + \frac{\sigma^2 \, \mathrm{tr} \, [(X'X)^{-1} \, X' \, (I - \Omega) \, X]}{n - k}. \qquad (3.15)$$

From (3.15) it follows that

$$E \, [\hat{\sigma}^2 \, (X'X)^{-1}] = \Sigma + \sigma^2 \, \frac{\mathrm{tr} \, [(X'X)^{-1} \, X' \, (I - \Omega) \, X]}{n - k} (X'X)^{-1}$$

$$= \Sigma_{\hat{\beta}} + \sigma^2 \, (X'X)^{-1} \, X' \, (I - \Omega) \, X \, (X'X)^{-1}$$

$$+ \sigma^2 \, \frac{\mathrm{tr} \, [(X'X)^{-1} \, X' \, (I - \Omega) \, X]}{n - k} (X'X)^{-1} \qquad (3.16)$$

In other words, the consequences of using (3.2) to estimate β instead of using (3.5) are two-fold:

(i) the estimates are inefficient in that they have larger sampling variances than necessary,

(ii) the estimated covariance matrix is biased so that standard tests of statistical significance are inappropriate. The bias is given by the last two terms in (3.16).

The importance of these two points clearly depends on the quantitative significance of the bias and inefficiency. This is in turn a function of both the nature of the X's and the form of Ω. As far as Ω is concerned, the two points noted above are valid for any covariance matrix. In other words, these results apply to situations involving both autocorrelation and heteroscedasticity. If we restrict ourselves to the latter, then Ω is simply a diagonal matrix in which the diagonal elements are not all identical. Even in this case it is difficult in general to compare analytically (3.8) and (3.6) or to evaluate (3.16). As a result, one is forced to evaluate some simple cases.

Empirical consequences

One standard econometrics textbook[4] assesses the relative efficiency of OLS and GLS [i.e. compares (3.6) and (3.8)] by considering two possible specifications for Ω in the context of a single independent variable. It considers both $\sigma_i^2 = \sigma^2 x_i$ and $\sigma_i^2 = \sigma^2 x_i^2$, where σ_i^2 is the variance of the ith disturbance and x_i is the independent variable. Using a sample of size 5, Johnston reports results ranging from 50 to 80% efficiency.[5] Goldberger, in an-

---

[4] J. Johnston, *Econometric methods*. New York, McGraw–Hill, 1963.
[5] That is the ratio of the variance of the GLS estimator of the slope (given by (3.6)) to that of the OLS estimator runs from 0.5 to 0.8.

other standard textbook[6], considers a single regressor and evaluates the bias of the classical estimator of the residual variance as given in (3.16) for a simple case in which (3.16) reduces to the following

$$E\left[\hat{\sigma}^2 (X'X)^{-1}\right] = \Sigma + \sigma^2 \frac{(n-1)\,\Sigma\,(1-k_t)\,x_t^2}{(n-2)\,(\Sigma x_t^2)^2}, \qquad (3.17)$$

where the variance of the tth disturbance is given by $\sigma^2 k_t$.[7] On the basis of this, Goldberger concludes that the classical variance estimator understates the true variance of the OLS estimator whenever high variances of the errors correspond to high values of the independent variables.

Finally, one particularly illuminating elaboration on (3.16) is contained in a paper by Theil.[8] The paper is based on the assumption that heteroscedasticity takes the form

$$\sigma_i^2 = E(u_i^2) = \gamma\,[E(y_i)]^2,$$

i.e., the variance of the ith disturbance is proportional to the square of the mean of the dependent variable.[9] For this specific case, Theil derives a more useful expression for (3.16). Let us consider the case of a single regressor[10] x and let μ_k be the kth moment about the mean of the regressor, i.e.,

$$\mu_k = \frac{1}{n} \sum_{i=1}^{n} (x_i - \bar{x})^k.$$

Further, let r be the correlation coefficient of the regression, let c be the coefficient of variation of the dependent variable[11], and let σ_β^2 and s_β^2 be the true and estimated variance of the slope coefficient. Theil then shows

$$\sigma_\beta^2 = s_\beta^2 \left[1 + \frac{2rc\,\dfrac{\mu_3}{(\mu_2)^{3/2}} + r^2 c^2 \left(\dfrac{\mu_4}{\mu_2^2} - 1 \right)}{1 + r^2 c^2} \right].$$

---

[6] A.S. Goldberger, *Econometric theory*. New York, Wiley, 1964.

[7] Expression (3.17) assumes the normalizations $\Sigma k_t = n$ and $\Sigma x_t = 0$.

[8] H. Theil, Estimates and their sampling variance of parameters of certain heteroscedastic distributions. *Revue de l'Institut International de Statistique* **19** (1951), 141–7.

[9] As indicated before, Johnston considered the case in which the variance is a function of the independent variable. As we shall see below, both these cases can be accomodated in a more general specification.

[10] Theil actually considers the general case.

[11] That is, $c^2 = \mathrm{var}\,(y)/[E(y)]^2$.

In other words, the bias in the estimated standard error depends in part on the skewness of the independent variable (as measured by the third moment μ_3) as well as on the fourth moment, the correlation coefficient, and the coefficient of variation of y. Theil reports a particular example in which the estimated variance underestimates the true variance by about 25%.

Up to this point we have described only some general tendencies implied by the heteroscedasticity of the error term and have presented a few shreds of empirical evidence. It is therefore desirable to conclude this section with a more comprehensive indication of the inefficiencies and biases created by heteroscedasticity. For the sake of simplicity we assume a model with a single regressor given by

$$y_i = \alpha + \beta x_i + u_i, \quad \text{where} \quad E(u_i^2) = a + b x_i + c x_i^2.$$

In other words, the variance of the ith disturbance is a quadratic function of the ith observation on the independent variable. It should be noted that this specification includes all of the previous specifications as special cases. More particularly, it encompasses $\sigma_i^2 = \sigma^2 x_i$; $\sigma_i^2 = \sigma^2 x_i^2$; and $\sigma_i^2 = \gamma [E(y_i)]^2$.[12] In order to assess the consequences of heteroscedasticity we resorted to Monte-Carlo calculations. More particularly, we assumed values for α, β, a, b, and c, generated a sample of x's, and explicitly computed the values of expressions (3.6), (3.8), and (3.16) above. The x's were assumed to have a given mean and variance in the population and were randomly generated in such a way as to follow either a uniform or lognormal distribution. The calculations were hardly meant to be exhaustive. Rather they are supposed to indicate the quantitative significance of heteroscedasticity under a variety of assumptions. Table 3.1 reports some of these calculations. The two statistics shown are: (1) the ratio of the true standard error of the OLS estimators of α and β to the standard error of the GLS estimators; and (2) the ratio of the true standard errors of the OLS estimator to the classical estimator of the standard errors for OLS. That is, the first statistic is the ratio of the square root of the diagonal elements of (3.8) to (3.6) and the second is the ratio of the square root of the diagonal elements of (3.8) to (3.16).

The results can be quickly summarized under the following points:

(i) Heteroscedasticity can produce gross inefficiencies if one uses OLS rather than GLS.

---

[12] Since $E(y_i) = \alpha + \beta x_i$, this last specification is simply $\sigma_i^2 = \gamma \alpha^2 + 2\gamma \alpha \beta x_i + \gamma \beta^2 x_i^2$, which is clearly of the form given in the text.

TABLE 3.1 A

Effects of heteroscedasticity-uniform distribution*

b	c	μ_x	σ_x	Eq. (3.8)/Eq. (3.6)		Eq. (3.8)/Eq. (3.16)	
				α	β	α	β
1	0	200	80	1.08	1.07	0.85	1.01
1	0	239	138	1.43	1.26	0.73	0.98
1	0	308	178	1.32	1.21	0.74	0.97
1	0	533	308	1.61	1.30	0.71	1.02
10	0	200	80	1.10	1.08	0.84	1.00
10	0	239	138	1.46	1.23	0.69	1.02
10	0	308	178	1.64	1.36	0.77	1.03
10	0	533	308	2.36	1.50	0.72	1.01
1	0.1	200	80	1.44	1.30	0.76	0.99
1	0.1	239	138	4.17	1.83	0.65	1.06
1	0.1	308	178	3.14	1.63	0.62	1.06
1	0.1	533	308	3.93	1.87	0.69	1.14
1	0.2	200	80	1.46	1.33	0.78	1.00
1	0.2	239	138	4.21	1.87	0.66	1.06
1	0.2	308	178	5.84	2.16	0.71	1.03
1	0.2	533	308	9.57	2.05	0.65	1.12
1	0.3	200	80	1.38	1.27	0.80	1.04
1	0.3	239	138	7.11	1.97	0.64	1.08
1	0.3	308	178	6.71	2.03	0.65	1.07
1	0.3	533	308	11.73	1.88	0.54	1.01

* The x's are uniformly distributed with mean μ_x and standard deviation σ_x. For all experiments in the table $\alpha = 2$, $\beta = 2$, and $a = 20$.

(ii) The classical variance estimator may considerably understate the true variances of the OLS estimator.

(iii) For a given mean and variance of the independent variable, a more skewed distribution of the x's produces greater biases and inefficiencies.

(iv) Variations in the parameters which underlie the variance of the disturbances can markedly influence the consequences of heteroscedasticity.

Both the theoretical and empirical results presented above suggest that heteroscedasticity may be a severe problem. If the covariance matrix Ω of the disturbances is known, then GLS is applicable and nothing more needs to be said. Unfortunately, in realistic situations Ω is unknown and consequently the presence of heteroscedasticity may also be unknown. We turn now to the more general problems presented by the need to test for heteroscedasticity and by estimation in the face of an unknown Ω.

TABLE 3.1 B

Effects of heteroscedasticity-lognormal distribution*

b	c	σ_x	Eq. (3.8)/Eq. (3.6)		Eq. (3.8)/Eq. (3.16)	
			α	β	α	β
1	0	80	1.15	1.13	1.13	1.27
1	0	160	1.28	1.21	1.00	1.27
1	0	240	1.41	1.27	1.16	1.94
1	0	500	1.58	1.27	0.98	2.26
10	0	80	1.11	1.10	1.03	1.16
10	0	160	1.46	1.30	1.02	1.41
10	0	240	1.66	1.36	1.12	1.84
10	0	500	2.15	1.46	1.18	2.40
1	0.1	80	1.46	1.37	1.11	1.35
1	0.1	160	4.31	2.48	1.47	2.41
1	0.1	240	4.33	2.27	1.24	2.39
1	0.1	500	9.20	2.86	1.42	3.45
1	0.2	80	1.82	1.64	1.48	1.78
1	0.2	160	4.29	2.49	1.51	2.27
1	0.2	240	13.81	5.00	3.56	9.32
1	0.2	500	8.88	2.79	1.25	3.35
1	0.3	80	1.50	1.38	1.15	1.43
1	0.3	160	4.31	2.59	1.62	2.66
1	0.3	240	14.87	5.41	3.73	9.05
1	0.3	500	11.48	2.70	1.05	3.13

* The x's are lognormally distributed with mean 200 and
standard deviation σ_x. For all experiments $\alpha = 2$,
$\beta = 2$ and $a = 20$.

3.3. Testing and estimation

Thus far we have assumed known both the presence of heteroscedasticity
and, what is an even stronger assumption, the relevant covariance matrix of
the disturbances. More generally, however, we will need to perform statistical
tests for the presence of heteroscedasticity and find estimation methods that
produce reasonable estimates even if Ω is unknown.

The literature on this subject has several different strands. At one end of
the spectrum there is what might be called nonconstructive tests for heteroscedasticity. Here the primary interest is to establish the presence or absence

heteroscedasticity and the estimation aspects are ignored. The other end of the spectrum consists of assuming a particular form for heteroscedasticity and then directly facing the estimation problem. The middle ground consists of what might be termed constructive tests for heteroscedasticity. Here the test is tied up with the estimation problem and if the test rejects the hypothesis of homoscedasticity it provides a direct method of estimation which takes account of the nonspherical character of the disturbances.

We shall discuss these various types of tests below. It should be noted at the outset, however, that in the most general case, when nothing is known about Ω except that it has form (3.18) below, estimation will be impossible since there are

$$\Omega = \begin{bmatrix} \sigma_1^2 & 0 & \cdots & 0 \\ 0 & \sigma_2^2 & \cdots & 0 \\ \cdot & & \cdots \cdots & \cdot \\ 0 & \cdot & 0 & \cdots & \sigma_n^2 \end{bmatrix} \tag{3.18}$$

more parameters to be estimated than there are observations. Only when one is willing to impose some further structure on Ω does the problem become tractable. Generally, however, in economic applications one has some notion of the relevant variables that account for the variation in σ_i^2. The precise functional nature of this variation may be unknown and we return to this below.

Nonconstructive tests

The tests that are considered in both this and the next section, with one exception, all utilize the residuals from an OLS regression. The basic method is to compare the distribution of the residuals under the hypothesis that the full set of standard assumptions holds with the distribution of the residuals in the presence of heteroscedasticity. The use of residuals for analyzing specification errors has become increasingly more common and indeed has been applied to a wide range of situations including serial correlation, nonnormality, and incorrect functional forms. Work by Anscombe and Tukey, Theil, and Ramsey, is characteristic of these efforts.[13] In addition to formal

---

[13] F.J.Anscombe and J.W.Tukey, The examination and analysis of residuals. *Technometrics* **5** (1963), 141–60; H.Theil, The analysis of disturbances in regression analysis. *Journal of the American Statistical Association* **60** (1965), 1067–79; J.B.Ramsey, Tests for specification error in classical linear least-squares regression analysis. *Journal of the Royal Statistical Society* **B31**, 2 (1969), 250–71.

efforts, researchers often use heuristic approaches including various plots of residuals. As a practical matter, using such techniques is generally wise no matter what formal tests are employed. The present authors had earlier presented two tests for heteroscedasticity based on least squares residuals. These are described below as is a test presented by Ramsey. Before doing this, however, it will be helpful to outline the standard test for heteroscedasticity in a non-regression context.

The classical situation, as developed, for example, by Pearson, assumed drawings x_{ij} from k independent normal samples with mean μ_i and variance σ_i^2, where n_i observations were available for the ith sample ($i = 1, \ldots, k$). The hypothesis to be tested is that $\sigma_1^2 = \sigma_2^2 \cdots = \sigma_k^2$. Using the likelihood ratio method, Pearson presented the test statistic

$$l = \prod_{i=1}^{k} (s_i^2/s^2)^{n_i/2}, \tag{3.19}$$

where

$$n_i s_i^2 = \sum_{j=1}^{n_i} (x_{ij} - \bar{x}_i)^2, \quad ns^2 = \sum_{i=1}^{k} n_i s_i^2, \quad \text{and} \quad n = \sum_{i=1}^{k} n_i.$$

A subsequent modification by Bartlett replaced n_i by corresponding degrees of freedom (i.e., $n_i - 1$). Then, as is well known, $-2 \log l$ is asymptotically distributed as χ^2 with $k - 1$ degrees of freedom.

Now consider the regression model (3.1) given by

$$Y = X\beta + U,$$

where Y und U are $n \times 1$ vectors, X is an $n \times k$ matrix, and β is a $k \times 1$ vector. We wish to test for the equality of the variances against the hypothesis that the covariance matrix of the disturbances has the form given by (3.18). Of course, the true disturbances are unobservable, but we do have available the OLS residuals e given by

$$e = [I - X(X'X)^{-1} X'] Y.$$

By analogy, then, it would seem sensible to regard the square of the ith residual e_i^2 as an estimate of σ_i^2 and to attempt to apply the likelihood ratio criterion described earlier. Unfortunately this suffers from two difficulties. First, while under the null hypothesis the true disturbances are independently and identically distributed as $N(0, \sigma^2)$, the e_i are not independent nor identically distributed. Indeed

$$E(ee') = \sigma^2 (I - X(X'X)^{-1} X'),$$

which shows that e has a nonscalar covariance matrix. Second, and more important, is the fact that $-2 \log l$ will not be asymptotically distributed as $\chi^2(k-1)$ if we simply have one observation per sample, that is, if we obtain n different σ_i^2 each based on one observation. This means that some grouping of the residuals is necessary if this second problem is to be overcome. It then becomes reasonable to ask whether there is some natural grouping of the residuals and it is here where additional *a priori* information comes into play. For example, if we are dealing with a time series regression and one believes that residual variances increase over time, then a natural grouping would be by neighboring time periods. If the hypothesis is that variances are related to one of the independent variables, then groupings according to the range of this variable would be more natural. As we shall see both of these techniques have been used in actual tests that have been proposed. We first consider the parametric test proposed earlier by the authors.[14]

It is assumed for this test that σ_i^2 is monotonically related to the value of one of the regressors, say the mth, with individual observations x_{mi}. Further assume that σ_i^2 is positively related to the regressor x_m—obvious changes in the test can be made if the reverse is true. On the assumption that the error terms are normally distributed a test can be constructed in the following manner.

(a) Order the observations by the values of the variable x_m; i.e., the new ordering is given in terms of the second subscript of x_m, indexed so that $x_{mi} \leq x_{mj}$ if and only if $i < j$. The remaining variables are then indexed so that the index values correspond with those of the x_{mi}.

(b) Given some choice of the number of central observations, p, to be omitted, we fit separate regressions (by least squares) to the first $(n-p)/2$ and last $(n-p)/2$ observations, provided also that $(n-p)/2 > k$, the number of parameters to be estimated, and that the $(n-p)/2$ observations are distributed over at least k distinct points in the X-space.

(c) Denoting by S_1 and S_2 the sum of the squares of the residuals from the regressions based on the relatively small and relatively large values of x_m respectively, we form

$$R = \frac{S_2}{S_1}.$$

[14] S.M.Goldfeld and R.E.Quandt, Some tests for homoscedasticity. *Journal of the American Statistical Association* **60** (1965), 539–47.

The quantity R clearly has the F-distribution with $((n-p-2k)/2,$ $(n-p-2k)/2)$ degrees of freedom under the null hypothesis of homoscedasticity. Under the alternative hypothesis values of R will tend to be large since the values of x_m are larger for the second set of residuals than for the first and the corresponding sum of squares of residuals will tend to be larger as well.

The following observations are relevant:

(a) Since the sum of the squares of the residuals can be expressed as a quadratic form in the true errors as in (3.11) above, the ratio R is homogeneous of degree zero in the true error terms; hence the ratio is independent of σ^2 under the null hypothesis.

(b) The ratio R is independent of the regression coefficients β.

(c) The power of this test will clearly depend upon the value of p, the number of omitted observations; for very large values of p the power will be small but it is not obvious that the power increases monotonically as p tends to 0.[15]

(d) The power of the test will clearly depend on the nature of the sample of values for x_m as well as on the nature of the relationship between σ_i^2 and x_{mi}. If the variance of x_m is small relative to the mean of x_m the power can be expected to be small, and conversely.

(e) The test is analogous to the likelihood ratio rest where we have considered only two groupings. The problem of lack of independence between the OLS residuals has been bypassed by computing two separate regressions rather than taking the residuals from a single OLS regression.

The power of the test just proposed was previously investigated and generally found to be quite satisfactory.[16] Although it was not brought out in this earlier work, the cases in which the F-test failed to detect heteroscedasticity are precisely those cases in which the efficiency loss in using OLS is small (e.g., when the variance of x_m is relatively small). Additional evidence on both this point and the use of this test is provided below.

Ramsey's proposed test for heteroscedasticity also starts from the likelihood ratio test outlined above.[17] To get around the problem of lack of independence of the estimated residuals, Ramsey suggests using a set of $n-k$

---

[15] The reason for this conjecture is as follows. Although the two regressions will be based on relatively more observations when p equals or is near zero, thus leading to high power, the inclusion of the centrally located observations will cause the residual variances to differ from each other by less than they would if p were relatively large. This latter effect tends to diminish the power. It does not seem to be clear *a priori* which influence will predominate.

[16] S. M. Goldfeld and R. E. Quandt, *op. cit.*

[17] J. B. Ramsey, *op. cit.*

residuals whose distribution under the null hypothesis is $N(0, \sigma^2 I)$. Basically, Ramsey proposes to use Theil's BLUS residuals, which are 'best' linear unbiased estimators of the true disturbances and which can be derived from the OLS residuals.[18] To get around the second problem in applying the likelihood ratio test (i.e., lack of repeated observations), Ramsey proposes dividing the sample into three nonintersecting groups and estimating s_i^2, $i = 1, 2, 3$ in (3.19) above by using the Theil residuals. The groups are chosen so that roughly the first third of the observations fall in the first group, with the middle third in the second group and the remainder in the last group. Two points are worth noting about this technique. First, the choice of three groups is not critical and is simply suggested as a practical compromise. Second, the manner of grouping implicitly assumes that under the alternative hypothesis the variance of the disturbances is a function of the index i used to order the observations. As indicated above this may be appropriate for time series analysis but may not be for a cross sectional problem.[19] Of course, there is no reason why the groups could not be chosen according to some other criterion.

Ramsey and Gilbert provide an experimental test of the power of this test. They do not compare it with any other method, nor do they engage in extensive experimentation but the test seems to perform quite satisfactorily with the power increasing with sample size. One interesting finding of their study is that the power of the test is higher if OLS residuals are used rather than Theil residuals. The conclusion, at least in testing for heteroscedasticity, would seem to be that the simpler procedure is adequate.[20]

One final nonconstructive test for heteroscedasticity which may be mentioned is the so-called 'peak-test'.[21] The 'peak-test' is basically an attempt to formalize more heuristic graphical procedures that might be used when

---

[18] H. Theil, *op. cit.* Use of transformed residuals has also been proposed by Putter and Heyadat and Robson. See J. Putter, Orthonormal bases of error spaces and their use for investigating the normality and variances of residuals. *Journal of the American Statistical Association* **62** (1967), 1022–36, and A. Heyadat and D. S. Robson, Independent stepwise residuals for testing homoscedasticity. *Journal of the American Statistical Association* **65** (1970), 1573–81.

[19] In an experimental evaluation of this test done by Ramsey and Gilbert, the true disturbances are generated so that $\sigma_i^2 = i/25$. In other words, the data embody the implicit assumption noted above. See J. B. Ramsey and R. F. Gilbert, A Monte Carlo study of some small sample properties of tests for specification error. Michigan State University, Econometrics Workshop paper No. 6813, June 1969.

[20] It should be noted that the Theil residuals generally worked better for other types of misspecification, *ibid.*

[21] S. M. Goldfeld and R. E. Quandt, *op. cit.*

the variance of the disturbances is thought to increase with some variable. It is a nonparametric test and therefore, unlike the likelihood ratio test or its derivatives, does not depend on normality of the disturbances. The following steps are taken in carrying out the test where, as before, we have assumed the variance increases with x_m.

(a) Estimate the linear regression model by OLS.

(b) Let e_i be the ith residual corresponding to the ith value of x_{mi}. The set of residuals, $\{e_k\}$ is assumed to be ordered in the following manner. We order the values of the variable x_m so that $x_{mi} \leq x_{mj}$ if and only if $i < j$. We then index the residuals e_i so that the index values correspond with those of x_{mi}. Thus if $i < j$ then e_i appears to the left of e_j in the ordered list of residuals.

(c) Define a peak in the ordered residuals at observation i to be an instance where $|e_j| \geq |e_i|$ for all $i < j$. The first residual, e_1, does not constitute a peak.

(d) If the residuals are heteroscedastic such that the variance increases with x_m, the number of observed peaks will tend to be large.

(e) In order to test whether the number of peaks is significant, the number is compared with a critical number that is obtained by computing the cumulative distribution of the number of peaks under the hypothesis of homoscedasticity. A table for this is provided in the appendix to this chapter (see table 3.30).[22] Sampling experiments indicate that the power of the peak test compares favorably with that of the F-test described above.

Constructive tests and estimation

Up to this point the discussion has focussed on tests for establishing the presence of heteroscedastic disturbances but not on securing improved parameter estimates. As emphasized before, these tests implicity assume something about the nature of the heteroscedasticity and these assumptions may also be exploited for securing improved estimates. For example, if either the F-test or peak-test suggests that the variance is an increasing function of an independent variable x_m, one may then posit

$$\Omega = \begin{bmatrix} f(x_{m1}) & \cdots & 0 \\ \cdots & \cdots & \cdot \\ \cdots & \cdots & \cdot \\ \cdots & \cdots & f(x_{mn}) \end{bmatrix} \tag{3.20}$$

---

[22] This table is only valid asymptotically, but evidence presented in the appendix suggests that as a practical matter the test can be used for sample sizes greater than 15. One could also think of applying the test to the BLUS residuals, in which case the table is valid in small samples.

where f is some increasing function and apply GLS.[23] Unfortunately, in order to do this properly one may need more precision than the tests provide. For example, plausible forms for f could include $(a + bx)$, $(a + bx)^2$ or $\sqrt{a + bx}$. If a is known to be zero, then one must 'only' choose the proper form of the x-variable. However, if neither a nor b is known, there are further difficulties. The methods described in this section focus on securing estimates of parameters such as a and b. Since $b = 0$ corresponds to the case of homoscedasticity, these methods may employ tests of the significance of b as a further test for heteroscedasticity.

Glejser's test

Glejser has proposed a constructive test of this type.[24] Starting from the basic model

$$Y = X\beta + U \tag{3.21}$$

he posits

$$U = VP(z), \tag{3.22}$$

where $P(z)$ is a nonnegative polynomial, z is one of the independent variables, and V is a random variable. Assume for the moment that $P(z) = a + bz$. Further assume that we have estimated (3.21) by OLS where, as before, we denote the OLS residuals as e. From (3.22) we have

$$E(|U|) = E(|V|)P(z)$$

or

$$|e| = E(|V|)P(z) + |e| - E(|U|). \tag{3.23}$$

On the basis of this, Glejser suggests estimating a and b by regressing the absolute values of the OLS residuals on the variable z.[25] The estimates for a and b in $P(z) = a + bz$ are then compared with their standard errors via the 't-test' and the following possibilities are considered.

(i) If b is not significant, homoscedasticity is accepted along with the OLS estimates;

(ii) If b is significant but a not significant, then the equation is reestimated by GLS with $\sigma_i^2 = \sigma^2 z_i^2$ [26];

---

[23] Or, if Ramsey's test is used, one might take the estimates s_i^2 and use them in a pseudo-GLS procedure. The reason for the use of 'pseudo' is discussed below.

[24] H. Glejser, A new test for heteroscedasticity. *Journal of the American Statistical Association* **64** (1969), 316–23.

[25] The estimates obtained will only be valid up to a constant of proportionality, $E(|V|)$, but this is all one needs.

[26] This, of course, is equivalent to scaling all variables by z.

(iii) If both a and b are significant, then the equation is reestimated by GLS with $\sigma_i^2 = \sigma^2 (a + bz_i)^2$.

As Glejser generally recognizes there are a number of statistical and practical difficulties with his proposed test. The statistical problems are of two types. The first concerns the tests of significance on the parameters a and b. Estimates of these parameters are obtained from a regression of the form

$$|e_i| = a + bz_i + v_i, \quad \text{where} \quad v_i = |e_i| - E(|u_i|).$$

Unfortunately, the disturbance term, v_i has a number of undesirable properties: namely it has non-zero mean, it is autocorrelated, and it is heteroscedastic! We have already seen that standard tests do not apply in such cases so that testing a and b for significance in the present context is an uncertain procedure at best. Indeed Glejser reports some difficulty in pinning down an appropriate level of significance to assure a true probability for type I error of 0.05.

The second statistical difficulty concerns the nature of the estimation procedure in Glejser's test. If we wish to estimate the model given by (3.21) and (3.22), with $P(z) = a + bz$, then there is no particular reason (save perhaps computer resources) why we should estimate the model in two steps (i.e., first a and b and then transforming to get β) rather than estimating all the parameters simultaneously.[27] Indeed, as we shall see below, maximum likelihood estimates of all the parameters are readily available and ought to be considered.

A practical difficulty with Glejser's procedure concerns the ease with which (3.23) can be estimated. To date we have considered $P(z) = a + bz$, so that standard linear regression techniques are applicable. If however, $P(z) = \sqrt{a + bz}$, then eq. (3.23) must be estimated by nonlinear techniques. This particular example could be dealt with by using e_i^2 as a dependent variable without changing the spirit of Glejser's approach. In the experiments described below, this will be called the Modified Glejser Method.

In fact, a quite similar suggestion is found in a paper by Park.[28] Park posits a structure for the variance of the error term given by

$$\sigma_i^2 = \sigma^2 z_i^\gamma e^v,$$

---

[27] Under suitable assumptions, such two-step procedures can lead to an estimator with the same asymptotic distribution as the GLS estimator with known covariance matrix. See, for example, H. Theil, *Principles of Econometrics*. New York, Wiley, 1971, ch. 8. Of course, the appropriate (and somewhat complicated) conditions must be verified in each instance and this has not been done in the present case.

[28] R. E. Park, Estimation with heteroscedastic error terms. *Econometrica* **34** (1966), 888.

where v is a well-behaved error term. This can be rewritten

$$\log \sigma_i^2 = \log \sigma^2 + \gamma \log z_i + v. \tag{3.24}$$

Park suggests using e_i^2 as an estimate of σ_i^2 and estimating (3.24). The resultant estimate of γ can be tested for statistical significance and, if significant, may be used to transform the original equation. The error term in eq. (3.24) suffers from similar difficulties to those noted above for (3.23).

A final point to be noted about the Park-Glejser approach is that while their tests offer several options for the form of the dependent variable (e.g. $\log e^2$, $|e|$, e^2), there are still numerous specifications of $P(z)$ which do not lead to linear estimating equations.[29]

Glejser engaged in a limited set of sampling experiments in order to assess the usefulness of his procedure. The experiments used the following alternative specifications for $P(z)$:

$$z, \sqrt{z}, 1/z, 1/\sqrt{z}, z + a, \sqrt{z + a}, (z^2 + a)^{1/2}.$$

Glejser termed the first four types 'pure' heteroscedasticity while the latter three types were called 'mixed' heteroscedasticity. Glejser generally found that the power of his test was satisfactory for large sample sizes and large variances for z. In addition, he established the following conclusions:

(i) The power of his test is not greatly affected by using an incorrect functional form for $P(z)$;

(ii) Mixed heteroscedasticity is generally difficult to detect;

(iii) If mixed heteroscedasticity is detected when the generating mechanism involves only pure heteroscedasticity, efficiency gains are still to be made (from transforming and doing the second stage) relative to OLS;

(iv) If pure heteroscedasticity is detected in lieu of mixed heteroscedasticity, there may be an efficiency loss relative to OLS.

These findings suggest one should be particularly careful in ascertaining the presence of mixed heteroscedasticity.

Maximum likelihood estimation

The formulation of a heteroscedastic regression model as a maximum likelihood problem is both straightforward and computationally simple.[30]

---

[29] For example, $P(z) = az^b + c$.

[30] The formulation has always been straightforward but computational difficulties led earlier writers (e.g., Theil) to dismiss maximum likelihood as impractical. More recently, however, this has been proposed by H.C. Rutemiller and D.A. Bowers, Estimation in a heteroscedastic regression model. *Journal of the American Statistical Association* **63** (1968), 552–7.

We again start from

$$Y = X\beta + U,$$

where U is now assumed to be normally distributed with mean vector 0. The covariance matrix of the U's is given by

$$\Omega = \begin{bmatrix} P(z_1) & 0 & \cdots & 0 \\ 0 & P(z_2) & \cdots & 0 \\ \cdot & \cdot & \cdots & \cdot \\ 0 & 0 & \cdots & P(z_n) \end{bmatrix}$$

where $P(z_i)$ is some function of a variable z (typically one of the x's), whose parameters are unknown. For example, $P(z_i) = a + bz_i$ or $P(z_i) = (a + bz_i + cz_i^2)/(d + ez_i + fz_i^2)$. The function $P(z)$ may involve more than one variable although as a practical matter one will probably suffice.

The likelihood function can now be written

$$L = \left(\frac{1}{\sqrt{2\pi}}\right)^n |\Omega|^{-1/2} \exp\{-\tfrac{1}{2}(Y - X\beta)' \Omega^{-1}(Y - X\beta)\}, \quad (3.25)$$

which one maximizes with respect to β and the parameters in P. As an illustration assume a single independent variable and a quadratic function for P, i.e., $P(x) = a + bx + cx^2$. Then (3.25) becomes

$$L = \prod_{i=1}^{n} \frac{1}{\sqrt{2\pi}\sqrt{a + bx_i + cx_i^2}} \exp\left\{-\frac{1}{2}\frac{(y_i - \alpha - \beta x_i)^2}{a + bx_i + cx_i^2}\right\}, \quad (3.26)$$

from which one estimates the five parameters α, β, a, b, and c. As we have seen before, one can also obtain asymptotic variances and covariances for these parameters from the matrix of second partial derivatives of the likelihood function.

In terms of testing for heteroscedasticity we now have two options. The first is to use these estimated variances and use asymptotic normality to obtain significance tests on a, b, and c.[31] If either b or c is significant then heteroscedasticity is present. The second option is to apply the likelihood ratio test. Denote by L_1 the value of (3.26) at the maximum and let L_0 be its

---

[31] We are assuming that the basic form of the nonstochastic part of the model is not in question.

value at the OLS estimates. Then the statistic $-2 \log (L_0/L_1)$ has approximately a chi-square distribution with 2 degrees of freedom.[32] One could also use this test to consider the hypothesis that $P(x)$ is a quadratic against the alternative that $P(x)$ is linear.[33]

One difficulty with the above is that both these procedures appeal to large sample theory as a justification for statistical testing. Clearly some evidence is needed to support this procedure in small samples. A second feature of the above—which is common to all constructive tests described—is that the form of the heteroscedasticity is assumed known. It would be desirable to gain some insight into the effects of misspecifying this form. Unfortunately both of these questions are difficult to deal with analytically and we are forced to resort to some sampling experiments for tentative answers.

3.4. Sampling experiments

Fundamentals of experiments

The primary objective of the sampling experiments described in this section is to ascertain the relative success of several alternative estimators in the presence of heteroscedasticity. As indicated above, most prior work in this area has concentrated on the power of various tests for detecting heteroscedasticity. While we shall also examine this question, our primary concern will be the relative efficiency of various estimators.

With some exceptions to be indicated below, the bulk of the experiments were conducted in the following fashion. The underlying relation was of the form

$$y_i = \alpha + \beta x_i + u_i, \tag{3.27}$$

where

$$u_i = (\sqrt{a + bx_i + cx_i^2}) \, v_i. \tag{3.28}$$

The v_i are distributed as $N(0, 1)$ and are independent of each other. In other words the variance of u_i is given by

$$\sigma_{i_j}^2 = a + bx_i + cx_i^2. \tag{3.29}$$

---

[32] For the homoscedastic model, OLS and maximum likelihood estimates coincide. Two degrees of freedom are used since the quadratic specification involves two extra parameters.

[33] Here the ratio would be distributed as $\chi^2(1)$.

The x's, which are distributed independently of the v's, were generated by either a uniform distribution or a log-normal distribution. The v's were then generated and from (3.28) the u's were calculated. The y's were then computed from (3.27), and this was replicated 50 or 100 times (holding the x's constant). Each particular set of parameters (α, β, a, b, c) and x distribution—henceforth called a *case*—was utilized for three different sample sizes, $n = 30$, 60, and 90.

For each replication, estimates of α and β and estimates of their sampling variances were then computed by seven methods:

(1) Ordinary least squares.
(2) Generalized least squares.
(3) GLS/X.
(4) Maximum likelihood.
(5) Glejser.
(6) Park.
(7) Modified Glejser.

The first two methods are straightforward and need no detailed discussion. It should be noted that Method 2 represents a theoretical ideal and is unattainable in practice since it requires knowledge of the true values of a, b, and c. The third method is obtained on the assumption that $\sigma_i^2 = \sigma^2 x_i$. It is equivalent to scaling each variable by the $\sqrt{x}$ and is therefore the appropriate GLS estimator only if $a = c = 0$ in (3.29).[34] Maximum likelihood estimation involves maximizing the function given in (3.26). As is made more explicit in table 3.2, this was done under alternative assumptions about the nature of the generation of the error terms. As discussed earlier, the last three methods are all three-step procedures in which the first step is OLS. In the second step the OLS residuals are used to generate an estimate of the σ_i^2 in (3.29). In the third-step, these are then used in a GLS-like procedure. The three methods differ in the specification of the second step regression. Glejser uses the absolute value of the OLS residuals as the dependent variable, Park uses the logarithm of the square of the residuals, and Modified Glejser uses the square of the residuals.

For both α and β the following summary statistics were computed for each *combination* of a case, sample size, and estimating method: the mean

---

[34] This is the type of estimate that would be normally employed if one had decided via the 'peak' test or the 'F-test' that heteroscedasticity was present and that the variance increased with x. In some sense it is the cheapest and simplest way of correcting for heteroscedasticity that increases with x.

TABLE 3.2

Specification of sampling experiments

Case number	True values of parameters*			Parameters assumed non-zero in estimation	Replica- tions	X Distribu- tion
	a	b	c			
I	70.0	0.0	0.00	a, b	100	uniform
II	0.0	1.0	0.00	a, b	50	uniform
III	20.0	0.5	0.00	a, b	100	uniform
IV	20.0	5.0	0.00	a, b	100	uniform
V	20.0	0.5	0.00	a, b, c	50	uniform
VI	20.0	1.0	0.25	a, b, c	50	lognormal
VII	20.0	1.0	0.25	a, b, c	50	uniform
VIII	20.0	1.0	0.25	a, b	50	lognormal
IX	20.0	0.5	0.00	a, b	50	uniform

* In all cases, $\alpha = \beta = 2$.

bias, mean absolute bias, root mean square error, and mean absolute stand-ard deviation. The emphasis in this chapter is placed on the latter two statistics.[35]

In addition to the experimental results, for each case and sample size the following 'population' information was computed:

(i) The exact covariance matrix of the OLS estimates of α and β, i.e. (3.8).

(ii) The exact covariance matrix of the GLS estimator of α and β, i.e. (3.6).[36]

(iii) The exact covariance matrix of the GLS/X estimator of α and β.

(iv) The expected value of the OLS estimator of the covariance matrix for $\hat{\alpha}$ and $\hat{\beta}$, i.e. (3.16).

The information computed in (i), (ii), and (iii) may be directly compared with the experimental results for the root mean square error. Furthermore, (iv) may be compared with the mean standard deviations. In order to con-

---

[35] If $\hat{\theta}_i$ are the estimates of a parameter with true value θ, then the root mean square error (RMSE) is given by $(\Sigma_i (\theta_i - \theta)^2/K)^{1/2}$, where K is the number of replications. If $\hat{\sigma}(\hat{\theta}_i)$ is the (asymptotic) standard deviation of the estimate $\hat{\theta}_i$, then the mean (asymptotic) standard deviation (MASD) is given by $\Sigma \hat{\sigma}(\hat{\theta}_i)/K$. Except for maximum likelihood, all the methods involve a least squares regression, so that standard errors are readily available. For maximum likelihood one must resort to the Cramer-Rao variances.

[36] The GLS estimator assumes knowledge of (3.29) and hence is unattainable in practice. The fact that (3.29) must be known in order to compute GLS *estimates*, should not be confused with the fact that computation of the *exact covariance matrix of different estimators* [e.g., in (i) and (ii) above] also requires knowledge of (3.29).

serve space these comparisons will not be reported below. However, it should be recorded that the correspondence between the population and experimental results was generally quite good.[37] This leads to some confidence that the experimental results for the remaining methods will also be a reliable indication of the unknown population results.

Table 3.2 summarizes the various cases we have considered. The parameters a, b, c in the table refer to (3.29). In case II, for example, the error variance is proportional to x, whereas in the estimation process it is assumed that the variance of the errors is proportional to $(a + bx)$. In case VIII, on the other hand the true error variances are proportional to $(a + bx + cx^2)$, but we omit the x^2 term in our assumed specification.

Pure and mixed estimates

The simplest procedure is to obtain estimates of α and β by each of the seven estimating methods described earlier. The resulting estimates are referred to as pure estimates. The various summary statistics based on the pure estimates indicate how successful each method is in combatting heteroscedasticity. They do not provide an accurate description in a realistic setting where the presence of heteroscedasticity itself is subject to question. An alternative, therefore, is to apply statistical tests of significance for heteroscedasticity in conjunction with the estimating procedures. Depending on the outcome of the test for heteroscedasticity a second-pass estimating procedure is applied that utilizes the information gained in the test. The results of the second pass are referred to as mixed estimates. (The terms 'pure' and

---

[37] For cases I and III (see table 3.2) and for $n = 90$ we list below the population and experimental values for the four types of standard deviations for α and β discussed in the text:

	α-population	α-experimental	β-population	β-experimental
Case I:				
OLS (i)	1.969	2.058	0.0069	0.0072
GLS (ii)	1.969	2.058	0.0069	0.0072
GLS/X (iii)	3.395	3.225	0.0129	0.0120
E(OLS) (iv)	1.969	1.972	0.0069	0.0070
Case III:				
OLS (i)	2.175	2.256	0.0096	0.0095
GLS (ii)	1.784	1.677	0.0082	0.0074
GLS/X (iii)	2.128	1.987	0.0094	0.0086
E(OLS) (iv)	2.853	2.819	0.0106	0.0099

'mixed' as applied to estimates are not to be confused with these terms as applied to types of heteroscedasticity.) The specific details of the mixed estimating procedure depend on what the first-pass method is and are outlined below.

(1) OLS: Since OLS provides no opportunity for testing for heteroscedasticity, there is no difference between the pure and mixed estimates.

TABLE 3.3

Parameters assumed non-zero in estimation	Parameters found	Second-pass estimating method
a, b	a, b	FIML
	b	GLS/X
	a or none	OLS
a, b, c	c and a or b	FIML
	c	GLS/X^2
	b	GLS/X
	a, b	FIML (with just a, b)
	a or none	OLS

(2) FIML-t: According to this method parameters are estimated by the maximum likelihood technique and are tested for significance individually by employing the usual "t-type" statistics. The range of possible outcomes and the procedures followed are shown in table 3.3. FIML estimates are used only in cases I and IV, while at other times an alternative estimator is used.[38] For example, in the case represented by the fifth line of this table only the squared term in (3.29) is found to be significant, and so GLS/X^2 is used. That is, GLS estimates are computed under the assumption that $\sigma_i^2 = \sigma^2 x_i^2$, which is equivalent to deflation by x In the tables which report the percentage of the time that estimates of a, b, and c are significant (e.g., table 3.6) the percentages for FIML-t appear in the rows labeled FIML-A, FIML-B, and (wherever appropriate) FIML-C respectively

(3) FIML-χ^2: As indicated earlier, the null hypothesis of homoscedasticity was examined with respect to the alternative hypothesis that either both a

---

[38] In each instance, where estimates of the parameters a, b, c, are individually tested for statistical significance, a critical value of 1.96 was used for the absolute value of the ratio of a parameter estimate to its standard error. The same criterion is used for other methods as well. In the situation represented by the fourth line of table 3.3 when c and just one of a or b was significant, one might have specified $\sigma^2 = a + cx^2$ or $\sigma^2 = bx + cx^2$ and reestimated.

and b are significant or that a, b and c are all significant. In the first case the likelihood ratio is distributed as $\chi^2(1)$ and in the second as $\chi^2(2)$. If homoscedasticity was accepted, then the OLS estimate was used. Otherwise the FIML estimate was accepted. In the tables giving percent significance, this case is simply labeled χ^2.

(4) Glejser: The absolute values of the OLS residuals are regressed on x, i.e., $|e| = a + bx$. If both a and b are significant they are used to transform the equation. If just b is significant, then GLS/X is used.[39] In the percent significance tables, the results for a and b are listed under Glejser-A and Glejser-B respectively.

(5) Park: The coefficient γ_1 in $\log e^2 = \gamma_0 + \gamma_1 \log x$ is tested for significance and is used to transform the equation if it is significant. Otherwise OLS is accepted.[40]

(6) F-test: The 'F-test' described in section 3.3 was performed. The number of omitted observations was 16 for sample size 90, 16 for 60, and 4 for 30. If the F-ratio is significant then GLS/X is used, otherwise OLS is accepted.[41]

(7) Modified Glejser: The squared residuals (e^2) were regressed on x or on x and x^2 depending upon what was assumed about (3.29). The procedures followed parallel those described under FIML-t above, except that in two cases a pseudo-GLS estimator replaces the FIML estimator. These are (a) the case when a and b are assumed present and both are found significant, and (b) the case when a, b and c are assumed present and c and either a or b are found significant. For example, if only a and b are assumed present and if $\hat{a}$ and $\hat{b}$ are estimates of a and b, then GLS was performed with covariance matrix given by

$$\Omega = \begin{bmatrix} \hat{a} + \hat{b}x_1 & \cdots & 0 \\ \cdot & \cdots & \cdot \\ \cdot & \cdots & \cdot \\ 0 & \cdots & \hat{a} + \hat{b}x_n \end{bmatrix} \tag{3.30}$$

---

[39] In order to do Glejser's method in strict fashion in the case in which $c = 0$ and a and b are nonzero in (3.29), one would have to estimate $|e| = \sqrt{a + bx}$. While this could have been estimated using nonlinear techniques, the modified Glejser method avoids the difficulty. In addition, the element of misspecification should cast some further evidence on Glejser's contention that the functional form was not critical. This is further tested in the case when the true specification of (3.29) includes c as well.

[40] Strictly speaking, if both a and b are present, then the dependent variable should be $\log(a + bx)$. See the previous footnote.

[41] One could of course do other tests in conjunction with the GLS/X estimator, e.g., the peak test.

The one additional complication is that it is now possible for one of the diagonal elements in (3.30) to be negative. In this instance, GLS cannot be estimated. This problem was not widespread but was considerably more common in the case of pure estimates. A number of ways for dealing with this were tried. The method finally used to compute the results involved replacing negative entries in (3.30) by the estimate of the variance of the residuals from the first step Modified Glejser regression. In the percent significance tables, the entries corresponding to this case are labeled Mod. Glejser-A, Mod. Glejser-B, and Mod. Glejser-C.

Results of experiments

The first experiment, case I, was designed to calibrate the appropriate significance levels of the various tests and to gain some idea about the efficiency loss associated with the estimation of unnecessary parameters. More particularly, homoscedastic error terms were used in (3.28) to generate the observations (i.e., $b = c = 0$), but it was assumed in estimating the parameters that $\sigma^2 = a + bx$.

In the first instance all seven estimating methods were used to compute pure estimates of α and β *without* any statistical tests for heteroscedasticity. In the present case, since the disturbances are homoscedastic, these estimates should be less efficient than those obtained by applying tests for heteroscedasticity. In subsequent cases, when heteroscedasticity is present, the pure estimates will overstate the efficiency of the various methods because they take for granted that a heteroscedastic estimating method is needed.

The summary results for the instance in which no significance testing is performed are contained in tables 3.4 and 3.5 under the heading 'pure estimates'. The GLS/X estimator is labeled the F-test estimator in these and subsequent tables[42], since it is the natural second-pass estimator in the mixed estimate case when the F-test described in section 3.3 reveals the presence of heteroscedasticity.

Table 3.4 presents as a measure of relative efficiency the ratio of the RMSE of β for each estimating method to the RMSE of β for exact GLS (which in this case is simply OLS).[43] Except for the F-test estimator, there is at most a 5.4% loss in efficiency from estimating an additional parameter. The F-test

---

[42] Furthermore, maximum likelihood estimates appear in two places in the table—as FIML-t and FIML-χ^2 and are identical for the pure estimates case.

[43] Results are only presented for the slope coefficient.

TABLE 3.4

Relative efficiency: case I

Method	Pure estimates. Sample size			Mixed estimates. Sample size		
	90	60	30	90	60	30
OLS	1.000	1.000	1.000	1.000	1.000	1.000
Park	1.022	1.049	1.054	1.011	0.996	1.020
Glejser	1.013	1.027	0.983	1.024	1.033	0.989
FIML-t	1.016	1.029	0.983	1.015	1.033	1.010
F-test	1.547	3.611	1.483	1.027	1.286	1.000
Mod. Glejser	1.016	1.028	0.993	1.023	1.010	0.988
FIML-χ^2	1.016	1.029	0.983	1.007	1.000	0.995

TABLE 3.5

Relative accuracy of variance estimator: case I

Method	Pure estimates. Sample size			Mixed estimates. Sample size		
	90	60	30	90	60	30
OLS	1.040	0.897	0.998	1.040	0.897	0.998
Park	1.067	0.941	1.041	1.056	0.896	1.005
Glejser	1.064	0.930	0.992	1.067	0.929	0.985
FIML-t	1.071	0.935	0.991	1.064	1.008	1.022
F-test	1.795	2.391	1.193	1.075	1.146	0.993
Mod. Glejser	1.068	0.933	1.012	1.069	0.904	0.981
FIML-χ^2	1.071	0.935	0.991	1.052	0.899	0.995

estimator, since it is equivalent to dividing by $\sqrt{x}$, introduces heteroscedasticity and it is not surprising that significant inefficiencies result.[44]

For each estimator, table 3.5 gives the ratio of the root mean square error to the mean standard deviation. Under standard assumptions, the latter is a consistent estimator of the former so the ratio should tend to be near unity. Indeed for all but one estimator this is the case. The F-test method,

---

[44] A number less than unity in table 3.4 indicates for this particular experiment that a method outperformed GLS. Since we know that this cannot really be the case for large numbers of replications, the occurrence of such a result suggests that some additional replications might have been desirable.

again reveals the effects of heteroscedasticity since the estimate of the variance of the parameter tends significantly to understate its true variability.

Table 3.6 summarizes the extent to which the various methods detected heteroscedasticity where, of course, in the present case none is present. More

TABLE 3.6

Percent significance: case I

Method	Sample size		
	90	60	30
Park	5	6	6
Glejser-A	98	98	55
Glejser-B	5	4	3
F-test	4	7	5
χ^2	7	3	3
FIML-A	91	94	52
FIML-B	8	4	11
Mod. Glejser A	91	90	63
Mod. Glejser B	4	3	8

particularly, table 3.6 indicates the percentage of times that a particular test statistic is significant at the 0.05 level. Thus, for example, the estimate of b by Glejser's method was significant in 5, 4 and 3 times for the various sample sizes. For maximum likelihood, the χ^2-statistic was significant 7, 3 and 3 times, while the estimate of b (FIML-B) was significant 8, 4 and 11 times.[45] In general, the correspondence between the actual frequency of type 1 error and the theoretical 0.05 level is quite good so that we therefore employ the same critical values in the remainder of the experiments.[46]

In case I there is not much difference between the pure and mixed estimating procedures since there was little difference between OLS and the other estimators in the pure case.[47] The one exception to this is the F-test estimator where, as expected, performance significantly improves for the mixed esti-

---

[45] It should be noted that all the maximum likelihood estimates reported in this chapter were computed using modified quadratic hill climbing with analytic derivatives.

[46] Under standard assumptions, the estimates of a in (3.29) should be significant about 95% of the time. The assumptions are not met, but the 95% level is achieved reasonably well (see Glejser-A, Modified Glejser-A, and FIML-A) for the two larger sample sizes. See footnote 56 below.

[47] It should be noted that for OLS the mixed estimates and pure estimates results are identical since no hypothesis testing is performed in this case.

mates since roughly 95% of the time we are using the OLS estimator rather than the incorrect GLS/X.

In case II, which is the first case of heteroscedasticity, $\sigma^2 = bx$. This is Glejser's 'pure' case so that the F-test estimator is identical with the GLS estimator. The results for this case are contained in tables 3.7 to 3.9, which are patterned after the previous tables. The salient features of this case can

TABLE 3.7

Relative efficiency: case II

Method	Pure estimates. Sample size			Mixed estimates. Sample size		
	90	60	30	90	60	30
OLS	1.637	1.592	1.279	1.637	1.592	1.279
Park	1.120	1.184	1.043	1.258	1.408	1.256
Glejser	1.134	1.396	1.189	0.987	1.022	1.231
FIML-t	1.063	1.097	1.030	0.985	0.994	1.050
F-test	1.000	1.000	1.000	1.113	1.024	1.051
Mod. Glejser	1.740	1.589	1.264	1.003	1.008	1.105
FIML-χ^2	1.063	1.097	1.030	1.063	1.097	1.059

TABLE 3.8

Relative accuracy of variance estimator: case II

Method	Pure estimates. Sample size			Mixed estimates. Sample size		
	90	60	30	90	60	30
OLS	1.043	1.073	1.199	1.043	1.073	1.199
Park	0.983	1.021	0.992	1.083	1.172	1.178
Glejser	0.948	1.128	1.064	0.899	0.895	1.178
FIML-t	0.939	0.861	1.004	0.911	0.873	1.018
F-test	0.917	0.882	0.932	0.972	0.890	1.009
Mod. Glejser	1.386	1.178	1.124	0.893	0.872	1.059
FIML-χ^2	0.939	0.861	1.004	0.939	0.861	1.047

be readily summarized. We shall concentrate our remarks in the text on the mixed estimates. First, OLS produces the most inefficient estimates and the inefficiency increases with sample size reaching 60% for $n = 90$. Park is the next worst method, but among the other methods there is not a great deal

TABLE 3.9

Percent significance: case II

Method	Sample size		
	90	60	30
Park	90	80	22
Glejser-A	0	2	4
Glejser-B	98	96	52
F-test	88	92	66
χ^2	100	100	72
FIML-A	8	0	12
FIML-B	100	98	74
Mod. Glejser A	0	2	8
Mod. Glejser B	92	90	54

to choose from in terms of relative efficiency. The marginally superior performance of FIML-t over FIML-χ^2 probably reflects the fact that the χ^2-test examines both a and b, so that when the test statistic exceeds the critical value, it always accepts the hypothesis of 'mixed' heteroscedasticity.[48]

In terms of detection, most methods are relatively successful at finding heteroscedasticity. There is a distinct improvement with increasing sample size. For example, the Glejser method finds heteroscedasticity 52% of the time for $n = 30$ and 98% of the time for $n = 90$. The FIML tests do considerably better for $n = 30$ and rise to a 100% detection rate for $n = 90$. All three of these methods do better than the F-test, which was designed specifically for this situation.

The results for cases III and IV are contained in tables 3.10 to 3.12 and tables 3.13 to 3.15, respectively. Both cases deal with mixed heteroscedasticity and differ only in the degree of heteroscedasticity—case III with $b = 0.5$ is considerably milder than case IV with $b = 5.0$. Indeed the size of the population variance for the OLS estimator of β in the latter case is roughly nine times the variance in the former case. For case III, FIML-χ^2 does best with Park next. The remaining methods all perform comparably.[49] In terms of detection, neither FIML-t nor Glejser is terribly successful at finding

---

[48] One other point should be noted. The relatively poor performance of the Modified Glejser technique in the pure estimates case reflects the computational difficulty discussed above. This difficulty is of small importance in the case of mixed estimates.

[49] For case III there is a curious bulge at $n = 60$ for the relative efficiency of the remaining methods.

TABLE 3.10

Relative efficiency: case III

Method	Pure estimates. Sample size			Mixed estimates. Sample size		
	90	60	30	90	60	30
OLS	1.308	1.113	1.206	1.308	1.113	1.206
Park	1.088	1.067	1.044	1.165	1.087	1.141
Glejser	1.065	1.163	1.016	1.193	1.634	1.041
FIML-t	1.042	0.989	1.008	1.154	1.652	1.038
F-test	1.135	1.959	0.995	1.218	1.729	1.019
Mod. Glejser	1.349	1.179	1.087	1.193	1.663	1.080
FIML-χ^2	1.042	0.989	1.008	1.052	0.991	1.053

TABLE 3.11

Relative accuracy of variance estimator: case III

Method	Pure estimates. Sample size			Mixed estimates. Sample size		
	90	60	30	90	60	30
OLS	0.997	1.006	1.206	0.997	1.006	1.206
Park	1.033	1.110	1.025	1.038	1.079	1.126
Glejser	1.004	1.169	0.999	1.174	1.641	1.044
FIML-t	0.976	0.960	0.977	1.177	1.678	1.045
F-test	1.171	1.940	0.947	1.173	1.734	1.021
Mod. Glejser	1.213	1.130	1.046	1.145	1.653	1.082
FIML-χ^2	0.976	0.960	0.997	0.979	0.962	1.053

TABLE 3.12

Percent significance: case III

Method	Sample size		
	90	60	30
Park	58	51	25
Glejser-A	11	17	11
Glejser-B	83	78	48
F-test	78	85	47
χ^2	92	86	54
FIML-A	9	19	10
FIML-B	96	87	49
Mod. Glejser A	3	6	13
Mod. Glejser B	75	77	44

TABLE 3.13

Relative efficiency: case IV

Method	Pure estimates. Sample size			Mixed estimates. Sample size		
	90	60	30	90	60	30
OLS	1.541	1.366	1.245	1.541	1.366	1.245
Park	1.131	1.192	1.050	1.252	1.300	1.230
Glejser	1.093	1.230	1.190	1.037	1.116	1.167
FIML-t	1.043	1.037	1.003	0.997	1.103	1.038
F-test	1.009	1.108	0.999	1.097	1.109	1.064
Mod. Glejser	1.190	1.467	1.236	1.039	1.097	1.116
FIML-χ^2	1.043	1.037	1.003	1.042	1.025	1.078

TABLE 3.14

Relative accuracy of variance estimator: case IV

Method	Pure estimates. Sample size			Mixed estimates. Sample size		
	90	60	30	90	60	30
OLS	0.985	1.171	1.218	0.985	1.171	1.218
Park	0.984	1.265	1.025	1.061	1.342	1.202
Glejser	0.920	1.244	1.108	0.929	1.208	1.134
FIML-t	0.882	1.023	0.977	0.916	1.208	1.030
F-test	0.923	1.216	0.957	0.958	1.208	1.050
Mod. Glejser	0.943	1.358	1.142	0.920	1.170	1.103
FIML-χ^2	0.882	1.023	0.977	0.880	1.025	1.083

TABLE 3.15

Percent significance: case IV

Method	Sample size		
	90	60	30
Park	87	80	22
Glejser-A	0	5	5
Glejser-B	94	93	51
F-test	88	95	63
χ^2	99	97	65
FIML-A	7	2	8
FIML-B	100	100	58
Mod. Glejser A	1	4	9
Mod. Glejser B	91	84	50

mixed heteroscedasticity (i.e. in finding a significant), but both FIML methods do best in finding heteroscedasticity of at least some type. For case IV, except for Park, all methods do well in terms of relative efficiency, although there is a slight tendency for the FIML methods to do best. The FIML methods also do best in terms of power of detection.

Comparing tables 3.12 and 3.15 we see that all methods generally do better at detecting more extreme heteroscedasticity. In addition, the relative efficiencies are also better in case IV (see tables 3.10 and 3.13). As suggested earlier, there is a definite tendency for the power of the test to be related to the loss of efficiency involved in not detecting heteroscedasticity. It might also be noted that the larger value of b in case IV makes this case closer to one of pure heteroscedasticity so that the relatively good performance of the F-test method in case IV is not surprising.

Case V is analogous to case III, except that in the maximum likelihood estimation it was assumed that $\sigma^2 = a + bx + cx^2$ when in fact c was zero.[50] In other words, an additional parameter was estimated. The effect of this on the relative efficiency of the maximum likelihood methods is quite minor. For example, comparing the results for pure estimates in tables 3.16 and 3.10 for FIML-χ^2 yields only small differences. As would be expected the largest difference occurs for sample size 30. In terms of overall results, case V is quite analogous to case III with Park and FIML-χ^2 serving as the best methods. FIML-t is relatively successful at accepting the hypothesis that c is

TABLE 3.16

Relative efficiency: case V

Method	Pure estimates. Sample size			Mixed estimates. Sample size		
	90	60	30	90	60	30
OLS	1.216	1.010	1.052	1.216	1.010	1.052
Park	1.022	0.992	0.989	1.022	1.015	0.999
Glejser	1.003	1.104	1.448	1.084	1.504	1.044
FIML-t	1.041	1.022	1.119	1.191	1.247	1.046
F-test	1.082	1.491	1.033	1.100	1.499	1.119
Mod. Glejser	1.343	1.112	0.970	1.235	1.221	1.078
FIML-χ^2	1.041	1.022	1.119	1.041	1.035	1.117

[50] The x's used in case V, while drawn from the same underlying distribution, were different from those used in case III.

not significantly different from zero. However, the presence of x^2 considerably reduces the ability of FIML-t to find a significant b. For example, for $n = 90$, b is significant only 40% of the time in case V, but 96% of the time in case III. FIML-χ^2 retains its power of detection in this instance.[51] In summary, a mis-

TABLE 3.17

Relative accuracy of variance estimator: case V

Method	Pure estimates. Sample size			Mixed estimates. Sample size		
	90	60	30	90	60	30
OLS	0.971	0.965	1.068	0.971	0.965	1.068
Park	1.047	1.104	0.997	0.984	1.076	1.001
Glejser	1.022	1.182	1.342	1.179	1.643	1.051
FIML-t	1.082	1.043	1.136	1.075	1.184	1.074
F-test	1.199	1.638	1.054	1.126	1.642	1.166
Mod. Glejser	1.366	1.168	0.917	1.027	1.133	1.103
FIML-χ^2	1.082	1.043	1.136	1.082	1.055	1.138

TABLE 3.18

Percent significance: case V

Method	Sample size		
	90	60	30
Park	68	52	42
Glejser-A	4	6	4
Glejser-B	94	90	64
F-test	76	98	62
χ^2	100	92	48
FIML-A	4	4	0
FIML-B	40	22	16
FIML-C	4	10	8
Mod. Glejser-A	0	0	0
Mod. Glejser-B	14	16	8
Mod. Glejser-C	4	2	14

[51] As indicated above, the χ^2 test used in this instance compared the case of non-zero a, b and c to the case of non-zero a. FIML-χ^2 would undoubtedly do even better if the standard of comparison were non-zero a and b. In this instance it is likely that c would frequently be found insignificant and therefore a smaller number of parameters would actually have been estimated.

specification of the type considered in this case appears to be of minor consequence for FIML-χ^2 but presents greater difficulties for FIML-t.[52]

The next three cases we shall consider all have a true error specification which makes the variance a function of linear and quadratic terms in x. The results for the first of these, case VI, are contained in tables 3.19 to 3.21. The heteroscedasticity implicit in case VI is clearly more severe than in any of the previous cases—witness the fact that OLS is 460% less efficient than

TABLE 3.19

Relative efficiency: case VI

Method	Pure estimates. Sample size			Mixed estimates. Sample size		
	90	60	30	90	60	30
OLS	4.627	2.835	1.698	4.627	2.835	1.698
Park	2.312	1.642	1.242	3.021	2.079	1.413
Glejser	1.956	1.843	1.476	2.034	1.877	1.476
FIML-t	1.008	1.077	1.060	1.449	1.989	1.440
F-test	1.915	1.580	1.170	1.915	1.580	1.239
Mod. Glejser	2.122	2.088	1.731	2.044	2.213	1.517
FIML-χ^2	1.008	1.077	1.060	1.008	1.077	1.118

TABLE 3.20

Relative accuracy of variance estimator: case VI

Method	Pure estimates. Sample size			Mixed estimates. Sample size		
	90	60	30	90	60	30
OLS	5.066	2.992	1.453	5.066	2.992	1.453
Park	2.121	1.566	1.065	2.776	2.006	1.215
Glejser	1.455	1.436	1.346	1.508	1.447	1.295
FIML-t	0.834	0.881	0.786	1.348	2.055	1.228
F-test	1.811	1.509	1.010	1.811	1.509	1.076
Mod. Glejser	1.893	1.675	1.376	2.016	2.187	1.298
FIML-χ^2	0.834	0.881	0.786	0.834	0.881	0.840

[52] The results in table 3.18 suggest that it would have been better after rejecting the significance of c to re-estimate with $\sigma^2 = a + bx$ and re-examine the significance of b in the absence of x^2.

TABLE 3.21

Percent significance: case VI

Method	Sample size		
	90	60	30
Park	94	90	74
Glejser-A	66	60	24
Glejser-B	100	98	92
F-test	100	100	90
χ^2	100	100	88
FIML-A	2	2	2
FIML-B	2	4	6
FIML-C	94	50	12
Mod. Glejser-A	62	22	8
Mod. Glejser-B	92	60	98
Mod. Glejser-C	72	58	14

GLS! In terms of the various performance measures in tables 3.19 and 3.20, FIML-χ^2 far outstrips the other methods. It is the only method which consistently improves with sample size, and indeed by $n = 90$ it is within 1% of the unattainable GLS estimator. Furthermore, it is the only method with a reasonably accurate variance estimator. The Park, Glejser and F-test methods get consistently worse as sample size rises, both in terms of relative efficiency and relative accuracy of variance estimator. This occurs despite their consistently improving performance in terms of detecting heteroscedasticity. Glejser's method, for example, detects heteroscedasticity of some type 100% of the time for $n = 90$ and even detects mixed heteroscedasticity 66% of the time. Unfortunately the heteroscedasticity detected is of the wrong type so that efficiency suffers. The Modified Glejser Method, which does a reasonable job of detecting the true nature of the heteroscedasticity, does not perform appreciably better, but computational difficulties noted earlier may account for this. Indeed, FIML-t, which does a bad job of detecting anything but the quadratic term in the variance, does better than the Modified Glejser Method.

Case VII is comparable to case VI, except for the method of generating the x's. Case VI uses a lognormal distribution, whereas case VII uses a uniform distribution (of comparable mean and variance). Clearly, the reduced skewness is reflected in a lower degree of inefficiency for OLS. For $n = 90$, OLS is only 246% more inefficient than GLS, still however a rather sub-

TABLE 3.22

Relative efficiency: case VII

Method	Pure estimates. Sample size			Mixed estimates. Sample size		
	90	60	30	90	60	30
OLS	2.462	2.345	1.529	2.462	2.345	1.529
Park	1.257	1.387	1.127	1.257	1.424	1.300
Glejser	1.483	1.531	1.418	1.405	1.577	1.336
FIML-t	1.020	1.113	1.066	1.045	1.544	1.396
F-test	1.278	1.301	1.118	1.278	1.301	1.128
Mod. Glejser	1.796	2.402	1.646	2.215	2.296	1.496
FIML-χ^2	1.020	1.113	1.066	1.020	1.113	1.078

TABLE 3.23

Relative accuracy of variance estimator: case VII

Method	Pure estimates. Sample size			Mixed estimates. Sample size		
	90	60	30	90	60	30
OLS	1.113	1.408	1.297	1.113	1.408	1.294
Park	1.052	1.373	1.153	1.052	1.400	1.311
Glejser	1.088	0.912	1.060	0.975	0.986	1.234
FIML-t	0.850	0.991	1.038	0.914	1.4..	1.250
F-test	0.937	1.269	1.103	0.937	1.269	1.115
Mod. Glejser	1.154	1.470	1.251	1.129	1.524	1.324
FIML-χ^2	0.850	0.991	1.038	0.850	0.991	1.053

stantial inefficiency. As with case VI, FIML-χ^2 yields the most satisfactory results, again comparing favorably with the unattainable GLS estimator. Although the remaining methods do not do as well, when compared to case VI they improve dramatically both in terms of relative efficiency and relative accuracy of variances. In short, while FIML-χ^2 seems to do uniformly well, the performance of other methods seems to vary with the characteristics of the case.

Case VIII is analogous to case VI, except that it involves a misspecification of the structure of the error variance.[53] In particular, the quadratic

---

[53] While they are drawn from the same underlying distribution, the x's in cases VI and VIII are not identical. Due to some computational difficulties Modified Glejser is omitted from the tables for case VIII. Also the variance accuracy for FIML-χ^2 is not reported in table 3.26.

TABLE 3.24

Percent significance: case VII

Method	Sample size		
	90	60	30
Park	100	98	82
Glejser-A	40	30	20
Glejser-B	100	100	96
F-test	100	100	96
χ^2	100	100	98
FIML-A	6	6	2
FIML-B	10	22	4
FIML-C	100	100	22
Mod. Glejser-A	0	0	2
Mod. Glejser-B	6	6	16
Mod. Glejser-C	16	20	16

term in x is omitted from the specification. The relative performance of FIML-χ^2 deteriorates (compare tables 3.25 and 3.19), but FIML-χ^2 still outperforms other methods for case VIII. FIML-t does next best, primarily because it now is quite successful at detecting mixed heteroscedasticity, albeit of a misspecified type. While the omission of a parameter is clearly more serious than the estimation of an additional parameter, the maximum likelihood methods seem to stand up relatively well under both types of misspecification.

TABLE 3.25

Relative efficiency: case VIII

Method	Pure estimates. Sample size			Mixed estimates. Sample size		
	90	60	30	90	60	30
OLS	4.644	2.694	1.640	4.644	2.694	1.640
Park	2.337	1.762	1.118	3.027	1.885	1.292
Glejser	2.715	1.699	1.213	2.812	1.937	1.321
FIML-t	1.467	1.447	1.069	1.467	1.630	1.157
F-test	1.855	1.750	1.200	1.855	1.750	1.239
FIML-χ^2	1.467	1.447	1.069	1.467	1.447	1.093

One final case we shall deal with, case IX, concerns the possibility of mis-specifying the variable upon which the variance of the error term depends. In other words, we have a case where we posit

$$\sigma_i^2 = a + bx_{1i} + cx_{1i}^2, \tag{3.31}$$

TABLE 3.26

Relative accuracy of variance estimator: case VIII

Method	Pure estimates. Sample size			Mixed estimates. Sample size		
	90	60	30	90	60	30
OLS	5.017	3.660	1.666	5.017	3.660	1.666
Park	2.002	1.951	1.276	2.604	2.103	1.439
Glejser	1.954	1.653	1.144	2.021	1.860	1.257
FIML-t	1.241	1.458	1.275	1.241	1.749	1.374
F-test	1.669	2.022	1.378	1.669	2.022	1.424

TABLE 3.27

Percent significance: case VIII

Method	Sample size		
	90	60	30
Park	94	92	66
Glejser-A	48	60	16
Glejser-B	100	98	80
F-test	100	100	88
χ^2	100	100	94
FIML-A	100	44	50
FIML-B	100	100	94

where in fact

$$\sigma_i^2 = a' + b'x_{2i} + c'x_{2i}^2. \tag{3.32}$$

In realistic empirical situations this might often be the situation. At an intuitive level, one would suspect that the higher the correlation between x_1 and x_2, the less the consequence of this misspecification. In order to gain some experience concerning the nature of this relationship we performed the following experiment.

TABLE 3.28

Relative efficiency: case IX

Method	$\gamma = 0$ Sample size			$\gamma = 0.2$ Sample size			$\gamma = 0.5$ Sample size			$\gamma = 0.9$ Sample size			$\gamma = 1.0$ Sample size		
	90	60	30	90	60	30	90	60	30	90	60	30	90	60	30
OLS	1.276	1.254	1.228	1.162	1.095	1.181	1.110	1.049	1.149	1.139	1.130	1.172	1.142	1.239	1.364
Park	1.287	1.253	1.231	1.162	1.094	1.188	1.090	1.030	1.108	1.056	1.054	1.160	1.079	1.101	1.299
Glejser	1.295	1.231	1.230	1.249	1.084	1.187	1.180	1.048	1.152	1.151	1.390	1.150	1.077	1.188	1.341
FIML-t	1.293	1.291	1.330	1.165	1.115	1.295	1.137	1.073	1.397	1.098	1.134	1.176	1.066	1.055	1.184
F-test	1.391	1.265	1.228	1.259	1.120	1.342	1.203	1.083	1.327	1.180	1.361	1.227	1.161	1.273	1.210
Mod. Glejser	1.299	1.253	1.242	1.271	1.118	1.187	1.147	1.055	1.155	1.179	1.385	1.177	1.121	1.133	1.248
FIML-χ^2	1.286	1.275	1.275	1.165	1.107	1.246	1.104	1.040	1.199	1.036	1.053	1.147	0.995	0.992	1.225

The model was assumed to be

$$y = a + \beta x_1 + u, \quad \sigma^2 = a + bx_1,$$

where in fact

$$\sigma^2 = a + bx_2.$$

The variable x_2 was generated in the following fashion. First a variable x_3 was generated to be independent of x_1, but so as to have the same mean and variance as x_1. Then x_2 was defined by

$$x_2 = (1 - \gamma) x_3 + \gamma x_1,$$

where $0 \leq \gamma \leq 1$. It is easily verified that the correlation between x_2 and x_1 varies between 0 and 1 as γ varies between 0 and 1. Table 3.28 contains the information on relative efficiencies (for the mixed estimates) for five values of γ. For $\gamma = 0$, OLS performs best, although some of the other methods do quite comparably. Indeed this is to be expected since no method corrects properly for heteroscedasticity and OLS involves estimating fewer parameters. For $\gamma = 0.2$ the results are comparable to those for $\gamma = 0$. For $\gamma = 0.5$, both Park and FIML-χ^2 do better than OLS, although only marginally so, while the superiority of these methods over OLS is more pronounced for $\gamma = 0.9$.[54] Similar conlusions can be derived

TABLE 3.29

Percent significance: case IX

Method	$\gamma = 0$ Sample size 90	60	30	$\gamma = 0.2$ Sample size 90	60	30	$\gamma = 0.5$ Sample size 90	60	30	$\gamma = 0.9$ Sample size 90	60	30	$\gamma = 1.0$ Sample size 90	60	30
ark	4	18	6	0	12	8	14	16	12	58	30	16	66	52	24
lejser-A	100	96	64	96	92	48	92	84	24	34	38	6	28	16	6
lejser-B	6	16	8	6	14	4	24	16	6	76	58	18	92	76	20
test	8	6	0	8	12	6	40	18	8	86	70	24	90	92	22
	8	24	8	8	18	12	26	20	18	92	70	52	96	90	66
ML-A	100	98	34	100	96	22	94	82	4	38	44	6	16	12	20
ML-B	10	28	20	8	20	26	26	18	42	92	68	78	94	88	86
od. lejser A	96	90	34	88	84	24	74	54	12	18	24	4	6	6	4
od. lejser B	2	12	4	6	10	4	22	22	4	76	60	8	86	74	24

[54] The case $\gamma = 1.0$ corresponds to case III considered earlier, so it is not surprising that OLS does relatively poorly in this instance.

from table 3.29, which contains the detection rate. For $\gamma = 0.5$ heteroscedasticity is only detected about 25% of the time and it is not until $\gamma = 0.9$ that a marked rise in detection occurs.

Case IX is an example of a particular type of misspecification of the structure of the error variance, i.e., where x_1 in (3.31) is erroneously used in estimation instead of x_2 as in (3.32). From this simple example, it would seem that such a misspecification will lead to estimates that are more efficient than OLS (which also embodies a misspecification—that of homoscedasticity) only when x_1 and x_2 are highly correlated. Such a correlation may often be present in practice. Moreover, the present example is characterized by a relatively mild degree of heteroscedasticity (witness the OLS row in table 3.28). Undoubtedly, with more marked heteroscedasticity, a value of γ less than 0.9 would have improved matters.[55]

3.5. Concluding remarks

This chapter has focussed on the consequences of heteroscedasticity and on its detection and cure. Both the illustrative calculations in table 3.1 and the results from the sampling experiments suggest that heteroscedasticity can be a quantitatively severe problem. However, the sampling experiments also suggest that a variety of methods are successful in varying degrees in both detecting heteroscedasticity and in securing relatively efficient parameter estimates. Although it is recognized that the sampling experiments were of only limited scope, the following general conclusions would seem to be justified.

First, maximum likelihood offers both readily computable estimates and a highly efficient estimator, comparing quite favorably with the unattainable GLS estimator.

Second, the χ^2 likelihood ratio test appears to be the most powerful test for detecting heteroscedasticity. In general, it appears to be more successful than FIML-t which is based on individual tests of significance using Cramer-Rao variances and on an appeal to large sample normal theory. The relative lack of success of FIML-t does not seem to stem from any difficulties with the reliability of the Cramer-Rao variances. Rather tests on individual para-

---

[55]   It should be noted that no intermediate values of γ were tried so that even in the present case, a smaller value of γ might have still been satisfactory.

meters appear to suffer from the sampling correlation between parameters as well as from some theoretical difficulties.[56]

Third, the general performance of methods other than maximum likelihood was found to be moderately sensitive to the characteristics of the case considered. The cheapest method of correcting for heteroscedasticity—simply deflating the variables as in GLS/X—appears to work moderately well in a variety of cases. Nevertheless, in all cases maximum likelihood estimates offer further efficiency gains which are sometimes substantial.

Fourth, tests of individual coefficients either as in FIML-t or as in Glejser's method or its modified version appear to be relatively unsuccessful at detecting mixed heteroscedasticity. This confirms Glejser's finding reported above. This, in conjunction with the fact that the efficiency loss of estimating unneeded parameters appears to be much smaller than the efficiency loss due to estimating too few parameters, provides further support for the joint test of significance used in FIML-χ^2.

---

[56] The relatively good performance of the Cramer–Rao variances can be seen below, where for two cases we have given the RMSE's of the estimates of a, b, and c and the MASD's that are derived from the Cramer–Rao estimates.

Case III:

n	RMSE-a	MASD-a	RMSE-b	MASD-b
90	16.610	15.208	0.124	0.117
60	17.670	16.760	0.147	0.158
30	33.703	30.758	0.290	0.261

Case VI:

n	RMSE-a	MASD-a	RMSE-b	MASD-b	RMSE-c	MASD-c
90	865.7	883.2	23.42	22.07	0.124	0.109
60	1440.7	1513.0	37.09	35.98	0.166	0.174
30	2487.4	3054.9	63.14	68.62	0.319	0.343

Quite clearly the correspondence between RMSE's and MASD's is quite good even for $n = 30$. However, the absolute size of the RMSE's in case VI, especially for a and b, makes it clear why FIML-t was not terribly successful in this case. One theoretical difficulty which should be noted is that it is not sensible to test a for significance if b is not significant in $\sigma^2 = a + bx$.

Fifth, the ability of all methods to detect heteroscedasticity increases markedly with sample size. This is in keeping with the general finding that the power of the test is related to the efficiency loss associated with the use of OLS estimates.

Finally, it is clear that in general one does not know the precise form of the heteroscedasticity. As a consequence, one is forced to rely on what may be approximations to the structure of the variance. The limited evidence presented above suggests that even in these instances maximum likelihood estimates may remove much of the inefficiency inherent in OLS estimates.[57]

Appendix B: The peak-test of heteroscedasticity

Chapter 3 described a nonparametric test for heteroscedasticity based on the number of 'peaks' in the absolute values of OLS residuals. On the assumption that successive residuals are independent, the exact distribution of the number of peaks in a sequence of n residuals can be obtained as follows.

Define $N(n, k)$ as the number of permutations of n absolute values of residuals yielding k peaks. For convenience we define $N(1, 0) = 1$. We note that adjoining an nth residual to $n - 1$ others can create a total of k peaks in two ways: (i) if the preceding $n - 1$ residuals yielded k peaks and the last one creates no new one, and (ii) if the preceding $n - 1$ residuals yielded $k - 1$ peaks and the nth one does create an additional peak. This yields the following recursions:

$$N(n, n - 1) = 1$$

$$N(n, n - 2) = (n - 1)N(n - 1, n - 2) + N(n - 1, n - 3)$$
$$\vdots$$

$$N(n, k) \quad = (n - 1)N(n - 1, k) + N(n - 1, k - 1)$$
$$\vdots$$

$$N(n, 1) \quad = (n - 1)N(n - 1, 1) + N(n - 1, 0)$$

$$N(n, 0) \quad = (n - 1)N(n - 1, 0).$$

---

[57] Regardless of how complicated is the true structure of the error variances, one may approximate it by a Taylor series or as a ratio of rational functions. The sampling results would seem to argue for generosity in the number of terms one chooses prior to truncation.

TABLE 3.30

Cumulative probability distribution of the number of peaks in the homoscedastic case

Sample size n	Number of peaks k															
	0	1	2	3	4	5	6	7	8	9	10	11	12	13	14	15
20	0.050	0.227	0.502	0.753	0.906	0.972	0.993	0.999								
40	0.025	0.131	0.337	0.582	0.784	0.908	0.967	0.990	0.998	0.999						
60	0.017	0.094	0.262	0.487	0.700	0.852	0.938	0.978	0.993	0.998						
80	0.012	0.074	0.218	0.425	0.639	0.807	0.911	0.965	0.988	0.996	0.999					
100	0.010	0.062	0.188	0.381	0.592	0.769	0.887	0.952	0.982	0.994	0.998					
150	0.007	0.044	0.142	0.308	0.508	0.695	0.835	0.921	0.967	0.988	0.996	0.999				
200	0.005	0.034	0.116	0.263	0.452	0.641	0.793	0.894	0.952	0.981	0.993	0.998	0.999			
250	0.004	0.028	0.099	0.232	0.411	0.599	0.758	0.870	0.938	0.973	0.990	0.996	0.999	0.999		
300	0.003	0.024	0.087	0.209	0.380	0.565	0.729	0.849	0.925	0.967	0.986	0.995	0.998	0.999		
350	0.003	0.021	0.078	0.191	0.354	0.537	0.703	0.830	0.913	0.960	0.983	0.994	0.998	0.999		
400	0.002	0.019	0.071	0.176	0.333	0.513	0.681	0.813	0.902	0.953	0.980	0.992	0.997	0.999		
450	0.002	0.017	0.065	0.164	0.315	0.492	0.661	0.797	0.891	0.947	0.977	0.991	0.996	0.999		
500	0.002	0.016	0.060	0.154	0.299	0.473	0.643	0.783	0.881	0.941	0.973	0.989	0.996	0.999		

Since n absolute values of residuals can appear in a total of $n!$ permutations, the probability $P(n, k)$ of n absolute values of residuals yielding exactly k peaks is

$$P(n, k) = \frac{1}{n!} N(n, k).$$

The values of the cumulative probabilities

$$\sum_{i=0}^{k} P(n, i)$$

are displayed for selected values of n and k in table 3.30.

Of course, as noted above, the estimated residuals are correlated in finite samples. However, since the OLS residuals are asymptotically uncorrelated for large samples, the distribution provided in table 3.30 may be an acceptable approximation for sufficiently large samples. The appropriateness of table 3.30 for finite samples was investigated by means of sampling experiments. These experiments were designed to be similar to those reported earlier.[58] From experiment to experiment, each of which consisted of 1000 replications, the sample size, and both the mean and standard deviation of the single independent variable were varied. Homoscedasticity was assumed in the experiments, since it is the distribution of the estimated residuals under the null hypothesis that is of interest. For each experiment the empirical cumulative distribution of the number of peaks was computed and compared to the theoretical distribution reported in table 3.30. The comparisons were performed by use of the Kolmogorov-Smirnov test. Values of the test statistics are presented in table 3.31. To make it easy to reject the hypothesis that the distributions are the same, a significance level of 0.1 was used. As can be seen from the table, the null hypothesis is rejected in 7 out of 16 experiments for $n = 15$, in 1 out of 14 experiments for $n = 30$, and for none out of 15 for $n = 60$.[59] This would seem to suggest that there is a close approximation between the empirical and theoretical distribution, for $n \geq 30$ at least.

---

[58] S. M. Goldfeld and R. E. Quandt, *op. cit.*

[59] The reason for unequal numbers of experiments for different sample sizes is explained in *ibid.* It should be noted that table 3.31 is based on letting the disturbances follow a normal distribution. However, experiments with the uniform distribution indicate very similar results.

It is important to note that from the point of view of testing the hypothesis of homoscedasticity, what is relevant is the quality of the approximation in the upper tail of the distribution. It must therefore be pointed out that the larger differences between the empirical and theoretical distributions are all in the lower tail. Thus even for $n = 15$, where the tabulated probability of having five or more peaks is 0.0567, the empirically-generated probabilities all lie in the range 0.047 to 0.079. As a practical matter, the use of the peak test with OLS residuals seems acceptable for sample sizes of 15 or more.

In addition to applying the peak test to the OLS residuals, one may apply them to transformed independent residuals. In such cases the data in table 3.30 would provide exact significance points. This approach has been utilized in a paper by Heyadat and Robson, which is also noteworthy for its manner of constructing a set of independent residuals.[60]

TABLE 3.31

Kolmogorov–Smirnov test statistics

σ_x	μ_x	10	20	30	40	50
	$n = 15$	0.0117	0.0541*	0.0324	0.0103	0.0159
5	$n = 30$	0.0155	0.0175	0.0414*	0.0281	0.0301
	$n = 60$	0.0156	0.0201	0.0241	0.0274	0.0131
	$n = 15$		0.0793*	0.0863*	0.0353	0.0574*
10	$n = 30$		—	0.0284	0.0334	0.0294
	$n = 60$		0.0220	0.0241	0.0211	0.0210
	$n = 15$			0.0203	0.0584*	0.0534*
15	$n = 30$			0.0151	0.0175	0.0105
	$n = 60$			0.0401	0.0151	0.0280
	$n = 15$				0.0246	0.0324
20	$n = 30$				0.0074	0.0205
	$n = 60$				0.0351	0.0096
	$n = 15$				0.0573*	0.0144
25	$n = 30$				0.0186	—
	$n = 60$				—	0.0096

* Indicates significance at the 0.1 level.

---

[60] Heyadat and Robson, *op. cit.*

CHAPTER 4

ESTIMATION OF REGRESSIONS WITH DUMMY DEPENDENT VARIABLES

4.1. Introduction

There are many applications in which models are developed to explain the variation in discrete random variables. One of the most common of these instances is when there is a qualitative dependent variable of a dichotomous nature. For example, one may be interested in the effect of income on whether or not a household buys a consumer durable in a given period. Alternatively, one may be interested in investigating the response of a patient to various dosage levels of a drug. In the first example, one wants to explain whether 'buy' or 'not buy' occurs while in the second case one is concerned with 'cure' or 'non-cure'. In each of these cases the dependent variable may be represented by a dummy variable taking on the values of zero or one, with a one indicating that the quality under examination is present and a zero that it is absent.

The purposes of this chapter are several. We first briefly review some of the methods that have been proposed to analyze the variation of dichtotomous dependent variables.[1] We also consider several ways of estimating each of the proposed models[2], among which we include the method of maximum likelihood. As we shall see, this latter method leads to highly nonlinear estimating equations. In subsequent sections, we analyze the computational aspects of the maximum likelihood procedure and compare several alternative estimating methods. As in the previous chapter, these comparisons will be primarily based on the results of a sampling experiment study.

---

[1] Our review is hardly exhaustive. For a good recent survey of the field see D. R. Cox, *The analysis of binary data*. London, Methuen and Co., 1970.

[2] For additional estimation methods see *ibid*., and A. Zellner and T. H. Lee, Joint estimation of relationships involving discrete random variables. *Econometrica* **33** (1965), 382–94.

4.2. Some alternative models and estimation methods[3]

We consider a dichotomous variable y and a set of explanatory variables x, such that the expected value of y is a function of the explanatory variables.

Linear probability function

The first model we consider that has this property is the linear probability function in which y is specified to be an ordinary linear function of x's. Denoting, as usual, by Y the vector of observations on the y_i and by X the matrix of observations on the x_i's,

$$Y = X\beta + U, \tag{4.1}$$

where

$$E(U) = 0. \tag{4.2}$$

Since the elements of Y can only take on the values 0 and 1, we can deduce certain properties of the disturbance term in (4.1). In particular, letting X_i denote the ith row of the matrix X, we observe that the ith disturbance, u_i, can have one of two possible values:

$$u_i = \begin{cases} 1 - X_i\beta & \text{if} \quad y_i = 1 \\ - X_i\beta & \text{if} \quad y_i = 0 \end{cases} \tag{4.3}$$

Since these are the only two possible values of u_i, they must occur with probabilities p and $1 - p$ respectively. Moreover, the requirement $E(U) = 0$ implies

$$p(1 - X_i\beta) + (1 - p)(-X_i\beta) = 0,$$

and thus

$$\begin{aligned} p &= X_i\beta \\ 1 - p &= 1 - X_i\beta. \end{aligned} \tag{4.4}$$

The error variance is therefore

$$\begin{aligned} E(u_i^2) &= p(1 - X_i\beta)^2 + (1 - p)(-X_i\beta)^2 \\ &= X_i\beta(1 - X_i\beta)^2 + (1 - X_i\beta)(-X_i\beta)^2 \\ &= X_i\beta(1 - X_i\beta), \end{aligned} \tag{4.5}$$

which is not a constant but depends on the values of the regressors.

---

[3] This section draws heavily on the exposition of A. S. Goldberger, *Econometric theory*. New York, Wiley, 1964, pp. 248–51.

Aside from the somewhat unorthodox nature of the disturbance in (4.1), there is another difficulty with the linear probability model. In particular, given estimates of β, the predicted values $\hat{Y}$ will not, in general, equal 0 or 1. This suggests that it would be more useful to interpret the conditional expectation of Y given X as the conditional probability that the event will occur given X. Put another way, a predicted value between 0 and 1 may be interpreted as the fraction of individuals (in the appropriate range of the exogenous variables) that may be expected to have the quality in question.

The underlying statistical model is then one based on a discrete distribution of the disturbances, the variance of which depends on the regressors. One may conceptualize the generation of the values of the dependent variable by 'Nature' as follows: (1) For each observation, say the ith, Nature computes the probability $X_i\beta$; (2) Nature produces a random number R uniformly distributed on the (0, 1) interval; (3) If $R \leq X_i\beta$, Nature sets $y_i = 1$, otherwise y_i is set equal to 0. For reasons which should be apparent, with this interpretation we call (4.1) the Uniform Model.

There are at least three ways in which the Uniform Model may be estimated. The first consists of computing the ordinary least squares regression of Y on X. Unfortunately, as indicated above, the disturbances in (4.1) are heteroscedastic, so that OLS estimates suffer from all the difficulties outlined in the previous chapter. As a result, Goldberger has suggested an adaptation of generalized least squares, which consists of estimating the ordinary least squares regression as in the first method and then employing the predicted values of the dependent variable, $\hat{y}_i$, for estimating the diagonal elements of the covariance matrix Ω from (4.5): accordingly, the ith diagonal element of Ω will be $\hat{y}_i(1 - \hat{y}_i)$. The generalized least squares estimates can then be estimated from the well-known formula[4]

$$\beta = (X'\Omega^{-1}X)^{-1} X'\Omega^{-1}Y.$$

One further difficulty should be noted with the Uniform Model in the context of each of the two estimating methods mentioned above. This problem is that OLS can produce predicted values outside the range $0 - 1$. If this happens, the conditional probability interpretation does not carry through. Furthermore, when this happens certain diagonal elements of Ω will be negative, thus invalidating the straightforward application of Goldberger's two-

---

[4] The consistency of this procedure is proved in R. McGillivray, Estimating the linear probability function. *Econometrica* **38** (1970), 775–6.

stage GLS procedure. This problem can be dealt with by the imposition of constraints, which turns this from a computational point of view into a quadratic programming problem.[5]

An obvious alternative to these methods is estimation of β by maximizing the likelihood function implied by the Uniform Model. The likelihood function clearly is

$$L = \prod_{y_i=1} X_i\beta \prod_{y_j=0} (1 - X_j\beta), \qquad (4.6)$$

as can be seen from (4.4). The logarithm of the likelihood function is thus

$$\log L = \sum_{y_i=1} \log (X_i\beta) + \sum_{y_j=0} \log (1 - X_j\beta). \qquad (4.7)$$

Since the logarithm of a negative quantity is not defined, maximization of (4.7) cannot produce a $\hat{\beta}$ for which $X_i\hat{\beta} < 0$ for those observations for which $y_i = 1$, nor a $\hat{\beta}$ for which $X_j\hat{\beta} > 1$ for those observations for which $y_j = 0$. We are thus guaranteed, by virtue of the fact that the logarithm of a negative number is not defined, that when $y_i = 1$, the predicted $\hat{y}_i$ will be positive and when $y_i = 0$, the predicted $\hat{y}_i$ will not exceed unity. There is no general *guarantee*, however, that all predictions will be in the 0–1 range Of course, for predictions employing x-values outside the sample, the range problem may be even more serious and thus the conditional probability interpretation of the Uniform Model is not fully satisfactory.

One way of avoiding these difficulties is to specify an alternative model. In particular, one can apply a monotonic transformation to the probability in such a way that the resulting variable has range $(-\infty, \infty)$.[6] There are, of course, an infinite number of such transformations but there are two which have received considerable attention in the literature—the probit and logit transformations. We shall confine our attention to the Probit Model.[7]

---

[5] On this see G. G. Judge and T. Takayama, Inequality restrictions in regression analysis. *Journal of the American Statistical Association* **313** (1966), 166–81.

[6] There remains, of course, the question of whether this is an appropriate specification. For some evidence on the possible consequences of misspecification see the next two sections.

[7] A logit model specifies a probability in (4.8) below as $p_i = 1/(1 + e^{-X_i\beta})$ or alternatively as $\log [p /(1 - p)] = X_i\beta$. See D. R. Cox, *op. cit.* and J. Aitchison and J. A. C. Brown, The lognormal distribution. Cambridge, Cambridge University Press, 1957, Ch. 7. For some economic applications see H. Theil, *Economics and information theory.* Amsterdam, North-Holland Publ. Co., 1967.

Probit analysis

The Probit Model assumes that the dependent variable is generated by the following mechanism: (1) Nature computes for each observation, say the ith, the quantity $X_i\beta$; (2) Nature generates a normally distributed variable z with mean $= 0$ and variance $= 1$; (3) If $X_i\beta \geq z$, y_i is set equal to 1; otherwise y_i is set equal to 0.

Let $f(z)$ represent the normal density with $\mu = 0$ and let

$$F(z) = \frac{1}{\sqrt{2\pi}} \int_{-\infty}^{z} e^{-x^2/2} \, dx$$

be the corresponding cumulative distribution. We then have

$$\Pr\{y_i = 1 | X_i\beta\} = \Pr\{z \leq X_i\beta\} = \int_{-\infty}^{X_i\beta} f(z) \, dz = F(X_i\beta) \qquad (4.8)$$

and

$$\Pr\{y_i = 0 | X_i\beta\} = 1 - F(X_i\beta). \qquad (4.9)$$

The previous assumption that $E(u_i) = 0$ is no longer consistent with this model. Indeed, if we insisted on writing the model in ordinary regression form, the ith disturbance could be expressed as

$$u_i = y_i - X_i\beta$$

and

$$E(u_i) = E(y_i) - X_i\beta.$$

But, according to the Probit Model,

$$E(y_i) = (1) \int_{-\infty}^{X_i\beta} f(z) \, dz + (0) \int_{X_i\beta}^{\infty} f(z) \, dz = \int_{-\infty}^{X_i\beta} f(z) \, dz.$$

Hence[8],

$$E(u_i) = \int_{-\infty}^{X_i\beta} f(z) \, dz - X_i\beta \neq 0.$$

The most obvious estimating technique is maximum likelihood estimation of the β's.[9] From (4.8) and (4.9) we see that the likelihood function can be

---

[8] The exception being when $X_i\beta \approx 0.78$, since $\int_{-\infty}^{0.78} f(z) \, dz \approx 0.78$.

[9] Another common estimating method is the 'minimum normit χ^2', which yields an estimator with the same asymptotic properties as maximum likelihood. See J. Berkson, Estimate of the integrated normal curve by minimum normit chi-square with particular reference to bio-assay. *Journal of the American Statistical Association* **50** (1955), 529–49.

written

$$L = \prod_{y_i=1} \int_{-\infty}^{X_i\beta} f(z)\,dz \prod_{y_j=0} \left(1 - \int_{-\infty}^{X_j\beta} f(z)\,dz\right)$$

$$= \prod_{y_i=1} F(X_i\beta) \prod_{y_j=0} [1 - F(X_j\beta)] \qquad (4.10)$$

Maximization of (4.10), as is also true of (4.6), is obviously a problem with considerable nonlinearities.

4.3. Estimation in the uniform and probit models: some sampling experiments

We wished to investigate primarily three questions:

(1) Are there any particular difficulties in satisfactorily maximizing (4.6) and (4.10)?

(2) Are the results of maximum likelihood estimation preferable to the 'naive' methods of ordinary or quasi-generalized least squares in reasonably small samples?

(3) What are the consequences of misspecifying the Probit Model as the Uniform Model, and vice versa?

In principle the behavior of the various estimating techniques may well depend on how the data were generated. For this reason we performed two parallel sets of sampling experiments; in one set the dependent variable was generated by the Uniform Model and in the other by the Probit Model. Moreover, there seemed no reason why all four of the estimating techniques should not be applied to each set of data; thus whether they were generated by the Uniform or Probit Model, the coefficients $\hat{\beta}$ were estimated by ordinary least squares, quasi-generalized least squares, by maximizing (4.6) (referred to as Maximum Likelihood I) and by maximizing (4.10) (referred to as Maximum Likelihood II). Obviously, the maximization of (4.10) when the data come from the Uniform Model or maximizing (4.6) when they come from the Probit Model involves misspecification of the model.

In obtaining the various estimates certain conventions were desirable. As indicated earlier, in the case of quasi-generalized least squares the estimate of the covariance matrix makes no sense if one or more of the predicted values $\hat{y}_i$ are outside the 0–1 range, for then some of the estimated variances would be negative. This problem was handled by omitting in the second stage of the computations all those observations which produced $\hat{y}_i$'s outside the 0–1 range in the first stage. In the case of the maximum likelihood estimates it proved more convenient to maximize the logarithms of the likelihood functions (e.g. as in (4.7)) than (4.6) and (4.10) directly. After extensive experimentation with the quadratic hill-climbing method, Powell's conjugate gradient method and the Hooke and Jeeves pattern search algorithm, the quadratic hill-climbing method seemed to be the most robust one and it yielded higher maxima for the values of the logarithmic likelihood functions. This algorithm was therefore employed throughout the sampling experiments.

The sampling experiments employed three exogenous variables (including the constant term) throughout. The experiments employed true values of β given by 0.2, 0.5, 2.0. A sample of x values was chosen as follows: (1) $x_1 = 1$ for all observations (i.e., β_1 is the constant term in the regression), (2) x_2 was chosen to be uniformly distributed over the range $(0, 1)$, and (3) x_3 was uniformly distributed over the range $(-0.1, 0.1)$. For each sample size n a single sample of x's was generated and was held constant over the replications. In all cases 100 replications were used. The sample sizes in the experiments were $n = 15, 30, 60, 100, 200$.

4.4. Some results

In judging the results of the experiments we rely basically on the measures that we have utilized above—namely the root mean square error, the mean absolute deviation, and the mean estimate. The values of these statistics for the experiments are displayed in tables 4.1 to 4.3. In these tables Model I denotes the results from applying the estimating techniques to the Uniform Model and Model II refers to the Probit Model.

When we examine the experiments that used Model I for data generation, the first three estimating methods are intrinsically 'appropriate' and the last one involves misspecification. In the case of Model II only the last estimating method (Maximum Likelihood II) involves no misspecification. Observing the root mean square deviations we note the following:

(1) For each method of estimation that is appropriate for a particular set of data the root mean square errors decline markedly as the sample size increases.

(2) In the case of data generated by Model I, the asymptotically most appropriate estimating technique (Maximum Likelihood I) has the least root mean square error for all sample sizes of 30 and above.

TABLE 4.1

Root mean square errors

Data generated by		Model I UNIFORM				Model II PROBIT			
Model estimated by		OLS	GLS	Max Lik I UNIF	Max Lik II PROBIT	OLS	GLS	Max Lik I UNIF	Max Lik II PROBIT
β_1	$n = 15$	0.2554	0.2939	0.2219	0.1657	0.4056	0.4072	0.4230	0.3184
	$n = 30$	0.1718	0.1848	0.1547	0.1739	0.4154	0.4178	0.4263	0.2861
	$n = 60$	0.1135	0.1132	0.0916	0.1613	0.3944	0.3965	0.3992	0.2183
	$n = 100$	0.0829	0.0859	0.0639	0.1691	0.3941	0.3964	0.3925	0.2159
	$n = 200$	0.0649	0.0677	0.0530	0.1569	0.3855	0.3866	0.3861	0.1417
β_2	$n = 15$	0.5336	0.5961	0.4948	0.4153	0.5447	0.5709	0.5551	0.6300
	$n = 30$	0.3391	0.3571	0.3250	0.3579	0.4926	0.4970	0.5034	0.6195
	$n = 60$	0.1967	0.2090	0.1752	0.3508	0.3922	0.4011	0.3981	0.4485
	$n = 100$	0.1622	0.1693	0.1240	0.3453	0.3724	0.3808	0.3693	0.3864
	$n = 200$	0.1190	0.1250	0.0981	0.2732	0.3430	0.3463	0.3451	0.2483
β_3	$n = 15$	2.1144	2.3363	1.8195	1.4915	2.4058	2.6036	2.0906	1.888
	$n = 30$	1.3786	1.4162	1.2102	1.5057	1.9121	2.000	1.8896	1.8897
	$n = 60$	0.9540	0.9994	0.8144	1.4939	1.6091	1.6827	1.5942	1.7066
	$n = 100$	0.6653	0.7045	0.4608	1.5680	1.6439	1.6791	1.6515	1.6528
	$n = 200$	0.5311	0.5258	0.4441	1.5840	1.4131	1.4182	1.4211	1.2570

TABLE 4.2

Mean absolute deviations

Data generated by		Model I				Model II			
Model estimated by		OLS	GLS	Max Lik I	Max Lik II	OLS	GLS	Max Lik I	Max Lik II
β_1	$n = 15$	0.2027	0.2367	0.1776	0.1570	0.3446	0.3491	0.3618	0.2492
	$n = 30$	0.1308	0.1399	0.1228	0.1683	0.3841	0.3855	0.3944	0.2156
	$n = 60$	0.0955	0.0951	0.0734	0.1588	0.3778	0.3782	0.3823	0.1588
	$n = 100$	0.0694	0.0717	0.0541	0.1681	0.3822	0.3836	0.3796	0.1565
	$n = 200$	0.0522	0.0541	0.0404	0.1566	0.3800	0.3809	0.3804	0.0981
β_2	$n = 15$	0.4106	0.4682	0.3835	0.3797	0.4457	0.4720	0.4473	0.5108
	$n = 30$	0.2593	0.2668	0.2446	0.3259	0.4125	0.4180	0.4095	0.4931
	$n = 60$	0.1585	0.1683	0.1342	0.3387	0.3361	0.3431	0.3380	0.3488
	$n = 100$	0.1302	0.1351	0.0994	0.3373	0.3323	0.3377	0.3246	0.2742
	$n = 200$	0.0932	0.0969	0.0748	0.2699	0.3258	0.3282	0.3266	0.1900
β_3	$n = 15$	1.6995	1.8309	1.3811	1.3544	1.9722	2.1498	1.6528	1.4940
	$n = 30$	1.1291	1.1639	0.9241	1.4400	1.6335	1.7280	1.6194	1.5096
	$n = 60$	0.7680	0.8119	0.5664	1.4751	1.3630	1.4402	1.3778	1.2698
	$n = 100$	0.5409	0.5817	0.3107	1.5608	1.4093	1.4543	1.4487	1.2080
	$n = 200$	0.4136	0.4133	0.2901	1.5810	1.2626	1.2664	1.2745	0.8493

TABLE 4.3

Mean estimates. True values: $\beta_1 = 0.2$, $\beta_2 = 0.5$, $\beta_3 = 2.0$

Data generated by		Model I				Model II			
Model estimated by		OLS	GLS	Max Lik I	Max Lik II	OLS	GLS	Max Lik I	Max Lik II
β_1	$n = 15$	0.2429	0.2221	0.2332	0.0485	0.5179	0.5016	0.5362	0.2617
	$n = 30$	0.2021	0.1985	0.2065	0.0316	0.5841	0.5855	0.5944	0.2991
	$n = 60$	0.2013	0.1968	0.2069	0.0412	0.5778	0.5782	0.5823	0.2748
	$n = 100$	0.1928	0.1960	0.2045	0.0318	0.5822	0.5836	0.5796	0.2675
	$n = 200$	0.1948	0.1960	0.2034	0.0434	0.5800	0.5809	0.5804	0.2510
β_2	$n = 15$	0.4066	0.4274	0.3919	0.1610	0.2311	0.2672	0.2063	0.2607
	$n = 30$	0.4864	0.4950	0.4712	0.2000	0.1447	0.1382	0.1304	0.2362
	$n = 60$	0.4920	0.4988	0.4824	0.1612	0.1764	0.1728	0.1694	0.3198
	$n = 100$	0.5070	0.5061	0.4865	0.1626	0.1683	0.1634	0.1758	0.3506
	$n = 200$	0.5035	0.5015	0.4890	0.2301	0.1742	0.1718	0.1734	0.3889
β_3	$n = 15$	1.6012	1.5501	1.2248	0.6588	0.7228	0.7490	0.6449	0.8954
	$n = 30$	1.9150	1.9646	1.7264	0.5782	0.5912	0.5069	0.4742	0.8066
	$n = 60$	1.9913	1.9892	1.8677	0.5248	0.7075	0.6491	0.6744	1.2155
	$n = 100$	2.1016	2.0867	1.9461	0.4392	0.6034	0.5635	0.5627	1.1693
	$n = 200$	1.9970	1.9822	1.9585	0.4190	0.7451	0.7336	0.7271	1.5894

(3) For data generated by Model II the appropriate estimating technique (Maximum Likelihood II) has the unambiguously least root mean square error only for $n = 200$.

(4) For this set of data the other three estimating methods also exhibit root mean square errors that tend to diminish as sample size increases. Substantially the same conclusions emerge when the criterion of performance is the mean (absolute) deviation (table 4.2).

If we consider table 4.3 and the implied mean bias it is evident that Maximum Likelihood II for Model I and OLS, GLS and Maximum Likelihood I in the case of Model II produce unacceptable biases. In the cases in which the estimating method is 'appropriate' to the method by which the data were generated the biases are much more tolerable with the reservation that the Probit Model, even with Maximum Likelihood II, which is appropriate to it, involves generally larger biases and seems therefore harder to estimate. This appears to be consistent with the generally slower convergence of the Maximum Likelihood II results for this case noted in the discussion of the root mean square errors.

4.5. Conclusions

From these limited sampling experiments the following conclusions emerge:

(1) Maximization of the likelihood function associated with either the Uniform Model or the Probit Model is indeed tractable. Nevertheless, as with the case of other optimization problems encountered in this book, there is considerable variation in the success of alternative algorithms.

(2) In the Uniform Model, OLS, GLS, and Maximum Likelihood I all perform reasonably well although maximum likelihood is clearly superior. There appears to be no appreciable difference between OLS and GLS— although if anything OLS is somewhat to be favored. This may be accounted for by the computational difficulty inherent in the pseudo-GLS procedure. The use of Maximum Likelihood II, i.e., the misspecification of the Probit Model, yields distinctly inferior results with no tendency for estimator improvement as sample size increases.

(3) In the Probit Model, OLS, GLS, and Maximum Likelihood I (all based on a misspecification) tend to do quite comparably. Maximum Likelihood II is unambiguously better only for sample size 200, so that in the Probit Model the consequences of misspecification appear to be relatively less important.

CHAPTER 5

THE ESTIMATION OF COBB–DOUGLAS TYPE FUNCTIONS WITH MULTIPLICATIVE AND ADDITIVE ERRORS

5.1. Introduction

The estimation of functions of the type

$$y = \alpha_0 x_1^{\alpha_1} x_2^{\alpha_2} \cdots x_k^{\alpha_k} \tag{5.1}$$

occurs in economics in various contexts such as in the study of demand functions and production functions.[1] The stochastic term in models of type (5.1) is either specified to be additive,

$$y = \alpha_0 x_1^{\alpha_1} x_2^{\alpha_2} \cdots x_k^{\alpha_k} + u, \tag{5.2}$$

or, much more frequently, to be multiplicative as in

$$y = \alpha_0 x_1^{\alpha_1} x_2^{\alpha_2} \cdots x_k^{\alpha_k} e^u. \tag{5.3}$$

In either case it is customarily assumed that u is distributed according to $N(0, \sigma^2 I)$.

The differences between the two types of specification of the error term are several.

(1) The conditional expectation of the dependent variable in (5.2) is

$$E(y|x) = \alpha_0 x_1^{\alpha_1} x_2^{\alpha_2} \cdots x_k^{\alpha_k}, \tag{5.4}$$

whereas in (5.3) it is

$$E(y|x) = \alpha_0 x_1^{\alpha_1} x_2^{\alpha_2} \cdots x_k^{\alpha_k} e^{\sigma^2/2} \tag{5.5}$$

where the right-hand side in (5.5) without the term $e^{\sigma^2/2}$ represents the conditional median.

---

[1] Some of the literature in this area is discussed in R. C. Bodkin and L. R. Klein, Nonlinear estimation of aggregate production functions. *Review of Economics and Statistics* **49** (1967), 28–44; and also A. S. Goldberger, The interpretation and estimation of Cobb-Douglas functions. *Econometrica* **36** (1968), 464–72.

(2) The model given by (5.2) is homoscedastic, whereas (5.3) is hetero-scedastic, the conditional variance of y being

$$\text{var}\,(y|x) = [E\,(y|x)]^2\,(e^{\sigma^2} - 1).$$

The estimation of either (5.2) or of (5.3) is straightforward. The parameters of (5.2) can be estimated with the nonlinear techniques in chapter 1 by minimizing

$$\sum_{i=1}^{n} (y_i - \alpha_0 x_{1i}^{\alpha_1} x_{2i}^{\alpha_2} \cdots x_{ki}^{\alpha_k})^2$$

with respect to the parameters $\alpha_0, \alpha_1, \ldots, \alpha_k$. The resulting estimates are maximum likelihood estimates. The parameters of (5.3) are customarily estimated by taking logarithms on both sides and computing the resulting linear regression. Taking logarithms removes the heteroscedasticity noted in (2), but does create other problems. First, one does not obtain an unbiased estimate of α_0. Indeed, standard procedures lead to an estimator with an upward bias. Furthermore, in view of (1), care must be taken to secure an unbiased estimator of the conditional expectation.[2]

As should be clear from this discussion, the manner in which the error term enters the model is an integral part of specifying the model. In some instances there may be compelling *a priori* reasons for specifying the error as being of a particular type. A case in point for the multiplicative error is when the demand for a commodity is thought to be a function of the (ratio measurable) attributes of the commodity, as in the case of the abstract mode model of travel demand.[3] In such a case one may think of aggregating the various attributes $x_1, \ldots, x_k$ into a single scale and positing that the demand is a function of this scale. It can be shown[4], however, that the only non-constant differentiable function that maps ratio measurable variates into an aggregate that is itself ratio measurable is the power function $\alpha_0 x_1^{\alpha_1} \cdots x_k^{\alpha_k}$. Thus, if the error term is assumed to represent omitted attributes, it follows that it ought to be specified in the multiplicative form. Similarly, if (5.1) is taken to be a model of production to be estimated across firms, then α_0 may

---

[2] See A.S. Goldberger, *op. cit.*

[3] See R.E. Quandt and K.H. Young, Cross-sectional travel demand models: estimates and tests. *Journal of Regional Science* 9 (1969), 189–200; reprinted in *The demand for travel: theory and measurement*, edited by R.E. Quandt, Heath, 1970.

[4] See D.K. Osborne, From the many to the one: aggregation of goods, quality of goods, social welfare of individuals. University of Birmingham, Discussion Papers, Series A, April 1968, pp. 15–16.

be expected to vary as a result of technological differences. This too would call for a multiplicative specification of the error. As for an additive error, if the only source of a stochastic term in (5.1) is the fact that y (but not the x's) is observed with error, then (5.2) is appropriate.

In spite of the possibility that there might be *a priori* reasons for specifying the error term to be of a particular type, in most cases the multiplicative form seems to be chosen for its computational convenience. The two basic or pure alternatives given by (5.2) and (5.3) are rarely contrasted. Aside from contrasting the two pure cases, a rather natural question arises as to whether a more general model permitting both additive and multiplicative errors is possible. The primary purpose of this chapter is to show that this is indeed the case. The outline of the chapter is as follows. We first briefly consider some general ways of contrasting disparate sets of hypotheses such as might be expressed by (5.2) and (5.3). We then present a method of estimation devised to account simultaneously for additive and multiplicative errors. We subsequently illustrate the method on several simple and artificial examples. Finally, we indicate the workability of this new method by computing estimates for two alternative travel demand functions.

5.2. Testing disparate families of hypotheses

As indicated above, while there may be *a priori* reasons for specifying the error in (5.1) to be of a particular type, more often than not the multiplicative form is chosen for its computational convenience. Even if there are *a priori* reasons for expecting the error to be of a particular type, the proper statistical procedure is to test hypotheses about the error specification; i.e., the data ought to be allowed to reveal which of the two hypotheses is acceptable. Of course, the two pure cases are rarely both computed, and when they are the comparisons between them have been based on more or less informal procedures such as tightness of fit or conformity of the estimates to *a priori* notions.[5] Since the problem is essentially one of discriminating between two discrete specifications or theories, one might, at least in principle, employ any of three different approaches that have been suggested for this purpose.

---

[5] For two examples see R.C.Bodkin and L.R.Klein, *op. cit.*, and R.E.Quandt and K.H.Young, *op. cit.* In both of these cases the fits are good for both methods of estimation as measured by R^2. In the former the coefficient estimates are somewhat alike for models (5.2) and (5.3); in the latter they are not.

Comparison of forecasts

Let y represent the dependent variable and f_1 and f_2 the forecasts for y from two different models, with the forecasts f_1 representing the null hypothesis and f_2 the alternative. Hoel's test[6] can be reduced to regressing the quantity $y - f_1$ on the quantity $f_2 - f_1$. If the coefficient b in the regression

$$y - f_1 = a + b(f_2 - f_1) \tag{5.6}$$

is significantly positive, i.e., if the deviation of the f_2 forecasts from the f_1 forecasts tends to be positively related to the deviation between the actual observations and the f_1 forecasts, then f_1 would be rejected in favor of f_2. The test is, of course, not necessarily conclusive since we may fail to reject the hypothesis either in the form stated above or in the form obtained by interchanging the roles of f_1 and f_2. Worse still, the hypothesis may be rejected both in the form of (5.6) and after the roles of f_1 and f_2 are interchanged. In addition to these concerns is the practical experience that the test is not as powerful as might be desirable.

Discrimination based on minimum sum of squares of coverages

Let x be a random variable with cumulative distribution function $F(x)$. Let $x_1, \ldots, x_n$ be the order statistics for a sample of n observations. It has been shown[7] that consistent estimates of the parameters $\theta_1, \ldots, \theta_k$ of $F(x)$ can be obtained by minimizing the sum of the squares of the coverages:

$$S = \sum_{i=1}^{n+1} \left(F(x_i) - F(x_{i-1}) - \frac{1}{n+1} \right)^2, \tag{5.7}$$

where $F(x_0) = 0$ and $F(x_{n+1}) = 1$ by definition. If the null hypothesis F is true then $\lim_{n \to \infty} S = 0$, whereas if F is false and some alternative hypothesis G is true, then $\lim_{n \to \infty} S_a = K > 0$, where S_a is analogous to (5.7) with F replaced by G. Thus, for large n, the quantity $S_a - S$ is positive with high probability if F is true and G false, negative in the converse case and of indeterminate sign if both F and G are false. Unfortunately no critical values for the statistic $S_a - S$ are known and thus we cannot decide whether an observed positive value for $S_a - S$ is statistically significant or not.

---

[6] P.G. Hoel, On the choice of forecasting formulas. *Journal of the American Statistical Association* **24** (1947), 605–11.

[7] See R.E. Quandt, Old and new methods of estimation and the Pareto distribution. *Metrika* **10** (1966), 55–82.

Cox's likelihood ratio method

Let the null hypothesis H_f be given by the distribution function $F(x, \alpha)$ with probability density function $f(x, \alpha)$ and the alternative H_g by the distribution function $G(x, \beta)$ with density function $g(x, \beta)$, where α and β represent the vectors of parameters to be estimated. If $\alpha \in \Omega_\alpha$ and $\beta \in \Omega_\beta$, where Ω_α and Ω_β represent the parameter spaces, and if it is not true that either $\Omega_\alpha \subset \Omega_\beta$ or $\Omega_\alpha \supset \Omega_\beta$, we are dealing with separate families of hypotheses and the standard likelihood ratio approach cannot be employed. Cox has derived a test[8] based on the statistic

$$T_f = \{L_f(\hat{\alpha}) - L_g(\hat{\beta})\} - E_{\hat{\alpha}}\{L_f(\hat{\alpha}) - L_g(\hat{\beta})\},$$

where $\hat{\alpha}$ and $\hat{\beta}$ are maximum likelihood estimators, $L_f(\hat{\alpha})$ and $L_g(\hat{\beta})$ are the corresponding values of the logarithmic likelihood functions, and where $E_{\hat{\alpha}}$ denotes the expectation under H_f. Cox has shown that when H_f is true the quantity T_f is asymptotically normally distributed with mean zero and asymptotic standard deviation, which can be computed from the expected value of the derivatives of $\log f(x, \alpha)$ and $\log g(x, \beta_\alpha)$, where β_α is the limit to which the maximum likelihood estimate $\hat{\beta}$ converges when, in fact, H_f is true. The only disadvantage of this elegant method is that some of the computations are likely to be extremely difficult, such as those necessary to compute $E_{\hat{\alpha}}\{L_f(\hat{\alpha}) - L_g(\hat{\beta})\}$ and that the test cannot be performed routinely, i.e., alteration in, say, the nature of the alternative hypothesis necessitates repetition of the laborious computations.

In spite of the difficulties associated with the various tests, it may be desirable to perform them when estimates based on additive or multiplicative error specification are contrasted with each other.[9]

More generally, however, the question arises as to whether a tractable model can be developed encompassing both types of errors. Hurwicz, more than 20 years ago, suggested a similar possibility when he wrote: 'While at present in the systems treated each equation contains only *one* disturbance, in more

---

[8] See D.R.Cox, Test of separate families of hypotheses. In: *Proceedings of the fourth Berkeley symposium on probability and statistics*, vol. 1 (1961), pp. 105–123; and Further results on tests of separate families of hypotheses. *Journal of the Royal Statistical Society* **B 24** (1962), 406–23.

[9] J.D.Sargan, Wages and prices in the United Kingdom: a study in econometric methodology. In: *Econometric analysis for national economic planning*, Colston Papers No. 16, 1964, pp. 25–64, uses a variant of the maximum likelihood ratio test in a related context. In particular, he attempts to differentiate formally between a model which is linear in both the variables and the disturbances and a model such as (5.3).

realistic systems there might be equations each containing *several* disturbances. Moreover, some of these disturbances might enter in a nonadditive
fashion…'

As Hurwicz further indicated, there are numerous ways in which such
disturbances might be introduced.[10] It is the purpose of the remainder of this
chapter to consider one such generalization, which includes both the multiplicative and additive forms as special cases.

5.3. Estimation of a mixed model

Consider a model in which there are both additive and multiplicative errors,
as in

$$y = \alpha_0 x_1^{\alpha_1} x_2^{\alpha_2} \cdots x_k^{\alpha_k} e^u + v, \tag{5.8}$$

where u and v are distributed independently and normally with $E(u) = E(v)$
$= 0, E(u^2) = \sigma_u^2, E(v^2) = \sigma_v^2, E(u_i u_j) = E(v_i v_j) = 0, i \neq j$, and $E(u_i v_j) = 0$
for all i and j. We further assume that $x_1, \ldots, x_k$ are nonstochastic. The
computation of the density function of y in (5.8) is straightforward.

Let z be the random variable

$$z = \alpha_0 x_1^{\alpha_1} x_2^{\alpha_2} \cdots x_k^{\alpha_k} e^u = A e^u. \tag{5.9}$$

If u is distributed according to $N(0, \sigma_u^2)$, the density of z is clearly

$$f(z) = \frac{1}{\sqrt{2\pi}\,\sigma_u z} \exp \left\{ -\frac{\left(\log \dfrac{z}{A} \right)^2}{2\sigma_u^2} \right\}. \tag{5.10}$$

The density of v is simply

$$g(v) = \frac{1}{\sqrt{2\pi}\sigma_v} \exp \left\{ -\frac{v^2}{2\sigma_v^2} \right\}. \tag{5.11}$$

---

[10] For example, Hurwicz interpreting (5.1) as a production function argues that in addition to α_0 some or all of the α_i $(i = 1, \ldots, k)$ may also have error terms associated with
them. See L. Hurwicz, Systems with nonadditive disturbances. In: *Statistical inference
in dynamic economic models*, edited by T. C. Koopmans. New York, Wiley, 1950,
pp. 410–18. Such a model has in fact been analyzed by M. Nerlove, On measurement of
relative economic efficiency. *Econometrica* (Abstract) **28** (1960), 695, and more recently,
and in a different context, by H. H. Kelejian, Random parameters in a simultaneous
equation framework. Econometric Research Program Research Memo No. 125, Princeton University, 1971.

The density of y is then the convolution of (5.10) and (5.11)[11]

$$h(y) = \frac{1}{2\pi\sigma_u\sigma_v} \int_0^\infty \frac{1}{x} \exp\left\{-\frac{1}{2}\left[\frac{\left(\log\frac{x}{A}\right)^2}{\sigma_u^2} + \frac{(y-x)^2}{\sigma_v^2}\right]\right\} dx. \quad (5.12)$$

If n observations are available on the dependent variable y and the independent variables $x_1, \ldots, x_k$, the likelihood of the sample may be written as

$$\mathscr{L} = \prod_{i=1}^n h(y_i). \quad (5.13)$$

Instead of maximizing (5.13), it is convenient, as usual, to maximize its logarithm

$$L = \sum_{i=1}^n \log\left\{\frac{1}{2\pi\sigma_u\sigma_v} \int_0^\infty \frac{1}{x} \exp\left\{-\frac{1}{2}\left[\frac{\left(\log\frac{x}{A_i}\right)^2}{\sigma_u^2} + \frac{(y_i-x)^2}{\sigma_v^2}\right]\right\} dx\right\}$$

$$(5.14)$$

with respect to $\alpha_0, \alpha_1, \ldots, \alpha_k, \sigma_u$ and σ_v.

This is all that is necessary in principle to obtain maximum likelihood estimates.[12] However, as inspection of (5.14) reveals, it is not possible to find analytic expressions for the solutions. Rather, the maximization of (5.14) requires an algorithm for numerical maximization of a function of many variables. For this purpose we employed Powell's conjugate gradient method discussed in chapter 1. A further complication, the presence of a definite integral in (5.14) required that the maximization algorithm be used in conjunction with one for performing numerical integration.

Some initial attempts were made at maximizing (5.14) with the quadratic hill-climbing algorithms discussed in chapter 1 but Powell's algorithm gave uniformly higher values of L. This is presumably due to the fact that the Powell algorithm requires no derivatives, whereas the quadratic hill-climbing algorithms employ both first and second partial derivatives. Since the evaluation of the likelihood function, being based on numerical quadrature, may itself contain nonnegligible error, the compounding of this with the inherent error due to the numerical evaluation of derivatives may just have proved too much for reliably maximizing (5.14) by such algorithms.

---

[11] Here x is simply a dummy variable of integration. The range of integration is $(0, \infty)$ as the lognormally distributed variable is defined only for positive values.

[12] For a generalization see the appendix to this chapter.

As indicated, another complication that is not usually present in the typical (non-Bayesian) maximization problem faced in econometrics is the appearance of a definite integral in each term in (5.14). As closed expressions cannot be found for this integral, we must resort to numerical integration in order to accomplish the numerical maximization. The numerical quadrature was based on integrating over several finite intervals of width σ_v, starting with the two intervals $z = (y_i, y_i + \sigma_v)$ and $z = [\max(y_i - \sigma_v, 0), y_i]$. To the integral over these two intervals we add the integral over $z = (y_i + \sigma_v, y_i + 2\sigma_v)$ and over $z = [\max(y_i - 2\sigma_v, 0), \max(y_i - \sigma_v, 0)]$ and proceed outward in this fashion until the integral over the marginal intervals becomes less than 0.001 as a fraction of the integral already computed. The integration over each subinterval was performed by an 8-point Gaussian formula.[13]

Before presenting some sample estimates, it should be noted that the method described above does not yield estimates of the individual residuals u_i, v_i; it merely provides estimates of their variances. Nevertheless, we can still compute conditional expectations of y given x.

The techniques and procedures discussed above were first tested on artificial examples. The model assumed for test purposes was

$$y_i = \alpha x_i^\beta e^{u_i} + v_i \tag{5.15}$$

where $\alpha = 2.0$, $\beta = 1.5$, $\sigma_u = 0.4$, and $\sigma_v = 12.0$. For the x's we employed a sample of 10 uniformly distributed numbers over the interval $(5, 15)$ and another sample of 10 uniformly distributed numbers over $(15, 25)$. The y_i were generated according to (5.15), where the u_i and v_i were independent normal variates with zero mean and the indicated standard deviation. For each of the x-samples two independent sets of u's and v's were generated. Estimates

TABLE 5.1

Estimates in test samples

Method 1			Method 2			Method 3			
α	β	σ_u	α	β	σ_v	α	β	σ_u	σ^a
3.56	1.28	0.57	3.53	1.35	38.97	3.06	1.37	0.39	20.67
4.12	1.04	0.31	6.01	0.90	13.21	5.50	0.97	0.04	13.64
8.21	1.05	0.54	5.98	1.20	100.82	5.46	1.22	0.22	87.77
99.84	0.14	0.22	110.14	0.11	34.33	3.92	1.21	0.26	10.66

[13] Preliminary testing seemed to give better results for the Gaussian than for either Newton-Cotes or Romberg quadrature.

of the parameters were obtained by three methods: (1) Suppressing v_i and performing a linear regression on the logarithms of the variables;(2) suppressing u_i and directly minimizing the relevant sum of squares; (3) maximizing the likelihood function (5.14). The results are displayed in table 5.1, where the first two rows correspond to one x-sample, the second to the other.

Although the limited nature of these experiments makes them only suggestive, the finite sample properties of the estimates by the mixed method (Method 3) seem to be reasonable and in some cases startlingly better than the estimates from the other methods.[14]

5.4. Some concrete examples

Several models of the demand for passenger travel of the abstract mode type exist and two of these have been reestimated using the technique discussed in section 5.3.[15] The models are

$$T_{ijk} = e^{\alpha_0}(P_iP_j)^{\alpha_1} (C^b_{ij})^{\alpha_2} (C^r_{ijk})^{\alpha_3} (H^b_{ij})^{\alpha_4} (H^r_{ijk})^{\alpha_5} (D^r_{ijk})^{\alpha_6} R^{\alpha_7}_{ij} Y^{\alpha_8}_{ij} \quad (5.16)$$

and

$$T_{ijk} = e^{\alpha_0} (P_iP_j)^{\alpha_1} (C^r_{ijk})^{\alpha_3} (H^r_{ijk})^{\alpha_5} (D^r_{ijk})^{\alpha_6} \times$$

$$\times \exp\left\{\alpha_{10}\left[\frac{C^b_{ij}}{Y_{ij}}\right] + \alpha_{11}\left[\frac{H^b_{ij}}{Y_{ij}}\right]\right\}, \quad (5.17)$$

where T_{ijk} = volume of travel between nodes i and j by mode k; P_i = population at node i; Y_{ij} = population weighted mean per capita income in nodes i and j; C^r_{ijk} = relative cost of travel between i and j by mode k; C^b_{ij} = the best (cheapest) cost of travel between i and j over all modes; H^r_{ijk} = the relative travel time between i and j for mode k; H^b_{ij} = the best (fastest) travel time between i and j over all modes; D^r_{ijk} = the relative frequency of daily departures between i and j by mode k; and

$$R_{ij} = 0.75 \left[\frac{\max\limits_{k} C_{ijk} - \min\limits_{k} C_{ijk}}{\sum\limits_{k} C_{ijk}}\right] + 0.25 \left[\frac{\max\limits_{k} H_{ijk} - \min\limits_{k} H_{ijk}}{\sum\limits_{k} H_{ijk}}\right].$$

---

[14] Since the other methods involve a misspecification of the model, this suggests that the price one pays for ignoring the complexity of the mixed model if it is appropriate may be high.

[15] In an abstract mode model demand is assumed to be a function of some general economic-demographic variables and of variables measuring the attribute content of the various modes of travel. See R.E.Quandt and K.H.Young, *op. cit.*

The relative cost and travel time figures are the actual costs divided by the best costs or times. The best departure frequency variable was omitted since it is assumed that automobile travel always has the best departure frequency for all ij pairs, assumed to be 96 per day.[16] The admittedly artificial variable R_{ij} is intended to make the demand for travel a function of the density of travel mode configurations. It is reasonable to expect that the elasticity of demand with respect to R_{ij} will be positive. The data employed represent

TABLE 5.2

Estimates for the demand for transportation
(standard deviations in parentheses)

Coefficient	Model (5.16)		Model (5.17)	
	Loglinear estimates	Mixed estimates	Loglinear estimates	Mixed estimates
α_0	−32.10	−32.51 (2.06)	16.61	16.01 (1.01)
α_1	1.03 (0.15)	1.10 (0.13)	0.87 (0.12)	1.02 (0.18)
α_2	0.60 (0.94)	0.13 (0.58)		
α_3	−2.79 (0.57)	−2.83 (0.49)	−2.34 (0.51)	−3.01 (0.35)
α_4	−3.21 (1.61)	−2.99 (1.13)		
α_5	−1.95 (0.39)	−1.95 (0.35)	−1.72 (0.38)	−1.65 (0.48)
α_6	0.22 (0.27)	0.19 (0.23)	0.42 (0.24)	2.35 (3.50)
α_7	5.72 (3.71)	7.85 (3.40)		
α_8	6.14 (2.87)	6.14 (0.24)		
α_{10}			−401.96 (302.22)	−555.34 (225.25)
α_{11}			−1413.57 (560.94)	−1431.13 (77.10)
σ_u	0.85	0.79 (0.09)	1.26	1.26 (0.25)
σ_v	0.0	2026.97 (6.40)	0.0	1044.52 (4.74)

[16] This means that the traveler is assumed to think in terms of time quanta of a quarter of an hour.

observations on three modes (air, bus, automobile) for sixteen city pairs in California for 1960.

Both models have been estimated by (1) taking logarithms and computing the coefficients of the resulting linear regression, and (2) employing the technique discussed in section 5.3.[17] In the former case the standard errors of the estimated coefficients are available immediately; in the latter case they can be obtained by computing the Cramer–Rao bound.[18] The coefficient estimates and the corresponding standard errors are displayed in table 5.2.

In most cases the coefficient values obtained from the mixed estimating method are comparable with those obtained from loglinear estimation. The notable exceptions are α_2 and α_7 in model (5.16) and α_3 and α_6 in (5.17). Characteristically, the mixed method yields narrower confidence intervals for nearly all coefficients. An exception is α_6 in model (5.17) where the asymptotic standard deviation of the estimate increases markedly. Thus, even though the coefficient estimate is itself considerably greater, it can still not be considered statistically significant. Both the population as well as the cost elasticities of demand are somewhat higher in the mixed models. The disproportionate size in σ_u and σ_v appears sensible if one recalls that u enters the model multiplicatively and v additively.

5.5. Conclusion

This chapter has developed a model in which a Cobb–Douglas type function is coupled with simultaneous multiplicative and additive errors. This specification is a natural generalization of the 'pure' models in which either additive or multiplicative stochastic terms are introduced. The estimation problems posed by the mixed model are shown to be manageable and the model produces reasonable empirical results in a concrete application. At a formal level, several interesting and difficult statistical questions remain.

One question concerns the small-sample properties of the maximum likelihood method in the context of the mixed model. A second question would be the possibility of extending the estimation techniques described in this chap-

---

[17] The second method, minimizing the sum of squares resulting from the assumption of an additive error term, produced distinctly inferior results. See R.E. Quandt and K.H. Young, *op. cit.*

[18] This of course assumes that there exists a set of jointly sufficient statistics for the parameters. See chapter 2.

ter to alternative error structures. Finally, in some of the examples in section 5.3, the inappropriate estimation of either pure model produced highly inferior results. It would be extremely desirable to know more about the consequences of the various possible misspecifications of the error terms. More generally, how does one choose on statistical grounds among alternative specifications of the error term?

In the present instance, as the pure models appear to be special cases of the mixed model, one would expect that standard likelihood ratio tests might be applicable. The fact that the likelihood function (5.14) has a singularity when either σ_u or σ_v is zero should create no special difficulties since (a) there exists a well-defined likelihood function corresponding to the hypothesis that either $\sigma_u = 0$ or $\sigma_v = 0$, and (b) such a hypothesis represents a restriction to a subset of the entire parameter space. Of course, some of the techniques described in section 5.2 might also be applied to this problem. It is clear, however, that despite Hurwicz's long-standing challenge this remains a fruitful area for further research.

Appendix C: The density function for dependent error structures

In section 5.3 it was assumed that in the equation

$$y = \alpha_0 x_1^{\alpha_1} x_2^{\alpha_2} \cdots x_k^{\alpha_k} e^u + v$$

the errors u and v are independently distributed. It is this assumption that allows us to express the density function of y as the convolution of the normal and lognormal density functions.

If $E(u_i v_i) \neq 0$, we have to start from the joint density function of u and v. Let these random variables have the bivariate normal distribution with mean vector 0 and covariance matrix Σ. Denoting the elements of Σ by σ_u^2, σ_v^2 and σ_{uv}, and those of Σ^{-1} by σ^{uu}, σ^{vv} and σ^{uv}, the density function corresponding to (5.12) can be shown to be

$$h(y) = \frac{1}{2\pi (\sigma_u^2 \sigma_v^2 - \sigma_{uv}^2)^{1/2}} \int_0^\infty \frac{1}{x} \exp \left\{ -\frac{1}{2} \left[\sigma^{uu} \left(\log \frac{x}{A} \right)^2 \right. \right.$$
$$\left. \left. + 2\sigma^{uv} (y - x) \left(\log \frac{x}{A} \right) + \sigma^{vv} (y - x)^2 \right] \right\} dx.$$

The corresponding likelihood function is formed analogously to (5.14) and allows the estimation of the additional covariance parameter.

CHAPTER 6

ESTIMATOR BEHAVIOR FOR A NONLINEAR MODEL
OF PRODUCTION*

6.1. Introduction

The present chapter is devoted to comparing alternative parameter estimators
for a model involving complex nonlinearities. Its main purpose is to examine
and evaluate the conditions under which reliable estimators exist and the
standard variance approximations are accurate.

The basic estimating equations involve integrals which contain parameters
in not only the integrand but also the lower limits. The chapter discusses the
determination of the lower limits and it emerges that certain of the parameters are nearly indeterminate. The standard covariance approximations
are then computed, the degree to which they reflect the indeterminacy is
checked, and they are compared to covariance matrices based on a higher-
order approximation.

We next consider the question of whether certain data should be added, in
the form of a nonlinear constraint. It is possible to approximate both the
efficiency gained by imposing such a constraint in case it is correct and the
possible bias introduced by imposing it when it is incorrect. In the present
case, the question is the addition of wage data (and of the assumption that
the wage rate equals labor's marginal product) to a model of production and
technical change.

In general, the possible gains and losses from adding a constraint depend
upon both the true parameter values and the degree of discrepancy between
them and the imposed constraint. In the present example the discrepancies
often tend to follow a definite pattern—a systematic positive or negative
bias—which results from the possession of market power in the labor market
by either labor unions or firms. Thus we adapt the approximations which
produce the covariances to approximate the effects of biases in the wage data
that are added as a constraint.

---

* This chapter was prepared by D.E.Smallwood.

Another feature of the model is that, rather than postulating production relations which are invariant over time, the effects of technological change are acknowledged by introducing rates of change into the technical coefficients. While the assumption that parameters which characterize economic structures are constant over time might be universally questionable, it seems particularly tenuous for rates of technical change. Thus the approximations are also adapted to examine a likely error in specification, namely that the rates of technical change are not constant. The increment in the variance of estimators and predictors produced by random fluctuations in the rates of technical change is computed.

In summary, we examine, for estimators involving particularly complex nonlinearities, the basis on which the parameters are determined, the size of alternative covariance approximations and the validity of the standard approximations, the possible gains and losses from adding data in the form of a nonlinear constraint, and the effect of a likely error in specification. The purpose is to evaluate *a priori* the questions of how reliably the parameters of this nonlinear model can be inferred and how the estimators should be specified.

The nonlinearities are intrinsic in a significant aspect of the specification, namely that the production relations for different pieces of capital may depend on their vintage (the time they were produced). Integrals over the vintages of capital in use, in which the lower limit is a parameter, arise naturally from that assumption. Simplified estimating equations can be obtained only by restricting the types of technical change allowed or by adding a set of assumptions concerning investment behavior. Thus nonlinearities of this type are of more general interest, although this particular model is of interest in its own right.

Since the significance of the calculations is related to several basic questions of the specification of production relations, we discuss briefly the motivation for this model.

6.2. The fixed proportions vintage model

Elements of the model

Traditionally, the relationship among output and inputs has been modeled by assuming a fixed production function relating output to labor and a measure of capital. The latter is usually just the sum of plant and equipment, weighted by unit value after adjusting for depreciation by applying a fixed rate of exponential decay (that is, a unit of capital t periods after its construction is assumed to be equivalent to $e^{-\delta t}$ units of new capital of the same type, where δ is the rate of exponential decay). The capital measure may also be adjusted for a utilization rate, since the variable appearing in the theoretical functions actually represents the services of capital and many capital goods have been observed to lie idle during slack periods.

Recently, the simple, crude specifications of a log-linear relationship (Cobb–Douglas) or fixed proportions (Harrod–Domar) among output, labor, and capital have been supplemented by the use of functional forms that allow more general substitution possibilities (e.g., the constant elasticity of substitution production function) and by allowing the function to depend upon time, in order to let it reflect the effects of technological progress. The simplest way to include the effects of time is to assume that the production function increases at a constant rate for all labor and capital combinations, but such a specification obviously may not be an adequate representation of technical change.

While the changes just noted are significant, the innovation in the specification of the production function that introduces much greater complexity and troublesome nonlinearities into the problem of estimation—unless very restrictive assumptions are made—is the idea of capital vintages. While retaining, at least in the model presented here, the assumption of a single, homogeneous labor input and a single type of capital, the purpose of distinguishing vintages of capital is to recognize that new 'machines' will not usually be identical to older machines of the same type, but will incorporate improvements in design and general increases in knowledge. These differences will be retained throughout the useful life of the machines. Thus, instead of specifying a single production function,

$$Q = f(L, K)$$

relating maximum output, Q, obtainable from total labor, L, and the services of total aggregate capital, K, an entire class of production functions is postulated:

$$Q = f_v(L, K_v).$$

These functions relate maximum output obtainable from K_v units of capital of vintage v when it is combined with L units of labor.

The differences in the f_v represent technical change which can be exploited only by investing in machines of newer vintage; thus differences in the f_v are said to represent 'embodied technological change'. However, technical change transmitted through new machine designs and greater efficiency in machine production is not the only source of increased productivity gain. The functions f_v may shift over time, due to general increases in knowledge relevant to this production process such as better organization, cumulative adaptation and experimentation by labor, and so forth. The shifts in the f_v over time are said to be due to 'disembodied technical change'. Clearly, organizational improvements and learning may lead to productivity increases which are greater on some vintages and smaller on others, but problems of estimation and the lack of a better hypothesis concerning systematic differences produce the assumption that disembodied technical change shifts all the f_v equivalently.

The nature of these assumptions about production possibilities can be pictured (see fig. 6.1) by taking a particular value for Q and drawing the isoquants (level-curves) for different vintages and times.

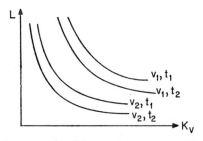

Fig. 6.1. Isoquants for different vintages, v, and times, t.

These isoquants are drawn in the tradition of classical economic theory, which assumes the possibility for continuous and unlimited substitution of labor for capital, and vice versa. In essence, this assumption implies that an increase in output can be accomplished either by increasing the labor employed on the capital in use or by adding some capital and reallocating the given labor.

The assumption of continuous substitution in economic models is due more to its theoretical convenience than to its empirical truth; observations of the use of particular capital goods usually suggest that efficiency implies rather rigid factor proportions. Typical arguments against a fixed-proportions assumption are that production activity in less developed countries sometimes reveals striking examples of substitution and that large changes in input prices often evoke responses such as automating or economizing on raw materials. But it does not follow that reversible substitutions often occur within a developed and highly capitalized economy.

Thus, in this model, the technical coefficients on a particular vintage at a particular time are assumed fixed. By assuming also that technical change of both the embodied and disembodied types proceeds at constant rates, the technical coefficients applying to capital of vintage v at time t can be written:

$$(Q/K)_{v,t} = ae^{gv+rt} \tag{6.1}$$

$$(Q/L)_{v,t} = be^{hv+st}. \tag{6.2}$$

Postulating these relationships excludes not only substitution on capital in place, but also the possibility that there is flexibility in the design of new capital which allows investors to respond to expected factor prices. While it is harder to argue that *ex ante* substitution possibilities should also be disregarded, it is even harder to believe that guesses about *a priori* substitution possibilities, expectations, and adjustment processes will be sufficiently accurate to compensate for the loss in efficiency and for the risks of drastically incorrect specifications.

Derivation of the estimating equations

Consider a decision maker, whether perfect or imperfect competitor, who has available, at time t, a vector of capital goods of vintage t and older:

$$(\ldots, I_{t-m}, \ldots, I_{t-3}, I_{t-2}, I_{t-1}, I_t),$$

where I_v represents the quantity of vintage v capital since the latter is simply equal to investment at time v.[1] In allocating a given amount of labor, L, it is sufficient to note that labor productivity on vintage v capital is be^{st+hv}. Then as long as $h > 0$, output will be maximized by applying the labor to the newest vintages until each is being run at capacity. In other words, no labor will be employed on a given vintage as long as there is a newer vintage which is not fully utilized.

If the decision maker is instead responding to a given wage rate, w, rather than allocating a fixed amount of labor, he will continue hiring labor as long as the value of the average product of labor on an idle vintage exceeds the wage rate:

$$p(Q/L) = pbe^{st+hv} \geq w \tag{6.3}$$

---

[1] Physical depreciation could be formally allowed, but exponential decay is actually equivalent to an increase in embodied and a decrease in disembodied capital augmentation.

since the average product of labor on the newest idle vintage is labor's marginal product. Thus the same conclusion applies in either case—when the allocation of labor is efficient, all vintages younger than a certain age (the 'marginal vintage') are fully in use, while the marginal vintage may be partially utilized, but all older vintages are completely idle.

If we make the transition, purely for reasons of convenience, to a continuous model in which a vector of capital goods is replaced by a stream

$$I(v), \quad -\infty < v \leqq t,$$

where each infinitesimal of capital with vintage between v and $(v + dv)$ operates with characteristics (6.1) and (6.2), then there are no partially utilized vintages. Production efficiency at time t implies that there is an interval $(t - m_t, t)$ of fully utilized vintages, where m_t is the age of the marginal vintage at time t, while all capital older than m_t will lie idle.

Let $L_{v,t}$ be the labor employed on vintage v capital at time t and $Q_{v,t}$ the output produced on it. Total output and labor are the integrals of these over the interval $(t - m_t, t)$:

$$Q_t = \int_{t-m_t}^{t} Q_{v,t} \, dv$$

$$L_t = \int_{t-m_t}^{t} L_{v,t} \, dv.$$

Using (6.1) and (6.2) gives:

$$Q_t = \int_{t-m_t}^{t} (Q/K)_{v,t} \, I(v) \, dv = \int_{t-m_t}^{t} ae^{rt+gv} I(v) \, dv \tag{6.4}$$

$$L_t = \int_{t-m_t}^{t} \{(Q/K)_{v,t}/(Q/L)_{v,t}\} \, I(v) \, dv = \int_{t-m_t}^{t} \{ae^{rt+gv}/be^{st+hv}\} \, I(v) \, dv, \tag{6.5}$$

which we can rearrange and then write the basic estimating equations for the vintage model as follows:

$$Q_t = ae^{rt} \int_{t-m_t}^{t} e^{gv} \, I(v) \, dv \tag{6.6}$$

$$L_t = (a/b) \, e^{(r-s)t} \int_{t-m_t}^{t} e^{(g-h)v} \, I(v) \, dv. \tag{6.7}$$

With these equations, the parameters of the model—a, b, g, h, r, and s—can be estimated along with the *simultaneous* estimation of the marginal vintage for each observation period, using only Q_t and L_t data.

If T observations on the pair (Q_t, L_t) are available, $(T + 6)$ parameters are estimated. Since two equations are fitted for each observation, T must be at least 6 in order that $2T \geq T + 6$. In fact, estimating the parameters on the basis of (6.6) and (6.7) seems rather dubious even for large T. Not only is a parameter added for each observation, but the basis for identifying the parameters is purely the differential effect of embodied technical change on productivity as the m_t are changed. Neither equation can be estimated by itself; the determination of the m_t depends on differences in the patterns of the Q_t and L_t.

Yet estimation based on just (6.6) and (6.7) provides very significant advantages. First, wage data are not used. In fact, there is no assumption that the marginal product of labor is related in any way to a wage rate (or even to the marginal cost of adding labor, if that is different). The derivation of (6.6) and (6.7) depends *only* on the specification of the production relations and on the assumption that whatever output is produced, it is produced by efficiently allocating labor over the different capital vintages. Thus the estimators are not based on the questionable assumption of competitive labor and product markets.

Second, the utilization of the capital goods is jointly estimated, rather than ignored or handled with a questionable 'adjustment' factor. In fact, as long as embodied labor augmentation (h) is positive, no theoretically valid method of aggregating capital exists. Thus a significant advantage of the vintage model is that the utilization of capital—indeed, the utilization of each vintage of capital—is simultaneously estimated rather than dealt with in rather crude and questionable ways.

We note that the ability to estimate the parameters without wage data or without even an assumption about wage rates is distinct from the simultaneous determination of capital utilization. Since the marginal product of labor is simply labor's average product on the marginal vintage, an assumption of competitive behavior (in *both* the labor and product markets) implies that:

$$w_t/p_t = be^{st+h(t-m_t)}. \tag{6.8}$$

This constraint can be added to (6.6) and (6.7); whether it should be or not depends upon a comparison between the resulting increase in the efficiency of the parameter estimators and the possible deleterious effects of the specification error committed if the competitive assumptions do not (approximately) hold.

Problems in computing maximum likelihood estimates

The conceptual framework outlined so far has three major advantages:

(1) The fixed proportions vintage model is more realistic than traditional models with respect to the utilization of capital goods.

(2) The joint estimation of capital utilization, using eqs. (6.6) and (6.7), is more satisfactory than the standard adjustments.

(3) The model can be estimated, at least in principle, without invoking assumptions of competitive behavior in either labor or product markets. Furthermore, the present model could be the building block for more complex, highly realistic, models involving several labor and capital categories and perhaps more than one production process.

Assume that we have discrete observations on the variables Q and L, indexed by the subscript $i = 1, \ldots, T$; the observations being made at times t_i, at which time the oldest capital still in use has age m_i. We postulate errors ε_i and u_i in the observations. Since the Q_i and L_i normally grow over time, and there is no plausible reason for the errors to become relatively less important over time, we postulate proportional errors[2]:

$$Q_i = \frac{ae^{rt_i} \int_{t_i-m_i}^{t_i} e^{gv} I(v) \, dv}{\{1 + \varepsilon_i\}} = F_i/\{1 + \varepsilon_i\} \qquad (6.9)$$

$$L_i = \frac{(a/b) \, e^{(r-s)t_i} \int_{t_i-m_i}^{t_i} e^{(g-h)v} I(v) \, dv}{\{1 + u_i\}} = G_i/\{1 + u_i\}. \qquad (6.10)$$

Employing the most manageable specification, we assume that the ε_i and u_i are normally distributed and independent—both of each other and across observations—and have the same variance, σ^2. The likelihood function for

---

[2] It may seem odd that the errors are placed in the denominators in (6.9) and (6.10) rather than using $(1 + \varepsilon_i)$ and $(1 + u_i)$ as multiplicative factors. The effect of this is to simplify the quadratic expansions of the estimators in terms of the errors, described below. In the present context, the more natural specification would compound the nonlinearities and complicate the approximations in exchange for a small increase in plausibility.

the observations on the Q_i and L_i for T periods is then an approximately monotonic function of[3]:

$$\sum_{i=1}^{T} \{\varepsilon_i^2 + u_i^2\},\tag{6.11}$$

so that maximum likelihood estimators are derived by minimizing the function:

$$S(\beta) = \sum_{i=1}^{T} \left\{ \left(\frac{ae^{rt_i} \int_{t_i - m_i}^{t_i} e^{gv} I(v)\, dv}{Q_i} - 1 \right)^2 \right.$$

$$\left. + \left(\frac{(a/b)\, e^{(r-s)\, t_i} \int_{t_i - m_i}^{t_i} e^{(g-h)\, v} I(v)\, dv}{L_i} - 1 \right)^2 \right\}\tag{6.12}$$

over all vectors β, where:

$$\beta = (a, b, g, h, r, s, m_1, m_2, \ldots, m_T),$$

subject only to nonnegativity constraints on a, b, and the m_i.

---

[3] Since the Jacobian of the transformation from the ε_i and u_i to the Q_i and L_i is not identically 1, the likelihood function in terms of the Q_i and L_i is not precisely monotonic in $\Sigma_i \{\varepsilon_i^2 + u_i^2\}$. The exact likelihood function becomes:

$$(2\pi\sigma^2)^{-T} \prod_i \left(\frac{F_i}{Q_i^2} \right) \left(\frac{G_i}{L_i^2} \right) \exp \left(-\frac{1}{2\sigma^2} \sum_i \{\varepsilon^2 + u_i^2\} \right),$$

where F_i and G_i are defined in (6.9) and (6.10). If we derive a concentrated (log) likelihood function by inserting the estimator for σ^2 into the logarithm of the likelihood function, the result is:

$$K - T \log \left\{ \sum_i (\varepsilon_i^2 + u_i^2) \right\} + \Sigma \{ \log (1 + \varepsilon_i) + \log (1 + u_i) \},$$

where K is a constant. We have ignored the third term throughout the approximations, which we justify on two grounds. First, the partials with respect to a particular error, say ε_i, of the second and third terms are:

$$-2T\varepsilon_i / (\Sigma \varepsilon_i^2 + u_i^2) \quad \text{and} \quad 1/(1 + \varepsilon_i)$$

respectively. For small ε_i and u_i, these are of order $1/\sigma$ and 1 respectively. We take $\sigma = 0.01$ below. Thus the change in the second term will tend to be 100 times as large as the change in the third term for a given change in a residual; maximizing the likelihood function is essentially equivalent to maximizing the second term. Second, including the term has no effect on any of the linear approximations derived below. The quadratic approximations would be altered slightly; these are completely valid for least squares estimators, but the latter are not, strictly speaking, maximum likelihood estimators for this model. Basically the quadratic approximations reflect the nonlinearities that enter because the F_i and G_i are not linear functions of the parameters, but ignore the nonlinearities that enter because of the error specification, which are much less significant in this case. Thus the quadratic approximations reflect the essential nonlinearities in the model, and are still sensible approximations for precise maximum likelihood estimators.

Two basic approaches to minimizing a nonlinear function of several variables are algorithms based on variations of the Seidel method and those based on variations of the gradient method, discussed in chapter 1. While gradient methods are generally more robust and reliable than Seidel methods, the form of $S(\beta)$—particularly the presence of parameters in the lower limits of the integrals—makes this problem seem tailor-made for a Seidel approach.

As indicated earlier, the Seidel method of solving a set of n equations in the components of the vector $\alpha = (\alpha_1, \ldots, \alpha_n)$ consists of manipulating the equations into the form:

$$\alpha = F(\alpha)$$

and finding a fixed point of this relation by iteration. The Seidel method can be used for minimization by applying it to the first order conditions, i.e., the equations

$$\frac{\partial S(\beta)}{\partial \beta_j} = 0 \quad (j = 1, \ldots, n).$$

This class of algorithms seems well suited for the minimization of (6.12), since tentative values for $\hat{a}$, $\hat{b}$, $\hat{g}$, $\hat{h}$, $\hat{r}$, and $\hat{s}$ can be used to obtain new estimates for the $\hat{m}_i$; the latter can then be used in the first-order conditions for the six basic parameters to obtain new estimates for them, and so forth.

Unfortunately, the basic method and numerous variations failed to produce a convergent algorithm. Even when hypothetical data, generated from given parameters, were used and the starting-points for the Seidel iterations were taken very close to the true values of the parameters, none of the Seidel modifications succeeded in converging to the true parameter point (and the actual minimum of 0 for $S(\beta)$). Instead, the algorithms not only diverged away from the true point but followed paths which appeared to be very unstable.

Although more robust, gradient methods which employ the matrix of second partial derivatives are expensive for the present problem simply because of the large number of parameters: normally 20 observations were employed, which implies 26 parameters. Very simple gradient methods were tried, in which just the first partials are computed and steps are taken in the direction of the gradient. These proved to be almost totally incapable of even moving toward the maximum.

More complicated methods which are based on a quadratic expansion of the function, such as the quadratic hill-climbing algorithm discussed in chapter 1, appeared to promise eventual convergence to the true maximum, but moved with small steps and resulted in extremely small increments in the function. Since these methods compute the inverse of the matrix of second partials at each step, they are quite expensive in this case. The small steps taken by the quadratic gradient methods seemed to follow ridges in the likelihood surface which were almost flat and quite meandering. While there was no evidence that, given sufficient time (which appeared to be a great deal—on the order of an hour of IBM 7094 time!), quadratic hill-climbing and similar routines would not eventually find the maximum, it was clearly not feasible to use these algorithms in explorations of the Monte Carlo type.

6.3. Problems of indeterminacy with the fixed proportions vintage model

The unusual difficulty encountered in minimizing the likelihood function suggested that sketching the general contours of the likelihood function and using search routines would be useful. The results of these attempts led to the conclusion that points in a large subset of the parameter space produced very good fits. Thus the question became whether, in this highly nonlinear model, a condition analogous to underidentification in the linear case exists when the estimation is based on only output and labor data.[4] The analysis below, showing the parameters to be nearly indeterminate for a large class of investment series, marginal vintage sequences, and parameter choices, certainly helps to explain the failure of the maximization routines.

The crucial point is that the determination of the parameters on the basis of just labor and output data depends entirely on the effect of h, embodied labor augmentation. If $h = 0$, the estimating equations reduce to:

$$Q_i = ae^{rt_i} \int_{t_i-m_i}^{t_i} e^{gv} I(v) \, dv \qquad (6.13)$$

$$L_i = (a/b) \, e^{(r-s)t_i} \int_{t_i-m_i}^{t_i} e^{gv} I(v) \, dv. \qquad (6.14)$$

Dividing (6.13) by (6.14) yields:

$$(Q_i/L_i) = be^{st_i}. \qquad (6.15)$$

---

[4] A definition of a condition called 'indeterminacy', similar to but distinguishable from underidentification, is contained in D. Smallwood, Problems of indeterminacy with the fixed coefficients, vintage model. *Yale Economic Essays*, Fall 1970.

Suppose, then, that data generated according to (6.13) and (6.14) are available, and that *arbitrary* $\hat{a}$, $\hat{g}$, and $\hat{r}$ are suggested, subject only to the restriction that $\hat{a}$ is not 'too small'. Specifically, let $\hat{a}$ satisfy

$$\hat{a} > \max_t \left[\frac{Q_i}{e^{\hat{r}t_i} \int_{-\infty}^{t_i} e^{\hat{g}v} I(v)\, dv} \right], \tag{6.16}$$

where $\hat{r}$ and $\hat{g}$ are arbitrary. Then a set of $\hat{m}_i$ can be found, by inverting (6.13), which makes the Q_i equations fit perfectly (the restriction (6.16) merely insures that finite $\hat{m}_i$ can be found). If $\hat{b}$ and $\hat{s}$ are then taken to satisfy (6.15)—thus equal to the true b and s—then the set $\{\hat{a}, \hat{b}, \hat{g}, \hat{h}, \hat{r}, \hat{s}, \hat{m}_1, ..., \hat{m}_T\}$ automatically satisfies (6.14) for each observation, since (6.13) and (6.15) together imply (6.14). Thus if $h = 0$, data generated by the vintage model can be explained with essentially any $\hat{a}$, $\hat{g}$ and $\hat{r}$ by choosing a suitable set of marginal vintages. Only b and s can be inferred.

While this dependence upon the effect of h is ominous, it is not clear that when h is relatively large the parameters will remain nearly indeterminate. The following result and the related computations suggest that they are.

Suppose Q_i and L_i data are given—not necessarily generated as in (6.6) and (6.7)—and that arbitrary α and β are chosen. We let:

$$\delta_i = \log (Q_i/L_i) - (\alpha + \beta t_i), \tag{6.17}$$

so that the δ_i can be considered the residuals when the natural log of (Q_i/L_i) is fitted to $\alpha + \beta t_i$.

Again let $\hat{a}$, $\hat{g}$ and $\hat{r}$ be arbitrary, subject only to the restriction that $\hat{a}$ is not too small, as above. If we choose $\hat{m}_i$'s such that

$$Q_i = \hat{a} e^{\hat{r}t_i} \int_{t_i - \hat{m}_i}^{t_i} e^{\hat{g}v} I(v)\, dv, \tag{6.18}$$

then we can rearrange (6.17) and (6.18) to give:

$$L_i = (e^{-\delta_i}) (\hat{a}/e^{\alpha}) e^{(\hat{r} - \beta) t_i} \int_{t_i - \hat{m}_i}^{t_i} e^{\hat{g}v} I(v)\, dv, \tag{6.19}$$

Let us assume for the moment that the δ_i are small enough so that

$$e^{-\delta_i} \approx 1 - \delta_i$$

is a reasonable approximation. Then (6.17) and (6.18) show that if the $\hat{m}_i$ are chosen correctly, arbitrary $\hat{a}$, $\hat{g}$ and $\hat{r}$ can 'explain' the Q_i data perfectly and the L_i data with percentage errors of $-\delta_i$, since, except for the term $e^{-\delta_i}$, (6.19) is precisely in the form of (6.14). Obviously if the m_i choices are adjusted, the discrepancies can be allocated between the Q_i and L_i; in fact, if $\bar{m}_i$ are chosen to solve the equation:

$$\int_{t_i-\bar{m}_i}^{t_i} e^{\hat{g}v} I(v)\, dv = \frac{1}{2}\left[\int_{t_i-m_i^*}^{t_i} e^{\hat{g}v} I(v)\, dv + \int_{t_i-\hat{m}_i}^{t_i} e^{\hat{g}v} I(v)\, dv\right],$$

where the m_i^* are defined by fitting the L_i data perfectly, then simple manipulations show that the discrepancies in the Q_i and L_i data become $\delta_i/2$ and $-\delta_i/2$. Thus we have the following result:

Let Q_i and L_i data be given, and let the δ_i be defined by:

$$\log (Q_i/L_i) = \alpha + \beta t_i + \delta_i,$$

where α and β may be chosen to minimize some function of the δ_i or may just be arbitrary. Then—independent of the investment stream given—the vintage model can be fitted to the Q_i and L_i data with $\hat{h} = 0$ and (essentially) arbitrary $\hat{a}$, $\hat{g}$ and $\hat{r}$, with percentage errors of at most $|\delta_i/2|$ in both the Q_i and L_i equations.

Obviously, a relevant question is how small the δ_i can be for optimally chosen α and β, such as the coefficients in a least squares fit. Mathematically, our result does not imply that the parameters of the model are necessarily nearly indeterminate; Q_i and L_i data can be generated for which the δ_i are very large for every α and β. However, Q_i and L_i data generated according to (6.6) and (6.7), using investment streams, marginal vintage sequences, and parameter values which appear to be at least generally plausible, are not arbitrary. For such data, the ratio (Q_i/L_i) almost inevitably closely follows an exponential time trend, implying that the determination of the vintage model parameters, except for b and s, is extremely tenuous.

This assertion is supported by the size of the δ_i's computed with a selection of illustrative examples. Twenty examples, produced by combining each of four investment series with each of five m_i sequences, were used in all the computations. In each example, 20 'observations' were assumed. The choices were meant to represent plausible examples with a bias toward high variability. Two of the investment series are essentially exponential with significant variance around the trend, while two do not even approximate an exponential trend. The m_i sequences have averages around 20 with absolute deviations from the trend which typically average 4 or 5.

For the set of 20 examples, which each reflect 20 observations, the $(\delta_i/2)$ that resulted from a least squares fit appeared to be proportional to $(1/h)$, averaging only 7.3% for $h = 0.04$ and 1.6% for $h = 0.01$! Even for large h, the basis for determining the parameters with this specification is extremely tenuous.

In fact, competitive forces will typically operate to keep $\log(Q_i/L_i)$ near its time trend. The competitive marginal vintage can be derived from (6.8):

$$m_i = \frac{1}{h}\{(s+h)\,t_i + \log b - \log(w_i/p_i)\}. \tag{6.20}$$

If the ratio of the wage rate to the price, (w_i/p_i), is constant or changes at a constant rate, the competitive m_i will follow a trend. But as long as $I(v)$ is even roughly exponential, this latter condition implies that $\log(Q_i/L_i)$ will tend to follow a time trend.[5]

In any case, it is clear that a large subset of the parameter space—essentially a three-dimensional surface consisting of (almost) arbitrary choices for $\hat{a}$, $\hat{g}$ and $\hat{r}$ with the corresponding $\hat{m}_i$ and with $\hat{b}$ near b, $\hat{s}$ near s, and $\hat{h} = 0$—provides points which come close to fitting each observation. This condition might seem to make further investigation of the estimator variances with this specification superfluous. Nevertheless, we proceed to approximate the estimators' sampling variances for several reasons:

(1) To determine whether this specification leads to unreasonably large variances even for large h and particularly favorable choices for $I(v)$ and m_i.

(2) To determine how the near-indeterminacy of a, g, r, and the m_i affects the sampling distributions of $\hat{b}$, $\hat{h}$, and $\hat{s}$.

(3) To provide a more direct comparison of this specification with a specification in which wage data are added. The results above suggest that the advantages of using wage data must outweigh the possible disadvantages, but approximating the estimator and predictor mean square errors (adjusted for possible biases) is the only feasible way to directly compare those alternatives.

(4) To investigate the validity of the standard variance approximations in the context of this highly nonlinear model, including whether the standard approximations indicate the nearly indeterminate state of some parameters.

(5) To determine whether estimators based on wage data are significantly more or less sensitive to fluctuations in the actual rates of technical change

---

[5] For more detailed support of these assertions, see D. Smallwood, *op. cit.*

than estimators based on just output and labor data, since the specification of perfectly constant rates obviously represents a sacrifice of realism for feasibility.

6.4. Linear and quadratic variance approximations

We now assume that the specification, in eqs. (6.9) and (6.10), of errors in the Q_i and L_i which are independent, normally distributed, and have equal variances, is correct. We further assume that maximum likelihood estimators are applied to Q_i and L_i samples and to a given (errorless) investment series, and approximate the sampling variances of the corresponding parameter estimators.

The derivation of the maximum likelihood equation employs all of the assumptions of the error specification; for instance, it is not only assumed that the ε_i and u_i have equal variances but also that the estimation method exploits this correct assumption. Obviously the resulting variances should be considered as lower bounds—probably significant underestimates—of the true variances in a realistic situation. If different variances for the ε_i and u_i, correlation between the ε_i and u_i, or autocorrelation among the ε_i and u_i were allowed for in the estimation, the sampling variances would be considerably increased even if those conditions did not obtain in reality. The assumption of uniformly favorable conditions is necessary to keep the computation of the approximations feasible.

The standard variance approximations for nonlinear maximum likelihood estimators, generally known as the Cramer–Rao variances and derived in chapter 2, can be written[6]:

$$-\left[\frac{\partial^2}{\partial \beta \, \partial \beta'} \log L(\beta) \right]^{-1}, \tag{6.21}$$

where $L(\beta)$ is the likelihood function. Using the definition of $S(\beta)$ in (6.12) and the error properties assumed, continuing to ignore a term as explained in footnote 3, we can write:

$$L(\beta) \approx \frac{1}{(2\pi\sigma^2)^T} e^{-S(\beta)/2\sigma^2}, \tag{6.22}$$

---

[6] The matrix in (6.21) should include partials with respect to σ^2, which is not a component of β. However, in this case the same covariance matrix for $\hat{\beta}$ results since the cross partials of $\log L$ with respect to σ^2 and the components of β are all zero when evaluated at the true parameter point.

where σ^2 is the common variance of the ε_i and u_i. Thus:

$$\frac{\partial^2}{\partial \beta \, \partial \beta'} \log L(\beta) \approx -\frac{1}{2\sigma^2} \frac{\partial^2 S(\beta)}{\partial \beta \, \partial \beta'}$$

and so the Cramer–Rao variances, in terms of $S(\beta)$, are:

$$\left[\frac{1}{2\sigma^2} \frac{\partial^2 S(\beta)}{\partial \beta \, \partial \beta'} \right]^{-1} = V^{-1}\sigma^2. \tag{6.23}$$

From (6.12), the second partials of $S(\beta)$ are simply:

$$\frac{\partial^2 S(\beta)}{\partial \beta_j \partial \beta_k} = 2 \sum_{i=1}^{T} \left[\left(\frac{F_i}{Q_i} - 1 \right) \frac{1}{Q_i} \frac{\partial^2 F_i}{\partial \beta_j \partial \beta_k} + \left(\frac{1}{Q_i} \frac{\partial F_i}{\partial \beta_j} \right) \left(\frac{1}{Q_i} \frac{\partial F_i}{\partial \beta_k} \right) \right.$$

$$\left. + \left(\frac{G_i}{L_i} - 1 \right) \frac{1}{L_i} \frac{\partial^2 G_i}{\partial \beta_j \partial \beta_k} + \left(\frac{1}{L_i} \frac{\partial G_i}{\partial \beta_j} \right) \left(\frac{1}{L_i} \frac{\partial G_i}{\partial \beta_k} \right) \right], \tag{6.24}$$

where

$$F_i = a e^{r t_i} \int_{t_i - m_i}^{t_i} e^{g v} I(v) \, dv \tag{6.25}$$

and

$$G_i = (a/b) e^{(r-s) t_i} \int_{t_i - m_i}^{t_i} e^{(g-h) v} I(v) \, dv. \tag{6.26}$$

Under very general conditions, maximum likelihood estimators are asymptotically normal, and when (6.23) is evaluated at the true parameter point, it is the asymptotic covariance matrix. The matrix of second partials is ordinarily evaluated at the parameter estimates, and an estimate of σ^2 is substituted. Since those estimators are generally consistent, the matrix obtained when (6.23) is evaluated at an estimate will converge to the asymptotic covariance matrix.

In the present problem, however, these asymptotic results do not apply, since they are derived for a sample coming from a *fixed* parent distribution with a *fixed* number of parameters. In this case, the mean of each Q_i and L_i depends upon a different function of β. While that aspect does not seem likely to affect the consistency of the estimators as long as the t_i, $I(v)$, and m_i behave reasonably as the sample is extended, the addition of a parameter with each observation may well do so. Various examples exist in which increasing the number of parameters along with the observations leads to inconsistent maximum likelihood estimators[7], even though the degrees of

---

[7] M. G. Kendall and A. Stuart, *The advanced theory of statistics*, vol. 2. New York, Hafner, 1961, pp. 61–2.

freedom approach infinity. Thus, although the matrix V, defined by (6.23), is evaluated here at the true parameter point, asymptotic properties cannot be invoked as a justification and the motivation for (6.23) will be considered.

In an actual estimation, (6.23) would be evaluated using $\hat{\beta}$. Having neither a sample for the ε's and u's nor the corresponding estimates, we choose the one set of errors, residuals, and estimates which we know are internally consistent, namely $\varepsilon_i = u_i = 0$ for all i and $\hat{\beta} = \beta$. For that choice, the first and third terms of (6.24) are zero since $F_i = Q_i$ and $G_i = L_i$. The (jk)th term of V becomes simply:

$$V_{jk} = \sum_{i=1}^{T} \left[\left(\frac{1}{Q_i} \frac{\partial F_i}{\partial \beta_j} \right) \left(\frac{1}{Q_i} \frac{\partial F_i}{\partial \beta_k} \right) + \left(\frac{1}{L_i} \frac{\partial G_i}{\partial \beta_j} \right) \left(\frac{1}{L_i} \frac{\partial G_i}{\partial \beta_k} \right) \right] \quad (6.27)$$

and V can be written as the sum of two matrix products:

$$D_1' D_1 + D_2' D_2,$$

where the (ij)th elements of D_1 and D_2 are

$$\left(\frac{1}{Q_i} \frac{\partial F_i}{\partial \beta_j} \right) \quad \text{and} \quad \left(\frac{1}{L_i} \frac{\partial G_i}{\partial \beta_j} \right)$$

respectively. This sum can alternatively be written as

$$\begin{bmatrix} D_1 \\ D_2 \end{bmatrix}' \begin{bmatrix} D_1 \\ D_2 \end{bmatrix} = X'X. \quad (6.28)$$

With $F_i = Q_i$ and $G_i = L_i$, the terms of X further simplify:

$$\frac{1}{Q_i} \frac{\partial F_i}{\partial a} = \frac{1}{F_i} \frac{\partial F_i}{\partial a} = \frac{1}{a} \quad (6.29)$$

$$\frac{1}{Q_i} \frac{\partial F_i}{\partial g} = \frac{1}{F_i} \frac{\partial}{\partial g} \left\{ a e^{rt_i} \int_{t_i - m_i}^{t_i} e^{gv} I(v) \, dv \right\} = \frac{\int_{t_i - m_i}^{t_i} v e^{gv} I(v) \, dv}{\int_{t_i - m_i}^{t_i} e^{gv} I(v) \, dv} \quad (6.30)$$

$$\frac{1}{Q_i} \frac{\partial F_i}{\partial r} = t_i, \quad (6.31)$$

and so forth. By writing:

$$\int_{t_i - m_i}^{t_i} v e^{gv} I(v) \, dv = t_i \int_{t_i - m_i}^{t_i} e^{gv} I(v) \, dv - \int_{t_i - m_i}^{t_i} (t_i - v) e^{gv} I(v) \, dv$$

and substituting into (6.30), it is immediate that

$$\frac{1}{Q_i} \frac{\partial F_i}{\partial g} = t_i - A_i(g),$$
(6.32)

where $A_i(g)$ is the average age of capital in use (augmented at rate g) at time t_i. Thus at the true parameter point, the matrix V can be written as $X'X$, where

$X =$

$$\begin{bmatrix}
1/a & t_1 & t_1 - A_1(g) & 0 & 0 & 0 & M_1(g) & 0 & \cdots & 0 \\
1/a & t_2 & t_2 - A_2(g) & 0 & 0 & 0 & 0 & M_2(g) & \cdots & 0 \\
\vdots & \vdots & \vdots & \vdots & \vdots & \vdots & \vdots & \vdots & & \vdots \\
1/a & t_T & t_T - A_T(g) & 0 & 0 & 0 & 0 & 0 & \cdots & M_T(g) \\
1/a & t_1 & t_1 - A_1(g-h) & -1/b & -t_1 & A_1(g-h)-t_1 & M_1(g-h) & 0 & \cdots & 0 \\
1/a & t_2 & t_2 - A_2(g-h) & -1/b & -t_2 & A_2(g-h)-t_2 & 0 & M_2(g-h) & \cdots & 0 \\
\vdots & \vdots & \vdots & \vdots & \vdots & \vdots & & \vdots & & \vdots \\
1/a & t_T & t_T - A_T(g-h) & -1/b & -t_T & A_T(g-h)-t_T & 0 & 0 & \cdots & M_T(g-
\end{bmatrix}$$

(6.33)

and where

$$M_i(g) = \frac{e^{g(t_i - m_i)} I(t_i - m_i)}{\displaystyle\int_{t_i - m_i}^{t_i} e^{gv} I(v)\, dv}$$
(6.34)

The easiest way to interpret these variance approximations is that they represent the approximations which result from linearizing the basic equations around the true parameter point. That is, one method of estimating (6.6) and (6.7)—and approximating the maximum likelihood estimator—is to pick a set of values for the parameters, β^0, and expand the F_i and G_i around $\beta = \beta^0$:

$$F_i(\beta) \approx F_i(\beta^0) + (\beta - \beta^0)' \left[\frac{\partial F_i}{\partial \beta}\right]_{\beta = \beta^0}$$
(6.35)

and similarly for $G_i(\beta)$. Estimates for the coefficients $(\beta_j - \beta_j^0)$ can then be obtained by linearly regressing the 'dependent variable' whose observations consist of both the $(Q_i - F_i(\beta^0))$ and the $(L_i - G_i(\beta^0))$ on independent variables, the jth of which consists of 'observations' on both the $\partial F_i(\beta^0)/\partial \beta_j$ and the $\partial G_i(\beta^0)/\partial \beta_j$. In this case, the point β^0 happens to be the true parameter point; in the ordinary application of the Cramer–Rao variances, β^0 corresponds to $\hat{\beta}$.

Suppose the model were linearized, once and for all, around the true parameter point. Suppose samples for Q_i and L_i were then repeatedly generated according to the error specification described above, and parameter estimates were obtained each time from the linear regression. The matrix $(X'X)^{-1} \sigma^2$ is the exact covariance matrix for such artificial 'estimators'. In that sense, the variables X_j, where

$$X_j = \begin{bmatrix} \dfrac{\partial F_1}{\partial \beta_j} \\ \vdots \\ \dfrac{\partial F_T}{\partial \beta_j} \\ \dfrac{\partial G_1}{\partial \beta_j} \\ \vdots \\ \dfrac{\partial G_T}{\partial \beta_j} \end{bmatrix} \tag{6.36}$$

play a role analogous to that of the independent variables in the linear regression context.

Thus singularity of the matrix V corresponds to perfect multicollinearity in the linear regression context. The matrix V clearly has rank less than $T + 6$ if and only if the matrix X has rank less than $T + 6$; that is, when these 'local independent variables' are linearly dependent. It is not surprising in the light of the previous analysis that when $h = 0$, so that $A_i(g) = A_i(g - h)$, the columns of X can be shown to be linearly dependent. Since the primary determinant of $\log(Q_i/L_i)$, given the parameters, is the average age of capital in use, it is also not surprising that when either

$$A_i(g) = \alpha + \beta t_i \quad \text{or} \quad A_i(g - h) = \alpha + \beta t_i$$

for all i and some α and β, the columns of X are again linearly dependent.

These results emerge from the previous analysis, but further examination of X produces new insights into the determination of the parameters. For instance, manipulation shows that X has less than full rank if:

$$M_i(g)/M_i(g - h) = \alpha + \beta t_i \quad (i = 1, \dots, T) \tag{6.37}$$

for some α and β. But the expansion of this ratio in h yields:

$$M_i(g)/M_i(g - h) = 1 - h(m_i - A_i(g)) + 0(h^2), \tag{6.38}$$

where $0(h^2)$ represents terms in h^2 and higher. Thus if

$$m_i - A_i(g) = \alpha + \beta t_i,$$

then the matrix X could be said to have rank less than $T + 6$ 'to order h'. This result suggests that even substantial fluctuations in the average age around its time trend may not be sufficient to produce reasonable estimator variances, since deviations in the A_i will usually correspond to deviations in the m_i around their trend in about the same proportion.

In the linear case, the singularity of the cross-product matrix of the independent variables, $(X'X)$, implies that the likelihood function has no unique maximum and, therefore, that coefficient estimators are indeterminate. In the nonlinear case, the likelihood function may have a unique maximum even though V is singular; the latter condition implies merely that in some direction in parameter space not only the first derivative but also the second derivative of the likelihood function is zero. While this condition does not translate easily into a statement about variance, the parameter combination corresponding to that direction will be close to indeterminate in normal cases.

We now employ a different approach to the motivation of (6.23) as the variance approximation which is useful in extending the approximation. The maximum likelihood estimator, $\hat{\beta}$, is implicitly defined by the $T + 6$ first order conditions, which from (6.12), (6.25), and (6.26) are:

$$\sum_i \left[\left(\frac{F_i(\hat{\beta})}{Q_i} - 1 \right) \frac{1}{Q_i} \frac{\partial F_i(\hat{\beta})}{\partial \beta_j} + \left(\frac{G_i(\hat{\beta})}{L_i} - 1 \right) \frac{1}{L_i} \frac{\partial G_i(\hat{\beta})}{\partial \beta_j} \right] = 0$$

$$(j = 1, \dots, T + 6). \tag{6.39}$$

This set of equations defines β as an implicit function of the Q_i and L_i. Thus, if partials in each of these equations are taken with respect to Q_k, for instance, the result is a set of $T + 6$ linear equations in:

$$\frac{\partial \hat{\beta}_j}{\partial Q_k} \quad (j = 1, \dots, T + 6),$$

which can be calculated for a particular choice of β; the natural choice is obviously the true parameter point. Since, according to (6.9)

$$Q_k = F_k/(1 + \varepsilon_k)$$

the partial derivatives of the $\hat{\beta}_j$ with respect to the ε_k can be computed. Similarly, partials with respect to the u_k can be calculated. Thus if we write:

$$\hat{\beta}_j \approx \beta_j + \sum_{k=1}^{T} \left[\frac{\partial \hat{\beta}_j}{\partial \varepsilon_k} \varepsilon_k + \frac{\partial \hat{\beta}_j}{\partial u_k} u_k \right], \tag{6.40}$$

then we can obtain an approximation to

$$E (\hat{\beta}_j - \beta_j)^2$$

by invoking the assumptions about the error distributions. Covariance terms can similarly be approximated.

These computations result in the same 'linearly approximated' variances as those produced by linearly expanding the F_i and G_i around the true parameter point.[8] The extensions to higher terms, however, do not give the same approximations. That is, (6.35) could be expanded to include quadratic terms:

$$F_i(\beta) \approx F_i(\beta^0) + (\beta - \beta^0)' \left[\frac{\partial F_i}{\partial \beta} \right]_{\beta = \beta^0} + \tfrac{1}{2} (\beta - \beta^0)' \left[\frac{\partial^2 F_i}{\partial \beta \, \partial \beta'} \right]_{\beta = \beta^0} (\beta - \beta^0) \tag{6.41}$$

and similarly for the $G_i(\beta)$, and the exact variances of the estimators based on fitting these quadratic functions could be determined.

But as long as the numerous interrelations of the coefficients in (6.41) are acknowledged, this is no solution at all. A linear regression subject to numerous nonlinear constraints is still a nonlinear problem, with no obviously easy way to approximate the covariance matrix. Applied to this new nonlinear problem, the Cramer–Rao solution simply generates again the linearized approximation to the covariance matrix. An easily computable alternative would be to compute the covariance matrix of the linear coefficients in (6.41) when the quadratic terms are included but the coefficient restrictions are ignored (thus producing an ordinary linear regression). This would certainly increase the approximated variances, but the procedure has no clear justification; if the method is extended by adding further terms but still ignoring the

---

[8] D. Smallwood, *op. cit.*

coefficient restrictions, the inevitable result (when the number of variables exceeds the number of observations) is a set of infinite variances. Indeed, for the problem at hand, this procedure could not be applied no matter how many observations were available.

Rather than trying to improve the variance approximations by using (6.41), an alternative is to extend the expansion implicit in (6.40). By taking partials in each of the first-order conditions a second time, say with respect to Q_k, $(T + 6)$ linear equations in the variables:

$$\frac{\partial^2 \hat{\beta}_i}{\partial Q_k \, \partial Q_j} \quad (i = 1, \ldots, T + 6)$$

result. If partials are taken the second time with respect to L_k instead, the partials

$$\frac{\partial^2 \hat{\beta}_i}{\partial L_k \partial Q_j}$$

can be computed, and so forth. The definition of the errors can then be used and we can write:

$$\hat{\beta}_j \approx \beta_j + \sum_i \left[\frac{\partial \hat{\beta}_j}{\partial \varepsilon_i} \varepsilon_i + \frac{\partial \hat{\beta}_j}{\partial u_i} u_i \right] + \frac{1}{2} \sum_i \left[\frac{\partial^2 \hat{\beta}_j}{\partial \varepsilon_i^2} \varepsilon_i^2 + \frac{\partial^2 \hat{\beta}_j}{\partial u_i^2} u_i^2 \right]$$

$$+ \sum_i \sum_{k>i} \left[\frac{\partial^2 \hat{\beta}_j}{\partial \varepsilon_i \partial \varepsilon_k} \varepsilon_i \varepsilon_k + \frac{\partial^2 \hat{\beta}_j}{\partial u_i \partial u_k} u_i u_k \right] + \frac{1}{2} \sum_i \sum_k \left[\frac{\partial^2 \hat{\beta}_j}{\partial \varepsilon_i \partial u_k} \varepsilon_i u_k \right]. \quad (6.42)$$

By applying the assumptions about the errors, a 'quadratically approximated' covariance matrix for the parameters can be evaluated. Whereas only the assumptions that the errors are independent, have zero means, and have a common variance of σ^2 were actually invoked in the linear approximations, the evaluation of the variance and covariance terms using (6.42) exploits more fully the assumption of normality, since the assumptions that $E(\varepsilon_i^3) = 0$ and that $E(\varepsilon_i^4) = 3 [E(\varepsilon_i^2)]^2$ are used.

Including the quadratic terms in (6.42) does not produce the exact sampling variances of estimators based on a quadratic expansion of the original function, as in (6.41). This follows from the fact that the cubic and higher terms in an extension of (6.42) are not generally zero for estimators derived from a quadratic function of the parameters. The class of functions for which (6.42) produces the exact sampling variances is not clear.

6.5. Computed covariance matrices

Since the approximated variances are taken around the true parameter values rather than the means of their estimators, their square roots are root mean square errors rather than standard deviations. We will abbreviate the linear and quadratic approximations as $RMSE_L$ and $RMSE_Q$. As they represent an extended approximation, the quadratic approximations are presumed to be more accurate. Some indirect evidence in support of this presumption is given below, where we argue that the patterns of the $RMSE_Q$ across different h are more plausible, given the analytic results of section 6.3, than the patterns of the $RMSE_L$.

When $E(\hat{\beta}_j - \beta_j)^2$ is computed using (6.42), the terms which have a non-zero expectation are either of the order σ^2 or σ^4. The terms involving σ^2 reproduce the linear approximations; the new terms are all of order σ^4. The ratio of the $RMSE_Q$ to the $RMSE_L$ thus approaches 1 if σ approaches 0.

For this model, the range of σ for which the $RMSE_L$ and $RMSE_Q$ are nearly equal is extremely small and depends crucially upon the size of h. Table 6.1 exhibits the $RMSE_L$ and the ratio $(RMSE_Q/RMSE_L)$ for $\hat{g}$, $\hat{h}$, and

TABLE 6.1

Linearly approximated root mean square errors and the ratio
of quadratic to linear, averaged over 20 examples

		$h = 0.04$ $\sigma = 0.01$	$h = 0.04$ $\sigma = 0.02$	$h = 0.01$ $\sigma = 0.01$	$h = 0.01$ $\sigma = 0.02$
$RMSE_L$	$\hat{g}$	0.0229	0.0458	0.0938	0.1876
	$\hat{h}$	0.0095	0.0136	0.0096	0.0191
	$\widehat{(g + r)}$	0.0055	0.0109	0.0224	0.0448
$RMSE_Q/RMSE_L$	$\hat{g}$	1.66	2.68	5.38	10.52
	$\hat{h}$	1.79	3.01	5.76	11.30
	$\widehat{(g + r)}$	1.53	2.37	4.42	8.57

$\widehat{(g + r)}$, averaged over the 20 examples described above. With $h = 0.04$ and 1% errors in the Q_i and L_i, the $RMSE_Q$ exceed the $RMSE_L$ by 50–80% on average. For smaller h or larger σ, the discrepancy becomes enormous. If high accuracy is desired, the inadequacy of the $RMSE_L$ is striking. For the $RMSE_L$

to be within 10% of the RMSE_Q on average, σ must be less than 0.4% if $h = 0.04$, and less than 0.1% if $h = 0.01$!

Two patterns, which are partially revealed in table 6.1 suggest that the RMSE_Q's more adequately reflect the indeterminacy of the parameters than do the RMSE_L's. First, the RMSE_L's for $\hat{a}$, $\hat{g}$, $\hat{r}$, and $(\widehat{g + r})$ are essentially proportional to $(1/h)$, whereas the RMSE_Q's increase much more than proportionately for small h. Second, the RMSE_L's for $\hat{b}$, $\hat{h}$, $\hat{s}$ and $(\widehat{h + s})$ are independent of h, whereas the RMSE_Q's show a substantial increase for $h = 0.01$, though not as great as for $\hat{a}$, $\hat{g}$ and $\hat{r}$. It is certainly plausible that the estimator reliability of $\hat{b}$, $\hat{h}$ and $\hat{s}$ is affected by its disintegration for the other parameters.

The RMSE_Q's thus indicate that unless σ is very small, the standard (i.e., linear) approximations drastically underestimate the variances of the parameter estimators. The RMSE_Q's are not only much larger, but have a more plausible pattern with respect to different values of h, particularly for $\hat{b}$, $\hat{h}$ and $\hat{s}$.

6.6. Alternative estimator specifications

The size of the RMSE's for estimators based on only output and labor data damages the case for ignoring wage data. The approximations are thus extended to determine how much the addition of wage data reduces the RMSE's. We then indicate how the approximations can be modified to evaluate the estimator bias implied by a bias in the wage data.

A comparison of specifications should include an examination of their robustness with respect to any particularly likely errors in both specifications. It is clearly implausible that the period-to-period rates of technical change are perfectly constant. The basic approximations are therefore also extended to compute the estimator variance added by random fluctuations in the actual period-to-period rates.

Last, the effects of the various assumptions are summarized by approximating the RMSE's for predictions implied by the different covariance matrices for a particular prediction situation. This also provides perspective on the magnitudes of the parameter RMSE's, and shows the significance of the correlation patterns among the parameter estimators.

The addition of wage data

It must be noted that adding wage data does not alter the indeterminacy of a, g, r and the m_i if $h = 0$. The marginal product of labor is labor's average product on the marginal vintage. Setting the value of labor's marginal product equal to the wage rate thus implies that (6.3) holds exactly for the marginal vintage:

$$(w_i/p_i) = be^{st_i + h(t_i - m_i)}. \tag{6.43}$$

With $h = 0$ this constraint is identical to (6.15), so that no new information is added in that case.

For $h > 0$, however, adding (6.43) sharply reduces the set of parameter vectors which allow close fits. It is no longer true that the numbers produced by fitting log (Q_i/L_i) to a time trend, and halving the residuals, are upper bounds for the errors in the Q_i and L_i equations which can be associated with arbitrary a, g and r. However, a modified condition can be demonstrated, which is:

If log (Q_i/L_i) fits $\alpha + \beta t_i$ with residuals of δ_i and log (w_i/p_i) fits the *same* trend, with residuals of θ_i, then essentially arbitrary a, g and r will fit the Q_i perfectly, the L_i data with absolute errors of less than $|\delta_i|\%$, and the (w_i/p_i) data with errors of less than $|\theta_i|\%$, for any investment stream.

Using (6.43), wage 'data' were computed for the 20 illustrative examples. When log (Q_i/L_i) and log (w_i/p_i) were then fitted by least squares to the same trend, weighting the residuals in the two equations equally, minimal δ_i and θ_i average 28 and 32% respectively for $h = 0.04$, and 7.3 and 8.3% for $h = 0.01$. These are more than 4 times as large as the corresponding bounds for the specification which ignores wage data.

It was assumed that (6.43) is added to (6.6) and (6.7), and that the corresponding 'data' contain errors of observation with a standard deviation of 2%. Linearly approximated root mean square errors (RMSE$_W$) were computed for the 20 illustrative examples. The average RMSE$_W$'s across the 20 examples are:

	$\hat{g}$	$\hat{h}$	$\widehat{(g + r)}$
$h = 0.01$	0.0139	0.0011	0.0037
$h = 0.04$	0.0039	0.0013	0.0011

These are an order of magnitude smaller than the RMSE$_L$. A smaller h still implies higher variances, but the introduction of wage data has drastically reduced their level.

The crucial question is whether the improvement depends upon 'high quality' wage data. We investigate this question by approximating the effects on the RMSE_w of larger errors or biases in the wage data. With wage data that include errors of observation, which we assume to be added, the generalization of (6.40) includes terms in the output, labor, and wage errors. Linear approximations for the effects of a larger variance or a non-zero mean for the wage errors can thus be obtained by applying those assumptions and taking expectations.

Computed for the 20 illustrative examples, the biases induced by a positive 5% bias in the wage data appeared systematically positive (i.e., the biases in at least 19 out of 20 examples were positive) for $\hat{a}$, $\hat{g}$ and $\hat{s}$, averaging 4.0%, 0.0044, and 0.0054 respectively with $h = 0.04$, and systematically negative for $\hat{b}$, $\hat{r}$ and $\hat{h}$, averaging -5.7%, -0.0048, and -0.0047 respectively. The relevant question is whether the effects of the wage bias dominate the reduction in variance. Crude extrapolations suggest that for $\hat{g}$ the critical level is a bias of about 25%, for $\hat{h}$ a bias of about 10%, and for $(\widehat{g + r})$ a bias of about 55%. Since one could rarely assume confidently that the bias in wage data was either definitely less than 10% or definitely greater than 55%, a comparison of the advantages and disadvantages of adding wage seems thus ambiguous. Computing the effects of a bias in the wage data on prediction allows the differing sensitivity among the parameters to be weighted appropriately.

Fluctuations in the rates of technical change

If parameter estimators are highly sensitive to deviations in the true period-to-period rates of technical change, they have questionable value. The assumption of perfectly constant rates is a fairly drastic simplification. Since embodied technical changes are improvements that can be realized only by acquiring new capital goods and thus reflect new machine designs, the assumption of perfectly constant embodied rates is particularly questionable.

Jorgenson has noted[9] that in a model which allows variable period-to-period rates, rates of embodied and disembodied technical change cannot be distinguished on the basis of just labor and output data (aggregated for each period over all vintages). His conclusion, that embodied technical change is not a meaningful concept, is not justified. The decomposition of productivity increase into that which will occur even with no new investment and that

---

[9] Dale W. Jorgenson, The embodiment hypothesis. *Journal of Political Economy* **74** (1966), 1–17.

attributable to new investment is certainly meaningful. The relevant question is how the distribution of parameter estimators, based on a specification of perfectly constant rates, will be affected by deviations in the rates about their means.

Thus we assume that the Q_i and L_i data are generated according to vintage model assumptions except that the rate of disembodied capital augmentation in the jth period, for instance, is not r but $(\bar{r} + \varepsilon_j^r)$. Thus the term rt is replaced by the term:

$$\bar{r}t + \sum_j \varepsilon_j^r$$

in the generating equations. The deviations are assumed to be independent, have zero means, and equal variances:

$$\sigma_{tc}^2 = E(\varepsilon_j^r)^2 = E(\varepsilon_j^g)^2 = E(\varepsilon_j^s)^2 = E(\varepsilon_j^h)^2.$$

A σ_{tc} of 0.005 implies that if $h = 0.04$, then about 95% of the period-to-period rates of embodied labor augmentation will be between 0.03 and 0.05. The estimator variance added by the deviations was approximated by combining the partial derivatives of the Q_i and L_i with respect to each deviation with the derivatives of the estimators with respect to the Q_i and L_i, derived above.

In table 6.2, we list some of the average RMSE's which result from adding the variance attributable to deviations in the rates of technical change to that attributable to errors of observation in the Q_i, L_i, and w_i data. For estimators based on just Q_i and L_i data with 1% errors, the increase ranges from 13 to 20% for $\sigma_{tc} = 0.005$, and from about 45 to 60% for $\sigma_{tc} = 0.010$.

TABLE 6.2

Average RMSE's with fluctuations in the rates of technical change

		$h = 0.04$		$h = 0.01$	
		$\sigma_{tc} = 0.005$	$\sigma_{tc} = 0.010$	$\sigma_{tc} = 0.005$	$\sigma_{tc} = 0.010$
Combined with	$\hat{g}$	0.0265	0.0347	0.1087	0.1432
RMSE_L	$\hat{h}$	0.0107	0.0136	0.0109	0.0142
	$\widehat{(g + r)}$	0.0064	0.0086	0.0259	0.0341
Combined with	$\hat{g}$	0.0062	0.0103	0.0219	0.0362
RMSE_W	$\hat{h}$	0.0032	0.0060	0.0029	0.0053
	$\widehat{(g + r)}$	0.0023	0.0042	0.0061	0.0102

The addition of wage data reduces the variance due to deviations in the rates, but not to the extent that it reduces the variance due to errors of observation in the data. Thus the relative increase is greater, particularly for parameters with small RMSE$_W$'s. For $\sigma_{tc} = 0.005$, the increases range from about 50 to over 140%, while for $\sigma_{tc} = 0.010$ the average RMSE$_W$'s are multiplied by factors ranging from 2 to 5. The standard variance approximations—computed on the assumption of perfectly constant rates—imply confidence intervals which are much too small even for $\sigma_{tc} = 0.005$ and are severe underestimates for $\sigma_{tc} = 0.010$.

6.7. Summary of the calculations

The effects of different covariance approximations, of the addition of wage data, and of deviations in the rates of technical change differ among the parameters (the effects differ across examples, also, but attempts to explain the differences in terms of characteristics of the $I(v)$ and m_i sequences were largely unsuccessful). Since a major purpose of estimating this model is to make conditional predictions, obvious summary measures are the RMSE's of particular predictors. They provide an appropriate weighting and are numbers whose significance is easier to evaluate.

Furthermore, when the parameter estimators are highly correlated, as they are here, their variances can be quite misleading since the variance of a predictor depends upon the interaction between the estimator correlations and the prediction conditions. For instance, errors in $\hat{g}$ and $\hat{r}$ have a high negative correlation, which allows the variance of $\widehat{(g + r)}$ to be much smaller than the variances of either $\hat{g}$ or $\hat{r}$. Since in most plausible prediction situations, offsetting errors in g and r produce largely offsetting prediction errors, the variances of g and r can be very misleading. This is a standard problem with multicollinearity; the situation is complicated in the nonlinear case by the fact that typical patterns for the independent variables cannot be calculated directly. At best, the surrogate 'independent variables' defined as in (6.36) can be used as indicators.

The addition of wage data and the assumption of deviations in the rates of technical change alter not only the parameter variances but also the correlation pattern among the estimators; the latter effect can be evaluated only by considering prediction variances.

In table 6.3, we list the root mean square (percentage) errors, averaged over the 20 illustrative examples, for the prediction of output 5 periods after the last observation period, with the projected investment stream and wage rate assumed to follow their observation period trends. Various predictors were considered, but the impact of the different assumptions was similar and the conclusions derived here would be altered only slightly by using another plausible prediction situation.

TABLE 6.3

Root mean square (percentage) errors, averaged over 20 examples, for the prediction of output at $t_T + 5$

| | h | 0.04 | 0.04 | 0.01 | 0.01 |
	σ	0.01	0.02	0.01	0.02
$\sigma_{tc} = 0$ (constant rates of technical change):					
Prediction RMSE's implied by:	$RMSE_L$	7.07	14.15	29.80	59.59
	$RMSE_Q$	12.97	43.57	165.06	646.65
$RMSE_W$ with: $\sigma_W = 0.02$	$B = 0$	1.33	1.93	4.43	5.39
$= 0.10$	$B = 0$	5.27	5.48	20.18	20.45
$= 0.02$	$B = 20\%$	13.20	13.34	51.26	51.50
$= 0.10$	$B = 20\%$	14.59	14.68	56.36	56.51
$\sigma_{tc} = 0.010$:					
Prediction RMSE's implied by:	$RMSE_L$	15.17	19.61	51.62	73.18
	$RMSE_Q$	19.59	46.76	173.48	649.46
$RMSE_W$ with: $\sigma_W = 0.02$	$B = 0$	9.74	9.85	14.36	17.76
$= 0.10$	$B = 0$	11.17	11.26	25.01	25.22
$= 0.02$	$B = 20\%$	16.68	16.75	53.47	53.67
$= 0.10$	$B = 20\%$	17.68	17.75	58.24	58.39

σ_W = Standard deviation of the errors in the wage data.
B = Bias in the wage data.

The prediction variances were approximated by linearly expanding the prediction error in terms of the parameter errors. The expected mean square errors were then computed with the aid of the previously calculated estimator covariance matrices. Monte Carlo tests, in which the actual predictions were repeatedly computed, indicated that the approximation error—assuming the adequacy of the estimator covariance matrices—is minor.

Table 6.3 shows that if $h = 0.01$, prediction errors would be extremely large unless high quality wage data were available. Even with perfectly constant rates of technical change, unbiased but variable wage data ($B = 0$, $\sigma_W = 0.10$) produce a prediction RMSE of over 20% on average, while a

20% bias in the wage data raises the prediction RMSE to over 50%. Even with good wage data, the effect of deviations in the rates of technical change, with $\sigma_{tc} = 0.010$, is to raise the standard deviation of the predictor to roughly 15%. With $h = 0.01$, a bias in the wage data has a severe effect. For small h, the specification based on just Q_i and L_i data is hopeless, and only high quality wage data together with highly stable rates of technical change will allow accurate prediction with this specification.

Even for $h = 0.04$, it appears justifiable to ignore wage data only if the Q_i and L_i data have very small errors and the bias in the wage data is large. Furthermore, the quadratic approximations indicate, not unexpectedly, that the constraint on the size of the errors in the Q_i and L_i is stringent.

Given the previous analysis, the inadequacy of the standard (i.e., linearly approximated) confidence intervals is not surprising for the specification based on only output and labor data. But even with wage data added, the calculations imply that the standard approximations are an order of magnitude too small when either a modest bias in the wage data or modest variations in the true rates of technical change are present. Furthermore, the derivation of the variance added by deviations in the rates of technical change suggests that adding quadratic terms would produce an increase comparable to that in the variance attributable to the errors of observation.

6.8. General conclusions

The computations indicate that the only reasonable circumstances in which wage data can be ignored are those in which the errors in the output and labor data are very small, h is large, and the biases in the wage data are considerable. If these stringent conditions are not met, the increase in efficiency attributable to using wage data easily dominates the effects of the estimator biases resulting from biased wage data. Furthermore, if h is small, such as $h = 0.01$, highly accurate wage data are needed to produce accurate predictions.

For the specification based on only output and labor data, the quadratic covariance approximations indicate that the standard (linear) approximations are accurate only for extremely small errors in the data. For errors with a standard deviation of 2%, the linear approximations appear to be drastic underestimates. With wage data added, the standard confidence intervals are also quite misleading if there is either more than minimal variation in the actual period-to-period rates of technical change or more than minimal biases in the wage data.

The very large prediction variances, except when accurate, bias-free wage data are available, raise questions of whether 'naive' prediction methods might not perform as well as the correct specification and whether constraints exist for which the increase in efficiency would dominate the possible bias. For instance, the constraint $h = 0$ leads to a much simpler estimation problem but also to unrealistic implications, such as that, depending upon the wage rate, either all capital or no capital is utilized. The performance of various 'naive' prediction methods is considered elsewhere.[10]

Probably the most illuminating results are the conditions which relate the deviations of $\log (Q_i/L_i)$ about its trend to the errors consistent with arbitrary choices for some of the parameters. These results illustrate the usefulness of specialized analyses for nonlinear estimators which arise when complex functions of the parameters are to be estimated.

---

[10] D. Smallwood, Estimation and prediction with the fixed coefficients, vintage model. Unpublished Ph.D. thesis, Yale University, 1970.

CHAPTER 7

AUTOCORRELATION IN SIMULTANEOUS EQUATION SYSTEMS

7.1. Introduction

One of the critical assumptions in the standard development of the linear model for a single equation[1], i.e. a model of the form

$$Y = X\beta + U \tag{7.1}$$

is that the disturbances have a variance-covariance matrix given by

$$E(UU') = \sigma^2 I \tag{7.2}$$

or

$$E(u_t u_{t'}) = \sigma^2 \quad (t = t') \tag{7.2a}$$

$$= 0 \quad (t \neq t'). \tag{7.2b}$$

In the general linear model, assumption (7.2) is replaced by

$$E(UU') = \sigma^2 \Omega, \tag{7.3}$$

where Ω is a positive definite matrix. This assumption naturally leads to estimation by generalized least squares (GLS). Generalized least squares estimation was briefly examined in chapter 3, in which we also investigated the consequences of estimating (7.1) by OLS when in fact GLS is the appropriate estimator. While this latter investigation was conducted in fairly general terms, the focus of chapter 3 was the special case of heteroscedastic disturbances. That is, assumption (7.2a) was relaxed but (7.2b) was retained.

Our concern in the present chapter will be with autocorrelated (but homoscedastic) disturbances. In other words, we shall relax assumption (7.2b), but retain (7.2a).

Unlike heteroscedasticity, the problem of autocorrelation in the context of a single equation has been extensively treated in the literature.[2] Some of

---

[1] See, for example, the brief development in chapter 2 above.
[2] See A.S. Goldberger, *Econometric theory*. New York, Wiley, 1964; and H. Theil, *Principles of econometrics*.

the more interesting and less exhaustively treated problems of autocorrelation occur in the context of simultaneous equations. As a consequence, the primary emphasis of the present chapter will be on autocorrelation in conjunction with simultaneous equation systems. As in earlier chapters, one of our principal concerns will be the use of maximum likelihood methods to estimate all relevant parameters. In particular we shall focus on the small sample properties of the maximum likelihood estimator.

A second objective of this chapter is an analysis of the tradeoff between accounting for the simultaneity in the equation system and the autocorrelation of the error term. As we shall see, the computational aspects of dealing with both simultaneity and autocorrelation are more burdensome than treating only one of these problems. As a consequence, empirical researchers typically tackle one or another of these problems but not both. As Goldberger has noted in general 'the researcher may well have to decide which complicating factor is most important in his data and adopt the model and procedure that would be appropriate if the others were absent'.[3] This type of research strategy is particularly evident in the construction of macroeconometric models where, characteristically, simultaneity is dealt with but autocorrelation is ignored.[4] In view of the rather widespread presence of autocorrelation in macroeconomic models, one may wonder whether this is a sensible strategy. Indeed, Fair concludes in the context of a recently developed small macroeconomic model 'that it is more important to account for serial correlation problems than it is to account for simultaneous equation bias'.[5] In the process of investigating the sampling properties of several alternative estimators, we shall attempt to gather some further evidence on this issue.

The present chapter is organized as follows. In section 7.2 we briefly re-

---

[3] See A.S. Goldberger, *op. cit.*, p. 388.

[4] This is true for many published large-scale econometric models such as the Wharton model and the Brookings model: M.K. Evans and L.R. Klein, *The Wharton econometric forecasting model* Wharton School of Finance and Commerce 1968; and J.S. Duesenberry, G. Fromm, L.R. Klein, and E. Kuh, *The Brookings quarterly econometric model of the United States.*, Rand McNally, 1965. In actual forecasting situations, autocorrelation is partially accounted for after the fact, by means of 'intercept adjustments'. See, for example, *Econometric models of cyclical behavior.* Conference on research in income and wealth (forthcoming NBER publication).

[5] See R.C. Fair, *A short-run forecasting model of the United States economy.* D.C. Heath and Co., 1971. Fair's model is noteworthy in that it has been estimated by a variant of two-stage least squares which also corrects for autocorrelation. Furthermore, Fair takes proper account of the presence of lagged dependent variables in his estimation. As indicated below, this can be of paramount importance.

view the consequences of autocorrelation for OLS estimates in a single equation context. We next consider several estimating methods for dealing with autocorrelation, first for a single equation and then in the context of a system of simultaneous equations. In section 7.3 we analyze a set of sampling experiments designed to shed some light on the small sample distribution for various estimators and on the tradeoff between simultaneity and autocorrelation.

7.2. Estimation with autocorrelated errors

Effects of autocorrelated errors in single equation models

In the present section we examine the model given by (7.1) and (7.3) with the further assumption of (7.2a). In other words, we deal with the general linear model but with homoscedastic disturbances.

As we have seen in chapter 3, the best linear unbiased estimator of the general linear model is the Aitken estimator given by

$$\tilde{\beta} = (X'\Omega^{-1}X)^{-1}(X'\Omega^{-1}Y) \tag{7.4}$$

with covariance matrix

$$\tilde{\Sigma} = \sigma^2(X'\Omega^{-1}X)^{-1}. \tag{7.5}$$

As a consequence, if Ω is known, then little more needs to be said. In general, of course, Ω will be unknown and must be estimated along with β. As in the case of heteroscedasticity, if nothing is known about the structure of Ω then estimation of Ω will be impossible since for n observations we must estimate $(n^2 - n + 2)/2$ parameters.[6]

It is, of course, always possible to estimate (7.1) by ordinary least squares. The consequences of estimation by OLS when assumption (7.2) is not fully met have been discussed in chapter 3. In particular, although the resulting estimator is unbiased[7], it yields inefficient estimates (relative to

---

[6] The symmetry of Ω means that generally there will be $n(n + 1)/2$ parameters, but the assumption of homoscedasticity reduces this by another $n - 1$.

[7] Throughout this discussion we are assuming that no lagged dependent variables appear in (7.1). As is well known, when such variables are present OLS will have a small-sample bias. When these variables appear in conjunction with autocorrelated disturbances, OLS will not even yield consistent estimates. For example, in the model $y_t = \beta y_{t-1} + u_t$, $u_t = \varrho u_{t-1} + \varepsilon_t$, it is easy to show that the OLS estimator $\hat{\beta}$ has the property that plim $\hat{\beta} = (\beta + \varrho)/(1 + \beta\varrho)$. Subsequent footnotes will further clarify the consequence of lagged variables.

(7.4)) and produces a biased covariance matrix. The relevant general expressions are given in chapter 3[8], but as with the case of heteroscedasticity, evaluation of these expressions is difficult unless a particularly tractable assumption is made about the form of Ω. Since, as indicated, such an assumption is needed for estimation purposes, we shall assume for simplicity that we are faced with a first-order autoregressive structure. In other words, we now write (7.2b) as

$$u_t = \varrho u_{t-1} + \varepsilon_t, \tag{7.6}$$

where ε_t are identically and independently distributed random variables with $E(\varepsilon_t) = 0$, $E(\varepsilon_t^2) = \sigma_\varepsilon^2$, and $|\varrho| < 1$.

Letting U be the column vector of the u_t's, it is well known that under the specification given by (7.6), the covariance matrix of the u_t's has the form[9]

$$E(UU') = \frac{\sigma_\varepsilon^2}{1-\varrho^2}
\begin{bmatrix}
1 & \varrho & \varrho^2 & \cdots & \varrho^{n-1} \\
\varrho & 1 & \varrho & \cdots & \varrho^{n-2} \\
\cdot & \cdot & \cdot & \cdots & \cdot \\
\varrho^{n-1} & \varrho^{n-2} & & \cdots & 1
\end{bmatrix}. \tag{7.7}$$

If we write (7.7) as $E(UU') = \sigma^2 V$, where $\sigma^2 = \sigma_\varepsilon^2/(1-\varrho^2)$ then the inverse of V can be written

$$V^{-1} = \frac{1}{1-\varrho^2}
\begin{bmatrix}
1 & -\varrho & 0 & \cdots & 0 & 0 \\
-\varrho & 1+\varrho^2 & -\varrho & \cdots & 0 & 0 \\
0 & -\varrho & 1+\varrho^2 & \cdots & 0 & 0 \\
\cdot & \cdot & \cdot & \cdots & \cdot & \cdot \\
0 & 0 & 0 & \cdots & 1+\varrho^2 & -\varrho \\
0 & 0 & 0 & \cdots & -\varrho & 1
\end{bmatrix}. \tag{7.8}$$

The relatively simple form of (7.8) allows us to make some more specific statements about the effects of autocorrelation on OLS estimates.

Consider, for example, the one variable regression model $y = a + bx + u$, where u obeys (7.6). It follows from (3.8) that the covariance matrix of the

---

[8] See (3.8) and (3.16).
[9] See J. Johnston, *Econometric methods*. New York, McGraw-Hill, 1963.

OLS estimator $\hat{\beta}$ is given by

$$\Sigma_{\hat{\beta}} = \sigma^2 (X'X)^{-1} (X'VX)(X'X)^{-1}.$$

In the present case this yields

$$\text{var}(\hat{b}) = \frac{\sigma^2}{\displaystyle\sum_{i=1}^{n} x_i^2} \left[1 + 2\varrho \, \frac{\displaystyle\sum_{i=1}^{n-1} x_i x_{i+1}}{\displaystyle\sum_{i=1}^{n} x_i^2} + 2\varrho^2 \, \frac{\displaystyle\sum_{i=1}^{n-2} x_i x_{i+2}}{\displaystyle\sum_{i=1}^{n} x_i^2} \right.$$

$$\left. + \cdots + 2\varrho^{n-1} \, \frac{x_1 x_n}{\displaystyle\sum_{i=1}^{n} x_i^2} \right] \tag{7.9}$$

where the x_i measure deviations around the mean. The first term in (7.9) is the classical expression for the sampling variance so that the OLS estimator of the sampling variance neglects all the remaining terms in (7.9). If ϱ is positive and, as is frequently the case with economic time series, x is positively autocorrelated, then the classical estimator will understate the true variance.

A further understatement will result when we replace σ^2 by the classical estimator of σ^2. This can be seen explicitly in the present case of a single regressor in which $s^2 = e'e/(n-2)$, where e is the vector of OLS residuals. From (3.12) we have that

$$E(e'e) = \sigma^2 [n - \text{tr}(X'X)^{-1}(X'VX)]. \tag{7.10}$$

In the present case the trace in (7.10) can be approximated by[10]

$$\text{tr}(X'X)^{-1}(X'VX) \approx \frac{2}{1-\varrho} + 2\varrho r, \tag{7.11}$$

where

$$r = \sum_{i=1}^{n-1} x_i x_{i+1} \Big/ \sum_{i=1}^{n} x_i^2.$$

---

[10] In the derivation of (7.11) we have ignored all terms in (7.9) except the first two. For further details on this derivation see H. Theil, *op. cit.*, ch. 6.3. For a related discussion see A. S. Goldberger, *op. cit.*, pp. 241–3.

Combining (7.10) and (7.11) we have

$$E(s^2) = \frac{\sigma^2 \left(n - \dfrac{2}{1 - \varrho} - 2\varrho r \right)}{n - 2},$$

which, for ϱ and r positive, clearly understimates σ^2.[11]

In addition to the inappropriateness of the classical variance estimator, we know that the OLS estimator is also less efficient than the corresponding GLS estimator given by (7.4). Some indication of this inefficiency in the simple case we are considering can be obtained by substituting (7.8) into (7.4) and comparing the result with (7.9). The aforementioned substitution yields

$$\text{var}\,(\tilde{b}) = \sigma_\varepsilon^2 \Bigg/ \left[(1 + \varrho^2) \sum_{i=1}^{n} x_i^2 - \varrho^2 (x_1^2 + x_n^2) - 2\varrho \sum_{i=1}^{n-1} x_i x_{i+1} \right], \quad (7.12)$$

where $\tilde{b}$ is the GLS estimator of b. Since we have $\sigma^2 = \sigma_\varepsilon^2/(1 - \varrho^2)$ we can obtain the following approximation[12]:

$$\frac{\text{var}\,\tilde{b}}{\text{var}\,\hat{b}} = \frac{1 - \varrho^2}{1 + \varrho^2 + 2\varrho^2 r\,(\varrho - 2r)}. \quad (7.13)$$

For example, for $r = \varrho = \tfrac{1}{2}$, the efficiency of OLS is about 67%, while for $\varrho = 0.9$, $r = 0$, the efficiency drops to about 10%.

It should be clear from this discussion, that if OLS estimation is used in the presence of autocorrelation, substantial inefficiencies may result and the validity of the standard procedures for testing hypotheses may be seriously impaired. On the other hand, since GLS estimates will not generally be available (due to the unknown covariance matrix), other methods of estimation must be sought.

Estimating methods in single equation models

For simplicity in exposition we confine our discussion to the model given by (7.1) and (7.6). While we focus on the first order autoregressive model, most of the methods discussed have natural generalizations to higher-order schemes.

---

[11] For high values of ϱ (and even low values of r so that the approximation in the previous footnote is good) the understatement in s^2 will be quite large for small or even moderate sized samples. For a more intuitive discussion on the bias in s^2 see J. Johnston, *op. cit.*, p. 189.

[12] The approximation ignores all terms but the first two in (7.9) and ignores the middle term in the denominator of (7.2). See H. Theil, *op. cit.*

We first consider the method of maximum likelihood and then indicate the correspondence with GLS. Rewrite the model given by (7.1) and (7.6) as

$$y_t = X_t\beta + u_t \quad (t = 1, \ldots, n) \tag{7.14a}$$

$$u_t = \varrho u_{t-1} + \varepsilon_t \quad (t = 1, \ldots, n), \tag{7.14b}$$

where X_t represents the tth row of the observation matrix X and where the ε_t are assumed to be normally distributed. Standard procedure would be to form the likelihood function of the ε_t. However, the likelihood of u_0, must be taken into account unless one is willing to assume that it is fixed. A more plausible assumption is that (7.14a) holds for $t = 0$, i.e. $y_0 = X_0\beta + u_0$, and u_0 is normally distributed with mean 0 and variance $\sigma_\varepsilon^2/(1 - \varrho^2)$ (i.e., the common variance of the u_t's). To facilitate comparison with the previous results in this section, however, it is simpler to rewrite (7.14b) as

$$u_1 = \varepsilon_1/\sqrt{1 - \varrho^2}, \quad u_t = \varrho u_{t-1} + \varepsilon_t \quad (t = 2, \ldots, n). \tag{7.14c}$$

We may further observe that if the $n \times n$ matrix T is defined as

$$T = \begin{bmatrix} \sqrt{1 - \varrho^2} & 0 & \cdots & 0 & 0 \\ -\varrho & 1 & \cdots & 0 & 0 \\ \multicolumn{5}{c}{\cdots\cdots\cdots\cdots\cdots} \\ 0 & 0 & \cdots & -\varrho & 1 \end{bmatrix} \tag{7.15}$$

then $TU = \varepsilon$. The likelihood function can now be written

$$L(\varepsilon_1, \ldots, \varepsilon_n) = (2\pi)^{-n/2} |\sigma_\varepsilon^2 I|^{-1/2} \exp\left\{-\frac{\varepsilon'\varepsilon}{2\sigma_\varepsilon^2}\right\} \tag{7.16a}$$

or, since the Jacobian of the transformation is $\det T = (1 - \varrho^2)^{1/2}$, as

$$L(u_1, \ldots, u_n) = (2\pi\sigma_\varepsilon^2)^{-n/2} (1 - \varrho^2)^{1/2} \exp\left\{-\frac{1}{2\sigma_\varepsilon^2} U'T'TU\right\}. \tag{7.16b}$$

After substitution for U from (7.1) this is then maximized with respect to ϱ, β and σ_ε^2.

It is straightforward to find the correspondence between maximizing (7.16) and minimizing the generalized sum of squares which is

$$(Y - X\beta)' V^{-1}(Y - X\beta)/\sigma^2 = [(Y - X\beta)' V^{-1}(Y - X\beta)] \left(\frac{1 - \varrho^2}{\sigma_\varepsilon^2}\right).$$
$$\tag{7.17}$$

To find the correspondence we observe that $T'T = V^{-1}(1 - \varrho^2)$, where T is the transformation which must be applied to (7.14a) such that it can be estimated by OLS. We note that given ϱ, minimizing (7.17) and maximizing (7.16) yield the same parameter estimates. However, if ϱ is estimated, the presence of the Jacobian term in (7.16b) implies that the two methods will give different answers. Of course, these differences disappear as sample size increases.

If there are k x's, the transformed equations have the following form:

$$y_1 \sqrt{1 - \varrho^2} = \sum_{h=1}^{k} \beta_h \left(x_{1h} \sqrt{1 - \varrho^2} \right) + \varepsilon_1 \sqrt{1 - \varrho^2} \qquad (7.18a)$$

$$y_t - \varrho y_{t-1} = \sum_{h=1}^{k} \beta_h (x_{th} - \varrho x_{t-1,h}) + (\varepsilon_t - \varrho \varepsilon_{t-1}) \quad (t = 2, \ldots, n). \qquad (7.18b)$$

In actual practice, whether one is dealing with either GLS or maximum likelihood, the added complication presented by the first observation is typically dropped. In GLS this means disregarding equation (7.18a). For maximum likelihood, this amounts to ignoring the first row of T in (7.15). Of course, ignoring the first observation makes no difference asymptotically.

For purposes of maximizing (7.16) or minimizing (7.17) one may use the techniques described in chapter 1. Alternatively one may use scanning techniques suggested by Hildreth and Lu and Dhrymes[13], or the iterative technique suggested by Cochrane and Orcutt.[14] The latter technique alternatively minimizes $\varepsilon'\varepsilon$ with respect to β conditionally on ϱ and then with respect to ϱ conditionally on β.[15]

---

[13] C. Hildreth and J. Y. Lu, *Demand relations with autocorrelated disturbances*. Technical Bulletin 276, Michigan State University, Agricultural Experiment Station, Nov. 1960. P. J. Dhrymes, On the treatment of certain recurrent non-linearities in regression analysis. *Southern Economic Journal* **33** (1966), 187–96.

[14] D. Cochrane and G. H. Orcutt, Application of least squares regression to relationships containing auto-correlated error terms. *Journal of the American Statistical Association* **44** (1949), 32–61.

[15] The convergence of this procedure has been discussed by J. D. Sargan, Wages and prices in the United Kingdom: a study in econometric methodology. In: *Econometric analysis for national economic planning*, Colston Papers No. 16, 1964, pp. 25–64; A. Zellner and G. C. Tiao, Bayesian analysis of the regression model with autocorrelated errors, *Journal of the American Statistical Association* **59** (1964), 763–78; J. P. Cooper, Asymptotic covariance matrix of procedures for linear regression in the presence of first order serially correlated disturbances (unpublished manuscript). The paper by Cooper also discusses the procedure of estimating the variance of $\hat{\beta}$ under the assumption that ϱ is known when it is in fact estimated.

There is also a one-iteration version of this method that is commonly used and worthy of a brief comment. On some general assumptions it is fairly straightforward to show that if a consistent estimate of ϱ, say $\hat{\varrho}$, is available, then the distribution of the $\hat{\beta}_h$ obtained by substituting $\hat{\varrho}$ and estimating (7.18b) by OLS, is asymptotically the same as the GLS estimate obtained with a known V.[16] Furthermore, if there are no lagged dependent variables among the x_h, then a consistent estimate of ϱ may be obtained by estimating (7.1) by OLS and using the residuals to compute $\hat{\varrho}$.[17] In the presence of lagged dependent variables, however, this does not produce a consistent estimate.[18]

Aside from GLS or maximum likelihood methods, one other technique worthy of mention is a procedure suggested by Durbin. In the case of the model given by

$$Y = X\beta + U$$

$$u_t = \varrho u_{t-1} + \varepsilon_t$$

one first regresses y_t on y_{t-1}, x_{ht} and x_{ht-1}. If the coefficient estimate of y_{t-1} is denoted by a, one then forms the variables $y_t - a y_{t-1}$, and $x_{ht} - a x_{ht-1}$ ($h = 1, \ldots, k$) and estimates β by using OLS applied to the transformed variables. Durbin shows that this estimator of β is consistent and asymptotically efficient.[19]

Autocorrelation in simultaneous equation systems

The literature on the problem of autocorrelation in the context of simultaneous equation systems is considerably sparser than the corresponding single equation case. Nevertheless, there have been several relevant theoretical developments. Sargan was the first seriously to investigate the use of

---

[16] For a proof of this see H. Theil, *op. cit.*

[17] For example, one can take

$$\hat{\varrho} = \frac{\dfrac{1}{n-1} \sum\limits_{t=1}^{n-1} e_t e_{t+1}}{\dfrac{1}{n-k} \sum\limits_{t=2}^{n} e_t^2}.$$

See *ibid.*, for a proof of consistency.

[18] For example, for the model considered in footnote 7, plim $\hat{\varrho} = \varrho \left[\dfrac{\beta (\beta + \varrho)}{1 + \beta \varrho} \right]$.

[19] J. Durbin, Estimation of parameters in time series regression models. *Journal of the Royal Statistical Society* **B 22** (1960), 139–53.

alternative maximum likelihood methods while more recently Hendry has further developed and applied one of the estimators proposed by Sargan. In addition, Amemiya has examined some two-stage least squares variants of one of Sargan's estimators while Fair has considered alternative TSLS estimators.[20] We shall briefly consider each of the estimators mentioned.

The full-information maximum likelihood estimator (FIML) is easily set out. Consider the standard model given by

$$By_t + \Gamma z_t = u_t \quad (t = 1, \ldots, T),$$ (7.19)

where y_t and z_t are vectors of observations at time t on the endogenous and predetermined variables respectively. If we set $x_t = \begin{pmatrix} y_t \\ z_t \end{pmatrix}$ and $A = (B\, \Gamma)$ we can rewrite (7.19) as

$$Ax_t = u_t.$$ (7.20)

As in our previous discussion we consider a first-order autoregressive process given by

$$u_t = Ru_{t-1} + \varepsilon_t,$$ (7.21)

where R is a matrix of autoregressive parameters[21] and the ε_t are jointly normally distributed with zero mean vector and covariance matrix Σ. Writing $X' = (x_1, \ldots, x_T)$, $U' = (u_1, \ldots, uT)$, and $E' = (\varepsilon_1, \ldots, \varepsilon_T)$, we can combine (7.20) and (7.21) to produce

$$AX' - RAX_1' = E',$$ (7.22)

where X_1 is the lagged matrix of x's. Since ε_t follows the multivariate normal distribution we have, using det for the determinant

$$P(\varepsilon_t) = (2\pi)^{-T/2} (\det \Sigma)^{-1/2} \exp\left(-\tfrac{1}{2}\varepsilon_t'\Sigma^{-1}\varepsilon_t\right)$$ (7.23)

[20] J.D.Sargan, The maximum likelihood estimation of economic relationships with autoregressive residuals. *Econometrica* **29** (1961), 414–26. D.F.Hendry, The estimation of complete models with errors generated by a vector autoregressive process, paper presented to the Meeting of the Econometric Society, Brussels, September 1969. T.Amemiya, Specification analysis in the estimation of parameters of a simultaneous equation model with autoregressive residuals. *Econometrica* **34** (1966), 283–306. R.C.Fair, The estimation of simultaneous equation models with lagged endogenous variables and first order serially correlated errors. *Econometrica* **38** (1970), 507–16.

[21] Specification (7.21) is somewhat more general than (7.6) since it permits the lagged value of the disturbances in all equations to influence a particular disturbance. If each disturbance is of the form (7.6), then R is a diagonal matrix. It should also be obvious that the methods described generalize easily to higher-order autoregressive processes.

so that the logarithmic likelihood function of (7.22) can be written

$$\log L = \text{constant} + T \log |\det B| - \frac{T}{2} \log (\det \Sigma)$$

$$- \frac{1}{2} \text{tr} \{(XA' - X_1 A'R') \Sigma^{-1} (AX' - RAX_1')\} = \text{constant} + T \log |\det B|$$

$$- \frac{T}{2} \log (\det \Sigma) - \frac{1}{2} \text{tr} \{\Sigma^{-1} [AX'XA' - 2RAX_1'XA' + RAX_1'X_1 A'R']\} \quad (7.24)$$

One then maximizes (7.24) with respect to Σ, R and A.[22] In principle this should be no more difficult than standard FIML calculations.

There are several things, however, to be noted about the presence of the matrix R. First, it is a simple matter to condense (7.24) with respect to R.[23] Second, there are several ways one can test the hypothesis $R = 0$. Perhaps the simplest is by use of the likelihood ratio test applied to (7.20) as compared to (7.20) and (7.21).[24] Alternatively, one may examine individual elements of R by use of the asymptotic covariance matrix. Finally, if R is known, it is a simple matter to maximize (7.24) with the imposition of the appropriate restriction.

Our discussion to date has focussed on the use of full information maximum likelihood methods. As indicated earlier, Sargan has proposed limited as well as full information methods. As one would expect, these limited information techniques possess two stage least squares analogues. For the case of a known covariance matrix of the disturbances in (7.20), such a technique was suggested by Theil who proposed 'generalized two stage least squares'. Basically, this method reduces to using Aitken's GLS estimator in both the first and second stages.[25] Amemiya has subsequently investigated such tech-

---

[22] Alternatively the likelihood function can be condensed with respect to Σ giving

$$\log L = k + T \log |\det B| - \frac{T}{2} \log (\det (AX'XA' - 2RAX_1'XA' + RAX_1'X_1 A'R')),$$

where the estimate for Σ is $\hat{\Sigma} = E'E/T$. For a more detailed derivation in the case of ho serial correlation see section 8.3.

[23] The expression in footnote 22 can be further condensed with respect to R yielding

$$\log L = k + T \log |\det B| - \frac{T}{2} \log (\det (AX'XA' - AX'X_1 A' (AX_1'X_1 A')^{-1} AX_1'XA')),$$

where the estimate for R is $\hat{R} = AX'X_1 A' (AX_1'X_1 A')^{-1}$.

[24] The appropriate ratio is distributed as a χ^2 statistic with m^2 degrees of freedom, where there are m stochastic equations. Hendry, *op. cit.*, proposes several alternative ways to test the hypothesis $R = 0$.

[25] H. Theil, *Economic forecasts and policy*, 2nd revised ed. Amsterdam, (North-Holland Publ. Co., 1965, p. 345.

niques more extensively in the case in which the covariance matrix is unknown but the form of the autoregressive structure is known.

Consider the problem of estimating the first equation of (7.19)

$$y = Y_1\beta_1 + X_1\gamma_1 + u_1 \tag{7.25}$$

with

$$u_{1t} = r_{11}u_{1t-1} + \varepsilon_{1t}, \tag{7.26}$$

where y is the observation vector on the endogeneous variable selected for
normalization, and where Y_1 and X_1 represent the observation matrices on
remaining included endogeneous and included exogenous variables respectively. Combining (7.25) and (7.26) (with $r_{11} = \varrho$) we obtain

$$y = \varrho y_{-1} + Y_1\beta_1 - \varrho Y_{1,-1}\beta_1 + X_1\gamma_1 - \varrho X_{1,-1}\gamma_1 + \varepsilon_1 \tag{7.27}$$

or

$$y^* = Y_1^*\beta_1 + X_1^*\gamma_1 + \varepsilon_1, \tag{7.28}$$

where $y_1^* = y_1 - \varrho y_{1,-1}$ and correspondingly for Y_1^* and X_1^*. For a given
value of ϱ (7.28) is estimated by obtaining a $\hat{Y}_1^*$ from a first stage regression
utilitizing Y_{-1}, X, and X_{-1} as instruments. As in the single equation case
one can then iterate or scan to provide estimates of both ϱ and β_1 and γ_1 that
minimize the error sum-of-squares of the second stage regression.[26] This then
provides an alternative technique which deals with the problem of simultaneity and autocorrelation.[27]

7.3. Some sampling experiments

In order to gather some experience with both the computational aspects and
the small sample properties of full-information maximum likelihood (FIML)
in the presence of autocorrelated errors and in order to shed some light on

---

[26] For details on this the reader should consult Amemiya, *op cit.*, who also provides alternative ways to choose instruments for the first stage. This problem is further considered
in Fair, *op. cit.*, who provides still additional methods that specifically deal with the
presence of lagged dependent variables.

[27] It should be noted that Amemiya's primary concern was the question of whether one
improved matters in terms of estimator efficiency if one assumed (7.26) was true but in
fact the disturbances were generated by $u_{1t} = r_{11}u_{1t-1} + r_{12}u_{2t-1} + \varepsilon_{1t}$. (He generally
does find an improvement.) This type of question is analogous to that considered in the
next section, where we examine methods which deal with simultaneity or autocorrelation separately.

some of the questions raised concerning the relative importance of simultaneity and autocorrelation, a number of sampling experiments were performed. For simplicity all the experiments were conducted with one two-equation model, which had the following form:

$$y_{1t} + b_{12}y_{2t} + c_{11}z_{1t} + c_{12}z_{2t} + c_{13}z_{3t} + c_{10} = u_{1t}$$
$$b_{21}y_{1t} + \quad y_{2t} \quad\quad\quad + \quad\quad\quad c_{23}z_{3t} + c_{24}z_{4t} + c_{20} = u_{2t}.$$

$$(7.29)$$

The error terms were assumed to be generated by a first-order Markov process of the form

$$u_{1t} = \varrho_1 u_{1t-1} + \varepsilon_{1t}$$
$$u_{2t} = \varrho_2 u_{2t-1} + \varepsilon_{2t},$$

$$(7.30)$$

where ε_{1t} and ε_{2t} were jointly normally distributed with a zero mean vector and a variance-covariance matrix given by Σ.

The procedures followed in the experiments were quite similar to those used at other points in this work. In particular, given a sample size n, the four non-constant exogenous variables were generated so as to have a given mean vector and covariance matrix. Three sets of exogeneous variables were employed in the experiments. One set was chosen to have zero correlations between pairs of exogeneous variables; the other two sets had varying degrees of multicollinearity. Given the type of intercorrelation employed in an experiment, and the size of the sample, the same exogeneous variables were employed in each replication. Furthermore, irrespective of the type of intercorrelation among the exogenous variables and the sample size, the exogenous variables were so generated as to have the same mean and variance throughout all experiments.[28] Next, given the covariance matrix Σ of the disturbances, a set of ε_{1t} and ε_{2t} were generated. Then given the values of the structural parameters (b's, c's and ϱ's) the endogenous variables were calculated.[29]

The next step was to secure estimates of the structural parameters by a number of different estimating techniques. The estimating methods utilized were ordinary least squares, standard two-stage least squares, and four variants of the maximum likelihood estimator. The first maximum likelihood

---

[28] The means for z_1, z_2, z_3, z_4 were 5, 10, 5, 5 and the corresponding variances were 8.33, 33.33, 8.33, 8.33.

[29] From (7.30) it is clear that starting values of the disturbances u_{10} and u_{20} are also needed to generate the data. In order to reduce the dependence of the results on the starting value, eqs. (7.30) were iterated for 100 periods before the beginning of the sample period for which y's were generated.

method (FIML 1) separately maximized the likelihood function associated with each of the two equations in the model. It is thus analogous to the Cochrane-Orcutt or Hildreth–Lu procedures in dealing with the autocorrelation of a single equation, but it ignores problems of simultaneity. The second maximum likelihood method (FIML 2) maximized the full likelihood function of the model but with the restriction that the ϱ's were zero. This is a misspecification which treats the problem of simultaneity but ignores autocorrelation. In this respect, FIML 2 is analogous to TSLS. The remaining two methods FIML 3 and FIML 4 each dealt with the full likelihood function. They differed in that for FIML 3 the ϱ's were estimated along with b's and c's while for FIML 4 the true values of the autocorrelation parameters were assumed known and only the b's and c's were estimated. FIML 4 is clearly unattainable in practice and in this respect is comparable to Theil's 'generalized two-stage least squares'.[30]

It should be noted that the four maximum likelihood estimates were computed with the aid of the modified quadratic hill-climbing algorithm using numerically evaluated derivatives. The estimates were computed in the order in which they have been discussed. The starting point for FIML 1 was the OLS estimate, for FIML 2 the TSLS estimate and for the remaining methods that one of all previous estimates that yielded the highest value for the likelihood function in question. It should also be mentioned that for purposes of computation the likelihood functions were concentrated with respect to the variances and/or covariances but not with respect to the autocorrelation parameters.

In addition to estimates of the structural parameters, we computed estimates of the sampling variances of the parameter estimates for each of the six methods. For the maximum likelihood methods these estimates were obtained by inversion of the appropriate matrix of second partial derivatives. Of course, for FIML 1 and FIML 2 (as well as for OLS and TSLS) there is an element of misspecification so that these estimates may be of questionable value. Indeed one of the purposes of this chapter is to examine the consequences of this misspecification.

For a given sample size, set of exogenous variables, and structural parameters, the above procedure was replicated 50 times. For each estimating

---

[30] The reader will note that we did not compute estimates by any of the variants of TSLS which are designed to deal with autocorrelation. While this might have been interesting, the main focus of the chapter is the behavior of FIML 3 estimates and the trade-off between simultaneity and autocorrelation.

method and for each structural coefficient (including the ϱ's where appropriate) we calculated a number of summary statistics. These included the mean estimate of a parameter (taken over all replications), the mean square error of a parameter estimate, and the mean of the estimated variances of the parameter estimates. These sample statistics were further refined, as detailed below, to provide overall measures on the performance of the various estimating methods.[31] In addition, within each experiment we also computed the percentage of the time that a given estimating method produced the 'best' estimate. In this context a 'best' estimator for a given parameter (in a given replication) is defined as the estimator producing the minimum absolute deviation from the true value of that parameter. These results are then aggregated over replications *and* coefficients to produce an overall 'percentage-win' statistic.

Before discussing the experiments in any detail it will be helpful to give an overview of their scope. Table 7.1 contains a brief outline of the salient features of the various cases examined. The structural parameters were fixed in all cases at the following values:

$$c_{11} = 1.0, \quad c_{12} = 2.0, \quad c_{13} = 3.0, \quad c_{10} = 10.0,$$
$$c_{23} = 1.0, \quad c_{24} = -2.0, \quad \text{and} \quad c_{20} = 20.0.$$

TABLE 7.1

Characteristics of the experiments

Case no.	ϱ_1	ϱ_2	b_{12}	b_{21}	n	Misc. comments
I	0.9	0.9	0.5	0.5	90	
II	0.9	0.9	0.5	0.5	180	
III	0.9	0.9	0.5	0.5	30	
IV	0.1	0.1	0.5	0.5	90	
V	0.1	0.1	0.5	0.5	30	
VI	0.0	0.0	0.5	0.5	90	
VII	0.0	0.0	0.5	0.5	30	
VIII	0.9	0.9	0.1	0.1	90	
IX	0.9	0.9	0.02	0.02	90	
X	0.1	0.1	0.1	0.1	90	
XI	0.9	0.9	0.5	0.5	90	Disturbance covariance = 0
XII	0.9	0.9	0.5	0.5	90	Correlated z's (Mild)
XIII	0.9	0.9	0.5	0.5	90	Correlated z's (More extreme)

---

[31] As indicated below, there were several instances where FIML3 estimates failed to converge for sample size 30 and big values of ϱ. This was taken into account in computing the summary statistics.

The variance-covariance matrix of the ε's was set at

$$\Sigma = \begin{bmatrix} 20 & 16 \\ 16 & 20 \end{bmatrix}$$

except in case XI, where

$$\Sigma = \begin{bmatrix} 20 & 0 \\ 0 & 20 \end{bmatrix}$$

i.e., the covariance between the ε's was set at zero. For all but the last two experiments, the exogenous variables were independently distributed. In cases XII and XIII, however, the exogenous variables are correlated with quite severe multicollinearity in case XIII.[32]

Case I is the benchmark experiment and as such will be discussed in somewhat more detail than the remaining cases. Cases II and III investigate the performance of the various methods with variation in sample size. Cases IV to VII examine the effects of reduced autocorrelation for two different sample sizes. For cases VI and VII the true ϱ's are zero, but both FIML 1 and FIML 3 attempt to estimate these parameters. Cases VIII and IX attempt to investigate effects on the empirical results of alterations in the structure. In some sense both experiments represent a reduction in the degree of simultaneity as compared with case I. Case X combines such a reduction with reduced autocorrelation permitting us to assess if the two different effects are in any way 'additive'. Case XI alters the structure in a different way—namely by eliminating the covariance between the disturbances in the two equations. It is thus another way of reducing the linkage between the two equations. Finally, as indicated, cases XII and XIII were designed to investigate the effects of multicollinearity on the empirical results.

The analysis of the results of the various experiments is first confined to a discussion of the b's and c's. The estimates of the autocorrelation parameters are treated next. Finally we undertake an analysis of the likelihood function for several of the experiments.

---

[32] The correlation matrices for the z's in the two experiments are

$$\begin{bmatrix} 1.00 & & & \\ 0.60 & 1.00 & & \\ 0.72 & 0.60 & 1.00 & \\ 0.72 & 0.60 & 0.72 & 1.00 \end{bmatrix} \text{ for case XII, and } \begin{bmatrix} 1.00 & & & \\ 0.87 & 1.00 & & \\ 0.90 & 0.87 & 1.00 & \\ 0.90 & 0.87 & 0.90 & 1.00 \end{bmatrix} \text{ for case XIII.}$$

Estimation of the b's and c's

We first consider experiment I which has a sample size of 90 and both values of ϱ equal to 0.9. Table 7.17[33] contains the mean estimates for each parameter for each estimating method. As this indicates, OLS produces the estimates with the largest mean biases. The biases are especially large for b_{12} and b_{21}, the coefficients most likely to be affected by simultaneity. FIML 1, the other method to ignore simultaneity, produces the next largest mean biases although its performance is clearly superior to OLS. The remaining four methods which all account for simultaneity both yield small biases and do quite comparably to each other. Since ignoring autocorrelation yields unbiased estimates in a single equation model in the absence of lagged dependent variables, these results are generally what one would expect.

Table 7.22 presents the corresponding mean square errors (MSE's) for case I. It is clear that the OLS estimator produces the largest MSE's and FIML 3 yields the smallest. It is perhaps even more illuminating to examine table 7.2 in which we have 'normalized' the MSE for each method and each

TABLE 7.2

Normalized MSE's: case I

	b_{12}	c_{11}	c_{12}	c_{13}	c_{10}	b_{21}	c_{23}	c_{24}	c_{20}
OLS	52.11	13.72	23.42	3.92	0.71	29.40	7.11	5.75	1.73
TSLS	7.10	12.97	5.78	3.42	0.71	4.28	3.81	6.15	0.71
FIML 1	2.11	2.13	1.90	0.96	0.66	1.45	0.91	0.88	0.75
FIML 2	8.13	4.52	5.73	4.00	0.62	4.27	4.41	6.90	0.71
FIML 3	0.94	0.95	0.88	1.00	0.81	0.87	0.97	0.97	0.91

parameter by dividing the MSE by the corresponding MSE for FIML 4. This table vividly reveals the extent to which the different methods have varying degrees of success. FIML 3, for example, is clearly the best method on this criterion as it has the lowest entries—save for the intercept. The additional fact that all the entries for FIML 3 are unity or less indicates that FIML 3 slightly outperforms FIML 4. The OLS estimates are clearly the worst yielding MSE's of over 50 times the MSE's of FIML 3 and FIML 4. The best estimator after FIML 3 is clearly FIML 1 which ignores simultaneity but does take into account the autocorrelation. FIML 1 is even slightly superior to

---

[33] Tables 7.17–7.31 are in Appendix D following this chapter.

FIML4. The two methods which treat simultaneity but ignore autocorrelation—namely TSLS and FIML2—do distinctly worse than FIML1 but appreciably better than OLS. They do, in fact, perform quite comparably to each other. Quite evidently, given the degree of simultaneity and the high autocorrelation present in case I, it is more important to take account of autocorrelation than simultaneity.

Some additional summary statistics for case I are contained in the first row of tables 7.3, 7.4, and 7.5. Tables 7.3 and 7.4 attempt to provide an overall summary of the MSE information. The entries are obtained by ranking the

TABLE 7.3

Sum of ranks for MSE's

Case no.	OLS	TSLS	FIML1	FIML2	FIML3	FIML4
I	48	37	20	37	19	28
II	51	44	22	38	11	23
III	45	39	13	35	39	18
IV	45	24	47	31	22	20
V	43	33	47	28	23	15
VI	49	34	36	$18\frac{1}{2}$	33	$18\frac{1}{2}$
VII	33	33	49	$17\frac{1}{2}$	39	$17\frac{1}{2}$
VIII	48	37	24	38	15	27
IX	49	38	24	36	16	26
X	42	31	42	31	24	19
XI	45	37	17	42	25	23
XII	52	38	25	36	20	18
XIII	48	43	28	35	19	16
Average	46.0	36.0	30.3	32.5	23.5	20.7

methods by the MSE's for each parameter and then summing over parameters. Since one is frequently less interested in the intercept than in the slope coefficients, table 7.4 reports the sums with the intercept omitted.[34]

Table 7.5 reports the 'coefficient-wins' statistic. The ranking of methods on the basis of this statistic generally agrees with the MSE ranking except that FIML1 appears to have a slight edge over FIML3. However, the pre-

[34] Since FIML3 and FIML4 tended to do worst in estimating the intercept this naturally improves their relative standing. The difficulties with the intercept are discussed more fully below.

TABLE 7.4

Sum of ranks for MSE's: intercept omitted

Case no.	OLS	TSLS	FIML1	FIML2	FIML3	FIML4
I	39	32	15	34	10	17
II	40	34	20	31	7	15
III	38	34	11	27	27	10
IV	33	16	37	25	20	16
V	32	27	36	20	21	11
VI	38	25	30	$14\frac{1}{2}$	25	$14\frac{1}{2}$
VII	27	27	39	$12\frac{1}{2}$	29	$12\frac{1}{2}$
VIII	37	32	19	35	8	16
IX	37	33	19	33	9	16
X	31	23	31	25	21	16
XI	38	31	15	36	13	14
XII	42	32	21	31	10	11
XIII	41	35	21	29	11	10
Average	36.4	29.3	24.2	27.2	16.2	13.8

TABLE 7.5

Percentage coefficient wins

Case no.	OLS	TSLS	FIML1	FIML2	FIML3	FIML4
I	0.093	0.140	0.231	0.109	0.222	0.204
II	0.056	0.087	0.193	0.078	0.302	0.284
III	0.120	0.100	0.256	0.107	0.162	0.256
IV	0.151	0.222	0.136	0.111	0.224	0.156
V	0.149	0.144	0.151	0.151	0.224	0.180
VI	0.169	0.236	0.147	0.193	0.256	—
VII	0.189	0.176	0.178	0.195	0.262	—
VIII	0.058	0.131	0.227	0.104	0.240	0.240
IX	0.071	0.133	0.193	0.109	0.262	0.231
X	0.104	0.207	0.144	0.149	0.227	0.169
XI	0.100	0.127	0.222	0.124	0.171	0.256
XII	0.071	0.098	0.244	0.138	0.198	0.251
XIII	0.089	0.089	0.184	0.129	0.236	0.273
Average*	0.097	0.134	0.198	0.119	0.224	0.227

* Average excludes cases VI and VII.

sence of FIML 4 in the calculations tends to muddy the direct comparison between FIML 1 and FIML 3.[35]

The final information available concerning case I is contained in table 7.27, which (for each parameter-method combination) reports the ratio of the mean square error to the mean of the variance estimate for each of the parameter estimates. As indicated in earlier chapters, if an estimating method is to provide a reliable indication of the precision of its estimates so as to permit significance tests, then the MSE's and the mean variances should correspond reasonably well to each other. In the present instance, the further an entry is from unity in table 7.27, the worse is this correspondence. Judged by this criterion both FIML 3 and FIML 4 provide quite reliable estimates of parameter variances. FIML 1, on the other hand, provides somewhat unsatisfactory parameter variances with the mean variances consistently understating the true variability of the estimates. TSLS and FIML 2 continue to perform quite comparably as both provide variance estimates which generally overstate the true estimator variability.[36] Finally OLS, as expected, provides the worst correspondence between MSE's and mean variances. What is even more troublesome, is that there is no consistent understatement or overstatement for OLS.

TABLE 7.6

Normalized MSE's: case II

	b_{12}	c_{11}	c_{12}	c_{13}	c_{10}	b_{21}	c_{23}	c_{24}	c_{20}
OLS	71.57	25.47	45.82	13.86	1.27	72.25	28.31	12.80	2.45
TSLS	8.25	20.32	6.40	19.13	1.39	5.14	6.42	9.15	0.97
FIML 1	4.22	3.10	3.03	1.26	0.72	2.05	1.26	0.86	0.69
FIML 2	8.24	5.94	6.57	19.10	1.23	5.05	6.28	9.15	0.96
FIML 3	0.86	0.84	0.89	0.99	0.83	0.97	0.95	0.84	0.77

[35] This is because FIML 3 and FIML 4 tend to be fairly similar and when FIML 4 obtains a coefficient win very often FIML 3 is next best. An upper bound to the performance of FIML 3 can be obtained by adding the last two columns of table 7.5. This would suggest that FIML 3 produces a coefficient win about twice as often as FIML 1. A slightly different statistic suggests this is not a marked overestimate. In particular, in case I 60% of the time FIML 3 was found closer to the true value of the parameter than was FIML 1.

[36] TSLS also does this in the context of the nonlinear simultaneous equation model reported in chapter 8.

We now turn to case II, which is identical to case I except that the sample size is 180. The mean estimates for this case are in table 7.18. It suffices to say, however, that the mean biases are comparable to the previous case except that the OLS estimates produce somewhat larger biases. The MSE's are presented in table 7.23. The MSE's for FIML3 and FIML4 are uniformly and substantially smaller than the corresponding MSE's in case I. For OLS, the MSE's are larger for six of the nine structural coefficients. The remaining three methods, FIML1, FIML2, and TSLS, generally produce smaller MSE's as compared with $n = 90$, but the improvement is not uniform nor is it as substantial as for FIML3 and FIML4. The normalized MSE information is summarized in table 7.6. This clearly shows the improved performance of FIML3 and FIML4 with increasing sample size.

As before the measures of overall rankings are given in tables 7.3 to 7.5. Both in terms of the coefficient wins and the sum-of-ranks, FIML3 is the best-performing method. This is followed by FIML4 and FIML1, then by the comparably performing FIML2 and TSLS, and finally by OLS. Table 7.28 presents the ratios of MSE's to mean variances (MV's). FIML3 and FIML4 continue to provide the best correspondence between MSE's and MV's and the comparison improves somewhat with sample size. FIML2 and TSLS also improve but the two methods which ignore simultaneity, OLS and FIML1, do somewhat worse as compared to $n = 90$.

We now turn to case III, which is identical to the previous two cases, except that $n = 30$. It should be noted at the outset that 5 of the 50 replications for FIML3 did not converge satisfactorily. This is discussed more fully below but should be borne in mind in interpreting the results for this case. Table 7.19 gives the mean estimates for this case and, as a comparison with table 7.17 reveals, except for OLS the mean biases are larger for $n = 30$ than they are for $n = 90$. Similarly, table 7.24 indicates that, again with the exception of OLS, the MSE's are appreciably larger than in the case of $n = 90$. The relative performance of the various methods can be gleaned from tables 7.3 to 7.5. These tables indicate that FIML1 performs comparably to FIML4, while the performance of FIML3 is not much better than TSLS or FIML2. OLS remains the worst method. As indicated in table 7.29, no method provides a very good correspondence between the MSE's and the MV's. FIML4 is the best but it consistently understates the true variability of the parameter estimates.

At this juncture, it will be helpful briefly to summarize the tendencies which emerge with the variation in sample size from $n = 30$ to $n = 180$. First, there is steady improvement in both the relative and absolute performance of FIML3. This is reflected in both the 'coefficient-wins', the sum-of-ranks and the improved correspondence between the MSE's and the MV's. Second there is a steady decline in the performance of OLS, as n increases while TSLS and FIML2 tend to hold their own. FIML1 loses ground as n increases, but nevertheless, given the high values of ϱ used in cases I–III, it is still true for $n = 180$ that FIML1, which only accounts for autocorrelation, is superior to both FIML2 or TSLS. We now turn to some experiments with a significantly reduced degree of autocorrelation.

Case IV is analogous to case I, except that $\varrho_1 = \varrho_2 = 0.1$. Table 7.20 contains the mean estimates from which it is evident that the largest mean biases occur, as before, for FIML1 and OLS. However, as compared to case I, OLS distinctly improves while FIML1 definitely worsens. Table 7.25 presents the MSE's while the normalized MSE's are presented in table 7.7.

TABLE 7.7

Normalized MSE's: case IV

	b_{12}	c_{11}	c_{12}	c_{13}	c_{10}	b_{21}	c_{23}	c_{24}	c_{20}
OLS	4.07	2.61	3.68	1.04	1.22	2.48	1.09	0.93	1.69
TSLS	0.99	2.71	0.97	1.00	1.12	1.03	1.00	0.91	1.04
FIML1	4.24	2.45	3.75	1.06	1.20	2.41	1.04	1.07	1.61
FIML2	1.04	1.03	1.02	1.05	1.01	1.02	1.06	0.96	1.03
FIML3	1.03	1.04	0.94	1.00	0.97	1.04	0.97	1.03	1.00

As inspection of this latter table indicates, FIML2 and FIML4 do quite comparably. Save for one coefficient, TSLS does about as well. On the other hand, FIML1 does appreciably worse than before, now ranking with OLS (which actually improves considerably in absolute terms). Clearly, the reduction of autocorrelation allows all of the methods which correct for simultaneity to do reasonably well. This general performance is also confirmed by the summary measures given in table 7.3 to 7.5. The improved performance of FIML2 and TSLS is also reflected in table 7.30 giving the ratio of MSE's to MV's. The most noteworthy thing about this table is the comparable performance of the four simultaneous methods. OLS still does relatively poorly on this score but improves considerably from case I.

The next three cases can be described quite rapidly. To conserve space we have omitted all the detailed results and simply report the overall summary statistics in tables 7.3 to 7.5. Case V is like case IV except that $n = 30$ and yields comparable findings. The MSE's obviously increase in absolute size but the general relative performance is as before. Noteworthy perhaps, is the fact that, relatively speaking, TSLS seems to do appreciably better for $n = 90$. Cases VI and VII are analogous to cases IV and V except that underlying true ϱ's are both zero. The difference between $\varrho = 0$ are $\varrho = 0.1$, however, is quite slight and the results are therefore quite comparable.[37] There is no noticeable effect on efficiency of estimating the two unneeded parameters (i.e., using FIML 3 instead of FIML 2) for $n = 90$. The average loss of efficiency is about 2 to 3 %. There is, as one would expect, a greater impact on efficiency for $n = 30$, but the effect still averages under 10 %. This is, generally, consistent with the relative performances of FIML 3 and FIML 4 in the earlier experiments. It should be noted, however, that although the absolute loss of efficiency is small, nevertheless comparing cases VI and VII with cases IV and V we see a marked improvement in the sum of ranks for FIML 2 and a noticeable decline for FIML 3.[38]

Cases VIII and IX differ from the basic case in that the parameters b_{12} and b_{21} are successively reduced from their values in case I. The purpose of these experiments is to examine the effect of reducing the degree of simultaneity in the model. In a two-equation model the reduction of the values of b_{12} and b_{21} is unambiguously equivalent to reducing the simultaneity, and in the limit when both b_{12} and b_{21} have gone to zero, and the two equations are parallel to the y_1 and y_2 axes respectively, there is no simultaneous equation bias in OLS.[39] This is true even if we include y_2 in the first equation when in fact it

---

[37] For cases VI and VII, FIML 4 and FIML 2 are, of course, identical estimators. In tables 7.3 and 7.4 these estimators were treated as having been tied. In table 7.5, the FIML 4 estimator is ignored.

[38] Another case, not separately reported in the tables, is one identical with case I except that $\varrho_1 = \varrho_2 = 0.5$. The results, as one might expect, are generally between those of case I and case IV. That is, the autocorrelation is sufficiently high so that FIML 1 still does reasonably well but the gap narrows between FIML 1 and the two methods that just correct for simultaneity (TSLS and FIML 2). FIML 3 and FIML 4 still remain the best two methods. The sums of the ranks for the MSE's for the six methods are 49, 34, 32, 42, 20 and 12 respectively. The percentage-win statistics for this case are 0.136, 0.164, 0.176, 0.173, 0.138, and 0.213 respectively and, once again, give a misleading comparison of the relative performance of FIML 3 and FIML 1. A direct comparison of these two methods shows that FIML 3 is actually closer to the true parameter values in about 63 % of the replications.

[39] In case there are more equations it is less obvious what changes in the B matrix reduce the degree of simultaneity. For a 4-equation example see R. E. Quandt, On certain small sample properties of k-class estimators. *International Economic Review* **6** (1965), 92–104.

does not belong there. Of course, including y_2 will reduce the efficiency of OLS, with the loss being greater the more y_2 is correlated with the included exogenous variables.[40] Furthermore, OLS will still suffer from ignoring both autocorrelation and the covariance between the disturbances. Because of these added complications, it is less clear that OLS will become uniformly more efficient as the b's are reduced. In addition, while the bias in OLS will disappear in the limit, there appears to be no reason to expect that the bias will get uniformly smaller as the b's are reduced. This is supported by Basmann who has indicated, although in a somewhat different context, that a change in the true value of a structural parameter can have opposite effects (on the mean biases and mean absolute standard deviations) in estimating the different structural parameters.[41] Furthermore these effects need not be monotonic with changes in the structural parameters.

We turn now to the results. Again to preserve space, we have omitted the detailed summary tables from the appendix. For the mean estimates, the most interesting information is summarized in table 7.8 below, which gives the absolute mean biases for OLS and FIML 3 for cases I, VIII and IX. As this table indicates, as b's change, the OLS bias increases for some coefficients and decreases for others. For FIML 3, there is a small but nevertheless uniform tendency for the bias to increase as the b's decrease. For both OLS and FIML 3, case VIII is closer in performance to case IX than to case I. Clearly it is somewhat dangerous to extrapolate changes on the basis of the limited evidence presented. Table 7.9 contains the information corresponding to table 7.8 for the MSE's. Here we find for both OLS and FIML 3 that some coefficients are estimated with greater precision, others with less. Generally speaking if the precision improves for OLS it also does so for FIML 3. In addition, as with the biases, case VIII is closer to IX than to I.

Table 7.10 presents the normalized MSE's for case VIII (they are omitted for case IX). Comparing table 7.8 with table 7.2 reveals the mixed changes

---

[40] In this case y_2 is a stochastic regressor but the exogenous variables are not. See A. S. Goldberger, *op. cit.* In the present case, there will be some correlation because y_2 depends on z_3 which appears in the first equation.

[41] Basmann deals with the GCL estimator in the absence of autocorrelation. See R. L. Basmann, Remarks concerning the application of exact finite sample distribution functions of GCL estimators in econometric statistical inference. *Journal of the American Statistical Association* **58** (1963), 943–76. For related expressions see D. H. Richardson, The exact distribution of a structural coefficient estimator. *Journal of the American Statistical Association* **63** (1968), 1214–26; and K. Takeuchi, Exact sampling moments of ordinary least squares, instrumental variables, and two-stage least squares estimators. *International Economic Review* **11** (1970), 1–12.

TABLE 7.8

Absolute mean bias

					OLS				
Case no.	b_{12}	c_{11}	c_{12}	c_{13}	c_{10}	b_{21}	c_{23}	c_{24}	c_{20}
I	0.245	0.151	0.228	0.171	1.164	0.102	0.233	0.071	4.540
VIII	0.516	0.010	0.027	0.418	3.465	0.258	0.632	0.076	9.988
IX	0.523	0.034	0.057	0.560	3.922	0.279	0.701	0.126	10.862

					FIML 3				
I	0.006	0.005	0.006	0.052	0.010	0.004	0.033	0.007	0.680
VIII	0.008	0.007	0.012	0.062	0.050	0.005	0.035	0.012	0.710
IX	0.009	0.008	0.014	0.065	0.060	0.005	0.035	0.013	0.710

TABLE 7.9

MSE's

					OLS				
I	0.0896	0.0824	0.1429	0.0895	19.78	0.0166	0.1838	0.0801	42.35
VIII	0.2972	0.0286	0.0105	0.2413	27.18	0.0780	0.5395	0.0709	120.80
IX	0.3095	0.0260	0.0117	0.3845	29.51	0.0879	0.6295	0.0789	141.30

					FIML 3				
I	0.0016	0.0057	0.0054	0.0227	22.63	0.0005	0.0252	0.0135	22.25
VIII	0.0029	0.0049	0.0038	0.0265	23.25	0.0009	0.0273	0.0150	22.59
IX	0.0030	0.0049	0.0039	0.0285	23.40	0.0009	0.0277	0.0154	22.67

resulting in OLS and FIML 1. In general FIML 2, FIML 3 and TSLS all perform (relative to FIML 4) quite comparably in cases VIII and I. As one would expect from this, the overall performance of the methods in cases VIII and IX is quite comparable to case I. On balance, tables 7.3 to 7.5 imply the following ranking for these cases: FIML 3, FIML 4, FIML 1, TSLS, FIML 2, and OLS. The ratios of the MSE's to the MV's (which are omitted to save space) generally reveal a steadily worsening performance for OLS and FIML 1 with not much change for the rest of the methods.

TABLE 7.10

Normalized MSE's: case VIII

	b_{12}	c_{11}	c_{12}	c_{13}	c_{10}	b_{21}	c_{23}	c_{24}	c_{20}
OLS	96.49	5.41	2.36	8.37	0.96	79.66	19.17	4.59	4.94
TSLS	7.45	14.16	4.29	3.24	0.72	4.15	3.83	6.20	0.78
FIML1	7.76	2.32	0.94	1.04	0.57	3.35	1.18	0.91	0.93
FIML2	8.82	4.21	4.03	3.25	0.64	4.21	4.48	6.97	0.77
FIML3	0.93	0.93	0.86	0.92	0.82	0.88	0.97	0.97	0.92

Taken as a whole, the results for cases VIII and IX indicate that overall performance in term of MSE's and the like may not be significantly changed by the types of parameter variations considered. Nevertheless, there are dramatic differences for particular coefficients (in both directions) and in the reliability of the sampling variances for the two single equation methods.

We now turn to case X which can be discussed quite briefly as it combines the features of cases IV and VIII—namely, reduced values for both the autocorrelation coefficients and the b's. As might be expected from the previous results, in overall terms this case behaves much more like case IV, which has reduced autocorrelation. This is reflected in the detailed mean estimates, and MSE's (not reported separately), the summary results in tables 7.3 to 7.5, and normalized MSE's in table 7.11. While case X (ϱ's $= 0.1$, b's $= 0.1$)

TABLE 7.11

Normalized MSE's: case X

	b_{12}	c_{11}	c_{12}	c_{13}	c_{10}	b_{21}	c_{23}	c_{24}	c_{20}
OLS	14.00	1.78	0.93	1.61	2.85	7.02	1.98	0.91	3.95
TSLS	0.99	2.63	1.06	1.02	1.12	1.05	1.00	0.91	1.04
FIML1	14.04	1.69	0.82	1.52	2.85	6.69	1.90	1.01	3.73
FIML2	1.04	1.03	1.05	1.05	1.02	1.03	1.06	0.98	1.03
FIML3	1.04	1.01	0.95	1.00	0.98	1.05	0.97	1.04	1.01

behaves overall like case IV (ϱ's $= 0.1$, b's $= 0.5$), the normalized MSE's indicate there are some striking differences for individual coefficients with OLS and FIML1. These differences, however, are precisely in the direction one would expect given the effects of changing the b's from 0.5 to 0.1 (i.e. compare table 7.2 and table 7.10).

Case XI can also be discussed quite briefly. It differs from the basic case I only in that the covariance between the disturbances has been set to zero. This fact, however, was not taken into account in the estimation by FIML 2, FIML 3, and FIML 4. Relative to case I, case XI produces a number of interesting differences. First, the mean biases tend to change sign (this is uniformly true for OLS) although not absolute magnitudes. As table 7.12 indicates, relatively speaking, TSLS does better uniformly for the first equation and worse, uniformly for the second. This is precisely the sort of effect that eliminating the covariance is likely to have. Despite these differences, the overall performance of the methods in case XI are quite analogous to case I.[42]

TABLE 7.12

Normalized MSE's: case XI

	b_{12}	c_{11}	c_{12}	c_{13}	c_{10}	b_{21}	c_{23}	c_{24}	c_{20}
OLS	28.66	5.14	14.86	3.77	0.62	44.89	10.16	5.70	1.02
TSLS	5.62	5.32	4.45	3.31	0.70	7.32	5.35	7.01	0.94
FIML 1	2.91	0.91	2.15	0.97	0.61	2.42	1.12	0.91	0.57
FIML 2	6.83	4.84	4.68	3.95	0.67	7.33	6.07	7.92	0.95
FIML 3	0.97	0.99	0.86	1.01	232.78	0.99	1.02	1.03	3.33

The final two cases to be considered differ from the benchmark case in that the exogenous variables are intercorrelated with case XIII representing the more severe multicollinearity.[43] Tables 7.21, 7.26 and 7.31 contain the relevant details (only for case XIII). The mean biases are generally quite comparable to case I for four of the methods but significantly exceed the case I biases for OLS and FIML 1. For these two methods the mean biases get steadily worse as the multicollinearity increases. On the other hand, all methods yield substantially larger MSE's for cases XII and XIII as compared with case I. Table 7.13 gives an example of the steady deterioration for FIML 4 as we pass from case I to XII to XIII. While all MSE's increase they

---

[42] One other change worthy of comment is the disastrous performance of FIML 3 in estimating the intercept in the first equation, as indicated by a MSE of 6283. This result is entirely due to a single sample which produced an estimate for the intercept of − 537. If this outlier were omitted and the MSE recomputed from the remaining cases, it would obtain the acceptable value of 5.05.

[43] The population correlation matrices are given in footnote 32. Of course, even in the case of independently generated exogenous variables, the actual samples will contain some intercorrelation.

TABLE 7.13

MSE's: FIML4

	b_{12}	c_{11}	c_{12}	c_{13}	c_{10}	b_{21}	c_{23}	c_{24}	c_{20}
I	0.0017	0.0060	0.0061	0.0228	27.90	0.0066	0.0258	0.0139	24.42
XII	0.0062	0.0202	0.0244	0.0396	27.73	0.0011	0.0720	0.0460	27.37
XIII	0.0120	0.0560	0.0375	0.1496	29.91	0.0015	0.1654	0.1451	27.18

TABLE 7.14

Normalized MSE's: case XIII

	b_{12}	c_{11}	c_{12}	c_{13}	c_{10}	b_{21}	c_{23}	c_{24}	c_{20}
OLS	21.65	19.72	17.87	8.66	4.06	70.24	28.02	17.13	0.50
TSLS	9.35	20.31	7.09	5.21	1.49	6.25	5.07	3.80	0.54
FIML1	4.69	3.75	3.88	1.90	1.13	3.26	1.78	1.40	0.60
FIML2	5.17	5.98	5.26	5.15	1.30	5.90	5.08	3.37	0.54
FIML3	1.06	0.96	1.11	1.05	1.01	1.11	1.00	0.94	1.08

do not do so uniformly. Table 7.14 gives the normalized MSE's for case XIII and this should be compared with table 7.2. Indeed as this comparison shows, the relative performance of FIML1 and TSLS is markedly deteriorated by multicollinearity. The same is true, although to a lesser extent, for OLS. Although FIML1 deteriorates, it remains, after FIML3 and FIML4, the best overall method for this case. In particular, it continues to outperform the two methods (TSLS and FIML2) which correct for simultaneity.

Estimation of the autocorrelation parameters

In discussing the results of the various experiments, we have thus far concentrated on the structural coefficients (i.e., the b's and the c's). We now turn to the estimates of ϱ_1 and ϱ_2. Only two of the methods, namely FIML1 and FIML3, provide estimates of the ϱ's, and tables 7.15 and 7.16 present some summary statistics for the various experiments for each of the two methods. More particularly, the tables contain estimates of the mean, the mean square error, and the mean square error—mean variance ratio.

The mean estimates of ϱ_1 and ϱ_2 by FIML3 consistently understate the true value of the parameters although not by a great deal. Furthermore, as the sample size increases there is a consistent and often marked improvement in the mean estimates. With the exception of ϱ_2 in experiment V the same

TABLE 7.15

FIML 1—estimation of ϱ

Case	Mean		MSE		MSE/MV	
	ϱ_1	ϱ_2	ϱ_1	ϱ_2	ϱ_1	ϱ_2
I	0.865	0.856	0.0042	0.0064	2.94	4.23
II	0.881	0.874	0.0011	0.0021	1.72	3.25
III	0.749	0.778	0.0404	0.0339	4.69	4.99
IV	0.095	0.097	0.0115	0.0094	1.92	1.60
V	0.062	0.102	0.0629	0.0392	3.26	2.06
VI	−0.006	0.003	0.0134	0.0092	2.21	1.53
VII	−0.045	−0.009	0.0477	0.0350	2.32	1.76
VIII	0.854	0.852	0.0056	0.0069	3.52	4.42
IX	0.851	0.851	0.0061	0.0070	3.72	4.48
X	0.074	0.093	0.0144	0.0093	2.38	1.58
XI	0.857	0.856	0.0058	0.0047	3.84	3.18
XII	0.864	0.855	0.0039	0.0067	2.71	4.40
XIII	0.862	0.852	0.0043	0.0072	2.86	4.68

TABLE 7.16

FIML 3—estimation of ϱ

	Mean		MSE		MSE/MV	
	ϱ_1	ϱ_2	ϱ_1	ϱ_2	ϱ_1	ϱ_2
I	0.876	0.865	0.0028	0.0040	1.69	2.37
II	0.889	0.878	0.0009	0.0014	1.36	2.00
III	0.727	0.819	0.0523	0.0301	7.07	3.80
IV	0.090	0.099	0.0057	0.0049	0.79	0.68
V	0.067	0.085	0.0416	0.0275	1.75	1.16
VI	−0.011	−0.004	0.0069	0.0061	0.93	0.83
VII	−0.025	−0.012	0.0293	0.0334	1.09	1.32
VIII	0.876	0.865	0.0028	0.0040	1.69	2.37
IX	0.876	0.865	0.0028	0.0040	1.69	2.37
X	0.090	0.099	0.0057	0.0049	0.79	0.68
XI	0.861	0.873	0.0066	0.0062	2.30	2.11
XII	0.877	0.864	0.0029	0.0042	1.67	2.33
XIII	0.877	0.866	0.0027	0.0042	1.71	2.54

two statements can be made about FIML1. As for a comparison between FIML1 and FIML3, FIML3 produces a smaller mean bias in 20 out of the 26 instances (2 ϱ's for each of 13 experiments). In terms of the MSE's, FIML3 yields smaller magnitudes in 23 out of the 26 cases.[44]

The MSE/MV ratio given in the tables can be compared with the correspondence statistics for the structural coefficients given in the appendix. In general, and especially when the true values of the ϱ's are 0.9, the correspondence between the MSE's and MV's for the ϱ's is worse than it is for the structural coefficients. The correspondence does, however, improve with increasing sample size. As between the two estimating methods, FIML3, as before, produces a more satisfactory correspondence than FIML1. In summary, insofar as one is concerned with estimating the ϱ's, FIML3 would seem to be a quite acceptable estimating method.[45]

---

[44] FIML3 produces a smaller mean bias in 21 out of 28 instances if we include the intermediate case with $\varrho_1 = \varrho_2 = 0.5$. It yields smaller MSE's in 25 out of 28 cases.

[45] The statistical significance of the ϱ's either can be tested jointly or individually by forming the variate $\hat{\varrho}/\text{st. dev.} (\hat{\varrho})$ and treating it as an approximately normally distributed variable. For purposes of testing we employed a 0.05 level of significance and, accordingly, used the critical value of 1.96. Testing was not done exhaustively but individual tests were performed for a number of cases. The table below gives the results:

Percent significance

Experiment	FIML1		FIML3	
	ϱ_1	ϱ_2	ϱ_1	ϱ_2
I	100	100	100	100
V	20	18	8	12
VI	10	6	2	2
VII	6	6	4	6
XIII	100	100	100	100

In the two cases when $\varrho = 0.9$, the estimated ϱ's are individually always significant. When both ϱ's $= 0.1$, FIML1 is more successful at detecting a significant ϱ, but this reflects the general understatement of the MV's for FIML1. This is further reflected in cases VI and VII where the two ϱ's are zero, and the apparently greater sensitivity of FIML1 to significant ϱ's leads to the incorrect statistical decision more often than in the case of FIML3.

Some properties of the likelihood surface

We now turn to two difficulties alluded to earlier in discussing the maximum likelihood estimates. The first difficulty concerns the behavior of the FIML 3 estimating method for case III (ϱ's $= 0.9$, $N = 30$). As indicated earlier, we experienced significant computational difficulties with FIML 3 for several of the replications for case III. The particular difficulty found was that after a number of iterations we reached a point where very small changes in the parameter estimates produced enormous changes in the value of the likelihood function.[46] Typically all of these cases involved a proposed iterative step, which would bring one of the ϱ's very close to (or some times over) unity. We attempted to circumvent these difficulties by fixing the relevant ϱ at 0.99 and then maximizing with respect to the remaining parameters, but the likelihood function nevertheless exhibited the same behavior. What seems to be the case here is that we have a situation in which there appears to be a near perfect fit. Furthermore, there may well be some difficulty with the accuracy of the numerical derivatives in such situations. The possibility of achieving a near perfect fit for some of the replications is enhanced by the relatively small sample size given the number of parameters to be estimated.[47] Indeed this difficulty disappears as the sample size increases.

The other difficulty noted earlier was the relatively poor performance of FIML 3 in estimating the intercept. We can examine this in a bit more detail by the use of likelihood contours. In particular for a given sample and for fixed values of all but two of the parameters, we may plot contour levels of the likelihood function as the two parameters of interest are varied. In fig. 7.1 we show one such contour map for case III ($n = 30$, ϱ's $= 0.9$), where the two parameters varied are ϱ_2 and c_{20} (the intercept in the second equation). The remaining parameters are held at their true (population) values. Figure 7.2 shows the same diagram for case V ($n = 30$, $\varrho = 0.1$) and there is a striking contrast between the two figures. In fig. 7.1, the contours are extremely flat with respect to the intercept indicating that a small change in the value of ϱ is consistent with a sharp change in the value of the intercept. By contrast, fig. 7.2 indicates exactly the opposite—namely the highest values

---

[46] This difficulty is exactly the opposite of the sort described in chapter 6. There near singularity due to multicollinearity and/or lack of identification yielded a likelihood function which was very flat. In the present case, the difficulty may reflect the fact that we have ignored the Jacobian term in (7.16b).

[47] The difficulty does not stem from sample size alone since it is not present in case V when $n = 30$ but the ϱ's $= 0.1$.

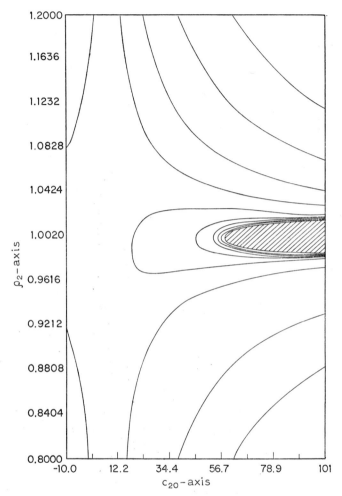

Fig. 7.1. Contours of the likelihood function for $n = 30$, $\varrho_1 = \varrho_2 = 0.9$ (Shaded area represents points at which function could not be evaluated).

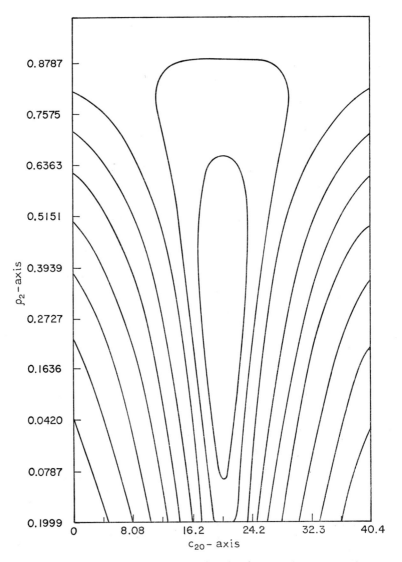

Fig. 7.2. Contours of likelihood function for $n = 30$, $\varrho_1 = \varrho_2 = 0.1$.

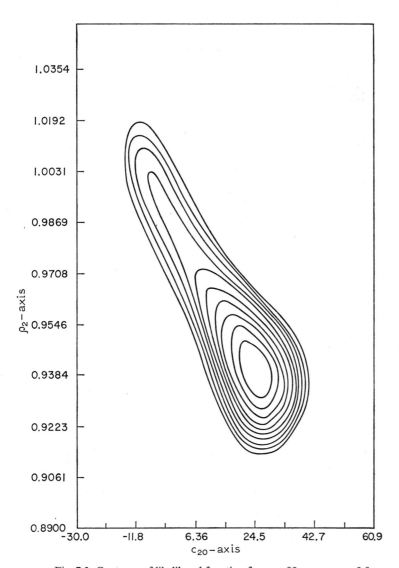

Fig. 7.3. Contours of likelihood function for $n = 90$, $\varrho_1 = \varrho_2 = 0.9$.

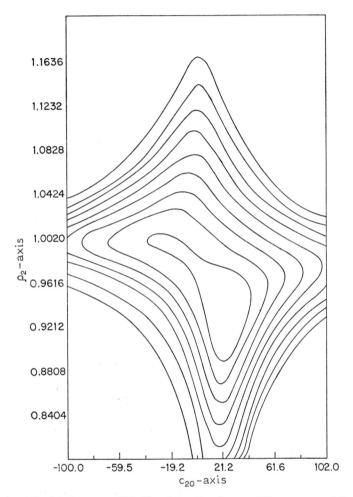

Fig. 7.4 Contours of likelihood function for $n = 180$, $\varrho_1 = \varrho_2 = 0.9$.

of the likelihood function are achieved over a fairly broad range of ϱ_2, but over a narrow range for the intercept. As one would expect, even from this rather partial examination of the likelihood surface, FIML 3 performs quite differently with respect to the intercept in cases III and V. Indeed, in case III, FIML 3 ranks last among all methods in terms of the MSE of both intercepts, whereas it ranks first for both intercepts for case V.[48]

Figures 7.3 and 7.4 present the analogous diagram for cases I and II, respectively. Quite evidently, there is substantially less flatness with respect to the intercept for the two larger sample sizes. This is reflected in the improved relative performance of FIML 3 for the two intercepts as sample size increases. This is shown in the MSE ranking given below:

MSE	Ranking of FIML 3	
n	c_{10}	c_{20}
30	6	6
90	5	4
180	2	2

7.4. Summary and conclusions

This chapter has focused on estimation in the presence of serially correlated errors in simultaneous equation systems. As in the case of heretoscedasticity examined in chapter 3, one of the most striking things that emerges is the extremely large impact of autocorrelation in terms of efficiency loss. Proceeding by the use of sampling experiments, we investigated the properties of several estimating methods. Of the methods considered, and given the range of the sampling experiments, the ranking of the methods would put

---

[48] The ratios for FIML 3 of the MSE's for case III to the MSE's for case V also demonstrate these same points. The ratios for the two equations including the ϱ's) are given below. They clearly show the relatively poor performance in case III for the intercept and the relatively good performance for the ϱ's.

	b's and c's				Intercepts ϱ's	
First equation	4.65	1.05	2.53	2.62	17.95	1.24
Second equation	6.06	2.90	2.76		40.22	1.07

FIML 4 and FIML 3 at the top, FIML 1 next, FIML 2 and TSLS next, and OLS last.[49]

Nevertheless, the overall rankings conceal a great deal of diversity. Given the 'extent of simultaneity', when autocorrelation is high (as it is in most of the experiments in this chapter), then a method that corrects for autocorrelation does better than a method that corrects for simultaneity. On the other hand, when autocorrelation is low, the reverse is true. Even when autocorrelation is high, however, there appears to be a significant further gain from correcting for simultaneity as well. This is in accord with Fair's findings in the context of a realistic macroeconometric model.[50] A further fact that argues for dealing with both simultaneity and autocorrelation is that the performance of FIML 1 is somewhat less impressive if one takes into account the mean variances it produces. In this regard, FIML 1 is like OLS, so that hypothesis testing in the context of FIML 1 becomes extremely risky.

While these conclusions would seem to have considerable practical application, since they are based on sampling experiments one should not overemphasize their generality. In the first instance, the conclusions need to be verified in a broader range of circumstances including alternative model structures and model sizes. One particular feature that appears worthy of further study is the behavior of the various methods when the true ϱ's are not all of the same sign.[51] Secondly, other difficulties that appear in realistic

---

[49] One indication of these overall rankings is given in the last rows of tables 7.3 to 7.5, which report average ranks and average percentage wins over the various experiments. A similar ranking results from the MSE 'wins' (i.e. smallest MSE for each parameterexperiment combination) which are tabulated below:

MSE wins

	Intercept	Other coeffs.
OLS	2	3
TSLS	3	5
FIML 1	10	14
FIML 2	$3\frac{1}{2}$	$4\frac{1}{2}$
FIML 3	5	38
FIML 4	$2\frac{1}{2}$	$25\frac{1}{2}$

[50] R.C.Fair, *A short-run forecasting model of the United States economy*, appendix B.

[51] Some extremely sketchy evidence on this point suggests that the general results of this chapter continue to hold when both ϱ's are negative but that FIML 3 and FIML 4 do less well when one ϱ is positive and the other negative.

situations such as nonlinearities and lagged variables must be brought into consideration. Finally, our results shed no light on the choice between alternative estimating methods that account for both simultaneity and autocorrelation. Clearly, as with most subjects in the volume, there remains considerable need for further research.

Appendix D: Additional tables for sampling experiments

TABLE 7.17

Mean estimates: case I

	b_{12}	c_{11}	c_{12}	c_{13}	c_{10}	b_{21}	c_{23}	c_{24}	c_{20}
OLS	0.255	1.151	2.278	3.171	8.836	0.398	0.767	-2.071	15.46
TSLS	0.503	1.014	1.990	3.078	9.658	0.498	1.073	-2.010	18.95
FIML1	0.450	1.007	2.070	3.059	9.612	0.481	0.989	-1.998	18.20
FIML2	0.506	0.993	1.988	3.064	9.790	0.500	1.062	-1.997	18.98
FIML3	0.506	1.005	2.006	3.052	10.010	0.496	1.037	-1.992	19.32
FIML4	0.505	1.011	2.005	3.055	9.623	0.496	1.033	-1.993	19.19

TABLE 7.18

Mean estimates: case II

	b_{12}	c_{11}	c_{12}	c_{13}	c_{10}	b_{21}	c_{23}	c_{24}	c_{20}
OLS	0.230	1.182	2.370	3.070	8.794	0.376	0.569	-2.168	15.72
TSLS	0.506	1.006	2.011	2.987	9.990	0.490	0.971	-2.025	19.36
FIML1	0.432	1.059	2.095	3.039	9.623	0.483	0.937	-2.023	19.20
FIML2	0.506	1.019	2.012	2.987	9.927	0.490	0.968	-2.024	19.36
FIML3	0.501	1.009	2.003	3.005	9.938	0.501	0.998	-1.997	19.82
FIML4	0.499	1.013	2.006	3.005	10.090	0.500	0.997	-1.999	20.07

TABLE 7.19

Mean estimates: case III

	b_{12}	c_{11}	c_{12}	c_{13}	c_{10}	b_{21}	c_{23}	c_{24}	c_{20}
OLS	0.263	0.974	2.328	3.130	10.180	0.418	0.757	-2.177	17.29
TSLS	0.464	0.978	2.097	2.991	10.120	0.472	0.923	-2.171	19.50
FIML1	0.420	0.960	2.105	3.027	9.907	0.482	0.999	-2.006	17.26
FIML2	0.467	0.936	2.075	2.953	10.590	0.484	0.935	-2.144	19.90
FIML3	0.555	0.924	1.883	2.928	10.270	0.512	1.038	-1.930	19.01
FIML4	0.511	0.975	1.983	3.002	8.773	0.499	1.040	-1.994	18.52

TABLE 7.20

Mean estimates: case IV

	b_{12}	c_{11}	c_{12}	c_{13}	c_{10}	b_{21}	c_{23}	c_{24}	c_{20}
OLS	0.411	1.049	2.118	3.073	9.360	0.466	0.932	-2.016	18.53
TSLS	0.508	0.997	2.006	3.033	9.723	0.492	1.013	-1.999	19.47
FIML1	0.409	1.042	2.121	3.080	9.378	0.467	0.933	-2.018	18.59
FIML2	0.507	0.995	2.009	3.038	9.711	0.493	1.019	-2.003	19.48
FIML3	0.507	0.996	2.007	3.033	9.750	0.493	1.008	-2.003	19.56
OIML4	0.506	0.997	2.010	3.035	9.714	0.492	1.010	-2.004	19.52

TABLE 7.21

Mean estimates: case XIII

	b_{12}	c_{11}	c_{12}	c_{13}	c_{10}	b_{21}	c_{23}	c_{24}	c_{20}
OLS	0.068	1.789	2.669	3.742	1.815	0.238	-0.681	-3.206	18.95
TSLS	0.555	0.876	1.905	2.989	10.630	0.500	1.018	-2.014	19.23
FIML1	0.274	1.344	2.349	3.422	5.931	0.439	0.618	-2.297	19.13
FIML2	0.505	1.110	1.965	2.970	9.837	0.496	1.021	-2.059	19.30
FIML3	0.507	0.983	1.971	3.040	9.792	0.502	1.056	-2.046	19.24
FIML4	0.499	1.009	1.989	3.028	9.761	0.499	1.040	-2.066	19.63

TABLE 7.22

Mean square errors: case I

	b_{12}	c_{11}	c_{12}	c_{13}	c_{10}	b_{21}	c_{23}	c_{24}	c_{20}
OLS	0.0896	0.0824	0.1429	0.0895	19.78	0.0166	0.1838	0.0801	42.35
TSLS	0.0122	0.0779	0.0353	0.0779	19.85	0.0024	0.0985	0.0857	17.29
FIML1	0.0036	0.0128	0.0116	0.0220	18.31	0.0008	0.0236	0.0123	18.29
FIML2	0.0140	0.0271	0.0349	0.0912	17.33	0.0024	0.1140	0.0961	17.31
FIML3	0.0016	0.0057	0.0054	0.0227	22.63	0.0005	0.0252	0.0135	22.25
FIML4	0.0017	0.0060	0.0061	0.0228	27.90	0.0006	0.0258	0.0139	24.42

TABLE 7.23

Mean square errors: case II

	b_{12}	c_{11}	c_{12}	c_{13}	c_{10}	b_{21}	c_{23}	c_{24}	c_{20}
OLS	0.0918	0.1029	0.1793	0.0681	15.32	0.0192	0.2956	0.0936	30.63
TSLS	0.0106	0.0821	0.0250	0.0940	16.76	0.0014	0.0670	0.0669	12.08
FIML1	0.0054	0.0125	0.0119	0.0062	8.69	0.0005	0.0131	0.0063	8.64
FIML2	0.0106	0.0240	0.0257	0.0939	14.84	0.0013	0.0656	0.0670	11.98
FIML3	0.0011	0.0034	0.0035	0.0049	9.99	0.0003	0.0099	0.0062	9.63
FIML4	0.0013	0.0040	0.0039	0.0049	12.08	0.0003	0.0104	0.0073	12.51

TABLE 7.24

Mean square errors: case III

	b_{12}	c_{11}	c_{12}	c_{13}	c_{10}	b_{21}	c_{23}	c_{24}	c_{20}
OLS	0.1034	0.1590	0.2677	0.2461	72.33	0.0202	0.2758	0.2602	97.95
TSLS	0.0378	0.1708	0.2061	0.2520	86.19	0.0098	0.1953	0.2866	80.01
FIML1	0.0134	0.0592	0.0400	0.0983	50.52	0.0024	0.0740	0.0829	70.88
FIML2	0.0351	0.1148	0.1653	0.2722	94.01	0.0084	0.1901	0.2522	81.08
FIML3	0.0464	0.0655	0.0989	0.2458	112.70	0.0103	0.2322	0.2355	244.30
FIML4	0.0117	0.0247	0.0331	0.0817	89.38	0.0022	0.0799	0.0899	89.70

TABLE 7.25

Mean square errors: case IV

	b_{12}	c_{11}	c_{12}	c_{13}	c_{10}	b_{21}	c_{23}	c_{24}	c_{20}
OLS	0.0097	0.0269	0.0192	0.0409	2.24	0.0018	0.0401	0.0149	4.79
TSLS	0.0024	0.0280	0.0051	0.0392	2.05	0.0008	0.0366	0.0146	2.94
FIML1	0.0100	0.0253	0.0195	0.0419	2.21	0.0018	0.0380	0.0172	4.58
FIML2	0.0025	0.0107	0.0053	0.0413	1.86	0.0008	0.0389	0.0155	2.94
FIML3	0.0024	0.0107	0.0049	0.0396	1.79	0.0008	0.0354	0.0165	2.83
FIML4	0.0024	0.0103	0.0052	0.0394	1.84	0.0007	0.0366	0.0161	2.84

TABLE 7.26

Mean square errors: case XIII

	b_{12}	c_{11}	c_{12}	c_{13}	c_{10}	b_{21}	c_{23}	c_{24}	c_{20}
OLS	0.2607	1.1040	0.6680	1.2950	121.40	0.1036	4.6350	2.4860	13.46
TSLS	0.1126	1.1370	0.2658	0.7792	44.53	0.0092	0.8382	0.5517	14.68
FIML1	0.0566	0.2097	0.1453	0.2837	33.69	0.0048	0.2934	0.2032	16.20
FIML2	0.0622	0.3349	0.1972	0.7702	38.79	0.0087	0.8404	0.4892	14.67
FIML3	0.0127	0.0538	0.0414	0.1571	30.19	0.0016	0.1647	0.1355	29.26
FIML4	0.0120	0.0560	0.0375	0.1496	29.91	0.0015	0.1654	0.1451	27.18

TABLE 7.27

Mean square error/mean variance: case I

	b_{12}	c_{11}	c_{12}	c_{13}	c_{10}	b_{21}	c_{23}	c_{24}	c_{20}
OLS	14.07	0.77	4.39	0.73	2.30	6.21	1.17	0.84	4.30
TSLS	0.79	0.60	0.72	0.53	1.89	0.70	0.56	0.84	1.51
FIML1	4.80	1.74	4.32	2.34	1.68	3.75	1.99	2.06	1.62
FIML2	0.85	0.53	0.72	0.59	1.84	0.67	0.64	0.92	1.51
FIML3	0.92	0.90	1.01	1.18	0.85	1.09	1.05	1.12	1.02
FIML4	0.95	0.91	1.09	1.15	1.24	1.21	1.05	1.13	1.03

TABLE 7.28

Mean square error/mean variance: case II

	b_{12}	c_{11}	c_{12}	c_{13}	c_{10}	b_{21}	c_{23}	c_{24}	c_{20}
OLS	25.12	1.83	8.82	1.25	3.42	12.67	3.87	1.49	6.00
TSLS	1.10	1.22	0.77	1.47	3.14	0.64	0.77	0.99	2.03
FIML1	11.69	3.29	6.85	1.79	1.80	4.39	2.64	1.51	1.77
FIML2	1.10	0.83	0.79	1.45	3.15	0.62	0.75	0.99	2.01
FIML3	0.99	0.97	0.90	0.68	0.75	1.00	0.98	0.73	0.78
FIML4	1.14	1.13	0.99	0.67	1.03	1.01	1.01	0.85	1.05

TABLE 7.29

Mean square error/mean variance: case III

	b_{12}	c_{11}	c_{12}	c_{13}	c_{10}	b_{21}	c_{23}	c_{24}	c_{20}
OLS	7.99	1.05	4.55	1.18	4.46	3.14	0.85	1.17	4.05
TSLS	1.33	0.92	2.29	0.97	4.23	1.27	0.56	1.22	2.96
FIML1	3.76	2.43	2.85	3.13	1.93	2.67	2.30	2.68	1.65
FIML2	1.22	1.37	1.76	1.03	4.83	0.95	0.54	1.03	2.86
FIML3	7.14	4.11	4.54	5.57	7.48	7.74	5.03	5.25	12.78
FIML4	1.40	1.13	1.18	1.39	1.84	1.23	1.23	1.46	1.59

TABLE 7.30

Mean square error/mean variance: case IV

	b_{12}	c_{11}	c_{12}	c_{13}	c_{10}	b_{21}	c_{23}	c_{24}	c_{20}
OLS	3.84	1.00	2.06	1.33	1.04	2.40	1.02	0.64	1.90
TSLS	0.72	0.99	0.48	1.22	0.91	0.93	0.91	0.62	1.13
FIML1	8.04	1.92	4.25	2.68	2.02	4.74	1.91	1.50	3.57
FIML2	0.74	0.90	0.51	1.23	0.92	0.92	0.95	0.65	1.12
FIML3	0.75	0.93	0.49	1.21	0.89	0.96	0.88	0.71	1.07
FIML4	0.73	0.90	0.53	1.20	0.91	0.92	0.91	0.70	1.08

TABLE 7.31

Mean square error/mean variance: case XIII

	b_{12}	c_{11}	c_{12}	c_{13}	c_{10}	b_{21}	c_{23}	c_{24}	c_{20}
OLS	24.41	1.97	4.90	2.30	15.47	15.88	5.91	3.89	2.91
TSLS	0.63	0.76	0.43	0.62	0.71	0.54	0.63	0.57	2.57
FIML1	18.95	4.57	9.73	5.97	3.31	5.48	3.86	4.24	1.57
FIML2	0.48	0.69	0.38	0.67	0.80	0.51	0.63	0.51	2.55
FIML3	1.05	1.08	0.85	1.29	1.03	0.80	0.98	1.33	1.34
FIML4	0.96	1.04	0.74	1.18	1.15	0.70	0.96	1.39	1.19

CHAPTER 8

NONLINEAR SIMULTANEOUS EQUATIONS

8.1. Introduction

The realization that economic variables are jointly dependent has led to the simultaneous-equation approach in econometrics. This approach recognizes that in a complete system of simultaneous equations (1) the conditions of the Markov theorem of least squares are not satisfied, and (2) the application of ordinary least squares to each equation does not yield consistent estimates.

The first developments along these lines dealt with linear structural models. For models of this type, considerable attention has been devoted both to establishing necessary and sufficient conditions for identifiability and to devising various alternative estimating methods that all share the property of consistency. Among these methods one may note full-information maximum likelihood, limited-information maximum likelihood, two-stage least squares, three-stage least squares, unbiased-k, indirect least squares, and others. Considerable research has also been aimed at deriving the asymptotic distribution of estimates from the various estimating methods. Despite the significant developments along the lines indicated, realistic empirical applications characteristically suffer from two additional problems—small sample sizes and nonlinearities—which have been less satisfactorily treated. The small-sample problem stems from the fact that asymptotic results provide no clear guide to finite sample distributions. Since rational choice among alternative methods requires knowledge of the small sample distributions of the various types of estimators, these have been examined in various ways. For a few special cases, exact finite sample distributions have been analytically derived.[1]

---

[1] See R. L. Basmann, A note on the exact finite sample frequency functions of generalized linear classical estimators in a leading three-equation case. *Journal of the American Statistical Association* **58** (1963), 161–71; D. G. Kabe, On the exact distributions of the GCL estimators in a leading three-equation case. *Journal of the American Statistical Association* **59** (1964), 881–94; D. H. Richardson, The exact distribution of a structural coefficient estimator. *Journal of the American Statistical Association* **63** (1968), 1214–26; and K. Takeuchi, Exact sampling moments of ordinary least squares, instrumental variables, and two-stage least squares estimators. *International Economic Review* **11** (1970), 1–12.

Other evidence has accumulated from a variety of sampling experiments.[2] Although these sampling experiments have yielded some results of broad usefulness, they have not been fully satisfactory, if for no other reason than the pervasive suspicion that the results are peculiar to the specification of the models and structures used in the experiments.[3]

Despite the widespread appearance of nonlinearities in virtually all major macroeconomic models, theoretical results about them have been slow in forthcoming. Nevertheless, progress has been made as in Fisher's results on identification and Kelejian's work on estimation.[4] In addition, there is a rather extensive body of literature on maximum likelihood estimation that can be applied to nonlinear econometric models.

The primary objectives of this chapter are to present some of the basic theoretical material on nonlinear simultaneous equations and to analyze the small-sample properties of the parameter estimates of two specific nonlinear systems. Our primary method of investigation is that of sampling experiments. Since nonlinearities can enter econometric models in a great variety of ways, all the criticisms that have been raised against sampling experiments as a research tool in this area can be repeated here with equal or even more justification. Although the results are limited, we nevertheless feel that they will prove of some usefulness in estimating the coefficients of nonlinear systems. More particularly, we shall address ourselves to the following questions:

(1) To what extent do previous experiments with linear models have relevance for nonlinear models, i.e., to what extent do the substantive conclusions derived from linear cases hold for nonlinear models?

---

[2] See A.L.Nagar, *Statistical estimation of simultaneous economic relationships*. Rotterdam, Netherlands School of Economics, 1959; R.E.Quandt, On certain small sample properties of k-class estimators. *International economic review* 6 (1965), 92–104; R.Summers, A capital intensive approach to the small sample properties of various simultaneous equation estimators. *Econometrica* 33 (1965), 1–41; and H.M.Wagner, A Monte Carlo study of estimates of simultaneous linear structural equations. *Econometrica* 27 (1958), 117–33.

[3] One interesting result in this regard is Kadane's finding that the relative efficiency of various estimating methods may depend on the size of the model. Most sampling experiments, of course, deal with quite small models. See J.B.Kadane, Comparison of k-class estimators when the disturbances are small. Cowles Foundation Discussion Paper No. 269.

[4] See F.M.Fisher, *The identification problem in econometrics*. New York, McGraw–Hill, 1966; and H.H.Kelejian, Two stage least squares and econometric systems linear in parameters but nonlinear in the endogenous variables. *Journal of the American Statistical Association* (forthcoming).

(2) Is there a variety of roughly equally sensible estimating methods for nonlinear models?

(3) Can an algorithm that has acceptable convergence properties (i.e., an algorithm that converges rapidly to the true maximum) be found for the calculation of full-information maximum likelihood estimates?

The next two sections are devoted to a discussion of the identification and estimation problems in nonlinear systems. Section 8.4 describes the models selected for study and the design of the experiments performed. Section 8.5 is devoted to an analysis of the results of the sampling experiments and the final section contains some conclusions.

8.2. Identification in nonlinear systems[5]

There are two types of nonlinearities that are of interest in the context of simultaneous equation models. The first nonlinearity concerns the variables while the second concerns nonlinear restrictions placed on the parameters. In the present chapter we shall only deal with nonlinearities of the first type. The nonlinearities we shall examine will, of course, be of the nontrivial type, which means that there is at least one endogenous variable that appears in the model in two linearly independent forms.[6]

To set out the general form of the model, let x be a vector of N 'basic' variables of which the first M are endogenous (denoted by y) and the remainder predetermined (denoted by z). Let $q(x)$ be an N^0-component column vector of functions of x. The general nonlinear model can then be written

$$A \, q(x) = u, \tag{8.1}$$

where A is an $M \times N^0$ matrix of parameters to be estimated, and u is a vector of disturbances. We further assume that (8.1) implicitly determines a single-valued continuous vector function such that $y = f(z, u)$, that the elements of $q(x)$ are linearly independent, and that the elements of u are distributed independently of the elements of z. We shall say more about the first assumption later on.

---

[5] The discussion in this section is largely based on F. M. Fisher, *op cit.*

[6] If a variable only appears, for example, in logarithmic form, then one could redefine variables so as to remove the nonlinearity.

As specific examples[7] of (8.1) consider the following two models. First

$$b_{11} \log y_1 + b_{12} \log y_2 + b_{13}z + b_{14} = u_1$$
$$b_{21}y_1 + b_{22}y_2 + b_{23}z \qquad = u,$$

$$(8.2)$$

where y_1 and y_2 are endogenous (t-subscript omitted) and z and a unit vector (denoted by 1) are predetermined. Then

$$q(x) = \begin{bmatrix} \log y_1 \\ \log y_2 \\ y_1 \\ y_2 \\ z \\ 1 \end{bmatrix}$$

$$(8.3)$$

and

$$A = \begin{bmatrix} b_{11} & b_{12} & 0 & 0 & b_{13} & b_{14} \\ 0 & 0 & b_{21} & b_{22} & b_{23} & 0 \end{bmatrix}.$$

As a second example, we have the following:

$$b_{11}y_1^2 + b_{12}y_2^2 + b_{13}y_1y_2 + b_{14}z + b_{15} = u_1$$
$$b_{21}y_1 + b_{22}y_2 = u_2,$$

$$(8.4)$$

where

$$q(x) = \begin{bmatrix} y_1^2 \\ y_2^2 \\ y_1y_2 \\ y_1 \\ y_2 \\ z \\ 1 \end{bmatrix}$$

$$(8.5)$$

and

$$A = \begin{bmatrix} b_{11} & b_{12} & b_{13} & 0 & 0 & b_{14} & b_{15} \\ 0 & 0 & 0 & b_{21} & b_{22} & 0 & 0 \end{bmatrix}.$$

We are now interested in examining conditions for identifiability of a particular equation of (8.1). Assume we are concerned with the first equation of

---

[7] F.M. Fisher, *op. cit.*, 133–4.

(8.1), i.e., we shall deal with the first row of A, say A_1. Before proceeding directly to the nonlinear case, it will be helpful to state the relevant results for the linear case, that is, when $q(x) \equiv x$. We shall only be concerned with identification under prior linear restrictions on the first equation, which take the form

$$A_1\phi = 0, \tag{8.6}$$

where ϕ is a matrix of constants. In this case, the necessary and sufficient rank condition for identifiability is that

$$\text{rank}\,(A\phi) = M - 1, \tag{8.7}$$

while the necessary order condition is that

$$\text{rank}\,(\phi) \geq M - 1. \tag{8.8}$$

An illuminating way to interpret this result is to consider the relative contribution of posterior (observational) and prior information (such as in ϕ) in achieving identification. If we rewrite eq. (8.1) for the linear case as

$$Ax = By + \Gamma z = u,$$

then the reduced form is given by

$$y = -B^{-1}\Gamma z + B^{-1}u = \Pi z + v.$$

If we define $W = \begin{bmatrix} \Pi \\ I \end{bmatrix}$, where I is an $(N - M)$ identity matrix, it is easy to verify that

$$A_1 W = 0 \tag{8.9}$$

and

$$AW = 0. \tag{8.10}$$

Eq. (8.9) simply states that A_1 is in the row kernel of matrix W, but as (8.10) indicates every row of A is in the row kernel as well so this does not distinguish A_1 from the other rows of A. The dimension of the row kernel of W is M and eq. (8.9) provides $N - M$ independent restrictions on A_1.[8] Since there are N parameters to identify in A_1, we need M more from prior restric-

---

[8] The row kernel of any $N \times S$ matrix P is the set of all N-vectors α such that $\alpha P = 0$. The statement follows from the theorem that the rank of a matrix plus the dimensionality of its row kernel equals the number of its rows. W is $N \times (N - M)$ and has rank $= N - M$.

tions and this is what is implied by the rank condition (8.7).[9] In other words the rank condition ensures that we can distinguish between the first equation and a linear combination of the equations in the model.

In the nonlinear case, unfortunately, this analysis does not go through without modification. The basic difference stems from the fact that whereas in the linear case only *linear* transformations of the equations of the model can generate restrictions on the equations that cannot be distinguished from the first one on the basis of observations (i.e., W above), in the general case one must also consider the possibility of nonlinear transformations. In particular, eq. (8.1) may imply that there exists a nonlinear function of the disturbances which is a *linear* function of the elements of $q(x)$. If the parameters of that function are linearly independent of the rows of A then this implied function generates an independent linear restriction on W. Put in another way, a linear combination of the implied function and the original structural equations may be indistinguishable from the true first equation.

The nature of the problem can best be illustrated by considering the second example given above in eq. (8.4). It is evident that squaring the second equation produces an equation which is linear in the elements of $q(x)$. In particular, it has the form

$$[b_{21}^2 \ b_{22}^2 \ 2b_{21}b_{22} \ 0 \ 0 \ 0 \ 0] \, q(x) = (u_2)^2,$$

which is clearly *linearly* independent of the original equations. Since any function of the disturbances is uncorrelated with any function of the predetermined variable, adding this implied equation to the first equation in (8.4) yields an equation that cannot be distinguished from the first equation, i.e., the first equation is not identified.[10] The possibility of nonlinear transformations yielding implied equations is thus the essential difference between the linear and nonlinear cases. With this in mind we can now concisely state Fisher's two main results on nonlinear identification.

Suppose there exist $M^* - M$ functions of the disturbances, such that

$$F^i(u_1, \ldots, u_M) = F^i[A_1 q(x), \ldots, A_M q(x)]$$
$$= h^i q(x) \quad (i = 1, \ldots, M^* - M), \qquad (8.11)$$

---

[9] The difference between M and $M-1$ in (8.7) reflects the fact that one fewer restriction is needed if we wish to identify coefficients only up to a factor of proportionality, i.e., if the equation is not normalized.

[10] The reader will note that squaring an equation would not produce a valid implied equation if, for example, we assumed the u's were normally distributed since the square of a normal variate is not normal. As in the linear case, specific assumptions about the disturbances can aid in achieving identification.

where the h^i are constant vectors such that the matrix

$$A^* = \begin{bmatrix} A \\ h^1 \\ \vdots \\ h^{M^*-M} \end{bmatrix}$$

has rank M^*, i.e., the vectors h^i are linearly independent both among themselves and with respect to the rows of A. Given this, Fisher has shown that if the prior restrictions take the form (8.6), i.e., $A_1\phi = 0$, then a necessary and sufficient condition for identifiability of the first equation is

$$\text{rank}\,(A^*\phi) = M^* - 1 \tag{8.12}$$

while a necessary condition is that

$$\text{rank}\,\phi \geq M^* - 1. \tag{8.13}$$

If we let $\tilde{u}_i \equiv F^i(u_1, \ldots, u_M)$ and define

$$u^* = \begin{bmatrix} u \\ \cdots \\ \tilde{u}_1 \\ \vdots \\ \tilde{u}_{M^*-M} \end{bmatrix}$$

then the rank and order conditions given in (8.12) and (8.13) are the same as those of the linear case applied to the expanded model $A^*q(x) = u^*$.

As a practical matter, of course, we need a method of determining M^* and all the vectors h^i, so that we can apply condition (8.12). Fortunately this is not very difficult. We shall first provide, however, an alternative interpretation of Fisher's results due to Kelejian, which further emphasizes the parallel between the linear and nonlinear cases.[11] As we shall see, this also has the virtue of bringing us directly to the estimation problem.

We again start from (8.1), i.e.,

$$Aq(x) = u,$$

---

[11] See H.H. Kelejian, Identification of nonlinear systems: an interpretation of Fisher. Princeton University, Econometric Research Program, Research Paper No. 22 (Revised), 1970, also paper delivered at the Second World Congress of the Econometric Society, Cambridge, Sept. 8–14, 1970. The reader should note that Kelejian's argument depends on the existence of certain expected values.

and we assume that the arguments in $q(x)$ are divided into M^0 endogenous functions (those involving the basic endogenous variables—the y's)[12] and $N^0 - M^0$ predetermined functions (those involving only the predetermined variables—the z's). We further assume that (8.1) can be solved for M endogenous functions in terms of the $M^0 - M$ remaining endogenous functions and the $N^0 - M^0$ predetermined functions.[13] We can rearrange the elements of q so that $q = (Y F G)$, where Y is the M component vector of endogenous functions for which we solve, F is the $(M^0 - M)$ component vector of the remaining endogenous functions and G is the $(N^0 - M^0)$ component vector of predetermined functions. With this we can rewrite (8.1) as

$$A_Y Y + A_F F + A_G G = u, \qquad (8.14)$$

where A_Y, A_F, and A_G are the appropriate submatrices of A.

The typical function in F, say f_i, can be written as

$$f_i = f_i(y, z), \qquad (8.15)$$

where y and z are the vectors of basic endogenous and predetermined variables respectively. The function f_i is a random variable so that, provided the expectation exists, we have

$$E[f_i | z] = b_i(z) \quad (i = 1, \ldots, M^0 - M) \qquad (8.16)$$

since the conditional expectation of a variable is generally a function of the conditioning variables.[14] From (8.16) we have

$$f_i = b_i + \varepsilon_i, \qquad (8.17)$$

where ε_i is a random variable such that $E[\varepsilon_i | z] = 0$. Substituting (8.17) into (8.14) we have

$$A_Y Y + A_F H + A_G G = v, \qquad (8.18)$$

where H is the $(M^0 - M)$ component vector with ith element b_i, and $v = u - A_F \varepsilon$, where ε is the $(M^0 - M)$ component vector of the ε_i.

Clearly $E[v | z] = 0$ and H is a function of the z's alone. Eq. (8.18) can now

---

[12] These functions may also include predetermined variables, e.g. $(y_1 z + y_2)$.

[13] M^0 cannot be less than M. If it were, we could replace each endogenous function by a new variable and (8.1) would then be a system of M equations linear in $M^0 < M$ (new) endogenous variables. But M^0 may be greater than M. For a particular equation this means that the same basic endogenous variable appears in both the endogenous function solved for and in the remaining functions.

[14] The b_i are, of course, generally unknown and in practice extremely difficult to compute. We return to this below.

be regarded as a linear model relating the elements of the vector of endogenous functions Y to the predetermined variables appearing in H and G.[15]

Assume for the moment that the $N^0 - M$ elements of H and G are linearly
dependent, i.e., they satisfy $J \le M^0 - M$ linear restrictions given by

$$BH + CG = 0, \qquad (8.19)$$

where B and C are constant matrices of order $J \times (M^0 - M)$ and $J \times (N^0 - M^0)$, respectively and B has rank J. Substituting (8.17) into (8.19)
produces

$$BF + CG = e, \qquad (8.20)$$

where $e = B\varepsilon$ and hence $E[e|z] = 0$. In other words, the J linear restrictions
given by (8.19) imply J additional equations for the elements of F which are
linearly independent of the M equations in (8.14). These implied equations
are precisely of the type considered above—that is they are the equations
that result from appropriate nonlinear transformations of the original structural equations.

That the existence of such equations implies a linear dependence between
H and G is also easy to see. Say we have J implied linearly independent equations of the form

$$D_Y Y + D_F F + D_G G = w. \qquad (8.21)$$

Solving (8.14) for Y and substituting into (8.21) yields

$$BF + CG = e, \qquad (8.22)$$

and if we now take conditional expectations of (8.22) with respect to z we get
(8.19) again.[16] In other words, the elements of H and G are linearly dependent if and only if implied equations exist.

The implications of this for identification of the first equation of (8.1) or
(8.14) are readily set out. First, consider the case in which no implied equa-

---

[15] There is a slight ambiguity here since we have not fully spelled out the functional form
of the basic variables. For example, if in model (8.2) we define y_1 and y_2 as the basic
variables and then solve for the endogenous functions $\log y_1$ and y_2, eq. (8.18) would
not yield the reduced form for variable y_1. On the other hand, one could assume the
basic variables are $\log y_1$ (say y_1') and y_2. The second equation in (8.2) would then have
a term in $\exp(y_1')$. However, if one is interested in predicting y_1, then this would not
be a desirable transformation. For an example of this in a related context see chapter 5.

[16] Clearly we must have

$$B = (D_F - D_Y A_Y^{-1} A_F), \quad C = (D_G - D_Y A_Y^{-1} A_G) \text{ and } e = w - D_Y A_Y^{-1} u.$$

tions exist.[17] Then one can apply standard linear identification theorems to eq. (8.18) and one has as a necessary and sufficient condition that rank $(A\phi) = M - 1$. In this case $M^* = M$ and $A^* \equiv A$ and the condition is identical to (8.12). In other words, for identification purposes we may count as valid prior restrictions the fact that certain predetermined *and* endogenous functions are excluded from the first equation.

The case in which implied equations exist is also easily treated. Assume known (8.14) and (8.20). Then partition F into F_1 and F_2, where F_1 is a vector of J functions in F for which (8.20) can be solved. If we set $E[F_2|z] = H_2$, then it is easily verified that H_2 and G are linearly independent. We can combine (8.14) and (8.20) into one system of $M^* = M + J$ equations as in

$$\begin{bmatrix} A_Y & A_{F_1} \\ 0 & B_1 \end{bmatrix}\begin{bmatrix} Y \\ F_1 \end{bmatrix} + \begin{bmatrix} A_{F_2} \\ B_2 \end{bmatrix} F_2 + \begin{bmatrix} A_G \\ C \end{bmatrix} G = \begin{bmatrix} u \\ e \end{bmatrix}, \qquad (8.23)$$

where A_{F_1}, A_{F_2}, B_1 and B_2 are the appropriate partitions of A_F and B. From the previous discussion, (8.23) can be regarded for purposes of identification as a linear system in $\begin{bmatrix} Y \\ F_1 \end{bmatrix}$. If we denote the complete (augmented) matrix of coefficients in (8.23) as A^*, the appropriate rank condition is rank $(A^*\phi) = M^* - 1$ or (8.12) again. In brief, we see that there is a closer relationship between the linear and nonlinear cases than appears at first blush.

There now remains the problem of how to determine M^* and the h^i vectors, i.e., the implied equations so that we can apply the identifiability conditions (8.12) and (8.13). In some instances, as in eqs. (8.4) above, the implied equations can be found by inspection but this is hardly a generally satisfactory technique. The discussion above related to eq. (8.20) in principle provides a way to compute the implied equations but this both requires detailed knowledge of the structure and is a nightmare to compute. Fortunately, Fisher has provided a simpler method.

Let $Q'(x)$ be the Jacobian matrix of $q(x)$, where the rows correspond to elements of $q(x)$ and columns to elements of x. That is, the ijth element is the partial derivative of the ith element of $q(x)$ with respect to the jth element of x.[18] $Q'(x)$ has only $N - 1$ columns since we cannot differentiate with respect to the constant. Furthermore, if the constant variable is the last element of

---

[17] It is easily seen that there must be at least one nonconstant predetermined variable for this to be the case.

[18] We, of course, need to assume the existence of the relevant partial derivatives.

$q(x)$, the N°th row of $Q'(x)$ is all zeros which we can omit from what follows. Given this, Fisher has shown that for all x satisfying $Aq(x) = 0$ we need only consider vectors h which satisfy

$$hQ'(x) = 0 \qquad (8.24)$$

in order to derive the implied equations.[19] As a practical illustration consider the two examples given above.

We first consider eqs. (8.4). For this model $q(x)$ is given by (8.5) and $Q'(x)$ by

$$Q'(x) = \begin{bmatrix} 2y_1 & 0 & 0 \\ 0 & 2y_2 & 0 \\ y_2 & y_1 & 0 \\ 1 & 0 & 0 \\ 0 & 1 & 0 \\ 0 & 0 & 1 \end{bmatrix}.$$

Suppose there exists a vector $h = (h_1, h_2, \ldots, h_6)$ such that $hQ'(x) = 0$ for x satisfying (8.4) with $u_1 = u_2 = 0$. We then have

$$2h_1 y_1 + h_3 y_2 + h_4 = 0$$

$$2h_2 y_2 + h_3 y_1 + h_5 = 0$$

$$h_6 = 0$$

and from (8.4) we have

$$y_1 = \frac{-b_{22}}{b_{21}} y_2,$$

so that

$$(b_{21} h_3 - 2b_{22} h_1) y_2 + b_{21} h_4 = 0$$

$$(2b_{21} h_2 - b_{22} h_3) y_2 + b_{21} h_5 = 0. \qquad (8.25)$$

Since (8.25) must hold for all values of y_2 which can be generated from (8.4) by varying z, the coefficients of y_2 and the constant terms in (8.25) must both be zero. Thus $h_4 = h_5 = 0$ and

$$h_1 = \frac{b_{21} h_3}{2b_{22}} \qquad h_2 = \frac{b_{22} h_3}{2b_{21}}.$$

---

[19] See F. M. Fisher, *op. cit.*, pp. 142–5. The primary advantage of working with (8.24) is that in general the unknown rows of A will not be in the row kernel of $Q'(x)$.

Thus there is only one linearly independent vector h satisfying (8.24). It is easy to verify that this h is proportional to $(b_{21}^2 \; b_{22}^2 \; 2b_{21}b_{22} \; 0\;0\;0)$. This is precisely the implied equation obtained from squaring the second equation of (8.24). The augmented matrix A^* is now

$$A^* = \begin{bmatrix} b_{11} & b_{12} & b_{13} & 0 & 0 & b_{14} & b_{15} \\ 0 & 0 & 0 & b_{21} & b_{22} & 0 & 0 \\ b_{21}^2 & b_{22}^2 & 2b_{21}b_{22} & 0 & 0 & 0 & 0 \end{bmatrix}$$

In model (8.4) there are two independent restrictions on the first equation so that the restriction matrix ϕ takes the form:

$$\phi = \begin{bmatrix} 0 & 0 \\ 0 & 0 \\ 0 & 0 \\ 1 & 0 \\ 0 & 1 \\ 0 & 0 \\ 0 & 0 \end{bmatrix}$$

Since $M^* = M + 1 = 3$, the order condition is satisfied. However,

$$A^*\phi = \begin{bmatrix} 0 & 0 \\ b_{21} & b_{22} \\ 0 & 0 \end{bmatrix}$$

and so the rank $(A^*\phi)$ is one, i.e. the rank condition fails and the first equation is not identified. As should be clear from this example, unlike the linear case, extreme care must be taken in using the order condition.

For the model given in eqs. (8.2) we have

$$Q'(x) = \begin{bmatrix} 1/y_1 & 0 & 0 \\ 0 & 1/y_2 & 0 \\ 1 & 0 & 0 \\ 0 & 1 & 0 \\ 0 & 0 & 1 \end{bmatrix}$$

and $hQ'(x) = 0$ implies

$$\frac{h_1}{y_1} + h_3 = 0$$

$$\frac{h_2}{y_2} + h_4 = 0$$

$$h_5 = 0,$$

which obviously can only be satisfied for $h = 0$. It follows that in this example $M^* = M$, and the matrix A^* is identical to A. The first equation is therefore identified.

These two examples provide a rather simple illustration of the steps necessary to examine the identification of a set of nonlinear equations. Clearly, while the above procedure works for larger systems[20], it may be tedious to find all the implied equations if the system is large. This is, however, a practical detail rather than a point of principle. Concerning the more basic question as to whether or not nonlinearities aid in identification, it is difficult to give a precise answer. They clearly do so in the linear-logarithmic example but this is not always the case. The most one can say in general is that nonlinearities never hinder identification and they may help. In view of the widespread nonlinearities in econometric models, this is nevertheless a reassuring result.

We have virtually concluded our discussion of nonlinear identification but there remains one further point that needs to be clarified—namely the problem of multiple solutions. As indicated earlier, Fisher derives his results by assuming a single-valued relationship between the endogenous variables and the predetermined variables and the disturbances. For nonlinear models, however, at least the formal possibility of multiple solutions may well exist. For example, the linear-logarithmic model given in (8.2) will possess two solutions for a broad range of the true parameter values.[21] If multiple solu-

---

[20] The reader may easily verify that the same type of calculation works when there is more than one implied equation, as for example in the model

$a_1 y_1 + a_2 y_2 = u_1$

$b_1 y_1 + b_2 y_3 = u_2$

$c_0 + c_1 y_1^2 + c_2 y_2^2 + c_3 y_3^2 + c_4 y_1 y_2 + c_5 y_1 y_3 + c_6 z = u_3.$

[21] For positive values of b_{11} and b_{12} the first equation will be asymptotic to the y_1, y_2 axes in the first quadrant. The reader may work out the conditions on the line given by the second equation (holding z and the disturbances constant) that will generate two intersections in this quadrant. For a particular instance of this see fig. 8.1 and also footnote 30.

tions are possible, a complete specification of the model must include a statement as to which of the several solution points 'nature' selects as an observation. Such a selection rule could depend on the value of one or more variables or disturbances that might be present in the model. In any event, the rule itself must, of necessity, be treated as part of the model. With such a rule, the univalence assumption cited above becomes more tenable. On the other hand, contrary to Fisher's implication, if a selection rule is necessary it must explicitly be taken into account in determining identification.[22] Unfortunately, this is easier said than done. Little is known about selection rules and how they would interact with the rest of the model.[23] This remains an interesting topic for future research.

8.3. Estimation in nonlinear systems

In discussing the question of estimation in a system of simultaneous equations in which nonlinearities are present in the variables we shall confine our attention for the present to two estimating methods—full-information, maximum-likelihood (FIML) and two-stage least squares (TSLS).[24] The former can, of course, be applied to either linear or nonlinear models in a fairly straightforward manner and has been employed in chapter 7. Conse-

---

[22] For a similar view see, H.H. Kelejian, *op. cit.*, Kelejian suggests that multiple solutions may aid in identification.

[23] Economic theory does provide some limited guidance on this. For example, in dynamic models stability conditions often rule out one or more possible equilibria. Furthermore, nonnegativity conditions often rule out some solutions.

[24] There are, of course, other methods that have been proposed for nonlinear systems. One approach would be an adaptation of the procedure suggested by H.Chernoff and H.Rubin, Asymptotic properties of limited-information estimates under generalized conditions. In: *Studies in Econometric Method*, edited by W.C.Hood and T.C.Koopmans. New York, Wiley, 1953. According to this procedure nonlinear functions of endogenous variables are written as new endogenous variables and for each such new variable a new (latent) equation is added to the model. The model can thus be linearized and, under very general conditions, its coefficients can be estimated by limited information maximum likelihood with the usual asymptotic properties. Another approach which has been utilized for several nonlinear models is the so-called 'repeated reduced-form' method. See, for example, R.L.Cooper, The predictive performance of quarterly econometric models of the U.S. (to appear in a forthcoming N.B.E.R. volume). Nevertheless, questions have been raised about the consistency of this method in the presence of nonlinearities. See S.M.Goldfeld, Comment on R.L.Cooper, *op. cit.* Finally, given a normalization rule, one can always fall back on ordinary least squares. This, in fact, is one of the methods we shall examine in the sampling experiments below.

quently, while we shall set out the problem for FIML, we shall not elaborate it at great length. TSLS, however, is a method which has been developed expressly in the context of linear systems and somewhat more justification is needed for its use in the present context.[25]

Full information maximum likelihood

Consider first a linear model that has the form

$$By_t + \Gamma z_t = u_t \quad (t = 1, \ldots, T), \tag{8.26}$$

where B is the $m \times m$ (nonsingular) matrix of coefficients of dependent variables, Γ is the matrix of coefficients of the predetermined variables, and y_t and z_t are vectors of endogenous and exogenous variables respectively. We further assume that the u_t have a multivariate normal distribution $N(0, \Sigma)$, where $\Sigma = E(u_t u_t')$ and that the disturbances in different periods are independently distributed.

The joint density of the u's is then given by

$$P(u_1, \ldots, u_T) = P(u_1) \cdots P(u_T)$$

$$= \frac{1}{(2\pi)^{mT/2} (\det \Sigma)^{T/2}} \exp\left[-\tfrac{1}{2} \sum_{t=1}^{T} u_t' \Sigma^{-1} u_t\right]. \tag{8.27}$$

For a particular t, the likelihood of the endogenous variables conditional upon the z's is then given by

$$P(y_t | z_t) = P(u_t | z_t) \left| \frac{\partial u_t}{\partial y_t} \right|, \tag{8.28}$$

where $|\partial u_t / \partial y_t|$ is the (absolute value of the) Jacobian of the transformation. From (8.26) we see that in the present case the Jacobian is simply $\det B$ (the same for all t). Consequently the likelihood function can be written

$$L = P(y_1, \ldots, y_T | z_1, \ldots, z_T) = |\det B|^T P(u_1) \cdots P(u_T). \tag{8.29}$$

Substituting (8.26) and (8.27) in (8.29) and taking logarithms yields

$$\log L = \frac{-mT}{2} \log 2\pi + T \log |\det B| - \frac{T}{2} \log (\det \Sigma)$$

$$- \tfrac{1}{2} \sum_{t=1}^{T} (By_t + \Gamma z_t)' \Sigma^{-1} (By_t + \Gamma z_t). \tag{8.30}$$

[25] H. Eisenpress and J. Greenstadt, The estimation of nonlinear econometric systems. *Econometrica* **34** (1966), 851–61, virtually rule out TSLS as a valid method in the context of nonlinear models.

Quite clearly maximizing (8.30) with respect to B, Γ and Σ is not a simple matter. Both the determinant of B and the last term in (8.30) are nonlinear functions of the unknown parameters and consequently the corresponding set of first-order conditions are nonlinear as well. Thus, as a practical matter, even in the case of a linear model, one must resort to numerical techniques for maximizing (8.30).

In the nonlinear case, one faces the same problem, in principle, although in practice the computations may be more difficult. If the model is written

$$F\,(y_t,\,z_t)\,=\,u_t, \tag{8.31}$$

then the corresponding log-likelihood function is given by

$$\log L \;=\; \frac{-mT}{2}\log 2\pi + \sum_{t=1}^{T}\log |J_t| - \frac{T}{2}\log\,(\det \Sigma) - \frac{1}{2}\sum_{t=1}^{T}u_t'\Sigma^{-1}u_t, \tag{8.32}$$

where u_t is given by (8.31) and where $|J_t|$ is the absolute value of the Jacobian $|\partial u_t/\partial y_t|$ which in general will no longer be constant for each observation. Thus in the general case (8.32) is the function to be maximized. One final point to note is that as in chapter 2, (2.48), we may obtain asymptotic variances and covariances by inverting the negative of the matrix of second partial derivatives of (8.32) evaluated at the estimates.

Two-stage least squares

For linear models this technique is applied by (a) designating one of the endogenous variables in each equation as dependent, (b) obtaining the reduced form, (c) replacing the values of the other endogenous variables by their values predicted from the reduced form, (d) regressing, by least squares, the designated dependent variable upon the new endogenous variables and the exogenous variables.

As should be evident from the discussion related to eq. (8.18) above, the major difficulty in applying TSLS to the nonlinear model stems from the nature of the reduced form. Fortunately, however, it can be shown that a procedure analogous to TSLS will work even in the nonlinear case.[26]

---

[26] The subsequent exposition is based on H.H. Kelejian, Two stage least squares and econometric systems linear in parameters but nonlinear in the endogenous variables. *Journal of the American Statistical Association* (forthcoming).

Consider again the nonlinear model given by (8.14), which we may rewrite for ease of exposition as

$$y_{it} = B_i F_{it} + C_i G_{it} + u_{it} \quad (i = 1, \ldots, m; \ t = 1, \ldots, T), \quad (8.33)$$

where y_{it} is the tth observation on the dependent variable in the ith equation, F_{it} is the vector of observations on the endogenous functions, and G_{it} is the vector of observations on the predetermined functions.[27] Let us consider the first equation of (8.33), which we assume has K_1 elements in F_{1t} given by $F_{1t} = (f_{1t}, \ldots, f_{K_1 t})$. The problem is now to remove the effects of the correlation between the f_{jt} and the disturbances.

It is clear that the first equation can be consistently estimated by TSLS if we can find K_1 instruments for the f_{jt} such that the instruments are uncorrelated with the disturbances, are linearly independent of the G_{1t}, and are correlated with the f_{jt}. We have seen in (8.17) that, provided the expectation exists, the f_{jt} may be written as

$$f_{jt} = E[f_{jt}|z_t] + \varepsilon_{jt} = h_{jt} + \varepsilon_{jt}, \quad (8.34)$$

where the h_{jt} are solely functions of the predetermined variables. As indicated above, if the first equation of (8.33) is identified then the h_{jt} and the elements of G_{1t} are linearly independent. Consequently if the h_{jt} were known they could be used as the TSLS instruments for the f_{jt}. Unfortunately, the h_{jt} are generally unknown. In the first instance the h_{jt} depend upon the unknown structural parameters of the original model. In addition, unlike the linear case, the h_{jt} depend on knowledge of the joint distribution of the original disturbances in order that the expectation operation in (8.34) can be carried out. Finally, the calculation of expected values in (8.34) may not yield an expression in closed form so the h_{jt} may only be expressible as multiple integrals.

A rather obvious way out of the difficulty created by the lack of knowledge of the h_{jt} is to approximate them by polynomials in the elements of G_t. More particularly, the analogue of the first stage in the linear case consists of regressing the f_{jt} on a polynomial in the elements of G_t and using the predicted values from this regression in the second stage. If we let M_t be the vector of observations on the elements of the polynomial with corresponding matrix M, and we let f_j be the vector of observations on f_{jt}, then the instruments we

---

[27] In going from (8.14) to (8.33) we have assumed that the basic endogenous variables can be isolated on the left-hand side of (8.33). As indicated in footnote 15 above, this may require a change in variables. Furthermore, it is possible that it cannot be done at all.

are using are $\hat{P}_{jt} = M_t \hat{\Pi}_j$, where $\hat{\Pi}_j = (M'M)^{-1} M' f_j$. We further define $\text{plim}_{T \to \infty} \hat{\Pi}_j = \Pi_j$, and $P_{jt} = M_t \Pi_j$. It is then easy to show that as the sample size tends to infinity $\text{plim } \hat{P}_{jt} = P_{jt}$, which is solely a function of predetermined variables, so that $\hat{P}_{jt}$ is uncorrelated in the limit with the disturbance term in the first equation, u_{1t}. Consequently, TSLS estimates based on these instruments will be consistent.[28]

Two additional points concerning the above argument are worthy of note. First, in regressing the f_{jt} on the polynomials in the elements of G_t, the same degree polynomial must be used for each $j = 1, \ldots, K_1$. If this is not done, the instruments $\hat{P}_{jt}$, will not, in general, be orthogonal to the estimated residuals $\hat{w}_{jt}$ defined by $f_{jt} = P_{jt} + \hat{w}_{jt}$, so that the procedure will not yield consistent estimates. More particularly, we require that $\hat{P}_{jt}$ and $\hat{w}_{kt}$ be uncorrelated ($j, k = 1, \ldots, K_1$) and the properties of least squares assure that this condition is met if we use the same variables (i.e., same degree) in each polynomial. Second, one must use the precise functional form as given by f_{jt}. One cannot regress the basic endogenous variables which comprise f_{jt} on the polynomial in the elements of G_t, and then transform these according to the functions specified by f. For example, if $f_{1t} = \log y_{1t}$, one may not proceed by first obtaining $\hat{y}_{1t}$ and then using $\log \hat{y}_{1t}$ as an instrument.[29]

This concludes our discussion of estimation in nonlinear systems. We have presented two methods—FIML and TSLS—which produce estimates having desirable large-sample properties. We now focus on the question of the small-sample distribution of these estimators. As indicated above, we shall approach this problem by conducting sampling experiments for some specific nonlinear models.

8.4. Models and design of experiments

Models

Two basic sets of structural equations have been employed in the study. They are as follows:

Model I:

$$b_{11} \log y_{1t} + b_{12} \log y_{2t} + b_{13} z_t + b_{14} = u_{1t}$$

$$b_{21} y_{1t} + b_{22} y_{2t} + b_{23} z_t = u_{2t},$$

---

[28] See *ibid.*, for a more detailed justification.

[29] This follows from the fact that the expectation of a function is generally unequal to the function of the expectation. Hence, if we write $\log y_{1t} = \log \hat{y}_{1t} + v_t$, v_t will be correlated with $\log \hat{y}_{1t}$.

with covariance matrix Σ_I, and
Model II:

$$b_{11}y_{1t} + b_{12}y_{2t}^2 + b_{13}z_t + b_{14} = u_{1t}$$

$$b_{21}y_{1t}z_t + b_{22}y_{2t} + b_{24} = u_{2t}$$

with covariance matrix Σ_{II}, where, in both models, z is an exogenous variable, (u_1, u_2) are jointly normally distributed with mean $= (0, 0)$ and the indicated covariance matrix and where $E(u_t u_{t-\theta}) = 0$ for all $\theta \neq 0$.

Sampling experiments were performed with both models. The experiments, the detailed characteristics of which are described below, consisted of generating normally distributed error terms, solving the structural equations for the values of the endogenous variables and using the resulting data series to estimate the coefficients of the equations in several ways. The estimates were then used to generate predictions for the endogenous variables.[30]

Estimating methods

For purposes of estimation we normalized the equations in both models. In Model I the first equation was normalized on $\log y_1$ and the second equation was normalized on y_2 (i.e., $b_{11} = b_{22} = 1$). In Model II the first equation was normalized on y_1 and the second on y_2 (i.e., $b_1 = b_{22} = 1$).[31]

---

[30] Since in general Model I cannot be solved for the endogenous variables in closed form, we obtained solution values by solving an equivalent problem which is to minimize $[(b_{11} \log y_{1t} + b_{12} \log y_{2t} + b_{13}z_t + b_{14} - u_{1t})^2 + (b_{21}y_{1t} + b_{22}y_{2t} + b_{23}z_t - u_{2t})^2]$. As a result of the minimization there is a minor element of approximation in the data. The approximation is not theoretical but computational in origin and is due to the fact that the minimization has been performed by iterative methods. Since the criterion for the acceptance of a sample point was that the equation had to be satisfied to within 10^{-3}, the effect will be negligible. Because this procedure is time consuming, no predictions were generated for Model I. The second model can be solved directly and posed no problem of this kind.

It may be noted that, for the particular structural parameters utilized in this paper, the problem of solving for the endogenous variables reduces to determining the real roots of a certain quintic polynomial. This polynomial arises from exponentiating the first equation and substituting from the second. Using Descartes' Rule of Signs it can be shown that it has three real roots in general of which one is extraneous, having been introduced by the exponentiation. Neglecting this extraneous root, two roots remain as admissible solutions to Model I.

[31] As has been noted before elsewhere, normalization, in the context of ordinary least squares and two-stage least squares, introduces an element of arbitrariness. However, since we have normalized in the same way for both methods they are, at least comparable. See R. Summers, *op. cit.*

It was not our intention to achieve completeness in the variety of estimating methods subjected to test. We simply confined our attention to three methods: (1) Ordinary least squares, (2) Full-information maximum likelihood, and (3) Two-stage least squares.

(1) *Ordinary Least Squares (OLS).* For OLS the variable of normalization in each equation was regarded as the dependent variable and all others were considered independent variables in that equation. The coefficients were then estimated by least squares.

(2) *Full-Information Maximum Likelihood (FIML).* According to this method we construct the likelihood function for each structure and choose as our estimates those values of the coefficients and variances and covariances that maximize the likelihood function. We used the quadratic hill-climbing algorithm in order to maximize the likelihood function.[32]

(3) *Two-Stage Least Squares (TSLS).* As indicated above, a general feature of nonlinear models is that reduced forms vary from model to model, are difficult to compute, and may not even have a representation in closed form. As a consequence, in computing TSLS estimates one must resort to the use of polynomials in the predetermined variables as an approximation to the reduced form. For both models we used approximating polynomials of the second degree.[33] We then computed TSLS estimates as indicated above.[34]

Identification

Examination of Model I reveals that it is identical to the model considered in (8.2) above and consequently it is identified. It can also easily be verified by the methods outlined above that Model II is similarly identified. There remains, however, the issue of multiple solutions. As indicated earlier, if it is

[32] The robustness of the computational technique was tested by computing the answers with several starting-points. These various estimates usually coincided to four significant digits. This suggests, but does not prove, that the likelihood function is unimodal in a fairly broad neighborhood about the true values of the parameters.

[33] We are indebted to L.R.Klein for pointing out that the use of polynomials of degree one would not allow the computation of estimates of the parameters of the first equation in each model since it would lead to an exact singularity. In S.M.Goldfeld and R.E.Quandt, *op. cit.*, we had reported estimates using such a polynomial for Model I. It was subsequently discovered that these results were based on a computer programming error.

[34] It should be noted that for Model I we performed a few computations in which we regressed y_2 on a polynomial in z to compute a $\hat{y}_2$ and then used log $\hat{y}_2$ for the second stage. As indicated in the text above, this will not produce consistent estimates. In fact, actual estimates resulting from this technique were completely unsatisfactory—indeed they were far inferior to the (also inconsistent) OLS estimates.

mathematically possible for several sets of values to satisfy the structural equations, the data-generating mechanism must have a criterion as to which set it should pick. The coefficients were chosen so that in each model there are two equilibrium points. Both are positive in Model I, and one is positive in Model II for all plausible values of the error terms. For Model II the positive equilibrium point was chosen. For Model I we generated some samples with all values for the endogenous variables from one intersection, all from the other and even one sample with an equal mixture of points. There is some sense in which the alternative intersections produce samples with different properties. The intuitive reason for this second peculiarity is that the nonlinearity of the structural equations makes the shapes of the scatters markedly different. This is indicated in fig. 8.1 representing Model I. In practice it was found in that model that when the data were drawn from region B in fig. 8.1[35]

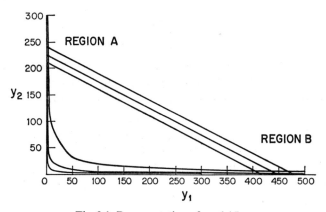

Fig. 8.1. Representation of model I.

the likelihood function appeared to be either (nearly) linear in the neighborhood of the maximum or (nearly) cylindrical in appearance, as indicated by the singularity of the matrix of second partial derivatives. Thus, in this instance, an infinity of linearly independent values for the structural coefficients can yield a maximum of the likelihood function.

---

[35] Figure 8.1 was obtained by letting z equal its mean value (15) and plotting each equation of the model at $u_i = 0$ and $u_i = \pm 3\sigma_i$, where σ_i is the standard deviation of u_i. The scatter generated in region A is seen to be smaller than the scatter from region B. Roughly speaking, the region A scatter is contained within a rectangle of size (3×30) while the region B scatter is contained within a rectangle of (80×7.5).

Model parameters

As indicated earlier, simplicity was a chief characteristic of the experiments. For given values of the number of observations, n, a single set of values for the one exogenous variable was used throughout the experiments. The set of $n z$'s to be used was generated by picking n numbers from a uniform distribution over the range 10 to 20. Three values of n were used in the various experiments, namely $n = 20, 40$, and 60. The u's were chosen to be normally distributed with zero mean and with covariance matrix

$$\Sigma_I = \begin{bmatrix} 0.5 & 1.25 \\ 1.25 & 25.0 \end{bmatrix}$$

for Model I and two alternative covariance matrices

$$\Sigma_{II,1} = \begin{bmatrix} 0.10 & 0.05 \\ 0.05 & 0.10 \end{bmatrix}$$

and

$$\Sigma_{II,2} = \begin{bmatrix} 0.10 & 0 \\ 0 & 0.10 \end{bmatrix}$$

for Model II. The number of samples generated for each experiment was 100.

An experiment thus consists of choosing a value of n, generating 100 times n pairs of u's with the appropriate covariance matrix and solving the relevant pair of structural equations for the endogenous variables 100 times.

Only a single set of structural coefficients was used for each model. The values of the structural coefficients are $b_{12} = 1.5$, $b_{13} = -0.5$, $b_{14} = 0.5$, $b_{21} = 0.5$, $b_{23} = -15.0$ for Model I and $b_{12} = 0.2$, $b_{13} = -1.5$, $b_{14} = -0.75$, $b_{21} = -0.05$, $b_{24} = 1.0$ for Model II. The list of all experiments is given in table 8.1.

TABLE 8.1

Model	n	Covariance matrix	Intersection
I	20	Σ_I	A
I	40	Σ_I	A
I	60	Σ_I	A
I	40	Σ_I	B
I	40	Σ_I	50–50 mixture of A and B
II	20	$\Sigma_{II,1}$	Positive orthant
II	40	$\Sigma_{II,1}$	Positive orthant
II	60	$\Sigma_{II,1}$	Positive orthant
II	60	$\Sigma_{II,2}$	Positive orthant

For each estimating technique we produced estimates of the coefficients of the equations, the elements of the covariance matrix and of the asymptotic variances of the coefficient estimates.[36] The order of computations was such that FIML estimates were computed last. This allowed us to use the reasonably realistic technique of starting the FIML computation at the estimates provided by either OLS or TSLS. In fact, we always started at the former. The reason for this procedure was our (not unexpected) finding that although OLS estimates are inconsistent, they exhibited a relatively small dispersion. Thus, we could be assured that the starting-point for the computation would almost never be extremely far from the true values of the parameters. On the other hand, as has been amply shown in experiments with linear models, TSLS tends, not infrequently, to produce estimates over a much wider range. It was hoped that by avoiding as starting-points the more extreme of the two-stage estimates, over-all computational time would be reduced.[37] It may be noted that the second covariance matrix employed for Model II involves a zero covariance. In the estimating procedures we did not impose this restriction. Hence, the results may cast some light on the consequences of a particular type of misspecification.

As noted before, predictions for the endogenous variables conditional upon the value of the exogenous variable were obtained only for Model II. In view of the importance of gauging the sensitivity of these predictions to the particular value of the exogenous variable chosen, predictions were made for two values of z, $z = 10.0$ and $z = 17.5$.

8.5. Analysis of results

The goodness of the various estimating techniques can be judged by their performance in terms of both the structural parameters and the conditional predictions for the endogenous variables. The reason for this are simple. The

---

[36] For the TSLS estimator of the asymptotic variances we used the standard formula. See, for example, A. S. Goldberger, *Econometric theory*. New York, Wiley, 1964. For FIML we used the Cramer–Rao variances.

[37] For Model I, OLS starting-points always produced an acceptable termination to the FIML computation. In Model II a small fraction of the computations did not terminate satisfactorily. In all of these cases a singularity or near-singularity of the matrix of second partial derivatives appeared to be involved. Some of these cases were brought to a satisfactory termination by restarting either at the TSLS estimates or at a point obtained by random perturbations of the OLS estimates. A few samples remained without full-information estimates.

economist is often interested in estimating the values of slopes and elasticities, and for this purpose it is relevant to know the performance characteristics of the individual methods with regard to individual coefficients. At the same time we are often interested in the accuracy of forecasts. In order to judge the latter question we explicitly have to consider the goodness of the various methods in terms of the conditional predictions. Otherwise, we would fail to allow for possible interactions among the various structural parameter estimates Clearly, the performances of a method with respect to these two criteria are not independent.

The various experiments performed enable us to draw conclusions (in the context of both structural parameters and predictions) with respect to different estimating methods and different sample sizes. In addition, for Model I we can examine the effect of choosing samples from various equilibrium points, and for Model II we can examine the effect of a simple type of misspecification.

Our analysis is conducted in terms of two sets of criteria:

(1) those involving comparisons of various statistics in an informal manner without any probabilistic implications or significance tests;

(2) those involving formal tests of significant differences.

To elaborate (1) we have to define the following quantities: Let θ be the true value of a parameter, let $\hat{\theta}_{ij}$ be its estimate in the jth sample (where i denotes a *combination* of an experiment and an estimating method) and $\hat{\sigma}(\hat{\theta}_{ij})$ be the (asymptotic) standard deviation of the estimate $\hat{\theta}_{ij}$. Then, analogously to chapter 3, we define for the ith combination

(a) Mean bias
$$\frac{\Sigma_j \hat{\theta}_{ij}}{100} - \theta,$$

(b) Mean absolute bias
$$\frac{\Sigma_j |\hat{\theta}_{ij} - \theta|}{100},$$

(c) Root mean square error
$$\sqrt{\frac{\Sigma_j (\hat{\theta}_{ij} - \theta)^2}{100}},$$

(d) Mean (asymptotic) standard deviation
$$\frac{\Sigma_j \hat{\sigma} (\hat{\theta}_{ij})}{100}.$$

Our informal analysis consists of making pairwise comparisons with (a), (b) and (c) (ranging over the subscript i—e.g., comparing methods or sample sizes) and from this obtaining informal rankings. For consistent estimating methods (d) provides a consistent estimate of (c). Hence, we also compare (d) and (c) in the expectation that the comparison will be worst for direct least squares. It has been pointed out by Basmann[38] that certain econometric estimators have exact finite sample distributions with no finite moments of some low order. Hence, these informal comparisons must be taken with a grain of salt.

Our second procedure made use of a frequently used non-parametric test to make formal pairwise comparisons.[39] The test, in fact, consisted of estimating the probability that the absolute deviation of the estimates for combination i is less than the absolute deviation of the estimates for combination k, i.e.,

$$P = \Pr\left[|\hat{\theta}_i - \theta| < |\hat{\theta}_k - \theta|\right].$$

This probability is easily estimated by the fraction of samples in each experiment for which $|\hat{\theta}_{ij} - \theta| < |\hat{\theta}_{kj} - \theta|$. This estimated relative frequency was used in a two-tailed binomial test of the null hypothesis that $P = 0.5$. We actually made use of the normal approximation to the binomial, and the tables below report the standardized normal variate.[40]

Model I results

In examining the results for Model I, we initially concentrate on the experiments utilizing the samples generated by choosing intersection A (see fig. 8.1). Tables 8.2–8.4 report the mean biases (MB), the mean absolute biases (MAB), the root mean square errors (RMSE) and the mean asymptotic standard deviations (MASD) for each parameter and for each estimating method. We first examine the relative performances of the various methods by making pairwise comparisons with respect to the first three criteria.

In terms of the (absolute) MB's, OLS is distinctly inferior to the other two methods. Between the latter two FIML is superior, save for the elements

---

[38] See R.L.Basmann, *op. cit.*
[39] See R.Summers, *op. cit.*
[40] It should also be mentioned that in the few instances when we did not have a full set of 100 samples for a particular combination we disregarded the missing samples in making pairwise comparisons. We, of course, adjusted the various reported statistics for this fact.

of the covariance matrix. In terms of both the MAB's and the RMSE's roughly the same ranking prevails—namely FIML, TSLS, OLS.

For our smallest sample size ($n = 20$), OLS performs well relative to both FIML and TSLS but the situation sharply, and not unexpectedly, changes for larger sample sizes.

TABLE 8.2

Model I: mean bias

Sample size	Inter-section	Method	σ_{11}	σ_{22}	σ_{12}	b_{12}	b_{13}	b_{14}	b_{21}	b_{23}
20	A	FIML	−0.040	−1.959	−0.138	1.099	−0.080	−4.705	−0.065	0.01
20	A	OLS	−0.078	−2.520	−0.956	−4.924	0.313	21.875	−0.785	0.07
20	A	TSLS	−0.018	−0.548	0.035	3.276	−0.219	−14.362	−0.099	0.01
40	A	FIML	−0.057	−1.049	−0.132	−0.365	0.040	1.347	0.039	0.00
40	A	OLS	−0.086	−1.499	−0.970	−5.296	0.365	23.064	−0.645	0.05
40	A	TSLS	−0.047	−0.372	−0.091	0.250	0.001	−1.387	0.118	0.00
60	A	FIML	−0.034	−0.800	−0.093	−0.106	0.016	0.308	0.124	−0.00
60	A	OLS	−0.057	−1.268	−0.933	−4.909	0.333	21.455	−0.548	0.04
60	A	TSLS	−0.029	−0.299	−0.083	0.212	−0.005	−1.087	0.151	−0.00
40	A/B	FIML	−0.064	−1.235	−0.163	−0.034	0.030	−0.307	0.001	0.00
40	A/B	OLS	−0.059	−0.670	−0.184	−0.061	0.030	−0.232	0.001	0.00
40	A/B	TSLS	4.376	16.391	−0.079	0.238	0.038	−1.276	0.002	−0.01
40	B	OLS	−0.499	−22.436	−0.251	−1.513	0.439	−5.656	−0.461	13.6
40	B	TSLS	−0.224	−9.875	−1.216	−1.559	0.448	−5.751	−0.155	4.6

TABLE 8.3

Model I: mean absolute bias

Sample size	Inter-section	Method	σ_{11}	σ_{22}	σ_{12}	b_{12}	b_{13}	b_{14}	b_{21}	b_2
20	A	FIML	0.135	7.473	0.982	6.673	0.450	29.174	0.955	0.0
20	A	OLS	0.129	6.961	0.961	5.839	0.386	25.778	0.999	0.0
20	A	TSLS	0.142	7.434	1.053	8.160	0.531	36.031	1.252	0.1
40	A	FIML	0.105	4.768	0.744	4.480	0.295	19.728	0.549	0.0
40	A	OLS	0.103	4.693	0.970	5.568	0.380	24.302	0.730	0.0
40	A	TSLS	0.110	4.958	0.797	4.985	0.323	22.034	0.810	0.0
60	A	FIML	0.080	3.819	0.578	3.258	0.214	14.385	0.448	0.0
60	A	OLS	0.083	3.732	0.933	4.938	0.335	21.604	0.612	0.0
60	A	TSLS	0.086	4.014	0.607	3.742	0.244	16.540	0.661	0.0
40	A/B	FIML	0.091	4.844	0.498	0.049	0.037	0.503	0.003	0.0
40	A/B	OLS	0.088	4.859	0.497	0.068	0.036	0.475	0.003	0.0
40	A/B	TSLS	4.400	18.403	4.451	0.542	0.050	1.701	0.015	0.2
40	B	OLS	0.499	22.436	1.252	1.513	0.439	5.656	0.461	13.
40	B	TSLS	0.641	16.764	1.268	1.764	0.499	6.434	0.215	6.

TABLE 8.4

Model I: sample root mean square errors and mean asymptotic standard deviations

Sample size	Inter-section	Method	σ_{11}	σ_{22}	σ_{12}	b_{12}	b_{13}	b_{14}	b_{21}	b_{23}
20	A	FIML	0.168	9.125	1.333	8.150	0.546	35.750	1.382	0.121
						7.870	0.519	34.684	1.069	0.107
20	A	OLS	0.159	8.335	1.051	6.945	0.454	30.666	1.168	0.122
						5.811	0.382	25.674	0.889	0.095
20	A	TSLS	0.180	9.905	1.346	10.683	0.702	47.083	1.603	0.138
						10.720	0.699	47.377	1.469	0.136
40	A	FIML	0.128	5.968	0.971	5.645	0.368	24.945	0.689	0.070
						5.325	0.353	23.437	0.773	0.074
40	A	OLS	0.128	5.809	1.011	6.651	0.449	29.136	0.868	0.083
						3.710	0.246	16.351	0.665	0.068
40	A	TSLS	0.138	6.391	1.056	6.456	0.418	28.573	1.110	0.085
						6.373	0.420	28.091	1.083	0.093
60	A	FIML	0.097	4.835	0.725	4.070	0.267	17.986	0.563	0.053
						4.332	0.288	19.062	0.612	0.060
60	A	OLS	0.099	4.747	0.967	5.637	0.380	24.712	0.737	0.068
						3.050	0.203	13.438	0.523	0.055
60	A	TSLS	0.103	4.958	0.751	4.805	0.316	21.218	0.877	0.072
						4.950	0.328	21.801	0.866	0.075
40	A/B	FIML	0.110	6.005	0.595	0.059	0.044	0.613	0.003	0.073
						0.043	0.033	0.534	0.003	0.071
40	A/B	OLS	0.108	6.060	0.595	0.079	0.045	0.595	0.004	0.074
						0.044	0.036	0.571	0.003	0.072
40	A/B	TSLS	14.741	28.762	7.710	0.878	0.071	2.670	0.018	0.283
						2.257	0.156	6.004	0.027	0.433
40	B	OLS	0.500	22.440	1.252	1.513	0.439	5.656	0.462	13.678
						0.011	0.003	0.042	0.026	0.758
40	B	TSLS	1.266	19.281	1.339	2.036	0.555	7.176	0.246	7.287
						7.147	1.771	23.119	0.226	6.674

Comparing the RMSE's and the MASD's reveals a number of interesting features. The correspondence is best for TSLS and FIML with both the RMSE's and the MASD's declining as sample size increases.[41] Comparatively, OLS does less well. The MASD's decrease somewhat faster than the RMSE's and hence RMSE/MASD tends to increase somewhat as the sample size increases.

---

[41] The basic data are presented in table 8.4. For each method the first row contains the RMSE's and the second the MASD's. One method performing better than another method in this context simply means that RMSE/MASD was closer to 1.

TABLE 8.5

Model I: normal variates

Sample size	Method comparisons	σ_{11}	σ_{22}	σ_{12}	b_{14}	b_{12}	b_{13}	b_{21}	b_{23}
20	FIML/OLS	−0.40	−3.40	2.40	−0.60	−0.60	−0.80	3.00	1.20
	FIML/TSLS	−0.20	−2.40	1.40	1.80	1.80	0.80	2.20	2.40
	OLS/TSLS	1.00	−0.80	−1.40	1.40	1.40	1.00	1.60	2.00
40 (intersection A)	FIML/OLS	0.20	−1.20	5.00	2.20	2.00	3.20	3.20	1.80
	FIML/TSLS	1.20	−0.20	1.20	1.80	1.80	1.40	1.60	0.60
	OLS/TSLS	0.40	−0.20	−5.20	−2.00	−2.00	−2.20	−1.00	−0.40
60	FIML/OLS	1.60	−1.00	5.80	3.40	3.40	3.80	2.40	2.80
	FIML/TSLS	0.80	0.40	0.40	1.60	1.80	1.20	2.60	2.00
	OLS/TSLS	−0.60	1.60	−6.00	−3.20	−3.40	−3.40	−0.40	−0.60
40 (intersection A and B)	FIML/OLS	−5.20	−2.00	1.20	−0.40	6.60	1.80	0.20	0.40
	FIML/TSLS	6.20	4.00	6.80	4.80	8.00	3.40	7.80	7.40
	OLS/TSLS	6.60	3.60	6.80	5.40	7.20	2.40	7.80	7.60
40 (intersection B)	OLS/TSLS	−9.20	−9.00	1.80	5.40	5.40	5.40	−9.60	−9.60

TABLE 8.6

Model I: normal variates

Method	Intersection comparison	σ_{11}	σ_{22}	σ_{12}	b_{14}	b_{12}	b_{13}	b_{21}	b_{23}
FIML	A/B								
	A/A and B	−1.00	−0.20	−2.60	−9.80	−10.00	−8.20	−10.00	0.
	B/A and B								
OLS	A/B	10.00	10.00	6.40	−7.60	−7.20	3.40	−3.60	10
	A/A and B	0.00	0.00	−7.80	−9.80	−10.00	−8.80	−10.00	−1
	B/A and B	−10.00	−10.00	−9.60	−10.00	−10.00	−10.00	−10.00	−10
TSLS	A/B	9.60	−8.40	5.00	−6.20	−6.00	4.80	−5.80	10
	A/A and B	6.20	4.20	5.60	−8.60	−8.40	−8.00	−9.40	7
	B/A and B	0.00	2.60	3.20	−8.80	−8.40	−9.80	−9.40	−9

Given the sample size, we estimated the probability P, defined above, for the purpose of comparing the performances of various methods more formally. Similarly, given the method, we estimated P for comparisons of various sample sizes. Tables 8.5–8.7 present the relevant normal variates that allow us to test directly the hypothesis that $P = 0.5$. As the tables are arranged, a significantly positive entry in a row labeled FIML/OLS (say) indicates that FIML beats OLS, i.e., the fraction of the samples for which FIML came closer to the true value of a parameter was significantly larger than one-half. In discussing the various comparisons in these tables we shall summarize our findings in terms of both a 5% cent level of significance and a 25% level.

Of the 24 possible pairwise comparisons between methods the summary

TABLE 8.7

Model I: normal variates

Method	Sample size comparison	σ_{11}	σ_{22}	σ_{12}	b_{14}	b_{12}	b_{13}	b_{21}	b_{23}
FIML	40/20	1.40	4.20	1.60	3.00	3.00	3.00	2.80	3.40
	60/20	3.00	4.40	2.00	4.40	4.60	5.40	3.20	4.80
	60/40	1.60	1.40	0.40	1.60	1.40	1.40	1.00	2.20
OLS	40/20	1.40	3.60	0.40	0.80	0.80	0.60	3.40	2.80
	60/20	2.60	4.60	0.20	2.20	2.20	1.80	4.00	2.20
	60/40	1.60	1.60	1.60	0.80	1.00	1.40	0.20	1.80
TSLS	40/20	1.40	2.40	1.40	2.60	2.60	2.20	3.60	3.80
	60/20	2.60	4.20	2.20	3.80	3.80	4.00	4.20	4.40
	60/40	2.60	1.20	1.80	1.40	1.40	1.20	0.60	1.00

TABLE 8.8

Comparison	Number of wins	Significant wins		Significant losses	
		5% level	25% level	5% level	25% level
FIML/OLS	17	13	16	1	2
TSLS/OLS	16	8	9	1	5
FIML/TSLS	21	4	16	1	1

statistics of table 8.8 can be deduced from table 8.5.[42] It would seem, on the basis of these summary measures, that the results imply a ranking of FIML, TSLS and OLS. This ranking is consistent with the results of the informal analysis presented above.

A more detailed analysis of table 8.5 supports another conclusion reached earlier, namely that OLS becomes more inferior to the other methods as the sample size increases.[43]

We now turn to the cases involving intersection B. The results for the experiments that used a sample from intersection B only are rather inconclusive and of limited interest.[44]

On the other hand, the results for the mixture sample are contrary to our earlier rankings. In particular, if we apply our estimating techniques to samples generated by choosing points in equal proportion from intersections A and B, we find that FIML and OLS become quite comparable and distinctly better than TSLS. The improvement in absolute terms of both OLS and FIML is quite remarkable. For example, for intersection A ($n = 40$) the RMSE's of the coefficients estimated by FIML are 5.6, 0.4, 24.9, 0.7, 0.07. The corresponding RMSE's for the mixture intersection are 0.06, 0.04, 0.6, 0.003, 0.07.

The effect of changing intersection points can be seen from table 8.6. As that table shows, OLS estimates for the mixture samples do distinctly better than corresponding estimates for 'pure' samples while for TSLS the situation is inconclusive.[45] The inferiority of the two-stage procedure may be explained by the fact that it is based on (local) expansions whereas the new information contained in the mixture samples has strong global characteristics.[46]

The final results of interest for Model I are reflected in table 8.7, which

---

[42] The 24 cases are obtained by aggregating, for intersection A, both across parameters and across sample sizes. In the above summary, a win is simply a positive entry in table 8.6.

[43] For example, 4 of the 5 losses of TSLS to OLS occur for $n = 20$. In comparing OLS and the two-stage methods, it was found that the former tended to do its worst for the coefficients of the first equation. It is interesting to note that the first equation is the only source of nonlinearity in Model I.

[44] Our inability to compute FIML estimates for this case made it impossible to make a complete set of pairwise comparisons.

[45] It is also interesting to note that OLS and TSLS applied to the 'A' sample produce distinctly better estimates of the variances and covariances as compared with the 'B' sample. This may reflect the shape of the regions alluded to above.

[46] We are indebted to A. Zellner for this point.

compares the performance of the various methods as the sample size changes. The significant thing about the table is the absence of a negative entry. Hence, in every pairwise comparison, including somewhat surprisingly, OLS, a larger sample size beats a smaller sample size. Except for two cases involving OLS the differences between $n = 60$ and $n = 20$ are more significant than those between $n = 40$ and $n = 20$. On the whole, the effect of increasing the sample size from 40 to 60 is less pronounced than the effect of going from 20 to 40.

Model II results

In terms of the MB's, the MAB's and the RMSE's, FIML tends to outperform TSLS and OLS. The choice between the latter two appears ambiguous. OLS does quite badly in MB comparisons but does better in terms of the MAB's and RMSE's. It seems to do best (against both FIML and TSLS) in pairwise comparisons involving variances and covariances. Examining table 8.11, to compare the RMSE's and MASD's, reveals that FIML provides a quite reasonable correspondence for these two quantities. TSLS performs next best and steadily improves as the sample size increases. OLS does the worst and exhibits no tendency for the RMSE's to decline or for the RMSE-MASD ratio to get closer to unity as n increases.

Table 8.12 reports the normal variates for the formal pairwise comparisons. In table 8.13 we have the summary statistics for the 32 possible pairwise comparisons.[47]

Both FIML and TSLS resoundingly beat OLS, winning every possible pairwise comparison. FIML is superior to TSLS, although by a smaller margin. As the sample size increases, FIML and TSLS become both more superior relative to OLS and less different when compared with each other. The effect of changing sample sizes is revealed more clearly by table 8.14. For FIML and TSLS both $n = 40$ and $n = 60$ beat $n = 20$ with the 60/20 comparison producing, on the whole, higher normal variates than the 40/20 comparison. Interestingly enough, the 60/40 comparison produced no significant (at 5%) differences for either TSLS or FIML. For TSLS $n = 60$ never loses to $n = 40$, but it loses in half the cases for FIML. This suggests, at least for Model II, that a 'large' sample may be something of the order of 60. In contrast to these results, the ones for OLS exhibit

---

[47] We have included in our 32 cases the experiment using covariance matrix $\Sigma_{II,2}$. As table 8.12 reveals, the comparisons for this experiment were extremely similar to those for the corresponding experiment using $\Sigma_{II,1}$.

TABLE 8.9

Model II: mean bias

Sample size	Covariance	Method	σ_{11}	σ_{22}	σ_{12}	b_{12}	b_{13}	b_{14}	b_{21}	b_{23}
20	0.05	FIML	0.067	−0.005	0.014	0.023	−0.187	1.450	−0.000	0.067
20	0.05	OLS	−0.069	−0.007	−0.066	−0.111	0.871	−6.494	0.001	−0.170
20	0.05	TSLS	9.170	−0.005	0.020	0.075	−0.584	4.308	−0.000	0.046
40	0.05	FIML	0.044	−0.007	0.001	0.013	−0.100	0.762	−0.000	0.013
40	0.05	OLS	−0.067	−0.009	−0.068	−0.112	0.878	−6.531	0.001	−0.173
40	0.05	TSLS	0.284	−0.007	0.002	0.010	−0.081	0.637	0.000	0.005
60	0.05	FIML	0.033	−0.006	0.002	0.013	−0.096	0.684	0.000	−0.021
60	0.05	OLS	−0.066	−0.007	−0.068	−0.112	0.876	−6.530	0.001	−0.215
60	0.05	TSLS	1.654	−0.006	0.007	0.019	−0.147	1.073	0.000	−0.016
60	0	FIML	0.044	−0.006	0.007	0.022	−0.164	1.185	0.000	−0.019
60	0	OLS	−0.038	−0.008	−0.040	−0.098	0.772	−5.758	0.001	−0.251
60	0	TSLS	0.273	−0.006	0.009	0.032	−0.245	1.790	0.000	−0.015

TABLE 8.10

Model II: mean absolute bias

Sample size	Covariance	Method	σ_{11}	σ_{22}	σ_{12}	b_{12}	b_{13}	b_{14}	b_{21}	b_{23}
20	0.05	FIML	0.124	0.025	0.055	0.083	0.655	4.900	0.002	0.341
20	0.05	OLS	0.069	0.025	0.066	0.111	0.871	6.494	0.002	0.357
20	0.05	TSLS	9.224	0.025	0.166	0.288	2.258	16.838	0.002	0.339
40	0.05	FIML	0.089	0.018	0.043	0.070	0.548	4.094	0.001	0.224
40	0.05	OLS	0.067	0.018	0.068	0.112	0.878	6.531	0.001	0.269
40	0.05	TSLS	0.326	0.018	0.077	0.134	1.050	7.834	0.001	0.221
60	0.05	FIML	0.081	0.016	0.037	0.062	0.483	3.568	0.001	0.195
60	0.05	OLS	0.066	0.015	0.068	0.112	0.876	6.530	0.001	0.251
60	0.05	TSLS	1.700	0.015	0.079	0.130	1.021	7.592	0.001	0.199
60	0	FIML	0.077	0.016	0.032	0.075	0.582	4.296	0.001	0.195
60	0	OLS	0.038	0.015	0.040	0.198	0.772	5.758	0.002	0.275
60	0	TSLS	0.304	0.016	0.054	0.125	0.976	7.240	0.001	0.199

significant instances of $n = 20$ beating both $n = 40$ and $n = 60$. Furthermore, the 60/20 comparison does not always produce normal variates higher than 40/20 comparison.

As noted earlier, predictions were made for two different values of the exogenous variable. Precisely the same statistics were calculated for the predictions as for the structural parameters. Thus, for example, table 8.15 reports

TABLE 8.11

Model II: sample root mean square errors and mean asymptotic standard deviations

Sample size	Covariance	Method	σ_{11}	σ_{22}	σ_{12}	b_{12}	b_{13}	b_{14}	b_{21}	b_{23}
20	0.05	FIML	0.213	0.030	0.079	0.108	0.860	6.513	0.002	0.430
						0.125	0.989	7.457	0.002	0.421
20	0.05	OLS	0.070	0.030	0.067	0.112	0.883	6.586	0.002	0.437
						0.018	0.143	1.088	0.002	0.413
20	0.05	TSLS	31.815	0.031	0.328	0.572	4.476	33.315	0.002	0.426
						2.153	16.837	125.159	0.002	0.418
40	0.05	FIML	0.146	0.021	0.058	0.098	0.767	5.732	0.002	0.288
						0.088	0.690	5.159	0.001	0.266
40	0.05	OLS	0.067	0.021	0.068	0.113	0.886	6.595	0.002	0.328
						0.014	0.107	0.805	0.001	0.263
40	0.05	TSLS	1.065	0.022	0.142	0.252	1.978	14.732	0.002	0.286
						0.386	3.029	22.608	0.001	0.266
60	0.05	FIML	0.133	0.019	0.047	0.083	0.646	4.779	0.001	0.234
						0.069	0.540	4.017	0.001	0.230
60	0.05	OLS	0.067	0.019	0.068	0.112	0.880	6.558	0.002	0.316
						0.011	0.085	0.643	0.001	0.226
60	0.05	TSLS	12.956	0.019	0.163	0.281	2.202	16.386	0.001	0.238
						0.462	3.615	26.860	0.001	0.230
60	0	FIML	0.182	0.019	0.046	0.115	0.888	6.541	0.001	0.234
						0.088	0.684	5.077	0.001	0.230
60	0	OLS	0.040	0.019	0.041	0.100	0.785	5.850	0.002	0.340
						0.018	0.139	1.041	0.001	0.225
60	0	TSLS	1.251	0.019	0.114	0.263	2.070	15.397	0.001	0.237
						0.385	3.019	22.479	0.001	0.230

TABLE 8.12

Model II: normal variates

Sample size	Method comparison	σ_{11}	σ_{22}	σ_{12}	b_{12}	b_{13}	b_{14}	b_{21}	b_{23}
20	FIML/OLS	4.29	2.04	4.69	4.29	4.69	4.69	1.63	1.43
	FIML/TSLS	2.45	0.41	2.25	2.32	2.32	1.90	1.02	0.61
	OLS/TSLS	−2.20	−2.80	−1.60	−1.65	−1.86	−1.86	−2.00	−1.60
40	FIML/OLS	4.92	2.71	7.74	6.73	6.73	6.93	2.71	2.71
	FIML/TSLS	0.90	−0.10	1.11	1.51	1.31	0.91	−1.31	−0.50
	OLS/TSLS	−3.00	−3.00	−5.60	−5.20	−5.20	−5.00	−3.00	−3.20
60	FIML/OLS	4.85	2.02	7.88	8.28	8.28	8.28	3.03	3.03
	FIML/TSLS	0.81	0.40	0.81	0.30	0.30	0.30	0.81	1.41
	OLS/TSLS	−4.40	−2.20	−5.80	−6.13	−6.33	−6.33	−2.60	−2.80
60 (covariance = 0)	FIML/OLS	4.04	2.22	5.45	6.26	6.26	6.26	4.04	3.43
	FIML/TSLS	−0.81	1.01	0.61	1.41	1.41	2.02	1.21	1.62
	OLS/TSLS	−3.80	−2.40	−3.40	−3.40	−3.60	−3.60	−4.00	−3.20

TABLE 8.13

Comparison	Number of wins	Significant wins		Significant losses	
		5% level	25% level	5% level	25% level
FIML/OLS	32	30	32	0	0
TSLS/OLS	32	27	32	0	0
FIML/TSLS	28	5	15	0	1

TABLE 8.14

Model II: normal variates

Method	Sample size comparison	σ_{11}	σ_{22}	σ_{12}	b_{12}	b_{13}	b_{14}	b_{21}	b_{23}
FIML	40/20	1.33	2.98	0.92	0.92	0.92	0.72	2.36	1.95
	60/20	1.03	2.68	1.44	1.03	1.65	2.06	2.68	3.30
	60/40	−1.32	0.30	−0.10	−0.30	−0.10	0.10	0.10	1.32
OLS	40/20	1.40	3.00	−2.00	1.00	1.20	1.20	1.80	1.20
	60/20	2.80	3.00	−2.80	−0.40	−0.40	0.40	2.60	2.60
	60/40	0.40	0.80	−0.60	0.80	0.80	0.20	−0.20	0.80
TSLS	40/20	2.20	3.00	1.40	1.44	1.44	1.44	3.00	2.30
	60/20	2.20	3.00	2.00	2.68	2.89	3.09	3.00	3.80
	60/40	0.40	0.60	0.20	1.11	0.90	0.90	0.00	0.60

the MB's, the MAB's and the RMSE's of the predictions for the various methods for each experiment. In terms of these measures the ranking of the methods is FIML, OLS and TSLS.[48]

Table 8.16 reports the results of the formal pairwise tests of the predictions. For the eight cases for each of the prediction values of z, these can be summarized as in table 8.17

Both values of z imply the same ranking, namely FIML, TSLS and OLS. Ranking is somewhat sharper for $z = 10$.[49] As in the case of the structural

---

[48] It should be noted that in several instances OLS beats FIML. TSLS performs quite badly in terms of these various measures, beating OLS only once in 48 comparisons and beating FIML not at all. Examination of the actual predictions revealed that this finding was the result of several extremely bad predictions generated by TSLS.

[49] It should be recalled that the z's in the sample were drawn from a uniform distribution over the range 10 to 20.

TABLE 8.15

Summary statistics for predictions (model II)

Sample size	Covariance	Method	Mean bias		Mean absolute bias		Sample root mean square errors	
			y_1	y_2	y_1	y_2	y_1	y_2
			Predictions for $z = 10.0$:					
20	0.05	FIML	0.010	−0.021	0.135	0.102	0.167	0.130
20	0.05	OLS	0.012	0.122	0.148	0.138	0.176	0.165
20	0.05	TSLS	−0.718	−0.378	0.888	0.476	3.125	1.612
40	0.05	FIML	0.031	0.008	0.126	0.088	0.326	0.169
40	0.05	OLS	0.111	0.114	0.124	0.120	0.147	0.139
40	0.05	TSLS	−0.439	−0.221	0.594	0.320	2.344	1.156
60	0.05	FIML	0.003	0.008	0.085	0.055	0.107	0.067
60	0.05	OLS	0.108	0.131	0.118	0.131	0.136	0.143
60	0.05	TSLS	−0.300	−0.148	0.404	0.215	2.112	1.074
60	0	FIML	0.002	0.007	0.107	0.049	0.136	0.060
60	0	OLS	0.073	0.127	0.109	0.127	0.130	0.137
60	0	TSLS	−0.153	−0.074	0.259	0.133	1.509	0.778
			Predictions for $z = 17.5$:					
20	0.05	FIML	0.000	−0.002	0.043	0.020	0.056	0.026
20	0.05	OLS	−0.001	−0.018	0.042	0.025	0.055	0.032
20	0.05	TSLS	−1.065	−0.953	1.103	0.971	4.345	3.883
40	0.05	FIML	−0.134	−0.126	0.171	0.142	1.143	1.027
40	0.05	OLS	0.005	−0.021	0.034	0.027	0.041	0.032
40	0.05	TSLS	−0.870	−0.759	0.905	0.775	3.849	3.338
60	0.05	FIML	0.004	−0.003	0.025	0.013	0.032	0.016
60	0.05	OLS	0.008	−0.018	0.024	0.020	0.032	0.024
60	0.05	TSLS	−0.442	−0.397	0.471	0.408	2.776	2.458
60	0	FIML	0.004	−0.002	0.029	0.011	0.037	0.014
60	0	OLS	0.014	−0.017	0.029	0.018	0.038	0.022
60	0	TSLS	−0.189	−0.174	0.223	0.186	1.903	1.699

parameters for Model II, FIML and TSLS improve relative to OLS and narrow relative to each other with increasing sample size.[50]

Finally, we can compare the methods with respect to the two alternative covariance matrices. The relevant normal variates are given in table 8.19.

---

[50] More detailed observations on the effect of increasing sample sizes can be gleaned from table 8.18. On the whole, the findings are similar to those noted above for table 8.14.

TABLE 8.16

Model II: normal variates

Sample size	Method comparison	Predictions for $z = 10.0$		Predictions for $z = 17.5$	
		y_1	y_2	y_1	y_2
20	FIML/OLS	1.84	3.06	−0.61	2.45
	FIML/TSLS	1.69	1.48	0.00	2.53
	OLS/TSLS	0.62	−1.86	1.24	−1.24
40	FIML/OLS	3.32	3.92	−0.70	3.52
	FIML/TSLS	0.90	2.91	0.10	−0.90
	OLS/TSLS	−1.80	−3.00	0.80	−2.80
60	FIML/OLS	4.24	7.68	−1.01	4.44
	FIML/TSLS	1.52	0.71	1.12	−0.51
	OLS/TSLS	−2.71	−6.33	0.50	−3.72
60 (covariance = 0)	FIML/OLS	−0.61	7.88	0.40	5.25
	FIML/TSLS	0.00	0.61	1.21	0.00
	OLS/TSLS	0.20	−7.20	0.20	4.20

TABLE 8.17

Compar-ison	$z = 10.0$					$z = 17.5$				
	Number of wins	Significant wins 5% 25% level		Significant losses 5% 25% level		Number of wins	Significant wins 5% 25% level		Significant losses 5% 25% level	
FIML/OLS	7	6	7	0	0	5	4	4	0	0
TSLS/OLS	6	4	6	0	0	4	3	4	0	1
FIML/TSLS	7 (1 tie)	1	4	0	0	4 (2 ties)	1	2	0	0

These results are, on the whole, rather ambiguous. For the experiment that misspecifies the covariance ($\Sigma_{\mathrm{II},2}$) all the methods do better at estimating the covariance and one of the variances. FIML and TSLS do better in the properly specified experiment for one of the equations while OLS does distinctly worse for that equation. The prediction results are similarly inconclusive. The limited experimentation with this type of misspecification is clearly not sufficient to establish over-all regularities.

TABLE 8.18

Model II: normal variates

Method	Sample size comparison	Predictions for $z = 10.0$		Predictions for $z = 17.5$	
		y_1	y_2	y_1	y_2
FIML	40/20	1.54	1.74	1.13	−1.13
	60/20	2.89	4.13	3.71	3.30
	60/40	1.52	1.52	1.92	3.35
OLS	40/20	1.20	0.40	0.60	−0.80
	60/20	2.20	0.80	3.80	1.80
	60/40	−0.20	−0.60	2.40	2.60
TSLS	40/20	1.86	1.44	0.62	0.62
	60/20	2.27	3.71	2.48	3.51
	60/40	−0.10	2.31	1.51	2.91

TABLE 8.19

	σ_{11}	σ_{22}	σ_{12}	b_{12}	b_{13}	b_{14}	b_{21}	b_{23}
FIML $\Sigma_{II,1}/\Sigma_{II,2}$	−6.26	1.82	−3.63	4.85	4.44	4.44	−0.40	−0.40
OLS $\Sigma_{II,1}/\Sigma_{II,2}$	−10.00	1.00	−10.00	−7.60	−7.60	−7.60	7.00	6.80
TSLS $\Sigma_{II,1}/\Sigma_{II,2}$	−3.20	1.60	−2.60	2.31	2.11	2.11	0.80	1.00

	Predictions for $z = 10.0$		Predictions for $z = 17.5$	
	y_1	y_2	y_1	y_2
FIML $\Sigma_{II,1}/\Sigma_{II,2}$	7.48	−3.64	8.69	−3.43
OLS $\Sigma_{II,1}/\Sigma_{II,2}$	−4.61	−1.80	4.80	−3.20
TSLS $\Sigma_{II,1}/\Sigma_{II,2}$	4.12	−2.51	6.33	−1.31

8.6. Conclusions

This chapter has analyzed the identification and estimation of nonlinear simultaneous equation models. The performance of two estimating methods, FIML and TSLS, was examined by sampling experiments. For both models investigated, FIML outperforms TSLS while each of these methods far outperforms OLS.

In summary then, the evidence thus far assimilated would seem to favor

FIML over the two-stage procedure and both over OLS for structural estimation as well as prediction. This conclusion is roughly similar to the findings from analyses of linear models. If anything, the strength of this conclusion is greater in the present case.

A number of other findings also emerge from an analysis of the results and we briefly list them:

(1) For both models OLS does progressively worse as the sample size increases.

(2) The ranking of the methods on the basis of predictive performance agrees with the ranking on the basis of structural parameter estimation.

(3) There are no reversals for FIML or TSLS in Model I in the sample size comparisons (i.e., a smaller sample size never beats a larger sample size—given the method—in a pairwise comparison). There are reversals, however, for Model II. This suggests that the definition of a 'large' sample size may vary from model to model.

(4) The performance of TSLS is affected by the choice of the degree of the polynomial used in the first stage.[51] There is the distinct possibility that the appropriate ('best') degree may vary from model to model.[52]

---

[51] Although not presented in the text, we did compute estimates based on a first degree polynomial for the second equation in Model I. The table below gives the RMSE's for this procedure (labeled TSLS1) as well as for the procedure employing a quadratic polynomial (labeled TSLS2 here for comparison). As is readily apparent, TSLS2 uniformly outperforms TSLS1.

Sample size	Intersection	Method	RMSE b_{21}	b_{23}
20	A	TSLS1	1.720	0.147
20	A	TSLS2	1.603	0.138
40	A	TSLS1	1.248	0.097
40	A	TSLS2	1.110	0.085
60	A	TSLS1	0.945	0.076
60	A	TSLS2	0.877	0.072
40	A/B	TSLS1	0.088	1.325
40	A/B	TSLS2	0.018	0.283
40	B	TSLS1	0.785	23.157
40	B	TSLS2	0.246	7.287

[52] The uniform superiority of TSLS2 over TSLS1 noted in the previous footnote, suggests it might have been interesting to examine the performance of a third-degree polynomial. There is no reason to expect continued improvement as the degree increases. See, for example, the lack of monotonicity cited by Klein in the use of principal components. See L.R. Klein, Estimation of interdependent systems in macroeconometrics. *Econometrica* **37** (1969), 171–92.

In conclusion, it is appropriate to indicate briefly some of the many directions in which the research described in this chapter could be expanded upon.

First, it would clearly be desirable to see if the substantive conclusions reached continue to hold for other (and larger) nonlinear models. Klein has already made some progress in this direction.[53]

Second, it is important to extend the type of results presented to cases where there are nonlinearities in the parameters. Of course, in this context, not only is TSLS not directly applicable but the treatment of identification in section 8.2 may have to be radically revised. In addition, the room for variation in specifications of nonlinear models far exceeds the range possible in the linear case. As indicated before, this suggests that the technique of sampling experiments may be even less satisfactory in the nonlinear case.

Third, it would be useful to know how various estimators perform in the face of multicollinearity, auto-correlated residuals and various types of misspecification.

Finally, there remains the question of multiple solutions. This needs to be examined from both the point of view of identification and estimation. The marked differences in estimator behavior associated with the different intersection points in Model I suggests this may be a particularly fruitful area of further research.

---

[53] *Ibid.*

CHAPTER 9

ESTIMATION OF DISCONTINUOUS PARAMETER CHANGES

9.1. Introduction

If a set of observations is available on a dependent variable y and on k independent variables $x_1, \ldots, x_k$, the customary linear model connecting y and the x's is

$$Y = X\beta + U, \tag{9.1}$$

where Y is the $n \times 1$ vector of observations on y, X the $n \times k$ matrix of observations on the x's and β the $k \times 1$ vector of unknown regression coefficients. It is, however, occasionally the case that the observations are thought, for theoretical reasons, to have been generated by two distinct regression regimes.[1] Thus, for some subset I of the n observations

$$y_i = \sum_{h=1}^{k} \beta_{1h} x_{hi} + u_{1i} \quad (i \in I), \tag{9.2}$$

and for the complementary subset J

$$y_j = \sum_{h=1}^{k} \beta_{2h} x_{hj} + u_{2j} \quad (j \in J), \tag{9.3}$$

where x_{hi} and x_{hj} represent the ith and ith observations on x_h respectively. The error terms in the two regimes would typically be assumed to have the usual properties of error terms in classical linear regressions, i.e., they would be assumed to be distributed normally and independently of one another with zero mean and constant variance, although the variances of the errors in the two regimes σ_1^2 and σ_2^2 may well be assumed to be different.

The formulations in (9.2) and (9.3) are completely general in the sense that they allow some independent variables to be missing in each regime that

---

[1] There is no intrinsic reason why the number of different regimes be limited to two. The complexity of any approach to this problem will, however, increase with the number of alternative regimes postulated.

are present in the other regime, i.e., some of the β_{1h} and β_{2h} may be set equal to zero on *a priori* grounds. The problem in any event is to estimate the parameters β_{1h}, β_{2h} $(h = 1, \ldots, k)$, σ_1 and σ_2 without knowing which of the n values of the dependent variable was generated by which regime.[2]

Efforts to cope with this problem have alternately focused on estimation of the parameters or on simply testing the null hypothesis that no change of regimes has taken place against the alternative that a change has taken place.[3] In the context of regression analysis the problem was initially posed as a time series problem in which the first t (t being unknown) observations come from regime 1 and the remaining $n - t$ observations are drawn from regime 2.[4] The essence of this simple formulation is that all the observations up to the unknown time point t come from one regime and all the observations after that point come from the other. Let the observation matrices X and Y be partitioned into submatrices X_t, X_{n-t}, Y_t, Y_{n-t} comprising respectively the first t and last $n - t$ rows of X and Y. On the assumption that t is the time at which the switch from one regime to the other occurred, the likelihood of the sample can be written as

$$L = \left(\frac{1}{\sqrt{2\pi}\,\sigma_1}\right)^t \left(\frac{1}{\sqrt{2\pi}\,\sigma_2}\right)^{n-t} \exp\left\{-\frac{1}{2\sigma_1^2}(Y_t - X_t\beta_1)'(Y_t - X_t\beta_1)\right.$$
$$\left. -\frac{1}{2\sigma_2^2}(Y_{n-t} - X_{n-t}\beta_2)'(Y_{n-t} - X_{n-t}\beta_2)\right\}.$$

Maximizing the logarithm of this with respect to $\beta_1, \beta_2, \sigma_1, \sigma_2$ yields the ordinary least squares estimates for the given separation of the sample into the two subsamples. Condensing the logarithm of the likelihood function with respect

[2] If it is known *a priori* which observations belong to which regime, the problem of testing the equality of the two sets of coefficients is fully solved by the Chow test. See G. Chow, Tests of equality between two sets of coefficients in two linear regressions. *Econometrica* **28** (1960), 561–605.

[3] Some of the earliest discussion of problems of this type is in E.S. Page, A test for a change in a parameter occurring at an unknown point. *Biometrika* **42** (1955), 523–7; and E.S. Page, On problems in which a change in a parameter occurs at an unknown point. *Biometrika* **44** (1957), 248–52. See also S. John, On identifying the population of origin of each observation in a mixture of observations from two normal populations. *Technometrics* **12** (1970), 553–63. These papers do not deal with regression problems but simply the problem of observations mixed from two populations.

[4] R.E. Quandt, The estimation of the parameters of a linear regression system obeying two separate regimes. *Journal of the American Statistical Association* **53** (1958), 873–80; and R.E. Quandt, Tests of the hypothesis that a linear regression system obeys two separate regimes. *Journal of the American Statistical Association* **55** (1960), 324–30.

to σ_1 and σ_2 yields

$$\log L = -n \log \sqrt{2\pi} - \frac{n}{2} - \frac{t}{2} \log \left[\frac{(Y_t - X_t\beta_1)' (Y_t - X_t\beta_1)}{t} \right]$$
$$- \frac{n-t}{2} \log \left[\frac{(Y_{n-t} - X_{n-t}\beta_2)' (Y_{n-t} - X_{n-t}\beta_2)}{(n-t)} \right]. \qquad (9.4)$$

The value of L may be evaluated for all possible choices of t and that value chosen as the estimate of the unknown switching point which maximizes L.[5]

Although this is estimation by maximum likelihood, it is somewhat unusual in that the variable t is discrete. Although the estimate of t is consistent[6] the discreteness of t may explain why the 'appropriate' likelihood ratio test does not seem applicable in practice.[7]

Various more practical test procedures have been suggested. A simple device analogous to the procedure designed to deal with heteroscedasticity in chapter 3 is to divide the total sample into two equal subsamples about the central observation, and to fit separate regressions to the two subsamples. Since the residuals in the two regressions are independent of another, an F-test becomes possible on the ratio of the residual variances. This test is obviously not useful against the alternative hypothesis that the switch occurred exactly at the midpoint *and* that the error variances of the two regimes are the same.

More recently it has been shown by Brown and Durbin that the residuals can be exploited in another and ingenious manner to test for the constancy of the regression coefficients.[8] If we denote by $\hat{\beta}_{rh}$ the regression coefficients estimated from the first r observations, they define the successive residuals $y_r - \sum_{h=1}^{k} \hat{\beta}_{r-1,h} x_{hr}$ for successive values of r. A certain generalization of the

---

[5] The problem of degrees of freedom implies that the switching point cannot be located so close to either end-point of the time series that the shorter of the two regimes does not have enough observations to estimate the parameters of the regime.

[6] See M. G. Kendall and A. Stuart, *The advanced theory of statistics*, vol. II. New York, Hafner, 1961, pp. 39–41.

[7] If we wish to test the hypothesis that there is no switch in regimes against the alternative of one switch, the appropriate likelihood ratio is $\lambda = \hat{\sigma}_1^t \hat{\sigma}_2^{n-t} / \hat{\sigma}^n$, where $\hat{\sigma}_1$ and $\hat{\sigma}_2$ are the standard deviations of the residuals for the two regimes with optimally estimated t, and $\hat{\sigma}$ is standard deviation of residuals from a single regression on the entire sample. It was shown empirically in R. E. Quandt, *op. cit.*, that the χ^2 distribution is a poor approximation to that of $-2 \log \lambda$ in the present case.

[8] R. L. Brown and J. Durbin, Methods of investigating whether a regression relationship is constant over time. Paper presented at the European Statistical Meeting, Amsterdam, 1968.

Helmert transformation yields transformed residuals which are independent and are distributed as $N(0, \sigma^2 I)$. They then propose testing the cumulative sums of the successive residuals for significant departures from zero as signals that a discrete change in parameter values have occurred.

An additional contribution to this problem is based on the assumption that any point in time is equally likely to be the switching point.[9] Farley and Hinich explore this assumption to develop a likelihood ratio test in which the appropriate test statistic is shown to have a normal distribution under the null hypothesis of no switch in regimes, and is shown to have a (generally multimodal) distribution that is an average of normal distributions under the alternative hypothesis of a single switch. They examine the power of their test by Monte Carlo methods and find it quite satisfactory.

All three of the above procedures are acceptable but suffer from two limitations. The first is the assumption that the observations belonging to a given regime are contiguous, i.e., that we first observe t points from one regime, then a switch to another regime occurs and the remaining $n - t$ points are all generated by the second regime. We thus rule out repeated switching back and forth between two regimes. This limitation applies to the procedures suggested by Quandt and by Farley and Hinich in principle. Although it does not apply to the Brown and Durbin procedure in principle, it seems that in practice it is important for theirs as well. The second limitation is the fact none of the procedures exploits the possibility that the investigator may be willing to specify on *a priori* grounds that nature's choice of which true regression regime to use for generating observations may depend on the value of some variable included in the regression or on some extraneous variable not included in the regression.

Both of these restrictions have been relaxed in a recent contribution to the analysis of markets in disequilibrium.[10] Fair and Jaffee implement their procedures empirically with data on the market for housing starts. In general, in a market in which trading may occur at disequilibrium prices one would find that the observed quantity lies on the demand function if the price is

---

[9] J. U. Farley and M. J. Hinich, A test for a shifting slope coefficient in a linear model. *Journal of the American Statistical Association* **65** (1970), 1320–9. See also the interesting approach based on hierarchical clustering by V. E. McGee and W. T. Carleton, Piecewise regression. *Journal of the American Statistical Association* **65** (1970), 1109–24.

[10] R. C. Fair and D. M. Jaffee, Methods of estimation for markets in disequilibrium. *Econometrica* (forthcoming); also delivered as a paper at the Second World Congress of the Econometric Society, Cambridge, England, Sept. 8–14, 1970.

greater than the equilibrium price and it lies on the supply function if the the price is less than the equilibrium price. An entire sample of observations thus represents a mixture of points, some tracing out the demand function and others the supply function; moreover, if the successive observations are made over time, the switching from demand points to supply points can occur every period according to whether the price that period is above or below equilibrium.

It is clear that the maximum likelihood method for estimating the para-meters of the two regimes (i.e., the demand and supply functions in the pre-sent case) becomes intractable; instead of evaluating the likelihood function as many times as there are ways of separating the sample into two contiguous subsamples (which is of the order of n), one would have to evaluate it as many times as there are ways of separating the sample into two subsamples with-out the restriction of contiguity (which is of the order of 2^n). Fair and Jaffee develop several alternative ways to estimate the parameters of the demand and supply functions. They all rely on the assumption derived from economic theory that if the price is below equilibrium there exists an excess demand and hence price must be rising and conversely for a price that is above equi-librium. Hence the sign of the change in the price level may be used to deter-mine whether a point belongs to regime 1 or regime 2. The quantity ΔP becomes the extraneous variable and for purposes of classifying observa-tions as coming from one or another regime, its value is compared with the *a priori* chosen cutoff point $\Delta P = 0$.[11]

9.2. A generalized approach

A generalization of the previously described procedure emerges from noting that it is not fully clear how one should classify observations for which the extraneous variable is near its cutoff value.[12] In fact, it need not be true that the appropriate cutoff value of the extraneous variable is known *a priori*. This might be the case if a demand function experienced a shift as a result of a

---

[11] Fair and Jaffee actually employ several alternative estimating methods. The one briefly described here is their Directional Method I. Directional Method II recognizes the presence of some ambiguity in the classification procedure when ΔP is near its cutoff value of zero and in such more dubious cases they allow the likelihood criterion (9.4) to make the choice.

[12] See also footnote 11.

change in an expectations variable measuring, say, consumer sentiment for which there might not be a 'natural' cutoff value.

For the sake of simplicity we shall develop a more generalized approach to the problem in terms of a regression model with a single explanatory variable. We posit two regimes:

$$y_i = a_1 + b_1 x_i + u_{1i} \tag{9.5}$$

and

$$y_i = a_2 + b_2 x_i + u_{2i}, \tag{9.6}$$

where the u_{1i} are independently distributed as $N(0, \sigma_1^2)$ and the u_{2i} are independently distributed as $N(0, \sigma_2^2)$. We assume that there are n observations and that there is an identifiable extraneous variable z with observations z_i which determines whether the ith observation is generated from (9.5) or (9.6). In particular, there is some *unknown* value z_0 such that when $z_i \leq z_0$ regime (9.5) holds and when $z_i > z_0$ regime (9.6) is relevant. Define a variable $D(z_i)$ as a step function of z_i: when z_i is less than or equal to the unknown value z_0, then $D(z_i) = 0$; if $z_i > z_0$, then $D(z_i) = 1$. Abbreviating $D(z_i)$ simply by D_i, (9.5) and (9.6) may be combined by multiplying (9.5) by $1 - D_i$, (9.6) by D_i and adding:

$$y_i = a_1(1 - D_i) + a_2 D_i + [b_1(1 - D_i) + b_2 D_i] x_i + u_{1i}(1 - D_i) + u_{2i} D_i \tag{9.7}$$

This procedures presumes that if z_i is greater than its unknown cutoff value, the regime given by (9.6) holds and if z_i is less than that value, (9.5) holds. In fact, as is obvious, (9.7) simply reproduces this set of assumptions.

In its stated form (9.7) might be considered as a regression with n observations from which $n + 6$ parameters must be estimated, namely $a_1, b_1, \sigma_1^2, a_2, b_2, \sigma_2^2$ and D_i $(i = 1, \ldots, n)$. In this form the regression is simply a restatement of the intractable combinatorial problem mentioned in section 9.1 of finding the regressions corresponding to all possible divisions of the sample into two subsamples. Since D_i is a step-function, it appears diagrammatically as in fig. 9.1. The problem would be considerably simplified if $D(z)$ could be approximated by a continuous function of z of the shape shown in fig. 9.2, where we have superimposed the continuous approximation on fig. 9.1.

One obvious functional form for such an approximation to $D(z_i)$ is the cumulative normal integral

$$D(z_i) = \int_{-\infty}^{z_i} \frac{1}{\sqrt{2\pi}\,\sigma} \exp\left\{ -\frac{1}{2}\left(\frac{\xi - \mu}{\sigma}\right)^2 \right\} d\xi, \tag{9.8}$$

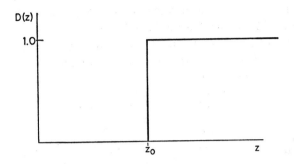

Fig. 9.1. The function $D(z)$.

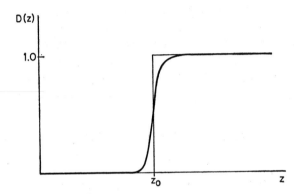

Fig. 9.2. The function $D(z)$ and its approximation.

where μ and σ are unknown. It is clear that μ plays the role of the unknown cutoff value z_0 and the value of σ expresses the tightness of the approximation to the ideal shape; indeed as $\sigma \to 0$ the approximation approaches the step function. We now have only 8 parameters to estimate instead of $n + 6$, namely $a_1, b_1, \sigma_1^2, a_2, b_2, \sigma_2^2, \mu$ and σ^2.

Eq. (9.7) has error variance equal to $\sigma_1^2 (1 - D_i)^2 + \sigma_2^2 D_i^2$ which is obviously heteroscedastic if $\sigma_1 \neq \sigma_2$. The appropriate logarithmic likelihood function is

$$\log L = -\frac{n}{2} \log 2\pi - \frac{1}{2} \sum_{i=1}^{n} \log [\sigma_1^2 (1 - D_i)^2 + \sigma_2^2 D_i^2]$$

$$- \frac{1}{2} \sum_{i=1}^{n} \frac{(y_i - a_1 (1 - D_i) - a_2 D_i - [b_1 (1 - D_i) + b_2 D_i] x_i)^2}{\sigma_1^2 (1 - D_i)^2 + \sigma_2^2 D_i^2}, \quad (9.9)$$

in which each value of D_i ($i = 1, \ldots, n$) is evaluated from (9.8). Maximum likelihood estimates are obtained by maximizing (9.9) with respect to the 8 parameters in question, with the substitution of (9.8) for D_i wherever D_i occurs.[13]

Whether such a model can be computed by the techniques of chapter 1 and whether it yields reasonably accurate estimates was tested with a limited number of experiments. The two regimes assumed for the purpose of the experiments were

$$y_i = 1.0 + 1.0x_i + u_{1i} \qquad (9.10)$$

for the first regime and

$$y_i = 0.5 + 1.5x_i + u_{2i} \qquad (9.11)$$

for the second.

In each case nature picked the regime for generating the ith value of the dependent variable by comparing a uniformly distributed variable with a cut-off point picked by the experimenter. If z_i was $\leq z_0$, (9.10) was selected, otherwise (9.11) was used for generating the dependent variable. Both x and z were uniformly distributed and, given the number of observations used in an experiment and the range of the variables employed, the same set of x- and z-values was used through all replications. The remaining characteristics of the experiments are summarized in table 9.1.

For all five cases the experiments were replicated 30 times. The likelihood function was maximized by the quadratic hill-climbing algorithm, which

TABLE 9.1

Characteristics of experiments

Case	No. of observations	Range of x-values	Range of z-values	z_0 cutoff value	σ_1^2	σ_2^2
I	60	10–20	0–400	200	2.0	2.5
II	120	10–20	0–400	200	2.0	2.5
III	60	10–20	0–400	300	2.0	2.5
IV	60	10–20	0–400	200	2.0	25.0
V	60	0–40	0–40	20	2.0	2.5

[13] It should be noted that if we reorder the (x_i, y_i) so as to correspond to increasing values of z_i, we could consider using the likelihood method given by (9.4) since there will be only one apparent switching point under the reordering. This technique, however, destroys whatever serial properties the disturbance term may have and breaks down completely when the model is extended to more than one z variable. These two circumstances are investigated in the next two sections respectively.

gave slightly superior results to Powell's method. The starting values for the algorithm were selected as follows: (a) z_0 was set at 150 in cases I II, III, and IV, and at 15 in case V; (b) σ^2 was arbitrarily set at 30 in all experiments; (c) the sample was divided into two subsamples according to whether $z_i \leq z_0$ or $z_i > z_0$ and OLS estimates were obtained for a_1, b_1, σ_1^2, a_2, b_2, σ_2^2. In approximately 25% of the 150 problems initiated (5 cases times 30 replications) convergence was sufficiently slow so that the computations were terminated before an optimum was reached. These cases are excluded from the summary tables. Table 9.2 displays the mean biases of the estimates. It also gives the quantity $\varDelta$, which is defined as the average over the replications of $\sum_{i=1}^{n} |\hat{D}_i - D_{i,\text{true}}|/n$, that is to say, the sum of the absolute deviations between the true values of the D_i's and the estimated ones. This quantity is obviously between 0 and 1 and gives in fact the average fraction of observations misclassified between regimes. Every observation being correctly classified implies that $\hat{D}_i = 0$ or 1 as $D_{i,\text{true}}$ is 0 or 1; misclassification of an observation implies the exact opposite. Finally the mean bias for σ^2 is the actual mean value for the estimated σ^2 since, if we posit the true shape of the $D(z)$ function to be a step function, the true value of $\sigma^2 = 0$ (The same applies to $\varDelta$).

TABLE 9.2

Mean biases

Coefficient	Cases				
	I	II	III	IV	V
a_1	−0.4972	0.0070	−0.1304	−0.5616	−0.1464
b_1	0.0287	0.0016	0.0078	0.0325	0.0003
a_2	0.6313	0.2674	0.2624	0.9600	0.2381
b_2	−0.0457	−0.0245	−0.1028	−0.0503	−0.0128
σ_1^2	0.0045	0.0030	−0.1661	−0.1393	0.0170
σ_2^2	1.6694	1.3295	3.6315	0.9974	2.8279
z_0	−14.5860	−15.1620	−40.0000	10.8490	−7.0450
σ^2	85.4111	36.7617	60.0583	202.0170	1.3391
$\varDelta$	0.0254	0.0206	0.1330	0.0297	0.0165

It is clear from every case that the b's and z_0 are estimated with considerable accuracy on the average.[14] The a's, i.e., the constant terms, are estimated considerably less accurately, a phenomenon that has been frequently observed in maximum likelihood procedures. Some of the noticeable mean biases

---

[14] A mean bias of say, 10, in z_0 is a 5% error if the true value is 200.

are obviously due to the sample size being only 60; in case II all mean biases (except that in z_0) are drastically reduced and even the constant terms seem to be estimated with fair accuracy. The quantity σ^2 measures the extent to which we approximate the step function in our estimate of $D(z)$; this is clearly very small when the range of z's is small (case V) and is worst when one of the regimes' error variance is fairly large (case IV). This is also the worst case in terms of the mean biases of the coefficient estimates, as might be expected. On the other hand, the worst mean bias in z_0, as well as the worst performance in terms of Δ, is for case III, when the number of observations coming from the two regimes is very uneven.[15] This case also results in the worst mean bias for z_0. In table 9.3 we display the corresponding MSE's.

The evidence of the MSE's is fairly similar.[16] Increasing the sample size reduces all MSE's. The slope coefficients have very much smaller MSE's throughout. Having a larger range of x-values (case V) dramatically improves

TABLE 9.3

Mean square errors

Coefficient	Cases				
	I	II	III	IV	V
a_1	2.0310	0.7009	1.3154	1.7264	0.2798
b_1	0.0074	0.0035	0.0050	0.0063	0.0004
a_2	1.7747	1.7629	6.7845	14.1377	0.4257
b_2	0.0076	0.0066	0.0288	0.0496	0.0008
σ_1^2	0.5413	0.1790	0.2241	0.3612	0.4167
σ_2^2	8.2325	5.6809	45.6505	45.5279	19.1851
z_0	503.2210	486.0580	5.4786×10^3	369.1550	2.2288
σ^2	2.9293×10^4	7.6830×10^3	1.8271×10^4	1.0645×10^5	4.3944

the MSE's, although the reduction in the MSE's for z_0 and σ^2 is probably attributable to the reduced range for the z-values. Cases III and IV do tend to perform somewhat worse than case I for some coefficients but not for others.

---

[15] This is somewhat analogous to the finding in the single-switch case that the power of the test suffers considerably if the single switch occurs near one of the endpoints of the time series. See J. U. Farley and M. J. Hinich, *op. cit.*

[16] In observing the very disparate sizes of the MSE's the reader should note (a) that the true values of the corresponding coefficients are very different (1.0 for b_1, 200 for z_0), and (b) these are MSE's, not root mean square errors.

It is interesting to compare the MSE's in table 9.3 with the exact variances of the regression coefficients based on (a) knowledge of the correct separation of the sample into two subsamples, and (b) knowledge of the true error variance. The exact variances of the coefficients in the two regimes are the diagonal elements of $\sigma_1^2 (X_1'X_1)^{-1}$ and $\sigma_2^2 (X_2'X_2)^{-1}$ respectively, where σ_1^2 and σ_2^2 are the two error variances, and X_1 and X_2 represent the matrices of observations on the independent variables in the two regimes. The exact variances are displayed in table 9.4.

Comparison of tables 9.3 and 9.4 indicates generally excellent correspondence. Table 9.4 also reveals why the MSE's for the constant term are so

TABLE 9.4

Exact variances of regression coefficients with correct sample separation

Coefficient	Cases				
	I	II	III	IV	V
a_1	2.3087	1.0721	1.1978	2.3087	0.3631
b_1	0.0091	0.0046	0.0049	0.0091	0.0006
a_2	2.4587	1.2266	10.9450	24.5874	0.3519
b_2	0.0104	0.0054	0.0438	0.1040	0.0006

TABLE 9.5

Ratio of mean asymptotic variances
to MSE's for case II

	MV/MSE
a_1	1.63
b_1	1.39
a_2	1.03
b_2	1.21
σ_1^2	0.88
σ_2^2	0.10
z_0	0.04
σ^2	0.78

much larger than for the slope coefficient: the model chosen for the sampling experiments is such that, even if we knew the exact separation point for the sample, the exact variances of the constant term are large compared to that for the slope coefficient.

Finally, we also computed for each replication in each case the Cramer-Rao variances and averaged them over the replications for each case. The ratios of these mean variances to the MSE's are not satisfactory for the smaller sample size of 60 in that they are not sufficiently close to unity, but are reasonable for case II for which $n = 120$. These ratios are displayed in Table 9.5.

It is to be noted that the ratios are unacceptably small for σ_2^2 and z_0. This is due to very large MSE's resulting from two outliers. Removing those outliers from the sample reduces the MSE's for these two quantities to 2.00 and 2.29 respectively; the corresponding MV/MSE ratios become 0.29 and 0.86. For most of the coefficients in question the ratio is reasonably close to the ideal of 1.0.

9.3. An economic example

In their recent paper analyzing markets in disequilibrium, Fair and Jaffee employed the market for housing starts as an empirical example and posited the following demand and supply functions for housing starts[17]:

$$y_t = \alpha_0 + \alpha_1 x_{1t} + \alpha_2 x_{2t} + \alpha_3 x_{3t} + u_{1t} \qquad (9.12)$$

and

$$y_t = \beta_0 + \beta_1 x_{1t} + \beta_4 x_{4t} + \beta_5 x_{5t} + \beta_6 x_{6t} + u_{2t}, \qquad (9.13)$$

where y_t = observed housing starts in month t; x_{1t} = time trend value in month t; x_{2t} = a measure of the stock of houses in existence in month t; x_{3t} = the mortgage rate lagged 2 months; x_{4t} = the 6-month moving average of flow of private deposits into savings and loan associations and mutual savings banks, lagged 1 month; x_{5t} = the 3-month moving average of borrowings by savings and loan associations from the Federal Home Loan Bank, lagged two months; and x_{6t} = the mortgage rate lagged 1 month; hence $x_{6t} = x_{3t+1}$.

The outside variable z_t associated with month t was the change in the mortgage rate $x_{6t+1} - x_{6t}$.

To estimate this with the technique of section 9.2, a further modification was necessary since it is reasonable to assume that the error terms are auto-

---

[17] R.C. Fair and D.M. Jaffee, *op. cit.*

correlated. To derive the appropriate likelihood function we introduce the following additional notation:

X_{dt} = the row vector of observations on the variables in the demand function in month t (the first element being unity to account for the constant term);

α = the column vector of coefficients in the demand function;

X_{st} = the row vector of observations on the supply variables in month t;

β = the column vector of coefficients in the supply function.

The two eqs. (9.12) and (9.13) can then be written:

$$y_t = X_{dt}\alpha + u_{1t} \tag{9.14}$$

$$y_t = X_{st}\beta + u_{2t}. \tag{9.15}$$

We posit the following error generating mechanism

$$u_{1t} = \varrho_{11}(1 - D_{t-1})u_{1t-1} + \varrho_{12}D_{t-1}u_{2t-1} + \varepsilon_{1t} \tag{9.16}$$

$$u_{2t} = \varrho_{21}(1 - D_{t-1})u_{1t-1} + \varrho_{22}D_{t-1}u_{2t-1} + \varepsilon_{2t}, \tag{9.17}$$

where D_t is the value of the previously defined $0 - 1$ variable in the tth period. According to (9.16) an error term in period t for regime 1 is generated either as $\varrho_{11}u_{1t-1} + \varepsilon_{1t}$ if in period $t - 1$ regime 1 was also in effect or it is generated as $\varrho_{12}u_{2t-1} + \varepsilon_{1t}$ if in that previous period regime 2 was operative. Similar considerations justify (9.17). Both for the sake of simplicity and for the sake of comparability with the Fair and Jaffee results, it was assumed that $\varrho_{11} = \varrho_{12} = \varrho_1$ and $\varrho_{21} = \varrho_{22} = \varrho_2$. Thus (9.16) and (9.17) become

$$u_{1t} = \varrho_1[(1 - D_{t-1})u_{1t-1} + D_{t-1}u_{2t-1}] + \varepsilon_{1t} \tag{9.18}$$

$$u_{2t} = \varrho_2[(1 - D_{t-1})u_{1t-1} + D_{t-1}u_{2t-1}] + \varepsilon_{2t}. \tag{9.19}$$

If we assume, as is customary, that the ε's are normally and independently distributed, (9.18) and (9.19) can be used to transform the original equations. Substituting from (9.14) and (9.15) into (9.18) and (9.19) (with appropriate lags, where indicated) we obtain

$$y_t - X_{dt}\alpha = \varrho_1[(1 - D_{t-1})(y_{t-1} - X_{dt-1}\alpha) + D_{t-1}(y_{t-1} - X_{st-1}\beta)] + \varepsilon_{1t} \tag{9.20}$$

$$y_t - X_{st}\beta = \varrho_2[(1 - D_{t-1})(y_{t-1} - X_{dt-1}\alpha) + D_{t-1}(y_{t-1} - X_{st-1}\beta)] + \varepsilon_{2t}. \tag{9.21}$$

Our composite equation is obtained by multiplying (9.20) by $1 - D_t$, (9.21) by D_t and adding. This yields

$$
\begin{aligned}
y_t &= (1 - D_t) \{ X_{dt}\alpha + \varrho_1 [(1 - D_{t-1})(y_{t-1} - X_{dt-1}\alpha) \\
&\quad + D_{t-1}(y_{t-1} - X_{st-1}\beta)] \} \\
&\quad + D_t \{ X_{st}\beta + \varrho_2 [(1 - D_{t-1})(y_{t-1} - X_{dt-1}\alpha) + D_{t-1}(y_{t-1} - X_{st-1}\beta)] \} \\
&\quad + (1 - D_t)\varepsilon_{1t} + D_t\varepsilon_{2t} \\
&= f(X_{dt}, X_{dt-1}, X_{st}, X_{st-1}, D_t, D_{t-1}, \alpha, \beta, \varrho_1, \varrho_2) + w_t, \quad\quad (9.22)
\end{aligned}
$$

where w_t is the usual heteroscedastic error term. The corresponding logarithmic likelihood function is similar to (9.9) and is

$$
\begin{aligned}
\log L &= -\frac{n}{2}\log 2\pi - \frac{1}{2}\sum_{t=2}^{n} \log [\sigma_1^2 (1 - D_t)^2 + \sigma_2^2 D_t^2] \\
&\quad - \frac{1}{2}\sum_{t=2}^{n} \frac{(y_t - f_t)^2}{\sigma_1^2 (1 - D_t)^2 + \sigma_2^2 D_t^2}, \quad\quad (9.23)
\end{aligned}
$$

where f_t represents the tth value of the f-function in (9.22) and n is one less than the original number of observations due to the lagging operation that led to (9.22).

Eq. (9.23) was maximized by the quadratic hill-climbing method with respect to the four α's, five β's, σ_1^2, σ_2^2, ϱ_1, ϱ_2 and the z_0 and σ^2 that appear in the cumulative normal integral (9.8). The asymptotic covariance matrix was also obtained and provided estimated standard errors for the coefficients. In table 9.6 we display the results for the Fair and Jaffee Directional Methods and for our procedure. The parenthesized figure under each coefficient value is the absolute value of the coefficient divided by its standard error.

The answers obtained by the method of this chapter are broadly compatible with those arrived at by Fair and Jaffee.[18] The following observations, however, are worthy of note:

(a) Demand is more responsive to the time trend and to the current stock of housing than is found by Fair and Jaffee;

---

[18] Some of the differences may be due to the fact that the Fair–Jaffee model included seasonal dummy variables. In order to reduce the number of parameters to be estimated we employed seasonally adjusted data.

TABLE 9.6

Results for the Fair and Jaffee model

	Fair and Jaffee Directional Method I	Fair and Jaffee Directional Method II	The new method
α_0	193.16 (3.10)	328.43 (6.06)	153.92 (1.67)
α_1	6.78 (2.01)	3.94 (1.69)	14.31 (2.22)
α_2	−0.055 (1.93)	−0.032 (1.63)	−0.123 (2.16)
α_3	−0.241 (2.27)	−0.471 (5.73)	−0.104 (0.78)
β_0	−40.84 (1.29)	−75.87 (1.74)	−32.55 (1.39)
β_1	−0.236 (3.12)	−0.332 (2.71)	−0.169 (2.64)
β_4	0.048 (6.20)	0.047 (4.32)	0.045 (6.85)
β_5	0.033 (2.76)	0.012 (0.62)	0.036 (4.26)
β_6	0.116 (2.69)	0.190 (2.74)	0.083 (2.29)
σ_1^2	76.38 —	65.45 —	106.07 (2.46)
σ_1^2	57.61 —	47.06 —	53.10 (5.63)
ϱ_1	0.731 —	0.499 —	0.992 (3.1×10^4)
ϱ_2	0.574 —	0.697 —	0.494 (6.06)
z_0	0.0 —	0.0 —	−0.003 (0.00)
σ	Not applicable		0.0012 (0.00)

(b) Demand is less responsive to the mortgage rate than they find by their Directional Method (but not so for their Quantitative method with which this result agrees better);

(c) Supply seems to have roughly similar responsiveness to the flow of funds to what they find but our finding of the supply responsiveness to the mortgage rate is lower than theirs;

(d) Their choice of separating supply and demand points according to whether the price change is of one sign or another is excellent (see our estimate for z_0);

(e) The estimated $D(z)$ function is nearly exactly the step function (see σ);

(f) Our estimate of ϱ_1 is perilously close to unity and its exceptionally small asymptotic variance may indicate problems in the numerical evaluation of the matrix of second partial derivatives;

(g) Since the value of z_0 is estimated at -0.003 and σ at 0.0012, from (9.8) we have that all points with a z_t value of exactly 0 have a computed D_t value of 0.991. Thus, when there is no price change 0.9 per cent of the observation is "allocated" to the demand function and remaining 99.1 per cent to the supply function,[19] which may explain why our estimate of $\hat{\sigma}_2^2$ agrees better with theirs than that of $\hat{\sigma}_1^2$. In general, we conclude that the method can work usefully in practical examples.

9.4. Extensions and concluding comments

Several extensions of the techniques discussed in the previous sections are possible, and we shall indicate them here even though no computational experience has been gained with them as yet.

Several extraneous variables

It might be hypothesized that which regime an observation belongs to depends not on a single extraneous variable z but on, say, a linear function of several variables $z_1, \ldots, z_k$.[20] Thus nature is assumed to choose regime 1

---

[19] If there are many points in the sample that can be regarded as equilibrium points the Fair–Jaffee procedure may be more efficient by allocating each such point both to the demand and supply regimes, whereas our procedure allocates a fraction of such points to one and the complementary fraction to the other regime.

[20] There is no intrinsic reason why only linear functions should be admissible.

for the ith observation if

$$\sum_{s=1}^{k} \gamma_s z_{si} \leqq z_0 \qquad (9.24)$$

and is assumed to choose regime 2 otherwise. It may normally be the case that both z_0 and the γ_s $(s = 1, \ldots, k)$ are unknown and must be estimated from the data. It is convenient to define a $(k + 1)$th variable $z_{k+1,i} = 1$ $(i = 1, \ldots, n)$ and to define $z_0 = -\gamma_{k+1}$. Eq. (9.24) then becomes

$$\sum_{s=1}^{k+1} \gamma_s z_{si} \leqq 0. \qquad (9.25)$$

The left-hand side is linearly homogeneous in the γ_s and obviously some normalization is required. Short of having a natural choice for one of the γ_s to be set $= 1$, the appropriate and symmetrical procedure would be to require $\sum_{s=1}^{k+1} \gamma_s^2 = 1$. Eq. (9.8) then becomes[21]

$$D_i = \int_{-\infty}^{\Sigma_s \gamma_s z_{si}} \frac{1}{\sqrt{2\pi}\,\sigma} \exp\left\{-\frac{1}{2}\left(\frac{\xi}{\sigma}\right)^2\right\} d\xi. \qquad (9.26)$$

The appropriate likelihood function will then be maximized with respect to the additional parameters appearing in (9.26) as well.

Continuous mixtures of regimes

It was assumed heretofore that nature generates a point from either regime 1 or from regime 2. It might be assumed, however, that each observation is a mixture (in varying proportions) of both regimes. Under these assumptions the analysis of section 9.2 can be applied with no change and the resulting estimate of σ^2 measures not so much the 'mushiness' or uncertainty in our ability to discriminate between the two regimes but rather the 'mushiness' exhibited by nature in generating data.

Several regimes

Imagine that observations come from three regimes

$$y = a_1 + b_1 x + u_1$$

$$y = a_2 + b_2 x + u_2 \qquad (9.27)$$

$$y = a_3 + b_3 x + u_3.$$

---

[21] An alternative normalization would be to set $\sigma =$ constant and leave the γ_s unrestricted.

Dependence of the regimes on an extraneous variable z is as follows:

if $z \leq z_0$, regime 1 is chosen

if $z_0 < z \leq z_1$, regime 2 is chosen

if $z > z_1$, regime 3 is chosen,

with z_0 and z_1 unknown cutoff points. We then define variables

$$D_i = \int_{-\infty}^{z_i} \frac{1}{\sqrt{2\pi}\,\sigma_L} \exp\left\{-\frac{1}{2}\left(\frac{\xi - z_0}{\sigma_L}\right)^2\right\} d\xi \qquad (9.28)$$

and

$$E_i = \int_{-\infty}^{z_i} \frac{1}{\sqrt{2\pi}\,\sigma_R} \exp\left\{-\frac{1}{2}\left(\frac{\xi - z_1}{\sigma_R}\right)^2\right\} d\xi, \qquad (9.29)$$

where σ_L^2 and σ_R^2 represent the variances of the left-hand and right-hand quasi-step-functions. Multiplying the first equation of (9.27) by $(1 - E_i)(1 - D_i)$, the second by $(1 - E_i) D_i$ and the third by $E_i D_i$, and adding, we obtain as the equation to be estimated

$$[1 - E_i (1 - D_i)] y_i = a_1 (1 - E_i)(1 - D_i) + a_2 (1 - E_i) D_i + a_3 E_i D_i$$
$$+ [b_1 (1 - E_i)(1 - D_i) + b_2 (1 - E_i) D_i + b_3 E_i D_i] x_i + w_i, \quad (9.30)$$

where the error term w_i has variance

$$[(1 - E_i)(1 - D_i)]^2 \sigma_1^2 + [(1 - E_i) D_i]^2 \sigma_2^2 + [E_i D_i]^2 \sigma_3^2.$$

The definition of the E_i and D_i insures that if the step functions are exactly estimated then for small values of z ($z \leq z_0$) both E_i and D_i are zero, for intermediate values ($z_0 < z \leq z_1$) $D_i = 1$, but $E_i = 0$, and for large values ($z > z_0$) both E_i and $D_i = 1$. It should finally be noted that in forming the likelihood function for (9.30) account must be taken of the fact that the dependent variable is multiplied by the exogenous variable $1 - E_i (1 - D_i)$ and the Jacobian of the transformation from the random variable w to the random variable y is no longer unity.

Concluding comments

This chapter has considered alternative ways to estimate models subject to discontinuous parameter changes. A particular case is examined in which observations are postulated to switch back and forth between two (or possibly more) distinct regression regimes depending on the values of some extraneous variables. In practical situations such behavior may arise in dealing with disequilibrium in supply-demand models; in macromodels where different relationships hold in the upswing or downswing of the business cycle; or in cross-section studies where 'small' and 'big' individuals and/or firms may behave differently. The solution proposed is clearly approximative in nature. Nevertheless, the evidence presented suggests that the method is feasible from a computational point of view and produces sensible results. Clearly more experience is needed, especially along the lines of some of the extensions above[22], but the method appears quite promising for handling certain types of structural shifts.

9.5. Some general conclusions

Since each of the applications chapters in this volume contains a brief conclusion, we shall not repeat any of our particular findings at this juncture. Rather, it will be more appropriate to confine our remarks to the general tendencies which emerge when this and the preceding six chapters are taken as a whole.

These several chapters have two general features in common: the presence of nonlinearities in the models considered and the use of maximum likelihood techniques for parameter estimation. From these features two findings emerge. First, the numerical techniques considered in chapter 1 seem fully up to the task of coping with the types of nonlinearities considered—i.e., nonlinearities can be handled more or less routinely. Secondly, the maximum likelihood technique performs impressively in a wide variety of applications and for relatively small sample sizes. Taken at face value, these two findings would argue for a greater willingness on the part of econometricians both to consider nonlinear specifications and to make greater use of maximum likelihood techniques. While we believe both of these statements to be true, it is important to emphasize the limitations of the evidence we present for their support.

In the first instance, the bulk of the evidence is from sampling experiments. By their very nature, these only permit the exploration of the behavior of estimators in a small part of the parameter space—a difficulty which may well limit the generality of our results. Secondly, most of the problems considered involve the estimation of a relatively small number of parameters (none exceeds 15). There is a clear need for a more extensive examination of larger problems. Thirdly, while four of the chapters do consider the consequences of certain types of misspecification (for which maximum likelihood holds

---

[22] One other possibility would be to investigate alternative specifications of the approximating cumulative distribution (i.e., alternative specifications of (9.8)). A second possibility would be to examine the estimator obtained by setting D_i equal to 0 or 1 according to whether $\hat{D}_i$ was less than or greather than $\frac{1}{2}$. The resulting estimator would be obtained by using least squares on the suitably partitioned samples.

up reasonably well), this hardly provides a significant amount of evidence on the robustness of maximum likelihood estimators. This is another subject which needs further work. Aside from the limitations of the evidence, some qualifications need to be made to the two general statements given above.

First, while the methods of chapter 1 were generally successful, the same algorithm was not uniformly best. In particular, while quadratic hill-climbing tended to be the most useful algorithm, for the problem discussed in chapter 5 the Powell algorithm was superior. Use of quadratic hill-climbing for that particular problem involved numerical differentiation of a function whose evaluation itself involved numerical integration. This undoubtedly made difficult the accurate evaluation of numerical second derivatives. In such instances, methods which avoid second derivatives are especially attractive.

A second qualification concerns the notion of what is an appropriately 'large' sample size. As we have seen, this depends on the characteristics of the problem. For some purposes a sample size of 30 is 'large', while for the probit model discussed in chapter 4, something of the order of 200 was 'large'. Furthermore, what is 'large' for a given problem depends on whether one is talking about the basic parameters or the accuracy of the estimator for their variances and covariances. For the latter, it seems to be the case that larger sample sizes are needed to obtain reasonable estimates.[23]

A third point to be noted is that maximum likelihood methods or, indeed, any other method should not be applied in automatic fashion to a particular nonlinear problem. It is generally desirable to learn as much as possible about the structure of the problem: for example, through the use of plotting likelihood contours or surfaces. In some ill-behaved problems, of course, one may be 'fortunate' enough to experience considerable difficulty with various numerical methods. This was vividly illustrated in chapter 6, where subsequent analysis revealed the reasons for the ill-behaved nature of the problem.

In conclusion we may say that nonlinearities are generally tractable and careful use of maximum likelihood techniques should considerably enhance the abilities of econometricians to obtain reliable parameter estimates. This volume has merely scratched the surface of the many ways in which this might be done.

---

[23] In some instances, where the variances are based on numerically evaluated derivatives, this may simply be a computational phenomenon. In other cases, it may reflect difficulties with the use of the standard formula, (2.48), for evaluating such variances. See chapter 2. It should also be borne in mind that what is 'large' depends on the size of the true error variances. As a consequence, the statements in the text need to be interpreted with care.

INDEX

Abstract mode model, 143–145
Aitchison, J., 127n
Amemiya, T., 187–188, 189n
Anscombe, F.J., 86
Asymptotic normality of maximum
   likelihood estimates, 63
Autocorrelation, 178–180, 270–271
  consequences of, 181–183
  estimation of, 183–189
  in simultaneous equation models,
   186–189
  in single equation models, 180–186
  tests for, 188

Bartlett, M.S., 87
Basmann, R., 201n, 219n, 243
Beale, E.M.L., 55n, 56, 57n
Beale contours, 55–57
Beale's function, 29
Berkson, J., 128n
Bodkin, R.C., 135n, 137n
Bowers, D.A., 94n
Bram, J., 4n
Brookings model, 179n
Brown, J.A.C., 127n
Brown, R.L., 260

Carleton, W.T., 261n
Chernoff, H., 232n
Chow, G.C., 17, 34n, 35n, 259n
Clustering, 261n
Cobb-Douglas function, 135–136
Cochrane, D., 185, 191
Confidence regions, 43–48
  in nonlinear models, 50–57, 68–74,
   169–176
Conjugate gradient methods, 13–16
Consistency of maximum likelihood
  estimates, 63

Convergence, 3–5, 8, 15
Cooper, J.P., 185n
Cooper, R.L., 38, 232n
Coverages, 138
Cox, D.R., 124n, 127n, 139
Cramer-Rao bound, 58–62, 98n, 119n, 145,
  161, 165, 167, 246

Davidon, W.C., 13n
Derivatives, use of, 18–21
Dhrymes, P.J., 185
Direct search methods, 16–17, 130
Discontinuous parameter changes, 258–276
Draper, N.R., 51n
Duesenberry, J.S., 179n
Dummy variables, 124–134
Durbin, J., 186, 260

Efficiency of maximum likelihood
  estimates, 63
Eisenpress, H., 233n
Errors, additive and multiplicative,
  135–146, 154n, 155n
Estimation, *see* least squares, maximum
  likelihood estimates
Evans, M.K., 179n

Faddeev, D.K., 18n
Faddeeva, V.N., 18n
Fair, R.C., 179, 187, 189n, 214, 261–262,
  269–273
Farley, J.U., 261, 267n
Fisher, F.M., 220, 221n, 222n, 224, 225,
  229, 231, 232
Flanagan, P.D., 15n
Fletcher, R., 5n, 13n, 29n
Fromm, G., 179n
Full-information maximum likelihood,
  see maximum likelihood